THE CHRISTIAN HERITAGE
in the
HOLY LAND

Edited by
Anthony O'Mahony
with Göran Gunner and Kevork Hintlian

**SCORPION
CAVENDISH**

Front Cover: Crusader silver coin. Photo courtesy of the Franciscan Museum, Jerusalem.

First published in 1995 by
Scorpion Cavendish Ltd
31 Museum Street
London WC1A 1LH
England

ISBN 1 900269 06 6

Editor: Leonard Harrow
Design: Knowles Thompson PLC, London WC1
Printed and bound in England by Butler & Tanner Limited, Frome

Preface

The Conference on the Christian Heritage in the Holy Land (6-9 July, 1994) held in the Holy City was an essential gathering not only for the local churches, but for the Universal Church. It was important that such an occasion took place in Jerusalem, where religion is a vital part of daily life and where the religious history of the city, not only unites it, but also divides it. The history of the religious and Christian heritage of Jerusalem and the Holy Land is of great importance and enrichment for us all. So many people today live in increasingly pluralistic societies, where different cultural and religious traditions have to live together. This makes the question of identity important. Without knowing of our roots it is hard to develop positive ways in which to coexist. It is within this perspective that we would like to place this conference on our Christian heritage in the Holy Land. Dialogue between religions is also about a dialogue between cultures. In confessing the Christian faith we need reflect upon the beginnings of our Christian heritage. The land in which the first Christians gathered is still of deep importance for the future of Christianity. This conference helped us understand the importance of the continuing presence of the Christian communities in Jerusalem and the Holy Land and deepened our knowledge of their long and significant history, and this also aids us in our deliberations on the future of our shared Christian faith.

So many scholars, theologians and church people associated with the various Christian communities came and participated in this conference and in their own created history, with their discussions and sharing of thoughts and reflections. We would like to thank all the participants and in particular Anthony O'Mahony and Kevork Hintlian who did such excellent work in preparing this conference. We would also like to thank Mgr Mathes and the Notre Dame Centre and Revd Thomas Stransky for their outstanding hospitality and for all at Swedish Christian Study Centre (SCSC) and the Mission Covenant Church of Sweden for their vital support in making this conference possible and a great success.

Jerusalem, July 1994

Per Olof Öhrn
President of the Educational
Association of Free Churches in Sweden

Dr Gösta Stenström
Secretary of World Missions
Mission Covenant Church of Sweden

The Swedish Christian Study Centre (SCSC) was established by the Educational Association of Free Churches in Sweden (FS). FS is a study association working with popular education together with 41 different Swedish Christian denominations and organisations, including Christian youth and peace movements. SCSC will provide facilities where Christians from Sweden and other countries can study their Christian roots in Jerusalem and at the same time take part in the life of the Christian communities in Jerusalem today.
Mailing address: PO Box 14233, 911 41, Jerusalem
Visiting address: Omar Ibn El-Khattab Square,
Jaffa Gate, Old City, Jerusalem
Phone: 02-89 42 43. Fax 02-28 58 77

Swedish Christian Study Centre   Mission Covenant Church of Sweden

Foreword

The task successfully undertaken by the Swedish Christian Study Centre, to sponsor the First International Conference on the Christian Heritage of the Holy Land and to subsequently publish the proceedings of the Conference, should be considered an important landmark. For too long the Church of the Holy Land has lived in shadow, known primarily for its struggle for physical and spiritual survival. The studies gathered in this collection reflect the tremendous importance of two thousand years of presence of the Christian faith in the land of its birth and at the centre of the monotheistic world. When one experiences Christianity in the Holy Land, one is immensely enriched by this cultural, human and religious encounter, which over the centuries has unfolded in so many traditions, ways of worship, liturgy and forms of witness. The so-called 'local church' in all its variety is spiritually extremely rich, and it depends on, and hopes for, the passing on of its unique religious message from its source to wherever the Christian community finds itself.

The Church of the Holy Land, on the other hand, will be challenged by the questioning, the sincere dialogue and peaceful desire which these studies present, a brotherly and sisterly search for the religious history and the significance of the Christian faith in this land.

It is my hope in sharing the richness of our faith, the Christians of the Holy Land will enable the rebirth of a common Christian theology in and of the Holy Land. This is more than a passing trend of contextual theology but rather an urgent need for the well-being of the whole Church: not just a return to its origins, but an endeavour which enables a living and creative access to the sources of our belief which is in contact with the land and which is within the historical context sanctified by the history of salvation.

As Chargé of the Holy See for the Pontifical Institute of Notre Dame of Jerusalem Centre, which was conceived in the spirit of the Second Vatican Council and in which the First International Conference on the Christian Heritage of the Holy Land was held, I am certain that these studies will make an important contribution to our knowledge and understanding of the Church in the Holy Land, and that they will break the ground for many meetings to come.

Mgr Dr Richard Mathes
Chargé of the Holy See for the Pontifical Institute of
Notre Dame of Jerusalem Centre

Contents

Preface   iii
Per Olof Öhrn

Foreword   iv
Mgr Dr Richard Mathes

Notes on Contributors   vii

Introduction   ix
Anthony O'Mahony

1   Pre-Constantinian Christian Jerusalem   13
    Jerome Murphy-O'Connor

2   Jerusalem and the Holy Land in the 4th Century   22
    Peter Walker

3   The Egyptian Relations of Early Palestinian Monasticism   35
    Samuel Rubenson

4   The Christians in Palestine during a Time of Transition:
    7th-9th Centuries   47
    Michele Piccirillo

5   Artistic and Cultural Inter-Relations between the Christian
    Communities at the Holy Sepulchre in the 12th Century   57
    Lucy-Anne Hunt

6   Tommaso Obicini (1585-1632) Custos of the Holy Land
    and Orientalist   97
    Giovanni-Claudio Bottini

7   Grigor the Chainbearer (1715-1749): the Rebirth of the
    Armenian Patriarchate   102
    Roberta Ervine

8   The Copts in Jerusalem and the Question of the Holy Places   112
    Otto Meinardus

9   The *Qeddusan*: the Ethiopian Christians in the the Holy Land   129
    Kirsten Stoffregen Pedersen

10 Travellers and Pilgrims in the Holy Land: the Armenian
Patriarchate of Jerusalem in the 17th and 18th Century   149
Kevork Hintlian

11 English Protestant Pilgrims of the 19th Century   160
Thomas Hummel

12 Culture and Image: Christians and the Beginnings of Local
Photography in 19th Century Ottoman Palestine   181
Ruth Victor-Hummel

13 Jerusalem and the Holy Places in European Diplomacy   197
Roger Heacock

14 The Greek Orthodox Patriarchate and Community of Jerusalem   211
Sotiris Roussos

15 Palestinian Christians: Politics, Press and Religious
Identity 1900-1948   225
Qustandi Shomali

16 The Religious, Political and Social Status of the Christian
Communities in Palestine, c. 1800-1930   237
Anthony O'Mahony

17 Church-State Relations in Jerusalem since 1948   266
Michael Dumper

18 Contemporary Christian Pilgrimage to the Holy Land   288
Glenn Bowman

19 Who is the Church? A Christian Theology for the Holy Land   311
Naim Ateek

Notes on Contributors

Jerome Murphy-O'Connor is a Dominican scholar at the Ecole Biblique, Jerusalem, and is the author of numerous works including *Holy Land: An Archaeological Guide from the Earliest times to 1700* (Oxford, 1986) and *The Ecole Biblique and the New Testament: a century of scholarship (1890-1990)* (Freiburg, 1990).

Peter Walker: Tyndale House, Cambridge, is the author of *Holy City, Holy Places? Christian Attitudes to Jerusalem and the Holy Land in the Fourth Century* (Oxford, 1990) and the editor for *Jerusalem Past and Present in the Purpose of God* (Cambridge, 1992).

Samuel Rubenson: Professor of Religious Studies, Lund University, and the author of *The Arabic Letters of Saint Anthony* (Lund, 1984).

Michele Piccirillo is a Franciscan friar based at the Studium Biblicum Franciscanum, Jerusalem, and is a specialist on the Christian archaeology in the Holy Land; he is the author of *Chiese e mosaici di Madaba* (Jerusalem, 1989) and *La Custodia di Terra Santa e l'Europa* (Jerusalem, 1983).

Lucy-Anne Hunt is a lecturer in the History of Art, University of Birmingham, and has published numerous articles in *Dumbarton Oaks Papers, Byzantine and Modern Greek Studies,* and *Orientalia Christiana Periodica.*

Giovanni-Claudio Bottini is a Franciscan friar based at the Studium Biblicum Franciscanum, Jerusalem, and is a specialist on the Franciscan community in the region; he has written and edited studies including *Studio Hierosolymitana: Nell' Ottavo centenario francescano (1182-1982)* (Jerusalem, 1982) and *Christian Archaeology in the Holy Land. New Discoveries* (Jerusalem, 1990).

Roberta Ervine: Armenian Patriarchate of Jerusalem; she has worked extensively in the Jerusalem archives and has done important work the history of the patriarchate.

Otto Meinardus has published extensively on the Coptic community, including *The Copts in Jerusalem* (Cairo, 1960), *Christian Egypt Faith and Life* (Cairo, 1970) and *Monks and Monasteries of the Egyptian Desert* (Cairo, 1989).

Kirsten Stoffregen Pedersen is a specialist on the Ethiopian community in Jerusalem and Ethiopian Christianity and is a long term resident of Jerusalem; she is the author of several studies including *The History of the Ethiopian Community in the Holy Land from the time of Emperor II till 1974* (Jerusalem, 1983), *Les Ethiopiens* (Editions Brepols, 1990), *The Ethiopian Church and its Community in Jerusalem* (Jerusalem, 1994).

Kevork Hintlian: Armenian Patriarchate of Jerusalem and the author of *History of the Armenians in the Holy Land* (Jerusalem, 1989, 2nd edition) and a forthcoming book on Europe and Palestine.

Thomas Hummel: Professor of Church History, Virginia Theological Seminary, Alexandria, Virginia, and an Episcopalian priest; he is the author of numerous studies on the English Protestant community in the 19th century and a forthcoming book on comparative Russian and English pilgrimage to Palestine.

Ruth Victor-Hummel: Department of History, Holton-Arms-School, Bethesda, Maryland; she has undertaken a special study of the development of photography in 19th century Palestine.

Roger Heacock: Professor of History, Bir Zeit University, and the author of studies on historical and contemporary Palestine, especially in the *Journal of Palestine Studies*.

Sotiris Roussos: School of Oriental and African Studies, London, has prepared a study on Greece and the Greek Orthodox Patriarchates and the Arab Orthodox Christian communities in the Middle East between 1917-1945.

Qustandi Shomali: Associate Professor, Department of Arabic, Bethlehem University, and a specialist on the Palestinian Arabic Press; he has published several books including *Literary and Critical Trends in Modern Palestinian Literature* (Jerusalem, 1990), *The Arabic Press in Palestine Mir'at al-Sharq (1919-1939)* (Jerusalem, 1992) and *The Arabic Press in Palestine Falastin 1911-1967* (Jerusalem, 1990-92).

Anthony O'Mahony: Department of History, School of Oriental and African Studies, London, and the author of several articles and a forthcoming book on the Christian communities in Palestine (1800-1948).

Michael Dumper: Lecturer in Politics, University of Exeter, and the author of *Islam and Israel: Muslim Religious Endowments and the Jewish State* (Washington DC, 1993) and studies in the *Journal of Palestine Studies*.

Glenn Bowman: Lecturer of Anthropology, University of Kent, and the author of numerous studies on Christian pilgrimage to the Holy Land in *Man*, *Middle East International* and in various collections.

Naim Ateek is an Anglican Priest, St Georges Cathedral, Jerusalem, and a well-known Palestinian Christian theologian; he is the author of *Justice and Only Justice: A Palestinian Theology of Liberation* (Maryknoll, 1989) and co-editor of *Faith and the Intifada: Palestinian Christian Voices* (Maryknoll, 1992)

Göran Gunner: Lecturer in History of Religion, Stockholm School of Theology, and the author of several books in Swedish on Christianity in the Middle East and further forthcoming work on apocalyptic interpretations of the Middle East in the Swedish Free Church.

Introduction

The idea for this conference, from which this work derives, was conceived in the Armenian quarter of Jerusalem in the early summer of 1993 over a casual cup of coffee. With substantial amounts of good will and the physical and financial support of the Swedish Christian Centre in Jerusalem, the conference planning took root, which grew into a large gathering of historians, social scientists theologians and laypeople, at the Notre Dame Centre and Tantur in the summer of 1994. The conference was conceived as an ecumenical event which would gather participants from all the different Christian traditions and from those with a special interest in Christianity in the Holy Land. The endeavour was framed around the wish to explore the history of Christianity in the Holy Land and the individual histories of the Christian communities and peoples in a continuous narrative from its beginnings until the contemporary period. It was hoped that exploration across various disciplines and between different points on the historical map, the early Christian era, the Islamic conquests and Crusaders, Ottoman and British rule and more recent times, would stimulate academics, churchmen and women and lay people to deeper and new reflections on the history of their Christian heritage. The collection of papers presented here is the fruit of that encounter. The studies unfold in a broadly chronological metre and whilst the collection cannot claim for itself comprehensives, however, it does attempt to present new and well-trodden avenues of research. The gaps in what we have achieved and what we would wish to know are large and obvious, but if we have stimulated others to pursue further these and other areas in which our knowledge of Christianity in the Holy Land is clouded then our efforts will have been greatly rewarded.[1]

---

[1] There have been other academic gatherings which have sought to present the history of Christianity in the Holy Land; see: D-M A Jaeger (ed): *Papers read at the 1979 Tantur Conference on Christianity in the Holy Land* (Jerusalem, Ecumenical Institute for Theological Research, Tantur, 1981). The excellent conference hosted by Alistair Duncan and the World of Islam Festival Trust at Cumberland Lodge, Windsor Great Park, England in 1993, which gathered Palestinian Christians and Churchmen and women to reflect upon their living Christian heritage in the Holy Land today and which was subsequently published as Michael Prior and William Taylor (eds): *Christians in the Holy Land* (London, WIFT, 1994) and the important annual seminars on Christian-Muslim Relations and Christianity in the Holy Land organized by Al-Liqa centre in Jerusalem, since 1983. See also the collection: Naim S Ateek, Marc H Ellis and Rosemary Radford-Ruether (eds): *Faith and the Intifada: Palestinian Christian Voices* (Maryknoll, New York, Orbis Books, 1992) and the important studies by Bernard Sabella on important questions of population and emigration for the Christian communities: 'Palestinian Christian Emigration from the Holy Land' (in *Proche-Orient Chrétien*, vol XLI (1991), 74-85). For the early history of Arabic Christian culture in the Holy Land see the outstanding collection by Sidney H Griffith: *Arabic Christianity in the Monasteries of ninth-century Palestine* (London: Variorum, 1992).

Jerome Murphy-O'Connor (Ecole Biblique, Jerusalem), describes the growth of the Christian community in Jerusalem prior to the convergence of the Constantinian state and the early Christian Church. Peter Walker (Tyndale House, Cambridge) develops the narrative through to 4th century Christian presence in the Holy Land. Samuel Rubenson (University of Lund), makes us aware of the strong connections between Egyptian and Palestinian monasticism and the formers influence upon its growth in the Holy Land. M Piccirillo (Studium Biblicum Franciscanum, Jerusalem) examines some of the archeological and literary evidence for the life of the Christian community in the Holy Land during the early Islamic period. Lucy-Anne Hunt (University of Birmingham) shows us the fruitful artistic relationship which developed between the Latin Catholic world and the Oriental and Eastern Christians in Palestine during the Crusader period.

Claudio Bottini (Studium Biblicum Franciscanum, Jerusalem) describes the work and career of Tommaso Obicini (1585-1632) who on resigning from being the Franciscan Custos in the Holy Land started a series of scholarly peregrinations to the various Christian communities in the region. Roberta Ervine (Armenian Patriarchate of Jerusalem) analyses the contribution of Gregory the Chain-Bearer (1712-1749) who created the successful foundations for the development of the Armenian Patriarchate in Jerusalem during the Ottoman period. Otto Meinardus (Hamburg, Germany) narrates the historical presence of the Coptic community in the Holy Land from its origins until today. Kirsten Stoffregen Pedersen (Jerusalem), examines the historical record and presence and continuous pilgrimage of the Ethiopian community to Jerusalem and the commitment of Christian Africa to the Holy Land. Kevork Hintlian (Armenian Patriarchate of Jerusalem) assesses the various travel accounts and pilgrim itineraries to uncover the life and history of the Armenian Patriarchate in the 17th and 18th century.

Palestine from the beginning of the 19th until the present has experienced a deep transformation of its political, social and cultural character, this process of change greatly affected the Christian communities and which fundamentally changed the world in which they lived. Robert L Wilken in his important work, *The Land Called Holy: Palestine in Christian History and Thought*, writes:

> Land, alas, is immovable; like the mountains and seas it is stationary. If it should happen that the only Christians to survive in the Holy Land were caretakers of the holy places, Christianity would forfeit a precious part of its inheritance. Like Judaism and Islam, Christianity . . . is not a European religion. Its homeland is in the Middle East, and continuity with its past is dependent on the Christians who continue in that land in which the faith is native. Were the holy places turned into museums or archaeological curiosities, as they have been in Turkey and Tunisia, the tangible links that stretch back

through history to the apostles and to God's revelation in Christ would be severed. Without the presence of living Christian communities, the witness of the Holy Land can only be equivocal. The martyrs and teachers, the monks and bishops, the faithful who lived in Bethlehem and Beit Jalal and Nazareth and Jerusalem, would no longer be signs of a living faith, but forgotten names from a distant past. Bethlehem would become a shrine, and Christian Jerusalem a city of ancient renown. Only people, not stones and earth and marble, can bear an authentic witness.[2]

The following papers attempt to assess the nature and variety of events which combined to create this moment of transformation. Thomas Hummel (Virginia Theological Seminary, Alexandria) describes the mental and physical impact the Holy Land had on the theological world of 19th century English protestants as they rediscovered the pilgrimage as a religious endeavour. Ruth Victor-Hummel (Bethseda, Maryland) opens up to us the development and use of photography upon the Christian communities in the 19th century. Roger Heacock (Bir Zeit University) narrates the role and impact of European diplomacy on the Holy Land in the period of expanding interest in destiny of late Ottoman Palestine. Sotiris Roussos (University of London) writes upon the history of the Greek Orthodox patriarchate of Jerusalem and the Arab Orthodox community in the 19th and 20th century. Qustandi Shomali (Bethlehem University) explains the extent and importance of Christians to the growth in the press in Palestine 1900-1948. Anthony O'Mahony (University of London) describes various aspects of the religious, political and social status of the Christian communities in Palestine c. 1800-1930. Michael Dumper (University of Exeter) analyses the nature of church-state relations in Jerusalem since 1948. Glenn Bowman (University of Kent) writes on the cultural and religious world of contemporary Christian pilgrimage to the Holy Land. And finally Naim Ateek (St George's Cathedral, Jerusalem) ends with some reflections on a Christian theology for the Holy Land.

Within such a widely spread collection of studies which try to cover such a vast historical and religious terrain as they attempt to survey and reflect upon the history and heritage of Christianity in the Holy Land, there will be found many omissions and lacunae. However, much has been achieved and it is hoped we have made some contribution to the dialogue between faith and history, theology and the Land.

We would like to thank Leonard Harrow of Scorpion Cavendish for all his care and patience in the preparation of these studies for publication.

---

[2] Robert L Wilken, *The Land Called Holy: Palestine in Christian History and Thought*, New Haven, Yale University Press 1992, 254.

1

Pre-Constantinian Christian Jerusalem

Jerome Murphy-O'Connor, OP

How much time Jesus spent in Jerusalem is not a topic that has exercised the sagacity of scholars. Normally those who advert to the problem are content to accept the witness of the Fourth Gospel that he was in Jerusalem at Passover (2: 13), on an unnamed festival (5: 1),[1] at Sukkot (7: 2, 10), at Hanukkah (10: 22), and finally on the occasion of another Passover (11: 55; 12: 12). The impression that Jesus was no more than an occasional visitor, whose motivation was the duty of pilgrimage,[2] is reinforced by the Synoptic gospels, for whom Jesus ministry was located exclusively in Galilee. For Matthew, Mark and Luke Jesus died on his first and last visit to Jerusalem for Passover.

A close reading of John, however, yields a different picture. Not only did Jesus preach and baptize in Judea as John the Baptist's assistant for some considerable time (3: 22-24), but he never returned to Galilee after going up to Jerusalem for Sukkot (7: 10). The hostility of the Jerusalemites forced him to take refuge in Perea (10: 40), but his stay there apparently was not prolonged, and he had enough friends in Bethany (11: 1-53; 12: 1-11) and Ephraim (11: 54),[3] to shelter him when he returned to Judea.

It is well known that John intended his gospel to be complementary to those of the Synoptics. Thus he does not mention events which he considered them to have treated adequately, e.g., the transfiguration and the agony in the garden, to which he alludes in 12: 27-28, or the institution of the eucharist, whose meaning he brings out in 6: 51-59. It

---

[1] All three pilgrimage feasts have been proposed; see R E Brown, *The Gospel according to John (I-XII)*, AB 29; Garden City: Doubleday, 1966, 206.

[2] Exod 12: 14-20, 43-49; Lev 23: 4-8; Deut 16: 1-8.

[3] Identified as et-Taiyibeh or En Samieh; see Brown, John, 441. Both are within a couple of hours walk from Jerusalem.

would be entirely in keeping with this approach for John to highlight a dimension of the ministry of Jesus, which the Synoptics do not mention, namely that he invested as much time and energy in Jerusalem as he did in Galilee.

Confirmation of this hypothesis comes from a surprising source, the Second Gospel. Mark contains a series of stories which present Jesus in conflict with Pharisees.[4] From this A Saldarini concluded, 'Mark sees them [the Pharisees] as active only in Galilee.' Not a single such story, however, contains any element which would permit us to identify the location. One is given the impression of a location in Galilee by juxtaposition in some but not all cases. There is no reliable evidence for Pharisees permanently based outside Jerusalem. Hence, it is most probable that it was in the Holy City that Jesus encountered them, and that the controversies were spread out over a period of time.

Nothing, in fact, is more likely than a prolonged mission of Jesus in Jerusalem. If 'prophets do not arise in Galilee' (John 7: 52), neither had they preached there since the fall of the northern kingdom. Those with a message from God delivered it in Jerusalem where Jewish power was concentrated. The reason why Jesus began to preach in Galilee was not any conviction of its importance, but simply to replace the arrested John the Baptist (Mark 1: 14), with whom he was then confused (Mark 6: 14-16).[5] Once Jesus had become conscious of his own unique mission, and had proclaimed the good news in Galilee, his thoughts inevitably turned towards Jerusalem, to which he had the same duty.

Jesus' success in Jerusalem was probably no greater than his achievement in Galilee, but it seems most improbable that he made no converts. From the beginning, therefore, the core of the Jerusalem church came from the city. Even though transplanted Galileans occupied the positions of power in the post-paschal period, the membership was essentially Jerusalemite.

The gradual shift of power from Peter to James the brother of the Lord, which is perceptible in Acts, is confirmed by Paul's reports of his two visits to Jerusalem (Gal 1: 18-19; 2: 9). Persecution marked the life of the church. Some was undertaken on private initiative, as exemplified by Paul's activities (Gal 1: 13, 23; Phil 3: 6; 1 Thess 2: 14). The rest was much more official, but sporadic and limited. Under Agrippa I (41-44) James the son of Zebedee was executed and Peter imprisoned (Acts 12: 1-12).[6] The religious authorities executed Stephen (Acts 6: 8-7, 60) and James the

---

[4] Mk 2: 16, 18, 24; 3: 6; 7: 1, 3, 5; 8: 11; 10: 2; 12: 13.

[5] See my 'John the Baptist and Jesus: History and Hypotheses', *New Testament Studies* 36, 1990, pp. 359-74.

[6] D R Schwartz suggests that the violent temperaments of Peter (John 18: 10; Matt 16: 17) and the of the sons of Zebedee (Mark 3: 17; Luke 9: 54) might have led to their involvement in public disturbances ('Agrippa I. The Last King of Judaea' [*STAJ* 23; Tübingen: Mohr, 1990], 123).

brother of the Lord and other believers.[7] In neither case, however, is there question of a systematic pursuit of Christians. This makes it difficult to know how much weight to give Luke's portrayal of Jerusalem as becoming steadily more inimical to Christianity. The contrast between the Holy City and Caesarea, whose Roman authorities afford a warm welcome and protection to the new faith, (Acts 21: 8-9, 12; 23: 23; 25: 2-4) smacks of propaganda in its simplicity.[8]

After the death of James, Eusebius reports the selection of Symeon as the second bishop of Jerusalem,[9] gives a list of the thirteen bishops who succeeded him up to the Second Revolt,[10] and notes the departure of Jerusalem Christians to Pella to escape the siege of Jerusalem, which ended the First Revolt.[11] All of these texts contain problems of interpretation, which have given rise to extensive debates. Here it must suffice to note the problems and what appear to be the most plausible solutions.

Eusebius accepts the report of Hegesippus that the martyrdom of James was immediately followed by the siege of Jerusalem,[12] and so dates the selection of Symeon after the fall of the city.[13] James, however, was executed in the interregnum between the death of Festus and the arrival of Albinus, his successor as procurator, i.e. AD 62, four years before the beginning of the First Revolt.[14] Since a leadership vacuum of some ten years is not plausible, we must assume that Symeon took power shortly after the death of James, and ruled until 'he was martyred at the age of 120 years when Trajan was Caesar and Atticus the governor.'[15] Unfortunately Trajan had a 19 year reign (AD 98-117) and the tenure of Atticus cannot be dated.[16] However, Symeon must have been middle-aged when elected, and even were he not martyred, he is unlikely to have lived beyond the first years of the reign of Trajan.[17] Hence, it would be prudent to infer that he ruled for about 40 years, and that Justus succeeded him at the beginning of the 2nd century.

If this conclusion is correct, the problem of the list of bishops becomes apparent. There are 13 bishops and only some 33 years until the establishment of Aelia Capitolina by Hadrian in AD 135; in other words an

---

[7] 'And so Ananus convened the judges of the Sanhedrin and brought before them a man named James, the brother of Jesus who is called Messiah (*ton adelphon Iēsou tou legomenou Christou*), and certain others. He accused them of having transgressed the law and delivered them up to be stoned.' (Josephus, *Antiquities of the Jews*, 20: 200).

[8] Schwartz, 'Agrippa I', 156.

[9] *Church History*, 3: 11; 4: 22.4

[10] *Church History*, 4: 5. An identical list is furnished by Epiphanius, *Panarion*, 66: 21-22).

[11] *Church History*, 3: 5.3.

[12] *Church History*, 2: 23.18.

[13] *Church History*, 3: 11.

[14] E Schürer, *The History of the Jewish People in the Age of Jesus Christ (175 BC-AD 135)*, ed. G Vermes et al.; Edinburgh, Clark, 1973, 1.468.

[15] *Church History*, 3: 32.3.

[16] E M Smallwood, 'Atticus, Legate of Judaea under Trajan', *Journal of Roman Studies* 52 (1962), 131-33.

[17] Schürer, *History*, 1.516.

average reign of only 2.5 years! of Eusebius' note that they were very short-lived,[18] is unacceptable as an explanation; it merely betrays his awareness of the problem. Various solutions have been proposed,[19] but the most probable explanation seems to be that the first three listed (James, Symeon, Justus) were in fact bishops and the remaining twelve – a highly symbolic figure – were a college of elders, who inherited the mantle of the elders who appear alongside the apostles in Acts (15: 2, 4, 6, 22, 23; 16: 4).[20]

The problem with the Pella story is that Eusebius contradicts himself. According to his Church History the believers departed from Jerusalem and 'dwelt in one of the cities of Perea which they call Pella' (3: 5.3). Yet in his Proof of the Gospel he asserts, 'Until the time of the siege by Hadrian there was an extremely significant Church of Christ at Jerusalem, which consisted of Jews' (3: 5.108). We have a choice between permanent departure and perfect continuity, and opinion is deeply divided. The traditional view, which accepts the historicity of the flight, has been defended most recently by V S Balabanski,[21] and attacked by G Lüdemann.[22] The latter, in my view, makes the more convincing case. The three allusions to the flight by Epiphanius[23] depend on Eusebius, whose probable source is Aristo of Pella. The possibility of special pleading diminishes the credibility of Aristo's late and lone voice. Moreover Pella is improbable as a city of refuge.[24]

If there was no flight to Pella, did the Christian community remain in Jerusalem for the duration of the siege? By the spring of AD 68 only the rich could buy their way out of Jerusalem; others who attempted to leave were cut down.[25] Those who escaped the year before must have been very farsighted. Did Christians belong to this group? Eusebius mentions 'an oracle given by revelation' which warned the church.[26] Just such an oracle appears as one of Mark's sources in ch. 13. As reconstructed by Balabanski

---

[18] *Church History*, 4: 5.1.

[19] 'The disproportionately long list of bishops Theodor Zahn believed to have included the names of bishops of neighbouring sees. Louis Duchesne considered it a list of bishops of Pella and of other colonies of the Jerusalem church. Adolph Schlatter held that it was a list of Jerusalem presbyters, while Rudolph Knopf thought that the names of the relatives of Jesus (*despósynoi*) were included; Harnack accepted and combined both explanations. Erich Caspar suggested that the transmitters of the apostolic tradition were named as well as the first bishops.' (J J Gunther, 'The Fate of the Jerusalem Church. The Flight to Pella', *Theologische Zeitschrift* 29 [1973], 81-94, here 92-93).

[20] R Bauckham, *Jude and the Relatives of Jesus*, Edinburgh Clark, 1990, 73-77.

[21] 'Eschatology in the Making: Mark, Matthew and the Didache' (PhD Dissertation, University of Melbourne, 1993), 96-127.

[22] *Opposition to Paul in Jewish Christianity*, Minneapolis, Fortress, 1989, 200-11.

[23] *Panarion*, 29: 7.7; 30: 2.7; *De menuris et ponderis*, 15.

[24] A gentile city which had been laid waste by Alexander Jannaeus (Josephus, *Jewish War*, 1: 1104), and again by Jews at the beginning of the First Revolt (*War*, 2: 458) would have had little sympathy for Jewish Christian refugees. The case of Gerasa (*War*, 2: 480) proves nothing; there is no question of it accepting the enemy as refugees.

[25] Josephus, *Jewish War*, 4: 377-79.

[26] *Church History*, 3: 5.3.

it reads, 'When you see him, the abomination of desolation, standing where he ought not to be – let the reader understand – then flee to the mountains. But pray that it does not happen in winter' (vv. 14-18).[27] She also establishes a most plausible *Sitz im Leben* for the oracle, namely, the struggle of the Zealots to wrest power from the high priestly families, and in particular their campaign to change the procedure by which high priests were appointed.[28] This goal they achieved by the nomination by lot of Phanias in the winter of AD 67.[29] That the oracle survived to be incorporated in Mark's gospel would suggest that it was heeded by at least some of the Christians in Jerusalem.

To be safe they did not have to go as far as Pella. Anywhere 10 to 20 km north of Jerusalem would have provided adequate security. Vespasian had left the hill country north of the city untouched until the early summer of AD 69.[30] At that stage Judeans would have acquired a very precise idea of the operational tactics of the legions, and it would have been relatively easy for Christians to move out of danger to the edge of the desert. The Romans attacked only where resistance was offered. The believers could have returned to the ruins of Jerusalem before the end of AD 70.

The martyrdom of Symeon under Trajan has already been mentioned. The historicity of this persecution of descendants of the house of David has been questioned by Schürer because it may represent 'an apologetical legend intended to emphasize the Davidid-Messianic status of Jesus.'[31] In any case the persecution was not directed against Christians as such. This sort of threat, however, became a reality during the Second Revolt. The fact that Christians used the messianic name Bar Kokhba 'Son of a Star' (cf. Numbers 24 : 27), which was invented by Rabbi Akiba for Bar Kosiba the leader of the revolt,[32] suggests that they had come under pressure to accept his leadership, something, of course, they could not do, having accepted Jesus as the Christ. Writing only 20 years after the event, Justin, in fact, reported that Bar Kokhba had attempted to force Christians to deny that Jesus was the Messiah.[33]

The fact of having been persecuted by the rebels was probably what saved the Jewish Christian survivors when Hadrian expelled the Jews from

---

[27] 'Eschatology in the Making', 87. 'To the mountains' may not have belonged to the original form of the oracle. It is lowland language and inappropriate for Jerusalemites living on the mountain of the Lord, even though the city is surrounded by higher ground.

[28] 'Eschatology in the Making', 121-25.

[29] Josephus, *Jewish War*, 4: 147-57. Ananus commented, 'How wonderful it would have been if I had died before seeing the house of God full of countless abominations' (*War*, 4: 163). See also S. Sowers, 'The Circumstances and Recollection of the Pella Flight,' *Theologische Zeitschrift* 26 (1970), 305-20, particularly 318-19.

[30] Josephus, *Jewish War*, 4: 550-51.

[31] *History of the Jewish People*, 1.528.

[32] Eusebius, *Church History*, 4: 6.2; see Schürer, *History of the Jewish People*, 1.543, note 130.

[33] 1 *Apologia*, 31: 6., which is quoted by Eusebius, Church History, 4: 8. For a contemporary hint of this persecution in the Apocalypse of Peter, see R Bauckham, 'The Two Fig Tree Parables in the Apocalypse of Peter', *Journal of Biblical Literature* 104 (1985), 269-87, especially 285-86.

the territory of Aelia Capitolina in AD 135.[34] The impression given by Eusebius that the church of Aelia was composed exclusively of believers of Gentile origin is too neat to be historical.[35] Where did the members of this Gentile church suddenly spring from? With the benefit of hindsight Eusebius simplifies a complex process. The new members who joined the surviving Jewish Christians were all Gentiles and inevitably changed the character of the church, particularly since the Jewish institutions and practices, which had reminded pre-Hadrianic believers of their roots, no longer existed. With the exception of Narcissus and Alexander, little or nothing is known of the pastors who governed the church in Jerusalem for the next 180 years.[36] It is unknown who among them 'discovered' the throne of Saint James, which became the chief treasure of the church.[37]

The new Roman colony developed north of the camp of the Tenth Legion, which was located in the area today occupied by Armenian and Jewish Quarters. On the west side of the Cardo Maximus Hadrian built the Capitoline temple;[38] which dominated the western forum with its triumphal arch from the north. This area is evoked by Melito of Sardis, who visited Jerusalem,[39] sometime before composing his Paschal Homily, which is to be dated between 160 and 170.[40] 'Had the murder [of Jesus] taken place at night, or had the deed been done in an uninhabited place, it would have been easy to keep silence, but it was in the middle of the colonnaded street and of the city – in the middle of the city – that the unjust murder of the Just One was carried out'.[41] Clearly Melito did not derive his information from the New Testament (NT), which implies that Jesus was crucified outside the city.[42] Melito must have been shown a specific area of the city expanded by Agrippa I, whose northern line was

---

[34] The decree mentioned by Eusebius, *Church History*, 4: 6.3, has been reconstructed by M Avi-Yonah, 'It is forbidden for all circumcized persons to enter or stay within the territory of Aelia Capitolina; any person contravening this prohibition will be put to death' (*The Jews of Palestine. A Political History from the Bar Kokba War to the Arab Conquest* [Oxford: Clarendon, 1976], 50-51).

[35] *Church History*, 4: 6; 5: 12.

[36] *Church History*, 5: 12 (the names of Maximus and Antoninus must be supplied after Capito from the Chronicle of Eusebius); 6: 10-11; 6: 39; 7: 14; 7: 32.

[37] Eusebius, *Church History*, 7: 19.

[38] See my 'The Location of the Capitoline Temple in Aelia Capitolina', *RB* 101 (1994), 407-15. An unsuccessful effort has been made to site the Capitoline Temple on the ruins of the Antonia fortress; see Shimon Gibson and Joan E Taylor, *Beneath the Church of the the Holy Sepulchre. The Archaeology and Early History of Traditional Golgotha* (Palestine Exploration Fund: Series Major 1; London, Palestine Exploration Fund, 1994), 70.

[39] Eusebius, *Church History*, 4: 26.14, quotes Melito, 'I visited the east and arrived at the place where it all happened and the truth was proclaimed.'

[40] O Perler, 'Méliton de Sardes, Sur la Pâque et fragments' (*SC* 123; Paris: *Cerf*,1966), 24.

[41] *Paschal Homily*, 94.

[42] 'They led him out (*exagousin*) to crucify him' (Mk 15: 22). 'As they went out (*exerchomenoi*) they found a man of Cyrene' (Mt 27: 32). 'Because the tomb was close at hand, they laid Jesus there' (Jn 19: 42). Jewish law prohibited tombs within towns; graves had to be 25 metres outside the built-up area (m. Baba Bathra 2: 9).

taken over by Hadrian.[43] Unfortunately his rhetorical formulation means no more than Jesus was executed, not in secret, but in the full glare of publicity. It cannot be forced to specify the western forum.[44] The same vagueness mars Eusebius' pre-Constantinian localization of Golgotha, 'in Aelia near the northern parts of Mount Sion'.[45]

Our inability to determine a precise spot is less important than the evidence of interest in places associated with Jesus on the part of visitors from abroad, who of course depended on local Christians to guide them. This feature of Jerusalem Christianity must have been reinforced in the 3rd century. In 212 Alexander, bishop of Cappadocia, came to Jerusalem 'in order to worship there and to examine the historic sites'.[46] Against his will, he was forced to become the auxiliary of the aged bishop, Narcissus,[47] whom he succeeded. During his long pontificate of 39 years he fostered pilgrimage. He commanded the admiration of Origen, whom he invited to preach in Jerusalem.[48] It may have been Alexander's example which inspired Origen 'to come to see the traces of Jesus, of his disciples and of the prophets'.[49] The specific point at issue is the name of the place where John baptized – 'Bethany' or 'Bethabara' – but this is unlikely to be the only site that Origen visited.[50] He appears to have been the first to identify the double pool now in the grounds of St Anne's with the pool near the Sheep Gate where Jesus cured a cripple (John 5: 1-9),[51] although it is improbable that he actually saw 'four porticos around the edges and another across the middle'.[52] Epiphanius of Salamis mentions that in the time of Hadrian there was 'a little church of God' on Mount Sion.[53]

---

[43] Josephus, *War*, 5: 147-148. Hadrian did not wall Aelia Capitolina. The commonsense assumption that a wall became necessary only after the departure of the Tenth Legion under Diocletian is confirmed by the aqueduct west of Herod's Gate, which was taken out of commission only at the beginning of the 4th century; see L-H Vincent, 'Encore la troisième enceinte de Jérusalem,' *RB* 54 (1947), 104.

[44] *Pace* J E Taylor, *Christians and the Holy Places. The Myth of Jewish-Christian Origins* (Oxford: Clarendon, 1993), 116-17.

[45] *Onomasticon*, 74: 19-21. This work should probably be dated c. 293; see P W L Walker, *Holy City, Holy Places? Christian Attitudes to Jerusalem and the Holy Land in the Fourth Century* Oxford Early Christian Studies, Oxford, Clarendon, 1990, 407. Eusebius here uses Mount Sion of the entire western hill.

[46] Eusebius, *Church History*, 6: 11.2.

[47] Narcissus was known as a miracle-worker. Disgusted by a baseless slander, he retired to the desert, and only after many years returned to take up his office. At the age of 116 he still participated in public worship (Eusebius, *Church History*, 6: 9-11).

[48] Introduction to his first sermon on Kings, *Patrologia Graeca* 12: 995. His preaching in the Holy City is also mentioned by Epiphanius, *Panarion*, 64: 2. See Eusebius, *Church History*, 6: 27.

[49] Commentary on John, 1: 28.

[50] So rightly Taylor, *Christians and the Holy Places*, 105.

[51] Commentary on John, 5: 2.

[52] The galleries are mentioned by Eusebius as a thing of the past (*Onomasticon*, 58: 22, s.v. *Bêzatha*).

[53] *De mensuris et ponderibus*, 14. On this edifice and its importance for the local church, see my 'The Cenacle and Community. The Background of Acts 2: 44-45', forthcoming in R Bauckham (ed.) *The Book of Acts in its Palestinian Setting*, Grand Rapids, Eerdmans.

Eusebius also benefited from an initiative of Alexander, namely, 'the library established at Aelia by the man who then presided over the church there, Alexander – the library from which I myself have been able to bring together the materials for the work now in hand.'[54] This library should be understood as an institution of the city rather than as a purely ecclesiastical library, although a concern for theological resources may have been its primary motivation. It was a time when cities felt that they owed themselves libraries, and the initiative of citizens was welcomed.[55] The allusion of Julius Africanus to 'the archives of our ancient homeland, the colony of Aelia Capitolina in Palestine' in a work dated about 230 is probably a reference to Alexander's library.[56]

The foundation of such an institution by Christians in Jerusalem manifests the strength and vitality of the church there. It certainly was not an isolated beleaguered community. It had regular contacts with neighbouring churches, whose leaders supervised the selection of bishops.[57] Visitors from abroad may have been numerous. There is no justification for thinking that Eusebius' mention of Melito, Origen, and Alexander implies that they were the only visitors to the Holy City.[58] Their scholarship and/or office demanded attention. Many other visitors were too insignificant to be mentioned by name in the great historian's wide-ranging story. Some may have stayed and infused new blood into the community.

Prior to the 3rd century persecution of Christians was conditioned by local factors, notably the attitude of the local governor. The consequences of the favour shown Christians by Alexander Severus (222-35) could hardly have been foreseen. Subsequently the stance of the emperor became critical and a cyclical policy developed. If one emperor tolerated Christianity, his successor repressed it.[59] Such swings were unfortunate for the flourishing Jerusalem church, because Philip the Arabian (244-49) – Eusebius 'had reason to believe' he was a Christian[60] – was succeeded by Decius (249-51), who initiated the first systematic persecution of Christians. It would have been impossible for the imperial representative in Palestine not to have summoned bishop Alexander of Jerusalem to Caesarea to put him to the test. Alexander refused to sacrifice but, before

---

[54] *Church History*, 6: 20.1.
[55] See C Wendel, 'Bibliothek', *Reallexikon für Antike und Christentum*, 2.231-74; F Granger, 'Julius Africanus and the Library of the Pantheon', *Journal of Theological Studies* 34 (1933), 157-61.
[56] The nature of the manuscript which prompted the reference – a bizarre incantation in which the name of Yahweh is combined with the gods of the Greek and Egyptian pantheons – shows that it could not have belonged to the 'public records' of Aelia, nor to a Jewish library. See J-R Villefond, *Les 'Cestes' de Julius Africanus. Etude sur l'ensemble des fragments avec édition, traduction et commentaires*, Firenze, Sansoni/Paris, Didier, 1970, 278, 288-91.
[57] Eusebius, *Church History*, 6: 10-11.
[58] As Taylor attempts to suggest (*Christians and the Holy Places*, 307-13).
[59] H. Chadwick, *The Early Church (Pelican History of the Church 1)*, London, Penguin, 1974, 117.
[60] Eusebius, *Church History*, 6: 34. His conclusion is universally rejected.

he could be put to the torture, he died in prison in 251.[61] It is not known if commissioners were sent to Jerusalem to check the certificates of those who had sacrificed to the gods.[62] J E Taylor deduces a climate of fear from the fact that the throne of James was not kept in one place.[63] According to Eusebius, 'the brethren look after it in turn.'[64] However, this may mean no more than each successive bishop kept it in his residence.

In 261 the rescript of the emperor Gallienus (253-68) guaranteed Christians the freedom to practice their faith.[65] In the 40 years which followed the menace to the church came from within. Eusebius lamented that, 'Increasing freedom transformed our character to arrogance and sloth; we began envying and abusing each other, cutting our own throats, as occasion offered, with weapons of sharp-edged words.'[66] None of these theological controversies, however, touched the church of Jerusalem, which became more and more a place of pilgrimage.[67]

---

[61] Eusebius, *Church History*, 6: 39.2-3.

[62] As elsewhere, the authorities in Caesarea would have had their hands full with local believers. 'Only prominent Christians were pursued, but there was no effective prison service where they could be detained for long periods. For the rest, the authorities, overwhelmed by their apparent success, were content to let matters be. In both Carthage and Alexandria there is evidence that about a score of confessors were imprisoned for obduracy, and there were some executions. but on the whole surprisingly little force had to be used' (W H C Frend, *The Early Church*, Philadelphia, Fortress, 1982, 99).

[63] *Christians and the Holy Places*, 209.

[64] *Church History*, 7: 19.

[65] Eusebius, *Church History*, 7: 13.

[66] *Church History*, 8: 1.7.

[67] *Proof of the Gospel*, 6: 18.23.

2

Jerusalem and the Holy Land in the 4th Century

Peter Walker

1 Introduction

When considering the Christian heritage in the Holy Land, the 4th century must rank as the 'jewel in the crown'. This is the century in which Jerusalem and the Holy Land first come into prominence within the Church world-wide, and in many ways the land of Palestine has been marked indelibly ever since with the imprint of what happened during this fascinating century. In the following we shall focus chiefly on the historical matters relating to the church during this period, but also note (briefly) the changing theological attitudes to Jerusalem and the Holy Land that took place as well.[1]

The contrast between the years 300 and 400, as far as Christianity in Palestine is concerned, is startling. At the close of the century we find a land transformed by the building of numerous churches, the influx of pilgrims from all quarters of the Byzantine empire and beyond, and the beginnings of monastic settlements in the Jerusalem area. In the 390s Jerome is living and studying in Bethlehem, encouraging his friends to travel to the 'holy places',[2] and claiming that every nation is now

---

[1] Much of this material is discussed more fully in my book: P W L Walker, *Holy City, Holy Places? Christian Attitudes to Jerusalem and the Holy Land in the Fourth Century*, Oxford, 1990, hereafter *HCHP*; cf. also 'Jerusalem in the Early Christian Centuries' in P W L Walker (ed.), *Jerusalem Past and Present in the Purposes of God*, Tyndale House, Cambridge, 1992; revd. ed., Paternoster/Baker, 1994, 79-98. Two key works on the historical and archaeological aspects of this subject should also be consulted: E D Hunt, *Holy Land Pilgrimage in the later Roman Empire AD 312-460*, Oxford, 1982, and J Wilkinson, *Egeria's Travels* (revd. ed.), Warminster, 1981.

[2] Jerome, *Ep.* 46; cf. *Ep.* 47.

represented in the Christian visitors to Palestine.[3] The Holy Land is being frequently visited by members of Theodosius' imperial court,[4] and the opinion of the Jerusalem bishop is being increasingly sought on matters of doctrinal controversy within the wider Church. Jerusalem and the Holy Land are on the 'centre stage'. What was believed and practised in Jerusalem was of vital interest to Christians elsewhere.

Yet contrast this with the beginning of the century! According to the the *Onomasticon* of Eusebius, written probably in the late 290s,[5] there were just three Christian villages in the entire province;[6] a few of the most important Gospel sites were indeed visited by pilgrims (Bethlehem, the Mount of Olives, Gethsemane, and the River Jordan),[7] but Jerusalem was still known by its pagan name of Aelia Capitolina.[8] The church in Aelia, whilst growing in strength throughout the previous century, was still comparatively insignificant,[9] and the only place where Christianity had put down strong roots was the provincial capital, Caesarea Maritima.[10] Moreover, the early years of the 4th century saw the revival of imperial persecution against the Church: Palestine was one of the provinces where the force of Diocletian's edict was felt most strongly, with the Christian community in Caesarea taking the brunt of the attack. Who could have foreseen the great reversal of fortune which the Palestinian Church would experience in the course of the next 100 years?

Eusebius, himself a resident in Caesarea (and its bishop from 313), has preserved for us a detailed account of those early years of persecution in his book, *the Martyrs of Palestine*. One story in particular reveals clearly the contrast with what was to follow. While travelling north through Palestine an Egyptian Christian, named Pamphilus, was arrested and brought before Formilianus, the provincial governor, and subsequently put to death because of his profession of Christian faith. During his interrogation, the governor asked him where he came from: 'from Jerusalem', he replied. Firmilianus then asked him where precisely this was, but even under torture Pamphilus only replied that 'it lay toward the far East and the rising sun' clearly intended as a description of the 'heavenly Jerusalem', his ultimate homeland.[11]

---

[3] Jerome, *Ep.* 108.3.3.

[4] See Hunt, *op. cit.*, 157 ff.

[5] T D Barnes in *Constantine and Eusebius* (Cambridge, MA, 1981), 110–11, dates it to 293; contra Wallace-Hadrill, *Eusebius of Caesarea*, London, 1960, 55–7.

[6] The villages of Anea, Iethira and Caraiatha: *Onom.* 26, 108, 12.

[7] See *Onom.* 58, 74; cf. *Dem. Ev.* 1.1.2, 3.2.47, 7.2.1–17, 6.18.23.

[8] See *HCHP*, 5, note 9. Indeed 'Aelia' continued to be used after 325 both in the official Byzantine lists and also on occasions by Christians such as Eusebius (*Theoph.* 4.20), Egeria (9.7): see Hunt, *op. cit.*, 149.

[9] See J Murphy O'Connor (above): cf. also *HCHP*, 9, and J. Wilkinson, *Jerusalem as Jesus knew it*, London, 1978, 176: 'the story of Christianity in Jerusalem makes depressing reading.'

[10] See Barnes, *op. cit.*, 81–105.

[11] See Eusebius, *Mart. Pal.* 11.9-12, discussed in Hunt, *op. cit.*, 4–5.

For our purposes the incident is intriguing on several accounts; for example, it shows the spiritual focus on the heavenly Jerusalem, rather than on the earthly Jerusalem, that was characteristic of much Christian spirituality in that pre-Constantinian period.[12] Yet it also reveals the complete ignorance of the governor in Caesarea that there was in his own province of Palestine (and not that far away) a city that had once been the world-famous city of Jerusalem. 'Jerusalem: where is that?', he asked. A century later, we may safely presume, few people in the empire let alone any government official in Palestine itself! would have needed to ask such a question.

2 The years after 325

The changes were indeed dramatic. With the Edict of Milan (313) persecution of Christians was officially brought to an end within the empire, though the emperor in the East, Licinius, revived a hostile approach to the Church before too long.[13] This would have been one of the contributory factors to the increasing tension between Constantine and Licinius which culminated in the battle of Adrianople in 324. Constantine's victory brought a Christian emperor to the eastern half of the empire, and within a year bishops were being invited to meet with him at the Council of Nicaea (July 325). One of the items on their agenda was Jerusalem.

Evidently a tension was already developing between the see of Caesarea (the metropolitan bishopric of the province) and the up-and-coming see of Aelia/Jerusalem: for the seventh canon promulgated at Nicaea declared:

> Since a custom and ancient tradition has held good, that the bishop of Aelia should be honoured, let him have his proper honour, saving to the metropolis [Caesarea] the honour peculiar to it.

Bishop Macarius of Aelia had clearly taken this opportunity to have his position as head of the 'mother' church in Jerusalem recognised. Since Eusebius, the bishop of Caesarea, had arrived at the council very much 'under a cloud' because of his Arian sympathies, he was hardly in a strong position.[14] Macarius' tactics thus seem undeniably opportunistic. This is the first appearance of an ecclesiastical dispute which would colour Eusebius' subsequent writings and his dealings with Jerusalem,[15] which would re-

---

[12] See below at n. 71ff.
[13] See Eusebius, *VC*, 1.51-53; EH. 10.8.15-18; cf. Barnes, *op. cit.*, 71-2.
[14] J Stevenson, *Studies in Eusebius*, Cambridge, 1929, 96; cf. also H Chadwick, 'Faith and Order at the Council of Nicaea', *HTR* 53 (1960), 173-4.
[15] See *HCHP*, ch. 4, 9, 11.

appear in the following generations,[16] and which would lead eventually to Bishop Juvenal's successfully establishing Jerusalem in the year 451 as the fifth patriarchate (alongside Constantinople, Alexandria, Antioch, and Rome).

Yet it is likely that Macarius discussed Jerusalem issues with the emperor *in private* as well. For he returned from Nicaea with Constantine's personal permission to set about the demolition of the Venus Temple in the centre of Jerusalem which the local church believed to mark the site of the Crucifixion and Resurrection of Christ.[17] So began one of the few archaeological excavations of antiquity, and certainly the most exciting! Eusebius' description of it in his Life of Constantine brims with excitement as 'contrary to all expectation' and their wildest dreams, 'the venerable and hallowed monument of our Saviour's Resurrection' was discovered.[18] Its appearance, after nearly 300 years of oblivion, was itself for Eusebius a powerful symbol of Resurrection light overcoming darkness, a 'faithful similitude of his return to life' and a 'testimony to the Resurrection clearer than any voice could give'.[19]

Most probably, some pieces of wood were also uncovered during these excavations, which were swiftly identified as none other than the *lignum crucis,* the wood of the cross. Constantine may be referring to this second significant discovery when he writes a note of congratulation to Macarius and comments on the 'fresh wonders' that are being brought to light.[20] Concerning this, as opposed to the tomb, Eusebius would appear to have been more sceptical: he probably doubted its authenticity as a historian, and for reasons both ecclesiastical and spiritual was wary of how the Jerusalem

---

[16] See e.g., Z Rubin, 'The tenure of Maximus, Bishop of Jerusalem, and the conflict between Caesarea and Jerusalem during the fourth century', *Cathedra* 31 (1984), 31–42.

[17] For the authenticity of the general site, see *HCHP*, 241-247. A more sceptical view is taken by Joan Taylor in *Christians and the Holy Places*, Oxford, 1992, 113-142, who sees a purely anti-pagan motivation for the selection of this site. Yet the reference in Melito of Sardis (c. 160?) to the crucifixion taking place 'in the middle of the city' (*On Pascha.* 72, 94) surely indicates that he had been shown a location in the middle of Aelia during his journey to the East (Eusebius, *EH.* 4.26.14); the silence concerning Golgotha, especially compared to the references to pilgrims visiting Bethlehem and the Mount of Olives (see above n.7), thus indicates a known inaccessibility. Eusebius himself, we suggest, was far from being an incredulous observer (see below at n. 21) and his simple reference in *Onom.* 74.19-21 to Golgotha being 'in Aelia to the north of Mt Sion' fits well with the site of the eventual church of the Holy Sepulchre.

[18] *VC.* 3.28. Eusebius never mentions that other tombs were found at the time (as the *kokim* tombs now visible by the wall of the Rotunda suggest they must have done) and therefore gives no indication of how they decided which was the right tomb.

[19] *Ibid.*

[20] *VC.* 3.30, as argued well by H A Drake in 'Eusebius and the True Cross', *JEH* 36 (1985), 1-22; cf. also Z Rubin, 'The Church of the Holy Sepulchre and the conflict between the sees of Caesarea and Jerusalem' in L I Levine (ed.), *Jerusalem Cathedra* 2 (Jerusalem and Detroit, 1982), 82-7; *contra* Hunt, *op. cit.*, 39.

church might develop a 'cult of relics' focused on this object.[21] Certainly the Jerusalem church would make much of this find: twenty years later, the Jerusalem bishop can boast that the 'wood of the cross is now filling the world',[22] whilst what remained was by Egeria's day being brought out on display each Good Friday to be venerated though kept firmly on the bishop's knee and supervised by a posse of deacons, since on one occasion a devotee had succeeded in biting off a chunk for home consumption![23]

It is unlikely that the emperor's mother, Helena, was directly involved in the discovery of this 'true cross': the connection is not in the earliest sources and is first attested only in the 390s by Ambrose of Milan.[24] Yet that this important imperial personage did come on pilgrimage in those early years after 325, there is no doubt.[25] According to Eusebius her involvement was more to do with the extension of the Constantinian programme to include the building of churches at Bethlehem and on the Mount of Olives.[26] Eusebius himself may have been personally involved in this extension since he waxes lyrical about the 'triad' of churches now built over the 'three mystical caves' which themselves were associated with the three central events in the Creed: Jesus' Birth, Death/Resurrection, and Ascension.[27]

Eusebius' fondness for 'caves' is slightly puzzling.[28] In certain locations 'caves' may have been useful fixed landmarks for Christian pilgrims and indeed provided necessary shelter for acts of worship (and there would thus be other sites in the 4th century associated with caves); yet Eusebius seems to attach some more mystical meaning to them which is somewhat out of keeping with his otherwise fairly 'cerebral' approach to the Gospel sites. Moreover, it forced him effectively to associate the cave on the Mount of Olives with the unlikely event of the Ascension.[29] For understandable reasons the idea of a cave for the Ascension was a little confusing for pilgrims,[30] and later in the century a small church, the Imbomon, was built

---

[21] See *HCHP*, 126-130. The rapid growth of the 'relic trade' is well discussed in Hunt, *op. cit.*, ch. 6. 'Towards the end of the century there was a sudden awakening of the impetus to discover hitherto unsuspected remains: thus revelations unearthed a succession of OT prophets, Habakkuk, Micah, Zechariah, to be capped only by the emergence in Dec. 415 of the tomb of St Stephen' (*op. cit.*, 131); Jerome in defending the relic trade to Vigilantius describes the transportation of the bones of the prophet Samuel to Constantinople in extremely colourful terms.

[22] Cyril, *Catech.* 4.10, 10.19, 13.4; cf. also *ibid.* 13.39 and *Ep. Const.* 3.

[23] Egeria 37.2; see Hunt, *op. cit.*, 128.

[24] *De Obitu Theodosii*, 41ff (AD 395).

[25] See Hunt, *op. cit.*, ch. 2, for a full discussion of the date and the motivation of this famous 'pilgrimage'.

[26] *VC* 3.41-3.

[27] *L Const.* 9.16-17; VC. 3.41-3. See *HCHP*, 184-198.

[28] Most notably the cave for the Sermon on the Mount at Heptapegon (modern Tabgha). For this tension in Eusebius, see *HCHP*, 41-50 compared with *ibid.*, 188-194.

[29] See Hunt, *op. cit.*, 162; *HCHP*, 190.

[30] It is possible that the famous mistake of the Bordeaux Pilgrim (595.4-596.1) in believing the Mount of Olives to be the site of the Transfiguration might have been occasioned by a general confusion at the site resulting from Eusebius' over-tight schema: see *HCHP*, 213-14.

on the summit of the Mount of Olives: appropriately, this time, it had no roof, being open to the skies![31]

Eusebius died in 339, Constantine in 337. The emperor had never visited the Holy Land. At his baptism shortly before his death he said that he had wished to be baptized 'in the waters of the river Jordan', but it was not to be.[32] So he never saw the great Martyrium church, built over Golgotha and was absent from its Dedication in September 335. The bishops who had been at a council in Tyre discussing the fate of Athanasius made their way on to Jerusalem for this great occasion,[33] and Arius was re-admitted to communion during the course of its proceedings a foretaste of the way in which Jerusalem would inevitably become embroiled in the controversies that were affecting the wider church during the course of the 4th century.[34]

Many speeches were delivered by the bishops, including one no doubt by Macarius' successor, Bishop Maximus. According to recent scholarship, Eusebius' speech on this occasion is to be identified with chapters 11-18 of the work known as de laudibus Constantini; if correct, as is likely, it is significant for our understanding of Eusebius that his focus is not on the Resurrection of Christ at all, but rather on his favoured concept of the 'theophany' of the Logos. Eusebius then travelled to Constantinople where he delivered the same address for the emperor's benefit.

It is likely that some time during the episcopate of Bishop Maximus, who died in 348, the local Jerusalem church was responsible for the building of a new church on Mt Sion to mark the site of Pentecost and the place where the local congregation had been meeting for many years.[35] This is referred to by Maximus' successor, Cyril, in the Catechetical Lectures which he delivered in the new Martyrium church to the baptismal candidates in the Lent of 350.[36] These lectures make fascinating reading,

---

[31] This was built by Poemenia some time after Egeria's visit in 384 (since she makes no reference to a 'church' but only to the 'place') but before 392 when Jerome (*Comm. in Zeph.* 1.15) refers to the resplendent cross which surmounted it. See Hunt, *op. cit.*, 162; on its archaeology, see J Wilkinson, *Egeria's Travels*, 49-53.

[32] *VC*. 4.62.

[33] Eusebius describes this in *VC*. 4.43-47: 'Thus Jerusalem became the gathering point for distinguished prelates from every province, and the whole city was thronged by a vast assemblage of God's servants . . . In short, the whole of Syria and Mesopotamia, Phoenicia and Arabia, Palestine, Egypt and Libya, all contributed to swell the mighty concourse of God's ministers.' The festivities included 'feasts and banquets' at imperial expense, and donations to the local poor.

[34] Many speeches were delivered by bishops, including one no doubt by Macarius' successor, Bishop Maximus. According to recent scholarship, Eusebius' speech on this occasion is to be identified with chapters 11-18 of the work known as *de laudibus Constantini* (see H.A. Drake, *In Praise of Constantine* (Berkeley, 1976). If correct, it is significant for our understanding of Eusebius that his focus is not on the Resurrection of Christ at all, but rather on his favoured concept of the 'theophany' of the *Logo* (see *HCHP*, 113-16). Eusebius then travelled to Constantinople where he delivered the same address for the emperor's benefit.

[35] See J Murphy-O'Connor (above) and B Pixner, 'Church of the Apostles found on Mt Zion', *BA* 16.3 (1990), 16-35, 60.

[36] Or, possibly, 348: see *HCHP*, 410.

both as an example of catechetical teaching of this period and for the attitude which Cyril conveys concerning the emerging 'holy places' and Jerusalem. Some of the marked contrasts between Cyril and Eusebius, but a half-generation apart, will be noted below.[37]

3 Egeria and the end of the century

The rest of the century sees a continued influx of pilgrims; an anonymous pilgrim from Bordeaux had come as early as 333 and in his brief notes of his travelogue has left some vital information about what was being 'pointed out' in the first decade after 325.[38] Many others followed in his steps, and Helena's example seems to have inspired many women from the western half of the empire: from the 380s onwards we know the names of several such female pilgrims for example, Poemenia, Paula, Fabiola, Melania, Sylvia of Aquitane and (most famously) Egeria.[39]

Egeria's travelogue (dating from 381-4) is far more detailed than that of the Bordeaux pilgrim and gives us a clear picture of the changes that had taken place in the intervening fifity years, no doubt in large part due to the influence of Bishop Cyril whose long episcopate only came to an end with his death in c. 384.[40] She indicates that several more churches had since been built in the Jerusalem area (including the Lazarium at Bethany and a 'graceful church' to mark the 'agony' in Gethsemane);[41] she refers to the Anastasis as a separate building from the Martyrium, indicating that the rotunda over Christ's tomb had now been completed;[42] she comments on the lavish decorations within the Constantinian basilicas;[43] and she witnesses to the elaborate pattern of services that had been developed to take full advantage of the proximity of these Gospel sites, especially during Holy Week. The development of Holy Week and of the 'Christian year' as a whole was to be one of the most significant and lasting legacies of Jerusalem to the rest of the Church.[44] As Gregory Dix amusingly observed,

---

[37] See below section 5.

[38] Hunt, *op. cit.*, 83-4; Wilkinson, *op. cit.*,153-164.

[39] Hunt (*op. cit.*, 164 ff) argues for Egeria's coming from NW Spain and being associated with the imperial court of Theodosius in Constantinople; she was in Constantinople before coming to the Holy Land whilst Theodosius himself came from Spain.

[40] See G Dix, *The Shape of the Liturgy*, London, 1945, 349-352.

[41] See Wilkinson, *op. cit.*, 53; on the apparently conflicting witness of Egeria (36.1) and Jerome (*Onom.* 75) concerning the church at Gethsemane, see *HCHP*, 229-234 and J Taylor, *op. cit.*, 192 ff.

[42] Originally Christ's tomb was in an open courtyard; since Cyril makes no mention of the Anastasis/rotunda in his Lectures, its construction is likely to date to between 348 and 381 (see Wilkinson, *op. cit.*, 40).

[43] Egeria 25.8-9: 'The decorations are really too marvellous for words. All you can see is gold and jewels and silk . . . You simply cannot imagine the number, and the sheer weight of the candles and the tapers and lamps and everything else they use for the services' (trans. Wilkinson).

[44] See Dix, *op. cit.*, esp ch. 11 ('the sanctification of time').

one can easily imagine how church-wardens throughout the empire were confronted by the likes of Egeria upon their return with the unbeatable argument, 'that's not how it is done in JERUSALEM'![45]

And so, once again, a 'word went forth from Jerusalem'.[46] Earlier in the century Eusebius had emphasized how Palestine was the 'source' from which the life-giving word of the Gospel had 'gushed forth' to the ends of the earth.[47] Now the ripple-pattern was being repeated. Space does not permit a full account of all the pilgrims whose names we know (such as Evagrius, Palladius and Rufinus), let alone the countless thousands whose names are lost to history; we know that a large number came from Egypt and from Mesopotamia and that the Greek services had to be translated into Syriac (and often into Latin).[48] Yet each one will have returned home with fresh liturgical experience, with tangible mementoes or 'relics' and almost certainly with a renewed faith in the events forever associated with the Holy Land. In this way Jerusalem and the Holy Land had a lasting impact on places far beyond its own borders, just as had the message of Jesus three hundred years before.

4 *Jerusalem tensions*

Yet, in concluding this brief section on the church's history, it must be said that not everything was straightforward or 'golden' in this period of the church's development in the Holy Land. There were clashes of opinion and episodes less than wholesome. Despite the impression that Cyril would prefer to convey, Jerusalem was far from a 'Christian city'.[49] The majority of the city's population would probably have been pagan throughout this period,[50] and Jerome on a bad day could describe Jerusalem as a:

> crowded city, with its council, its garrison, its prostitutes, actors, jesters, and everything which is usually found in other cities.[51]

He had once described Rome as 'Babylon',[52] but now he acknowledged that in Jerusalem too one was 'forced to endure everything that you seek to escape from elsewhere'. He also made an accusation (along with

---

[45] 'Christian human nature is endearingly the same': Dix, *op. cit.*, 379.

[46] Isa. 2.3c, quoted by Cyril in *Catech.* 18.34.

[47] *De Laudibus Constantini* 9.15, 11.2; cf. *Proph. Eclg.* 4.1.

[48] Egeria 47.3-4; see Hunt, *op. cit.*, 152

[49] 'The Jerusalem of old crucified Christ, but this Jerusalem worships him' (*Catech.* 13.7).

[50] See e.g. Hunt, *op. cit.*, 147 ff.

[51] Jerome, *Ep.* 58.4.4. On the number of Christians in the region, see e.g. J H W G Liebeschuetz, 'Problems arising from the conversion of Syria', *Studies in Church History* 16 (1979), 17-24.

[52] *Ep.* 45.6.

Epiphanius?) against Cyril's successor, Bishop John, that he was too extravagant in his life-style.[53]

Yet some of this anti-Jerusalem polemic in Jerome is itself the sad result of the tension that blew up between himself and the Jerusalem establishment (and between his own monastic settlements at Bethlehem and those of Rufinus and Melania on the Mount of Olives); this became so heated that he even described it as a *domestica bella*, a 'local war'.[54] The dispute about the theology of Origen that was affecting other parts of the Church at that time became inextricably entwined with this local feud. Twenty years later another controversy (concerning Pelagius) beset the wider Church and again the opinion of the Jerusalem bishop was sought. Christian unity proved hard to maintain.

Bishop John's experience was not dissimilar to that of his predecessor. Cyril too was involved in the wider theological controversies of his day: back in the 350s he had been exiled from his see on several different occasions because of his tenacious commitment to the Nicene theology at a time when 'the world awoke and groaned to find itself Arian';[55] Nicene theology was only re-established towards the very end of his life at Chalcedon (381). Meanwhile his financial dealings were also criticised, though on the opposite charge: he was accused – apparently not without cause – of selling some of the church's possessions (including some golden vestments presented by Constantine to Bishop Macarius for use in baptismal services) in order to pay for the ever-increasing throng of pilgrims who looked to the Jerusalem church for hospitality.[56] Then as now there was a price to be paid for being the 'mother-church'!

On a more serious note, although from a wider political perspective this was a period of comparative peace for the eastern provinces of the empire,[57] within Palestine itself there was the inevitable tension with the Jewish populace, for whom the coming of a Christian emperor posed further uncertainties.[58] Constantine reinstituted Hadrian's ban upon Jews entering Jerusalem (which, though never repealed, may have lapsed somewhat in practice), with the significant alteration that they were allowed to visit on one day in the year the 9th of Av, the anniversary of the Temple's destruction in AD 70).[59]

---

[53] Jerome, *Ep.* 5.12.5, 125.18; Epiphanius, as remembered in *Synaxarium Aethiopicum* (*PO* i 602ff).

[54] *Ep.* 77.8.

[55] Hilary, *De Synodis*, 10.

[56] Sozomen, *EH.* 4.25.3-4; Theodoret, *EH.* 2.27.1-2. Two centuries later the task of the Jerusalem church in this regard was likened to the 'feeding of the 5,000' (Justinian, *Nov.* 40)! Yet against this must be reckoned the great influx of wealth into the Holy Land as result of Christian beneficence: see Hunt, *op. cit.*, 137 ff and M Avi-Yonah, 'The Economics of Byzantine Palestine', *IEJ* 8 (1958), 39-51.

[57] In the winter of 394-5, however, there were rumours of barbarian invasions during the absence of Theodosius' army in the West (Jerome, *Ep.* 8.2.).

[58] See M Avi-Yonah, *The Jews of Palestine*, Oxford, 1976, 158-73.

[59] *Op. cit.*, 164.

This legislation (commented upon almost immediately by the Bordeaux Pilgrim[60,] and effectively the origin of the 'Wailing Wall') may have been a contributory factor behind the short-lived Jewish revolt against Gallus Caesar in AD 351 (which started in Sepphoris).[61] It will certainly have been influential on the thinking of the pagan emperor, Julian, who actively encouraged the Jews to return to Jerusalem and to begin rebuilding the Temple.[62] His intention was to overturn the Constantinian settlement, to prove Jesus' prophetic words false and to demonstrate that Christianity was illegitimate.[63]

This they attempted to do in the spring of 363 no doubt amidst an atmosphere in Jerusalem of great tension but proceedings were brought to a sudden halt on 27 May. Subsequent Christian legend embellished the tale, but the pagan historian, Ammianus Marcellinus, acknowledged that the project was abandoned because of an earthquake and subsequent fires probably in what are now known as 'Solomon's Stables' under the Temple platform.[64] The sudden death of Julian on 16 June, then brought their hopes to an end. Later in the century John Chrysostom would take this failed attempt as a clear sign that Christ was the truth and that his Gospel teaching did not 'allow for the rebuilding of the Temple'.[65] Jerusalem was ever a place of controversy and able to evoke strong emotions and conflicts.[66]

---

[60] *BP.* 591.5

[61] Avi-Yonah (*op. cit.*, 174-81) cites the new Constantinian laws forbidding Jews to have Gentile slaves as perhaps the major cause of the revolt, since it severely threatened Jewish industry, especially in Sepphoris, Tiberias and Lydda – the three towns to which the revolt spread before it was suppressed by Ursicinus.

[62] The Jewish leadership was probably unenthusiastic about Julian's programme, in part because they believed any such rebuilding should be brought about by the Messiah, not a pagan emperor: see Avi-Yonah, *op. cit.*, 191-204, who argues that Julian's intention was that Christian property in Jerusalem and perhaps Jerusalem itself should be returned into Jewish hands. See also M Adler, 'The Emperor Julian and the Jews', *Jewish Quarterly Review* 5 (1893), 591-651; F Blanchetire, 'Julien Philhellne, Philosmite, Antichrétien: L'affaire du Temple de Jérusalem (363)', *JJS* 31 (1980), 61-81; D B Levenson, 'A source and traditional critical study of the stories of Julian's attempt to rebuild the Jerusalem Temple' (Unpublished thesis, Hebrew Univ.).

[63] See R L Wilken, *John Chrysostom and the Jews*, Univ. of California, 1983, 145, who argues that Julian was motivated entirely by anti-Christian considerations, not through any pro-Zionism.

[64] Amm. Marc. 23.1; cf. also Rufinus *EH.* 10.39-40. The letter attributed to Cyril of Jerusalem is probably inauthentic but nevertheless dependent on early Jerusalem tradition about the events: see S P Brock, 'The Rebuilding of the Temple under Julian, a new source', *PEQ* 108 (1976), 103-7; *id.*, 'A Letter attributed to Cyril of Jerusalem on the rebuilding of the Temple', *BSOAS* 40 (1977), 267-86.

[65] John Chrysostom, *Homilia adversus Iudaeos*, 5; see Wilken, *op. cit.*, 157.

[66] Cyril, *Ep. Const.* 3, where he quotes Matt. 24.30 ('then will appear in heaven the sign that heralds the Son of Man'); cf. his *Catech.* 15.22 and Sozomen, *EH.* 4.5, 5.4. The evidence of Jerome (*Comm. in Zech.* 14.10) suggests that there was quite a considerable interest in questions of prophecy at the end of the 4th century: see Wilken, *op. cit.*, 146.

That the religious atmosphere could sometimes be quite intense is also indicated by the way the populace had responded earlier (in May 351) to a strange optical effect (known as a parhelion) when the the Jerusalem sky was filled with a bright light stretching from Golgotha to the Mount of Olives which outshone the sun and (according to some) was in the shape of a cross: crowds rushed to the new Martyrium basilica believing the return of Christ was imminent. Evidently for many Christians Jerusalem would play a central role in the events of the Second Coming. Jerusalem undeniably had a significant past, but it also had a glorious future!

5 Contrasting theologies

Finally, something must be said of the theological attitudes to Jerusalem and the 'holy places' that accompanied this developing history. From the time of Cyril's *Catechetical Lectures* onwards, there is a clear enunciation both in theory and in practice that Jerusalem is indeed a 'holy city' and that the Gospel sites are indeed 'holy places'. Yet this had not always been the case, and even at the end of the 4th century leading figures such as Jerome and Gregory of Nyssa could be disputing the validity of such sacramental ways of thinking.

The contrast between Eusebius and Cyril here is quite instructive. Contrary to the frequently-held notion that the Christian Holy Land was probably the brain-child of Eusebius, I have argued elsewhere that Eusebius' attitude to this new phenomenon were distinctly ambivalent.[67] He never spoke of Jerusalem as a 'holy city': the two uses of this phrase in the Gospels (Matt. 4:5; 27:53) he interpreted as references to the 'heavenly Jerusalem', and he argued strongly that if Jerusalem had indeed been the 'city of God' in Old Testament times, it was so no longer.[68] Twenty years later, Cyril would interpret those same Gospel verses as clearly referring 'to this city of Jerusalem in which we are now',[69] and would interpret verses from Isaiah and other parts of the Old Testament in such a way as to show the distinct continuity of Jerusalem and its unaltered special status in God's purposes.[70]

It is easy to suggest that personal bias may have coloured both these presentations. After all, Cyril was bishop of Jerusalem (who ever heard a Jerusalem bishop *play down* the importance of Jerusalem?!) whilst Eusebius as metropolitan of Caesarea stood to lose directly if Jerusalem rose to too great a prominence. Yet Eusebius' reasoning was more theological than that. For (as seen at the outset concerning the Egyptian Christian on trial) he shared with the pre-Constantinian church a spirituality that looked

---

[67] *HCHP*, esp. chs. 2–4, 11.
[68] See esp. *DE*. 4.12.4; 8.2.16; 10.8.64; *Comm. in Ps.* [87.11–13], *PG* 1064b; these are discussed in *HCHP*, 358–76.
[69] *Catech.* 14.16.
[70] For example, Isa. 1.26–7, 40.9, 65.18, 66.1, 10; see *HCHP*, 321–5.

beyond this world to the 'heavenly Jerusalem' (a natural thing for a Church still experiencing persecution); more importantly still, he had developed a consistent apologetic argument against Judaism which, at its simplest, caricatured an interest in the earthly Jerusalem as the distinctive hallmark of Judaism not of Christianity.[71] It was hard for such a theologian suddenly to acknowledge that Jerusalem was important for Christians after all.

In any period the Church's relationship to Judaism is a delicate issue: Eusebius' preference was to maintain as strong a contrast as possible, Cyril's to appropriate as much as possible. The Jerusalem beloved of the Jews thus became the Jerusalem sacred to the Christians. In some ways we have to acknowledge that this Christian emphasis on Jerusalem was indeed a new phenomenon within the Church's life, though Cyril (and perhaps many today) would have been keen to deny this: the 4th century simply provided, they believed, a new opportunity to express the importance which Jerusalem had always had for Christians.

A similar contrast (though less sharp) can also be detected between Eusebius and Cyril concerning the holiness of individual sites. For apologetical and spiritual reasons again Eusebius before 325 had emphasised that Christian worship was 'in spirit and in truth' and unlike Judaism was not tied to 'particular places' (*aphorismenois topois*).[72] He thus had a great historical interest in the Gospel sites, as revealed for example in his *Onomasticon*, but he did not inveigh them with any spiritual significance. After 325, though this framework remains, his language does begin to alter: the exciting discovery of Christ's tomb evidently made a strong impression upon him and he describes the 'cave' of the resurrection as like the 'holy of holies' in the former Temple,[73] and talks of Helena's journey to Jerusalem as an enactment of Psalm 91:7 in the Septuagint version ('let us worship at the place where his feet have stood').[74] Eusebius' thinking about the Gospel sites was beginning to move in a direction that would find a fuller expression in the teaching of Cyril, who constantly speaks of the Gospel sites as powerful 'witnesses' to the truth[75] and as themselves 'holy',[76] indeed 'all-holy'[77] and 'blessed'.[78]

[71] *DE.* 1.6.38-9; cf. also *ibid.*, 1.3.41, 1.6.43, 1.7.6, 2.3.38; see *HCHP*, 57, 67-70.

[72] *DE.*1.6.39-49, 44, 57. Such a line of argument reflects the teaching of Origen in Caesarea: see e.g. Origen, *Hom. in Josh.* 17.1.

[73] *VC.* 3.28. On the parallels developed between the church of the Holy Sepulchre and the former Temple (especially in relation to the Dedication festival), see J. Wilkinson, 'Jewish influences on the early Christian rite of Jerusalem', *Muséon* 92 (1979), 347-59. Once again there is the combination of a desire for both continuity and opposition. Eusebius is taking the contrary tack in *VC.* 3.33 when he describes the new church (not the whole city) as a 'new Jerusalem over against the one so celebrated of old' (the Temple): see further, *HCHP*, 399.

[74] *VC.* 3.42.

[75] See his three extended lists of such 'witnesses' in *Catech.* 10.19, 13.38-9, 14.22-3.

[76] *Catech.* 5.10, 10.19, 13.38-9.

[77] *Catech.* 1.1., 13.22.

[78] *Catech.* 4.10, 10.19.

Cyril's attitude would effectively win the day, yet it is worth noting that both Jerome and Gregory of Nyssa felt it necessary to sound some cautionary notes, *dis*suading people of the need to visit the Holy Land and warding off any excessive emphasis on 'holy places' as somehow essential to salvation: the 'door of paradise' lay wide open to those who had never seen Jerusalem and the important thing was not simply 'to have been to Jerusalem, but in Jerusalem to have lived a good life' (*'non Hierosolymis fuisse, sed Hierosolymis bene vixisse'*).[79] Such sentiments are clearly still timely and valuable in today's quite different contexts.

Conclusion

This is a fitting note on which to conclude this brief survey of both the history and the thought of the Church in Jerusalem and the Holy Land in the 4th century. As indicated above, there were some dark days but nothing as compared with what the Church would have to undergo in the many centuries that were to follow. In comparison with those, the period of the 4th century (and indeed, if there were time to recount, so too that of the 5th and 6th centuries) stands as a golden era. Without the events of the 4th century, our Christian heritage in this land would have been quite different and indeed much, much poorer. That era cannot come back to us, but its memory can live on, and its heritage treasured and passed on to them that come after.

---

[79] Jerome, *Ep.* 58.3 (to Paulinus of Nola); Gregory, *Ep.* 2 (c. 380 AD).

3

The Egyptian Relations of Early Palestinian Monasticism

Samuel Rubenson

Sixteen hundred years ago, in the early morning of the 13 September, 393 AD, a very dignified and ascetic bishop, more than 80 years old, but still very active, preached a sermon in the Martyrion, the great Constantinian cathedral of Jerusalem adjacent to the Anastasis, the rotunda surrounding the Holy Sepulchre. The bishop was Epiphanius, who had, for more than 25 years, been the metropolitan bishop of Salamis in Cyprus, but who was a man from Palestine and still head of the monastery he had founded half a century earlier at Besanduc, his native village, just outside the Graeco-Roman town of Eleutheropolis, present-day Bet-Guvrin.[1] The occasion for this visit in Jerusalem of the famous bishop of Cyprus was the feast of the dedication of the church linked to the Ascension of the Cross, which apart from Easter was the greatest feast of the year in the Church of Jerusalem. The church was undoubtedly packed with visitors from the land itself and from abroad, bishops and pilgrims from Palestine, Syria, Mesopotamia and Egypt as well as from Greece, Italy, Spain and Gaul. Notable among them was Jerome, who had come up from his monastery in Bethlehem to see his good old friend Epiphanius, and who is responsible for our eye-witness account of what happened that September-day in 393.[2]

Epiphanius of Salamis had for some years devoted most of his energy on a crusade against anything that could be termed heretic. His arch-foe was Origen, who to him seemed to be the source and instigator of all

[1] For the career of Epiphanius, see Pierre Nautin, 'Epiphane', *Dictionnaire d'Histoire et Géographie Ecclésiastique* 15, Paris, 1963, 617-631, and Jon F Dechow, *Dogma and Mysticism in Early Christianity: Epiphanius of Cyprus and the Legacy of Origen*, North American Patristic Society Monograph Series 13, Mercer University Press, 1988.

[2] The celebration of the dedication of the church and of the Cross is described by the contemporary eye-witness Egeria. See *Itineraium Egeriae*, chs. 48-49.

subsequent heresies. In his sermon Epiphanius could not withstand the temptation to air his suspicion about Origenistic tendencies in the teaching of the local bishop, John of Jerusalem.[3] What probably had made Epiphanius so concerned is the fact that the young and elegant bishop of Jerusalem was a close friend of the two famous Romans on the Mount of Olives, Rufinus of Aquileia and Melania the Elder, both well-known admirers of Origen and supporters of his followers among the monks in Egypt.[4] Bishop John of Jerusalem listened to the sermon but finally found that his guest had gone too far and while Epiphanius still spoke he sent his archdeacon to tell the honoured guest to shut up. This was not popular with the assembled congregation, to whom the old bishop of Salamis was known as a native and a ascetic holy man; and after the liturgy had ended he was immediately surrounded by people who wanted to be blessed by him. Bishop John lost his temper for a second time this same morning and accused Epiphanius for his vanity and his love for praise. Next day John took his revenge in a long sermon against all simple people who think that God has arms and legs and who condemn Origen while they themselves understand nothing. That it was Epiphanius who was the aim of his attack must have been obvious to all present.[5]

There is little reason to doubt the accuracy of Jerome's report, penned down in a letter to his friend Pammachius in Rome two and a half years later.[6] From other sources and subsequent events we know that Epiphanius was eager to eradicate Origenism in Palestine and that John of Jerusalem, as well as Rufinus and Melania, were sharply opposed to the aged saint of Cyprus.

Behind what occurred in the church we can detect some of the very close relations between Egyptian and Palestinian monasticism. According to his biographer, Epiphanius had, while still a very young man, stayed some years in Egypt in the 330s before he founded his monastery in

---

[3] For John of Jerusalem, see Daniel Stiernon, 'Jean de Jérusalem', *DSp (Dictionnaire de la Spiritualité)* 8, Paris, 1974, 565-574.

[4] Rufinus and Melania had arrived and set up their twin establishment in 378 and 381 respectively. For details on their lives and relations with John of Jerusalem see Thelamon, Françoise, 'Rufine d'Aquilée', *DSp* 13, Paris, 1988; Nicole Moine, 'Mélanie l'ancien', *DSp* 10, Paris, 1978, 955-960, and *idem*, 'Melaniana' in *Recherches Augustiniennes* 15 (1980); J N D Kelly, *Jerome. His Life, Writings and Controversies*, Duckworth, London, 1975, 121; Elizabeth Clark, *The Origenist Controversy. The Cultural Construction of an Early Christian Debate*, Princeton University Press, 1992, 11-16, 20-25, 188-193; and Derwas Chitty, *The Desert a City*, Oxford, 1966, 46-49.

[5] The events in the church are discussed in Kelly, *op. cit.*, 199f. The background for this conflict was Epiphanius's charge that Origen denied that man in his body was made in the image of God and the counter-charge by the Origenists that their opponents were anthropomorphists. See Clark, *op. cit.*, 43-75 and 86-104.

[6] Jerome, *Contra Ioannem* 11, 14. The text was written in early 397 in response to John's lost *Apologia* which he had sent to Theophilus of Alexandria in June 396.

Palestine.[7] And throughout his life the Egyptian monks remained his self-evident models as well as his bitter enemies. Undoubtedly strongly impressed and heavily influenced by the emerging Egyptian desert tradition he spent large parts of his writings condemning what he considered heretical tendencies among the Egyptian ascetics. In his list of heresies the Egyptian monks turn up again and again as the proponents of strange sects, usually characterized by immoral behaviour.[8] Jerome, who thought of himself as a disciple and heir to the cause of Epiphanius had also visited Egypt before settling in Bethlehem. Unlike Epiphanius he had, however, not managed to go to Egypt in his youth, nor had he been able to stay for any more extended period of time.[9] It does not seem as if he had made any friends there either. Even Didymus, with whom he stayed for 30 days, and hailed as a great exegete, is later censured for his Origenism. Like Epiphanius Jerome never had any success with his Egyptian relations, and both of them became rather critical of the Egyptian tradition, especially the influence of Origen.

Jerome's views on the Egyptian tradition is manifest in two of his most celebrated writings, the lives of Paul and Hilarion. In both he manages to give his heroes an Egyptian legitimacy at the same time as he takes his chance to discredit St Antony and the tradition emerging out of his footsteps. The first work, *The Life of Paul,* centres around the fact that Antony was not the founding father of the tradition, but the heir to an unknown hermit called Paul.[10] The second story, the *Vita Hilarionis,* is more interesting. It deals with a Palestinian monk, Hilarion, from a village outside Gaza, who went to Egypt to see the desert fathers. But it is rather significant that the Vita tells about his visit to Egypt *after* he had become a famous holy man and wonderworker at home, with a monastery of his own in the neighbourhood of Gaza, and that he goes to Egypt only to find that Antony had died and that nobody knew his grave and nobody cared for his monastery. Hilarion then leaves Egypt and ends up in Cyprus. It seems quite probable that Jerome actually modelled this story on the life of Epiphanius, his own favourite bishop, but somehow turns it upside down

---

[7] See Sozomenos, *Historia ecclesiastica* VI.32 and *Acta S. Epiphanii* 2 (*PG* 41: 1196C) and the very legendary *Vita Epiphanii* (*PG* 41: 24–112). For lack of evidence it can, howeverm be doubted that Epiphanius spent any longer period of time in Egypt or that he ever met with the leaders of emerging monasticism. He does not see to have had any personal relations with any of the monks and his assessment of the monastic tradition of Egypt in his own writings does not show any detailed knowledge.

[8] See *i.a.* Epiphanius, *Panarion* 26 and 39.

[9] Jerome arrived in Alexandria in the early summer of 386. His visit, together with Paula, to the desert was very short, and did only include Nitria. For their trip to Egypt see Jerome, *Ep.* 108. Rufinus, who had spent 8 years in Egypt a decade earlier scorns Jerome for his superficial knowledge of the Egyptian tradition.

[10] See *Vita Pauli* (*PL* 23). The origin of the story about Paul of Thebe has been intensely debated, but few, even in Jerome's own time, have believed it to rest on historical ground. See M Fuhrmann, 'Die Mönchsgeschichten des Hieronymus. Formexperimente in erzählender Literatur', *Christianisme et formes littéraires de l'antique ité tardive en occident,* Genève 1976.

to make the Palestinian monk a famous holy man before he goes to Egypt, where he virtually finds nothing. There is no other source mentioning Hilarion, nor any known disciples of his, except for Epiphanius himself.[11]

It was not, however, only Epiphanius and Jerome who had their relations with Egypt. Their enemies on the Mount of Olives, Rufinus and Melania, also had their own, albeit very different, experiences of the Egyptian scene before settling in Jerusalem in 378 and 381. They had actually met each other in Egypt when Melania visited Nitria and the desert fathers in 372. She was a young aristocratic widow who upon death of her husband and two children left Rome for the ascetics of the desert. She even became a friend of Abba Pambo, the first generation desert father who was thought of as a master of people like St Macarius and the four tall brothers, the inner circle among Nitriote Origenists.[12] While Melania set off for Jerusalem, the goal of her pilgrimage, Rufinus stayed on for eight years as a student of Didymus, the famous blind biblical scholar and heir to Origen's exegetical endeavour. He did not, however, spend all his time at the feet of Didymus, but paid regular visits to the desert including a trip to the desert retreat of St Antony some twenty years after the 'father of the monks' had passed away.[13] In contrast to Epiphanius and Jerome the visits of Melania and Rufinus were profitable for themselves and their relations with the Egyptians remained excellent. Rufinus did not only translate some of Origen's major works, he also contributed greatly to our documentation of the early monastic tradition, both by his continuation of Eusebius' *Historia Ecclesiastica,* and by his translation and revision of the *Historia Monachorum in Aegypto,* the famous guidebook to the desert fathers, written sometime in the 390s by a Jerusalemite deacon, most probably from his own monastery. The book soon became a major monastic classic in the East as well as in the West, where it was always attributed to Rufinus.[14]

Among the friends of Rufinus and Melania were some who had originally come to Palestine to visit the holy places, but who had moved down to Egypt attracted by what they were told about the desert fathers.

---

[11] Hilarion is treated as an historical person by Chitty and most modern authors. The only sources are Sozomenos and Jerome. See Sozomenos, *Historia Ecclesiastica* III.14; V.10. Sozomenos says that Hilarion met St Antony while he was young studying philosophy in Alexandria and that he became amonk in Palestine and died in Cyprus. All this could be taken from Jerome, whose *Vita Hilarionis* is largely based on the *Vita Antonii* as stressed in Philip Rousseau, *Ascetics, Authority and the Church in the Age of Jerome and Cassian,* Oxford, 1978, 136-139.

[12] Melania was one of the first prominent westerners to visit the desert fathers. She had come to Egypt after the death of her husband and spent half a year with the monks, generously assisting them out of her great wealth. Apparently it was only later that the monks thought it impossible to receive women into the desert. Her visit is recorded in Palladius, *Historia Lausiaca,* 46.

[13] Rufinus's stay in Egypt is first mentioned in a letter from Jerome to Rufinus (ep. 3) and later referred to in Rufinus's *Apologia* and in his *Historia Ecclesiastica* II.4.

[14] For the *Historia Monachorum* and its various versions in all the languages of the early Christian tradition see *CPG* 5620. The Latin version of Rufinus is edited with extensive commentaries by Ewa Schulz-Flügel as *Rufinus, Historia Monachorum* (Patristische Texte und Studien 34), Walter de Gruyter, Berlin 1990.

Two of them became important authors of works of primary importance for Palestinian as well as Egyptian monastic tradition, and both were from Asia Minor, Palladius from Galatia and Evagrius from Pontus. The latter had grown up under the direction of the great Cappadocian fathers, and had been a celebrated deacon in Constantinople before he had to flee the city after a love-affair in 382.[15] In Jerusalem he stayed with Rufinus and Melania, but did not manage to cure his soul, so Melania finally sent him on to the monks of Egypt. There he became an ardent student of the great fathers of the first generation, especially St Macarius the Great, and the leader of a circle of Origenists, including the four tall brothers, well-known leaders in Nitria and close associates of the bishop of Alexandria, who consecrated two of them as bishops. In his desert retreat Evagrius created his own bold synthesis between Origenism and desert monasticism.[16] But although he never left the desert again he remained in touch with his friends in Jerusalem through letters until his death in 399.[17] A close associate of St Gregory of Nyssa he cannot have been unknown to Jerome and Epiphanius, who had both been in Constantinople at the time when Evagrius was a celebrated young deacon there. But nevertheless Epiphanius never mentions Evagrius, and Jerome, for whom Evagrius must have been the main foe, does not mention him until some twenty years after his death, long after the debate had abated. Apparently it was not possible to criticize Evagrius as long as he lived.

Palladius had come to Jerusalem as a very young man some years after Evagrius, most likely around 386. He stayed for two years after which he went down to Egypt, where he could not resist the call of the desert and decided to stay. After being introduced to the austere ascetic tradition he associated himself with the group around Evagrius. Palladius soon became an ardent advocate and spokesman for the Origenists, and after Evagrius' death in 399 he left Egypt defending his friends in Palestine and finally at the court and in front of the patriarch of the imperial see, St John Chrysostom, who consecrated him bishop of Helenopolis in Bitynia.[18] Here he sat down and wrote one of the most famous accounts of the desert

[15] For Evagrius' life and career, see Gabriel Bunge, 'Evagrios Pontikos. Briefe aus der Wüste', *Sophia. Quellen östlicher Theologie* 24, Paulinus-Verlag, Trier 1986, 17-93.

[16] For Evagrius' relations with the desert tradition see Bunge, *op. cit.* and *idem*, 'Evagre le Pontique et les deux Macaire', *Irénikon* 56 (1983), 215-227 and 322-360, and Samuel Rubenson, 'Evagrios Pontikos und die Theologie der Wüste', *Logos. Festschrift für Louise Abramowski*, Beihefte zur Zeitschrift für die Neutestamentliche Wissenschaft und die Kunde der älteren Kirche 67, Walter de Gruyter, Berlin 1993, 384-401. It is important to note that view that Evagrius had his Origenism entirely from Gregory of Nazianzen and that he himself was responsible for the introduction of Origenism to Egyptian monastic tradition can no longer be upheld.

[17] The letters of Evagrius are now easily accessible with extensive commentaries in Gabriel Bunge, *Evagrios Pontikos. Briefe aus der Wüste*.

[18] For Palladius' life and career we are mainly dependent on his own writings and some notes in Rufinus, Jerome and the 5th-century Chruch historians. For a recent summary on the research on Palladius see E D Hunt, 'Palladius of Helenopolis: A Party and its Supporters in the Church of the Late Fourth Century', *JTS* 24 (1973), 456-480.

fathers, the *Historia Lausiaca,* as well as an apology for John Chrysostom, who had been exiled by the emperor.[19] To Jerome Palladius was a well-known and terrible roaming propagator of Origen's heresy.[20]

But even long before the visits of Melania, Rufinus, Jerome and Evagrius, people had gone down from Palestine to Egypt to visit the desert fathers. Theodoret, as well as St Ephrem, tell us about the pioneer of Syrian monasticism, Julian Saba, who went down to Sinai, some time before the middle of the 4th century, attracted by what he had heard about the ascetics of the desert.[21] The famous Syriac writer Philoxenus of Mabboug tells us that a man called Adelphius, a native of Syria and disciple of Julian, had stayed for some time as a disciple of St Antony, probably in the 330s, before he settled in Edessa and became famous as one of the founding fathers of Messalianism.[22] It was, however, in the 370s with the publication and spread of the famous *Vita Antonii* by Athanasius the Great, the first account of the rise of monasticism, that the Egyptian desert became internationally known. The primary sources tell us about numerous monks, who like Porphyrios, the famous bishop of Gaza in the early 5th century, went down to Egypt in order to spend years and even decades in the Egyptian desert before returning to Palestine.[23] It seems as if Egypt in the later part of the 4th century presented such an attraction that one simply had to go there, and that the Egyptian monks were considered to be the genuine examples to follow. It was essential to be able to claim an Egyptian experience and Egyptian precedence. To those who had not succeeded in establishing good relations with Egypt, like Epiphanius and Jerome, it seemed necessary to find a way to make the tradition suspect.

The flowering of the relations between Egypt and Palestine came in the last decade of the 4th century and in the early 5th century. In the 390s a steady flow of visitors travelled from Jerusalem and Bethlehem down to Gaza and then on to Pelusion and the Egyptian desert. Others came by sea to Alexandria, where they were received by the monastic co-workers of the Alexandrian bishop. From there they invaded not only Nitria, but also

---

[19] *Historia Lausiaca* and *Dialogus de Vita Ioanni Chrysostomi.*

[20] Jerome does not himself attack Palladius before 415, when he wrote his *Dialogus adversus Pelagianos (Prologus 2),* but he of course knew Epiphanius' statements in his *Epistula ad Ioannem Episcopum* (=Jerome, *Epistula* 51.

[21] See Theodoret, *Historia Religiosa* II and Ephrem, *Hymni de Juliano Saba* IX, XX. The historicity of the accounts about Julian Saba is, however, open to doubt, since no independent sources exist.

[22] See Philoxenus, *Ep. ad Patricium.* Although Adelphius is known from several sources as a prominent leader of the early Messalian movement – he was tried and sentenced by Flavian of Antioch in a synod in the 380s – it is only Philoxenos who tells us anything about his background and Egyptian connections. In his major work on the Messalian tradition Columba Stewart rejects the connection, regarding it as an invention by Philoxenos. His arguments are, however, not conclusive. See Columba Stewart, *'Working the Earth of the Heart' The Messalian Controversy in History, Texts and Language to AD 431,* Clarendon Press, Oxford, 1991.

[23] According to his biography (Marcus Diaconus, *Vita S. Porphyrii Gazensis*), Porphyrius was born in Thessalonika in 347 and spent the years 382-387 in Egypt before he was ordained Bishop of Gaza in 395.

the retreats in Kellia and Scetis, and many even ventured to see the inner monastery of St Antony. The most vivid description is the travel account of a group of Jerusalemites who went down to Egypt in 394 to visit all the monastic sites from Upper Egypt down to Alexandria, a visit recorded in the famous guide-book translated by Rufinus. The silence of the desert was gone and the old disciples of the first generation looked back upon the time when they were young followers of the founding fathers. For many of them the fact that the world had moved in meant that they had to move out. Some settled in Sinai, but others moved into the deserts of Negev and Judea. An interesting example is Abba Silvanus, who had come from Palestine to Egypt in his youth and had become a famous elder in Scetis, before he decided to search for a more silent retreat, probably sometime in the 380s. After some years in Sinai, where one of his disciples was ordained Bishop of Pharan, he finally ended up back home in Palestine. He settled with his disciples Zacharias and Zenon in the Wadi Ghazzeh near Gaza.[24] When he died in 415 Zacharias became his successor. Later Abba Zenon came to be known as the spiritual father of the famous anti-Chalcedonian Bishop of Maiuma, Peter the Iberian.

The constant move of people from Palestine to Egypt and vice-versa almost made the monasteries around Gaza and Bet-Guvrin part of the Egyptian desert tradition. But the Egyptian influence did not only come with wandering monks, a literature on the Desert Fathers was already on its way around 400 AD The letters of the old heroes like Antony and Pachomius, as well as the sayings and admonitions given by them and other famous pioneers, were copied and translated into Greek, Latin and Syriac.[25] With their own personal experiences the visitors could take with them collections of sayings and other material back home. The amount of early Syriac translations shows that there was no lack of interest in the Egyptian fathers among the Syriac-speaking Christians of Palestine and Syria.

In addition to the old and general connections between Palestine and Egypt two major factors were added around the year 400 AD greatly strengthening the Egyptian impact on Palestinian monasticism, and even moving the centre of gravity for monastic theology from Egypt to Palestine. The first was what came out into the open air on the feast of the 13 September, 393: the struggle about the legacy of Origen. Epiphanius was not content with what he had achieved that day. The next year he offended Bishop John of Jerusalem again by consecrating Paulinian, the younger brother of Jerome a priest, acting far outside his diocese and against the will of the metropolitan of Jerusalem, under whose jurisdiction Paulinian's monastery in Bethlehem lay. Jerome had himself by then

---

[24] See Chitty, *op. cit.*, 71-74 and Michel van Parys, 'Abba Silvain et ses disciples. Une famille monastique entre Scéte et la Palestine à la fin du IVe et dans la première moitié du Ve siècle', *Irénikon* LXI (1988), 313-330 and 451-480.

[25] In his *De viris inlustribus*, written around 392, Jerome tells us that Antony's letters had been translated from Coptic to Greek, and later he himself translates parts of the Pachomian material.

become a staunch opponent of all kind of Origenism and was soon involved in a fierce struggle with Rufinus which finally led Rufinus to return to Italy in 397 or 398.[26]

But the decisive scene for the conflict had moved to Egypt where Bishop Theophilus of Alexandria suddenly turned against the Origenists among the monks, including some who had been his close associates. In early 400 after a year of intense debates and even violent clashes in the desert between Origenists and anti-Origenists he had the leading group of the former exiled.[27] Although his reasons remain somewhat obscure it seems as if the very popular and highly educated ascetics had become too powerful and independent of the hierarchy. With the Origenists, all close friends of Evagrius, who had died a year before, all his disciples and hundreds of monks left for Palestine. They considered themselves the true heirs of St Antony, the Father of Monks, and St Macarius the Great. Exiled from the area under the jurisdiction of Theophilus of Alexandria, Palestine was their obvious choice. There they had numerous friends who had been with them for shorter or longer periods in Egypt, and there they hoped to be supported by John of Jerusalem, known as a defender of Origen. Only a minor group went on to Constantinople and St John Chrysostom, greatly contributing to his dethronement at the Synod of the Oak in 403.[28] Most of them must have remained in Palestine and Syria, where they undoubtedly spread the teachings of their masters: Origen, Antony, Macarius and Evagrius. The growth and consolidation of Palestinian monasticism in the first decades of the 5th century was partly their contribution.

The second factor had nothing to do with Origen. In the first decades of the 5th century the flowering of the monastic tradition in the deserts of Nitria and Scetis had attracted the attention of the nomads of Egypt and Libya. The cells, refectories, churches and stores of thousands of monks without much military protection seemed to be an irresistible temptation, and the whole area was repeatedly sacked by ancient 'Saracens'. In the year 407-408 the entire valley of Scetis and all the monastic habitations were devastated. Many monks were killed, but most fled. Some went south to Upper Egypt, others stayed closer to the Nile or in the area of Suez, but some also ventured into Sinai, the Negev and Judea.[29] The young Iberian prince Nabarnugi, who was later consecrated bishop of Maimounas, the port of Gaza, met with an Egyptian hermit in the Jordan valley in 429, and

---

[26] On these events and Jerome' struggle with Rufinus see Kelly, *op. cit.*, 195-209.

[27] The ultimate reasons behind his attack and the details of the struggle in the desert have not yet been convincingly presented. The most recent and most extensive attempt is made in Elizabeth Clark, *The Origenist Controversy*. Clark's main contribution is her emphasis on the connection between the debate on Origenism and anthropomorphism on the one hand and the attacks on pagan temples and statues on the other. But many questions still remain to be answered.

[28] Our main account for these developments is Palladius, *Dialogus de Vita Ioanni Chrysostomi*. For a description see Chitty, *op. cit.*, 53-61 and Clark, *op. cit.*, 44-51.

[29] For these events see Chitty, *op. cit.*, 60-61 and 65-77.

Porphyry, the later bishop of Gaza, had himself left Egypt after five years in Scetis in the late 4th century.[30] Although Scetis was not desolate for a very long period, some went back rather quickly, it was sacked again twenty years later, and never recovered its original status. To the monks in exile it became essential to collect the sayings that went back to the early teachers, and the first large collections were made. All evidence point towards Gaza as the region where this work was done and written down into the famous Apophthegmata Patrum, a collection dominated by Scetis, but with numerous sayings derived from the Palestinian scene. Gaza was the gate to Egypt and in addition to Scetis which is the dominant scene in the sayings, there is a great number of sayings connected with people who for some time lived in the monastic surroundings of Gaza and nearby Eleutheropolis. It is actually quite probable that the collections of sayings of the Egyptian fathers were first done in or around Gaza.[31]

It is also in this area that we find the first evidence for a Palestinian monastic tradition that has left writings clearly dependent on the Egyptian fathers. The central figure is the somewhat enigmatic Isaiah of Gaza, also known as Isaiah of Scetis.[32] Born in the late 380s he had been trained in a kenobion and had settled as an hermit in Scetis sometime around the year 420. Apparently he was a charismatic person who within a few years had his own disciples. After about ten years there he emigrated to Palestine, probably at the time of the destruction of Scetis in 438. After a pilgrimage to the holy places he settled near Eleutheropolis. His fame was so great already by then that monks from Egypt as well as from the Judean desert sought him out. To keep his solitude he decided to move again, and settling near Gaza, he decided to shut himself up in a cell, accepting no visitors, attended to only by his disciple, Peter the Egyptian. Isaiah's importance lies in his literary output, his *logoi,* apparently collected and arranged by his followers. Unfortunately no good edition of the Greek text has yet been published. The important Syriac version is edited by late Prof. Draguet in the Corpus Scriptorum Christianorum Orientalium (CSCO).[33] The collection of his teaching is the first literary product of Palestinian monasticism, and of primary importance as a link between the Egyptian tradition as represented by Evagrius and later Palestinian and Syrian monastic literature. Although to a large degree similar in thought to the letters of St Antony and to Evagrius, the *logoi* betray certain characteristics which we will find in subsequent literature from the region, primarily the writings of Dorotheus of Gaza and the correspondence of Barsanuphius and John. The cosmological speculations of Origen and Evagrius are

---

[30] For Porphyrius, see above, note 23. For Prince Nabarnugi, later Bishop Peter the Iberian, see John Rufus, *Vita Petri Iberiae.* See also Chitty, *op. cit.,* 88-93.

[31] See Lucien Regnault, 'Les Apophthegmes en Palestine aux V-Vi siècle', *Irénikon* 54 (1981), 320-330.

[32] On this problem see Lucien Regnault, 'Isaïe de Scété ou de Gaza? Notes critiques en marge d'une Introduction au problème isaïen', *Revue d'Ascétique et du Mystique* 46 (1970), 33-44.

[33] For his works see *CPG* 5555, 5556. An edition of the Greek texts is under way by the Göttinger Akademie der Wissenschaften.

absent, but allegorical exegesis and Evagrius' psychological insights are everywhere present. The most important element in his writings is, however, a very personal devotion to Jesus. Like St Antony, Isaiah uses the name Jesus without any addition of Christ. For him and his friends this devotion made it impossible to accept the decisions of the Council of Chalcedon, speaking of two natures in Christ. Christ was not to them a theological term, the basis for a Christology, but their friend Jesus, the heavenly Saviour. The opposition of the majority of the monks in Palestine, as well as in Egypt and Syria against the council has, no doubt its roots in the spirituality represented most forcefully by Isaiah of Scetis/Gaza.

With the devastation of Scetis in 438 and the Council of Chalcedon in 451 the Egyptian influence on Palestinian monasticism had had its zenith. But its contribution was widely felt in the two major controversies haunting the monasteries of Palestine from 451 to 614: Chalcedon and Origen. The majority of the monks were originally strongly opposed to the council and its deposition of the Alexandrian patriarch, Dioscorus, the nephew of the great Cyril of Alexandria. They joined Theodosius in rejecting the patriarch Juvenal when he returned after signing the decree. It was only after Euthymius, the famous founder of the Judean monastic tradition, accepted the council, and after the compromises made by subsequent patriarchs and emperors, most notably the *Henotikon* of emperor Zeno, that the monks started to agree.[34] Some, like Isaiah and his disciple Peter the Iberian, bishop of Maiuma, would, however, have nothing to do with the council, and a permanent split could not be avoided in Palestine either. Whereas the two theological and ecclesiastical centres of opposition to Chalcedon were Alexandria and Antioch, Palestine and especially the monasteries in the plain were an essential for support and for communication.

The Origenist controversy, silenced in the early 5th century, broke out again in the early 6th century. After Euthymius died his disciples, primarily St Sabas, started on ambitious building projects in collaboration with civic and ecclesiastical authorities in Jerusalem. Some of the monks felt that the old tradition of the Egyptian desert was thereby betrayed. To avoid unending internal debates in the Great Lavra of St Sabas the critics were in 506 allowed to found a New Lavra according to their own understanding of monastic life. As long as St Sabas lived the two monastic settlements got along with each other, but after his death in 532 the Judean desert became

---

[34] The successor of Juvenal, Anastasius, patriarch 459-478 tried to be neutral in the controversy about the Council of Chalcedon, and when the rebel emperor Basiliscus promulgated an encyclica in 475 anathematizing the council, Anastasius signed. Even his succesor, Martyrius, achieved a union between the Church of the bishops (pro-Chalcedon) and the the church of the monks (anti-Chalcedon) by accepting that Chalcedon should passed over in silence an agreeement pointing towards the *Henotiokon* of Zeno promulgated in 482.

the centre of a fierce struggle about the legacy of Origen.[35] In this conflict between the Old and the New Lavra one can sense the difference between the Egyptian and Origenist tradition with its austere asceticism and suspicion against Church authorities on the one hand and the Syro-Palestinian tradition with its close links to the imperial court and the bishops of Jerusalem and abroad on the other. The conflict was only solved by imperial decree and the decisions of the Fifth Ecumenical Council, held in Constantinople in 553.

Though this presentation has centred on the early relations between Egyptian and Palestinian monasticism, monasticism in Palestine was by no means simply a product of influence from Egypt. The first monastic communities in the Jordan valley and in the Judean desert were founded by pilgrims from Rome and Italy and from the north: Cappadocia, Syria, Armenia and Georgia.[36] What stands out is the international character of Palestinian monastic tradition and the major role Palestine played in linking the Egyptian tradition to Syria and Asia Minor. In the monasteries of Palestine people from all corners of the christianized world met and learnt to live together in monastic communities, which derived much of their inspiration and systems of organization from Egypt. Most of the monks spoke Greek and very many Syriac. It was for the ones coming from the outskirts of the hellenized world, the Armenians and Georgians, that the first ethnic monasteries were founded. But these were not isolated from the rest, and many who knew or learnt Greek could, no doubt, become abbots and bishops among the Greek and Syriac speaking majority.

A very good example of what the Palestinian milieu meant is given by the life of Peter the Iberian.[37] As a kind of hostage and token of friendship he, being the son of an Iberian ruler, had been brought up at the court in Constantinople. On a pilgrimage to the Holy Land in 428 he met with an Egyptian monk, and soon decided to become a monk himself. He received the monastic habit by Abba Gerontius, who had been brought up by Melania the younger in the monastery of the Romans on the Mount of Olives. With his Iberian friend he built a small monastic guest-house in Jerusalem where he lived under the spiritual direction of Abba Zeno, a disciple of Abba Silvanus, the Palestinian monk who had lived many years first in Scetis and then in Sinai. Peter barely escaped ordination as a priest by the patriarch Juvenal, only to be ordained bishop of Maiuma by Theodosius, the anti-Chalcedonian intruder on the throne of Jerusalem in 452. After the return of Juvenal in 453 Peter fled to Egypt. There he assisted in consecrating the first non-Chalcedonian patriarch of Alexandria.

---

[35] The main source for this later conflict is Cyril of Scythopolis (Bet She'an), who wrote the lives of many of the most prominent monks of the Judean desert. He had been called to become a monk by St Sabas himself, and his own biography was deeply marked by the struggle, as in 554 he was sent to the new lavra to replace the ousted Origenists.

[36] For some general accounts of early Palestinian monastic tradition, see Chitty. The archaelogical evidence is presented in Yizhar Hirschfeld, *The Judean Desert Monasteries in the Byzantine Period*, Yale University Press, 1992.

[37] On his life see John Rufus, *Vita Petri Iberiae*.

A few years later he was back in Palestine, settling near Ascelon and helping to consolidate the anti-Chalcedonian monastic tradition. Here he remained staunchly anti-Chalcedonian, even rejecting the compromise of emperor Zeno, the Henotikon. After the death of Abba Zeno, the disciple of Silvanus, his main spiritual advisor was another man from Scetis, Abba Isaiah, now around eighty years old.

Largely as a result of the interest in the Holy Places it was in Palestine that all the different Christian traditions met. Thus it was here that the monastic tradition originating in Egypt with Antony and Pachomius, and preserved in the Sayings of the Desert Fathers, was transmitted and transformed into the various Christian traditions. Egyptians and many who had stayed for years in Egypt settled in Palestine. The oral traditions of Scetis in Nitria as well as the writings of the fathers were read, copied and translated here, and subsequent generations wrote their own ascetic works in the traditions influenced by the Egyptian fathers. Of greatest importance is probably the role Palestinian monasticism played in translating early Christian writings into other languages. For almost all our monastic texts the oldest manuscripts are in Syriac, originating in the translations made in the monasteries in the 5th century. Significantly it is only in Syriac that most of the writings of the great Graeco-Egyptian monk Evagrius of Pontus have been preserved. But also the Armenian and Georgian translations of early monastic texts are generally important witnesses to otherwise lost texts or portions of texts. For the Letters of St Antony the Georgian version is the best one still preserved, and an important letter from the Egyptian bishop Serapion of Thmuis to the disciples of Antony is only preserved in Armenian.

I think it is difficult for us today, with modern national states and emphasis on ethnicity to imagine the cultural exchange in and natural cosmopolitan character of Palestine in the early Christian centuries. Christian Jerusalem was, of course, dominated by pilgrims and monastic guest-houses serving the needs of people coming from east and west, south and north, from India and Persia, Armenia and Georgia, Ethiopia and Arabia, Ireland and Gaul, Spain and Rome. Gaza, Maiuma and Caesarea were centres of communication and exchange where the different cultures of the christianized world had to cope with each other. The plains and the Judean hills were plotted with monastic settlements whose inhabitants had not other national identity than their heavenly civitas or polis. This did not change with the advent of Muslim rule, Arabic was only added to the languages into which the heritage was translated. The libraries of the monasteries like St Catherine in Sinai or St Sabas near Bethlehem, kept spiritual writings in Greek, Coptic, Armenian, Georgian, Arabic, Latin, Syriac. It seems as if it is only with the Crusades in the Middle Ages and with modern European expansion in the 19th century that the idea develops that people of different races, of different religion and different ethnic background are unable to live together.

4

The Christians in Palestine during a Time of Transition: 7th-9th Centuries

Michele Piccirillo, OFM

The dated inscriptions of the mosaic floors of the churches excavated in Jordan, where the Studium Biblicum Franciscanum has already been working for sixty years, have had a double merit. First, they illuminate in the history of the Near East a Christian community with biblical origins. The community has almost been forgotten by the contemporary sources, although we find it flourishing particularly in the 6th-7th centuries at the beginning of the Islamic conquest. Second, they illustrate the life of this community during the first two centuries of Islam.

In a moment of confrontation between the Christian-Western world with that of Islam (with the danger of the appearance of two opposing integralisms, both of which are dangerous), the experience of the Christian community of the Arab province and of Palestine acquires importance as a consequence of the Yarmuk battle fought in 636 that ended with the defeat of the Byzantine army and the abandonment of the southern provinces of the empire to Islamic troops.

There has been a growth of historical certainty from the timid attempt by Clermont-Ganneau, in the last century, of dating the church of the Virgin in Madaba with use in the Seleucid era, to the Arab Muslim epoch, to the discovery of the mosaic floor of the church on the acropolis of the village of Ma'in dated to AD 719/20 at the time of 'Umar II, to the mosaic floor of the church of the village of al-Quwaismah dated AD 717/18, to the discovery of the double mosaic floors of the church of St Stephen at Umm al-Rasas built in the Umayyad epoch, certainly still in use in AD 756 when the mosaic floor of the sanctuary was redone at the time of Bishop Job, as indicated by the inscription near the altar.

The reproposal of reading the date of the church of the Virgin of Madaba to 767, and in use during the Byzantine era from the creation of the world (Anno Mundi 6274 or 766/7), recently suggested by Professor Lea di Segni of the Hebrew University of Jerusalem, will not scandalize anybody, as Clermont-Ganneau feared in the last century, while proposing the year 662 for the same mosaic and precisely seeing in that date an archaeological counterproof of the climate of tolerance prevalent in the ex-Byzantine province under the Islamic occupation at the time of the Umayyad caliphs. According to the French scholar a climate of tolerance resulted already from the reading of the contemporary literary texts.

The discovery of the mosaic of Saint Stephen at Umm al-Rasas has provided evidence of a flourishing organised urban Christian community in the territory of the diocese of Madaba in the steppe of Jordan in the second half of the 8th century, a community administratively governed by a deacon, with an artistic vitality and a prosperous stable economy.

Moreover, these mosaics of the Umayyad period show traces of iconoclastic damage, which therefore are subsequent to their dates. In most of the cases the damage was restored with care. That means that the churches were still in use after the iconoclastic crisis which must be dated in the Umayyad period.

Archaeological research has once again fulfilled its task of giving concrete documentary witness to what could have already been obtained by reading the contemporary historical sources to discredit simple and unfounded preconceptions. .

In this paper I shall consider two recent edited works by the Custos of the Holy Land. Both are the fruit of labour and competence of Professor Bartolomeo Pirone of the Instituto Orientale di Napoli. Their publication was inspired by the far-sightedness of the late Father Bellarmino Bagatti. The two books are witnesses of an era. The first is a historical work written in Arabic, 'The Annals of Patriarch Eutichius of Alexandria'. The second is a hagiography, 'The Life of St Stephen from St Saba' written by his disciple Leontius from Damascus.

While the life of St Stephen, even with its critical details, results as a witness in favour of the continuity between the Byzantine and the Islamic period, 'The Annals of Eutichius' are to be seen as a calm and documented response to a tense situation which gradually developed between the two communities.

The Life of St Stephen from St Saba

The recent publication of the critical edition of the Arab text of the 'Life of St Stephen' in the series of monographs of the Studia Orientalia Christiana of our Muski Center in Cairo, has given me the occasion to remember once again the truth already known in the level of historical research and archaeology. After the battle of Yarmuk in 636, which ended in the defeat of the Byzantine army and the abandonment of the southern province of the empire to Arab Islamic armies, life continued as before, for the monks in the Judean desert as well as the Christian population in the cities or in the villages of Syria-Palestine.

Taking into account that the life of St Stephen unfolded between 725, the year of the his birth in the height of Islamic period, and 794, the year of his death, the biography written in Greek by his disciple Leontius from Damascus about 807 and translated in Arabic in 902 by the monk, John of Stephanos Fakkhoury, assumes a valuable documentary value for its contribution in bringing about the consciousness of life 'in the territories governed by the Arabs', in a completely new political situation after the preceding centuries of Christian Byzantine domination.

As a result of the biography, such political change is lived only by reflection and marginally by the monks of the *lavra* of St Saba who continued life with its usual problems; from the entrance and the acceptance to the school of the elderly, to the different tasks in the community, to the search for a harsher and more committed ascetic life, up to the voluntary seclusion in a hermitage or in a walled cell, as told about the monk Amba Martirius from Gerasa: 'Our Martirius, guided by his desire (of not seeing death before meeting a true monk) roamed for 15 years in all the territories that are under the jurisdiction of the Arabs' until he found St Stephen and decided to stay with him. According to the testimony of Leontius, the continuous roaming of monks between the monasteries of the Judean desert were not stopped by encounters with the ferocious dogs of the nomads and nor with the not always hospitable nomads themselves.

Leontius is rather critical of the monastic life that was conducted in his days in the Judean desert. It even came to be seen in 'the great earthquake' that had upset the region, probably in the year 746/7, the date of the weakening of the discipline. In spite of this, Leontius records various notable exceptions, like Amba Marianus, 'who belongs to the distinguished Christians of the noble city of Damascus, adorned with the virtue of work and of contemplation and who possessed a great knowledge of science and who was also well acquainted with philosophy.' Or Amba Cosmas, 'Superior of the al-Quwaismah monastery which is near the city of Amman, a virtuous man, perfect in sanctity, true servant of God, irreproachable among the monks.'

The life of the monks contrasts strongly with the preoccupations of the Christian population in the same territory. 'The monks of this time lead a life without preoccupations; it is a reposed and tranquil life,' - says Leontius through a rich doctor of Moab who was invited by St Stephen to abandon everything and become a monk - 'while those who live in the world today are subject to great misery, sadness, privation and continuous difficulty.' The greatest difficulties come from the oppression of the tax collectors imposed by the new lords, particularly the *kharaj*, the tax imposed on the real estate of the Christians and furthermore, the *jizya*, or the annual personal tax. The aunt of Leontius, who was gravely ill during her pilgrimage in Jerusalem, sheds light on the situation: 'I feel, my son, that the ruler of this country is a despot, prone to violence, plunders the properties of the population especially those of the sick and of the pilgrims. I am referring to those days when a pilgrim died in the house of a Christian from here, leaving much inheritance. However, they were not present at the time of death. The ruler learned about the situation and made himself the owner of all that belonged to the deceased.' To escape the oppression 'of the tax collectors that was raging in the regions of Moab', a rich Christian from there took refuge in Jerusalem.

In spite of the difficulties and the gloomy view of the situation, Leontius sufficiently documents that the life of the Christians continued its normal course. The pilgrimages to the Holy Places from the adjoining regions and even from Europe continued. The aunt of Leontius, who usually came every year to Jerusalem for Easter, could continue the pilgrimage up to Mount Sinai without difficulties. In the desert, a noble Roman lady was living 'for thirty years' with her two daughters, heirs 'of the noble archonts and patricians' who after having sold everything embraced the monastic life. Leontius records also several distinguished Christians of Damascus, Moab, Egypt, Gaza, Jericho and Jerusalem. Among them is the brother of the monk Theodore, personal doctor of the Muslim prince of Ramlah. Taking advantage of his brother's position, Theodore had Elia, the patriarch of Jerusalem, sent into exile and had himself elected in his stead.

Rich merchants like Petrona, brother of Amba Marianus, 'dealt in the trade of dates between Damascus and the Palestinian Ghor.' He normally shuttled between the capital city and Jericho. Moreover, we find a very detailed account of a fanatical Muslim who decided to accompany peacefully an Egyptian Christian in his pilgrimage to Jerusalem. 'He wanted to come to Jerusalem to pray in the mosque that the Muslims have' (the construction of the Dome of the Rock had been finished in 692). With the Christian, he went as far as the monastery of St Saba 'to go on a trip and admire the desert'. The Muslim ended up being converted to Christianity, putting his life at risk after having witnessed a miracle of St Stephen. 'Selected and trustful persons among the Muslims' have been requested by the aunt of Leontius to attest to her will and last testimony before her death. *Vice versa*, St Stephen intercepted a priest in the service of the Holy Sepulchre, reproaching him as the cause of the apostasy of a rather negligent monk 'who, because of him fled and repudiated Christ,' himself converting to Islam. The priest was twice guilty because he acted against his brother and because he acting as tax collector of the Christians on behalf of the Muslim authority.

In this rather complex and difficult situation, Leontius writes at the end of his impassioned work in memory of his master: 'St Stephen demonstrated compassion and pity not only for the Christians but also for the Muslims,' overcoming with the universality of Christian charity the difficulties and differences imposed by the political contingencies.

The Annals of Eutichius Patriarch of Alexandria

The Annals of Sa'id ibn al-Batriq, also called Eutichius, patriarch of Alexandria (877-940), which the Franciscan Center of Christian Oriental Studies presents for the first time in Italian translation, is a work of high-profile among those that written in Arabic by Christian authors during the first centuries of the Hijra. The book is dated at the end of about three centuries of crisis experiencced by the Christian communities of the Near East as a consequence of the Islamic invasion.

The serenity and the objectivity of Eutichius who shows a position of equilibrium, as noted and praised by Mas'udi, the contemporary Muslim historian, do not hide the reality of the problems lived in the first person by the Patriarch and by his faithful. The first part of the work (from the creation to the reign of Heraclius) is concerned especially with the information and formation of the Christian readers misguided by the aftermath of Christological controversies that divided the Church from the 4th to the 7th century (Arianism, Nestorianism, Monotheletism). The second part (from Heraclius to Caliph al-Radi, 610 to 934) deals more with the present, with references to the events that mark the difficult relationship of living together between the Muslim authorities and the Christian population.

'In the first year of the reign of Heraclius, king of the Rums, took place the Hijra of the Prophet to Medina,' begins Chapter XVIII, where Eutichius expatiated on the achievement led by Heraclius to liberate the Holy Land from the Persians. The same chapter ends: 'In the 11th year of the reign of Heraclius, Muhammad died . . . the Prophet of the Muslims.' It is followed by the stories of the occupation of Iraq, Palestine, Syria and Damascus, Jerusalem and Alexandria. The account of the war is accompanied by the precise recording of the conditions of peace imposed by the conquerors and negotiated and accepted by the ecclesiastical authorities of the cities in the absence of civil and military authority: conditions of surrender that are known by the name of 'The Covenant of 'Umar' in the Islamic tradition. In such context, the present , 'In these our days, the Muslims have contravened the *sijill* of 'Umar ibn al-Khattab . . .', became a precise act of accusation and a warning regarding the honouring of the pact. Eutichius, in addition to being a theologian and historian, shows himself with his scientific work primarily as a pastor who wanted to reach the practical scope of illuminating and protecting the faithful who were entrusted to him when he was appointed patriarch of Alexandria.

In the practical example of such accords, renewed and clarified in the light of episodes of a progressive Muslim intolerance, Eutichius dedicates an important position to the deference of the Holy Places as an inalienable condition of religious freedom, pausing on the vicissitudes of the Basilica of the Holy Sepulchre in Jerusalem, of the Basilica of the Nativity in Bethlehem, of the Church of John in Damascus and of the different churches of Alexandria.

The motives, that pushed the curators to insert the book in the collection of the Center of Oriental Studies of Cairo of the Custody of the Holy Land, are mainly connected with the interest that Eutichius demonstrates in the Christian community under the Muslim occupation in Jerusalem and the Holy Places for which the work, in some cases, becomes a unique historical source.

Among the sanctuaries of the Holy Land, he follows with particular care the vicissitudes of the Basilica of the Holy Sepulchre. He records the destruction in 614 by order of Chosroes and the task of carrying it out by General Harwazaih: 'Then, he ordered the demolition of the Skull and the Tomb of the church of Constantine by setting fire to these last two.' The arson was followed by the restoration undertaken by 'a monk named Modestus who was the superior of the monastery of St Theodosius. When the Persians left, Modestus went to Ramleh, Tiberias, Tyre and Damascus to ask the Christians to give him some offerings to help reconstruct the church of Jerusalem.' For the restoration, John the Almsgiver, patriarch of Alexandria, 'sent him a thousand beasts of burden, a thousand sacks of wheat, a thousand sacks of legumes, a thousand jars of sardines, iron and a thousand workers.'

When 'Umar ibn al-Khattab entered the city to possess it, the historian records scrupulously the minute details of what he did and what he ordered during his visit to the basilica, giving merit to having respected its Christian character to the foresight of the Muslim caliph, who at the hour of prayer, refused the invitation of Patriarch Sophronius to pray inside the basilica. As an exchange, he asked a place in the city where he could build a mosque. The patriarch showed him the esplanade of the temple which had been abandoned for centuries.

Eutichius records the reconstruction of the basilica's dome which was in danger of collapse at the time of Caliph Ma'mun (814-833). The Patriarch Thomas, taking advantage of a favourable occasion 'sent some men to Cyprus in order to cut 50 trunks of pine trees and cedar and to send them to Jerusalem.' Once again, a wealthy Christian from Egypt helped financially. Eutichius is the only historian who wrote that on the Day of Palms of 936, the time of Caliph al-Radi, 'the Muslims made an irruption in the church of Jerusalem, setting fire at the southern gate of the church of Constantine and at the middle of the porch. They laid waste at the place of the Skull and at site of the Resurrection.'

Handling the contemporary facts, Eutichius takes advantage of clarifying his view: 'In these days, the Muslims contravened the *sigill* of 'Umar ibn al-Khattab. They removed the mosaics of the Basilica of Bethlehem and wrote there what they wanted. They prayed there in common and the muezzin called the faithful to prayer. They did the same thing to the steps of the stair which was at the gate of the church of Constantine where 'Umar had prayed. Half of the atrium of the church was appropriated and they constructed inside a mosque which they called the Mosque of Omar.'

The progressive intolerance and abuse showed by the Muslim

authorities regarding the Christian community, always seen as a violation of the pact of surrender, is emphasized from time to time; be it about the occupation and transformation of the churches to mosques, as in the case of the church of St John in Damascus, of one apse of the Basilica of Bethlehem, or of the part of the atrium of the Basilica of the Holy Sepulchre, of the ciborium of copper covered with gold in the church of Baalbek utilized to cover the Dome of the Rock in Jerusalem, or the persecuting behaviour regarding the Christians, which reached its apex at the time of the Caliph al-Mutawakkil (847-861): 'He sent letters to all the countries ordering the Christians to wear clothes of the same style with patches, and also a mantle with a patch in front and one in the back. He prohibited for them to ride pure-bred horses. This procedure caused great harm, pain and worries to the Christians.'

Because of a serious drought in Egypt, at the beginning of the caliphate of al-Muktafi bi'llah (902-908), the historian who was an eyewitness, writes that 'the Muslims, Christians and Jews came out together in procession raising their arms in prayer so that God would send them rain.'

Life after the conquest

A continuity complicates the life of archaeologists. Only recently thorough studies have attempted to define the typological series of pottery of the late Byzantine period from the Umayyad period of the 7th-8th century. New discoveries of dated monuments in the last decades have aided in distinguishing a mosaic floor of the Umayyad period from a mosaic of the 6th century and the first half of the 7th century.

What is now left for discussion is another problem of a historical-archeological nature: when and why did the dissolution of this region occur, with the abandonment of cities, villages and farms happen, as evidenced in many regions of the Middle East?

The evidence remaining was more apparent to the travellers of the last and of the first half of this century. Still the phenomenon does not escape the modern traveller. In the Palestinian Negev we can still visit the ruins of cities like Shivta, Mampsis, Netzana, Elusa, Avdat. In northern Syria, we have the dead cities of the calcareous mountains in southern Syria, the villages of Hauran, and in Jordan, the villages along the northern frontier of Sabha, Umm al-Quttain, Umm al-Surab, Khirbat al-Samra, Umm al-Jimal. In central Jordan we remember that the abandoned ruins of Madaba were resettled by the Christian families only in December of 1880. Up to now, the ruins of the Umm al-Rasas have fortunately not been resettled.

The phenomenon is common to all the peripheral zones of the Middle East. The historical explanation generally accepted by the historians of the last century attributes the cause to the Islamic invasion of the 7th century. We know now that this explanation is insufficient, if not wrong and false.

Life certainly continued for more than a century after the invasion, although the changed conditions of the Christian population under the Islamic government are not to be undervalued. This is a fact that no historian presently puts in doubt, and it finds confirmation from contemporary writers, whether Christian or Muslim, and archaeologically in the buildings constructed during this period - such as the mosques of Jerusalem and Damascus and the buildings and the churches that date from the Umayyad era. Based on this continuity, a Danish scholar has written a booklet recently entitled *The Invisible Conquest*. The author concludes his research by affirming that the Syro-Palestinian conquest in the 7th century is totally invisible in archaeological terms. The archaeologist who searches some data for a break between the pre- and post-Muslim conquest searches in vain. Archaeology demonstrates an uninterrupted continuity between the two periods.

Publishing the nine churches paved with mosaics in Rihab, a village on the Syro-Jordanian boundaries, 40kms south of Bostra, capital of the province Arabia, I had already noted the fact that the church of St Menas and that of the Prophet Isaiah were finished at the time of the Metropolitan and Archbishop Theodore in AD 634/35, in the immediate period of the capture of Bostra and the decisive battle of 636 between the Byzantine empire and the Arabs which resulted in the total defeat of the imperial army and forced the Byzantines to abandon the southern provinces to the hands of the Muslims. I wrote: 'The two churches demonstrate that the on-going fight between the Arab tribes coming from Hijaz and the Byzantine Empire was not felt in the village in its drama and the military turnover was a surprise for them as it is for us, distant spectators of an achievement considered impossible.' The historical conclusion is supported by archaeological excavations conducted by the Ecole Biblique at Khirbat al-Samra, a fortified village and station of the Via Nova Traiana in the same region. Some churches of the village are contemporary with the two churches of Rihab. Moreover, the church of St George was constructed and adorned with mosaics in 637, a year after the battle of Yarmuk and two years after the capture of Bostra.

The historians and archaeologists of this century have changed the date of the abandonment to the 8th century, making it coincide with the end of the Umayyad dynasty and the transfer of the capital city of Damascus to Baghdad, the capital of the new 'Abbasid dynasty in 750 AD. For the cities of the Jordan valley, that date coincides with the disastrous earthquake of AD 747. On this premise, all of the post-Byzantine pottery typologies of the sites that were not occupied in the posterior Ayyubid or Mamluk eras, have been labelled as Umayyad.

The excavations of the last decades in Beit Shean, Pella, Umm al-Rasas and Aqaba have lead to a reconsideration of such dates and to paying more attention also to the historical sources. In Beit Shean, it appeared that after the earthquake of 747 which destroyed the Byzantine-Umayyad city and the remaining monuments of the Roman era, the new houses were constructed by levelling and burying the ruins. In Pella, the new village of the post-Umayyad era was moved a little towards the north with respect to the site of the preceding city. In Aqaba, the excavations of the Oriental Institute have brought to light the city constructed in the Umayyad epoch that demonstrate an uninterrupted occupation until the Fatimid period, from the 7th to the 11th centuries. Such a discovery is an invitation to reread the historical sources and to be more prudent in our conclusions.

From the excavations and from the geographic-historical texts, we have to correct previous opinion. The abandonment of the cities and villages of Syro-Palestine in the middle of the 8th century was not caused by the earthquake of 747, nor was it caused by the transfer of the capital from Damascus to Baghdad in 750. Presently, the cause is being sought in the change of climate and epidemics. Pentz wrote in a footnote of *The Invisible Conquest*: 'It seems that the explanation of the invasion of the barbarians/Arabians is about to be replaced by the climate/earthquake/epidemic explanation when it deals with the collapse of a complex society.' Others seek to explain the phenomenon with the process of 'bedouinization'.

Conclusion

Invasions, climactic factors, earthquakes and epidemics, bedouinization, desertification, and the subsequent erosion of the soil, could have acted as concomitant causes but not as the primary causes of such abandonment. A series of misfortunes of that type which plagued a society could only be the last blow to a community that was already in decline and did not know how to deal with such calamity. The motive is to be sought within the communities, but until now it evades us. In a volume in press dedicated to our excavations at Umm al-Rasas, I wrote as a conclusion: 'After eight seasons of excavation, the archaeological evidence brings to date the abandonment of the city of Kastron Mefaa to the 'Abbasid era. It is necessary to talk about the abandonment and not of destruction because until now we have not encountered traces of violent destruction. It is necessary to think about an exodus whose causes need to be specified: religious, economic, political causes or simply nature, like an epidemic?' There is not yet an answer.

Therefore, we can conclude that the literary and archaeological evidence complement each other in clarifying a period of difficult transition between the Christian Byzantine epoch in which the Christians were the majority, and the later epoch with Muslims as a majority of the population.

There still remain some unsolved problems, such as the causes of iconoclasm, which I prefer to call iconophobia, stressing the Islamic character of the evidence in the floor mosaics of the region, and more importantly the causes which brought the progressive decay of urban and agricultural life, and finally to the abandonment of the territory both by Christians and Muslims.

I am confident that the publication of minor works in Arabic or in Syriac, such as the two which we have dealt with in this paper, written in Syria-Palestine, will contribute to responding adequately to such questions.

NOTE

M Piccirillo, *Leonzio di Damasco, Vita di S. Stefano Sabaita* (Testo arabo, introduzione, traduzione e note di B Pirone, Jerusalem: 1991, (Studia Orientalia Christiana Monographiae 4).

5

Artistic and Cultural Inter-Relations between the Christian Communities at the Holy Sepulchre in the 12th Century

Lucy-Anne Hunt

Introduction

This paper seeks to examine aspects of the cultural relations and artistic activity of the Christian communities in the Holy Land during the Crusader period through the microcosm of the church of the Holy Sepulchre in Jerusalem. This, the church over the sites of Christ's passion and resurrection, was, as now, sacred to all Christians as the spiritual centre of Christianity. During the 12th century, the Latins performed a coordinating role amongst the Christian communities at the church, part of a wider programme of asserting their cultural and political authority. Art played a significant part in this process.

The Holy Sepulchre functioned as the focus of pilgrimage and the traditional place of worship by the indigenous communities, especially the Orthodox, as well as performing a new role as the seat of the Latin patriarchate and the burial place of the Latin kings. Existing ceremonies, serving the pilgrimage traffic to the site, had to be accommodated alongside the new requirements of the Latin clergy and monarchy. The rebuilding and redecoration of the church, culminating in the consecration of the new choir in 1149 bears this out. The sculpted lintels of the south portal are re-examined here in the light of this situation. Their imagery is interpreted as stressing a common humanity amongst Christians preparing themselves to enter the church to visit the holy sites and seek personal salvation. At the same time Latin authority is asserted in signalling an anti-clockwise progression of the pilgrimage route around the church, past the tombs of the Latin monarchy endowed with the prestige of proximity to the tomb of Christ. Ecclesiastical and royal interests and taste elide in the sculpture, in a collaboration which points to the political strategy developed by Queen Melisende of Jerusalem. The commissioning of work by the Orthodox is represented in particular by the reattribution of a group of enamels with

Passion scenes to the patronage of the Byzantine Emperor Manuel Comnenos at the Holy Sepulchre in the 1160s. The reworking of the enamels, again as the frame to an icon of Christ of Pity, by the Georgian Orthodox community in Jerusalem in the 13th-14th centuries demonstrates the appropriation of works of art in line with control over the Sepulchre itself. Interaction amongst the Christian communities, embracing competition and rivalry as powerful elements of coexistence at the Holy Sepulchre, remained fertile ground for artistic and cultural activity.

The approach will be to survey the relations between the different Christian communities and their position within the Resurrection church. The emphasis will be on the indigenous Christians and their relations with the incoming western settlers, the Latins. This will provide the basis for discussing artistic production at, or connected with, the church. Art provided channels of communication between communities, a visual discourse through which to express their interests and identities. The time-span is between the taking of Jerusalem by the Latins during the First Crusade in 1099 and its return to Muslim hands by Saladin's conquest in 1187, after which the Latin Kingdom was administered at Acre until its fall in 1291. There also followed a brief interlude (1229-1244) when Jerusalem itself was temporarily returned into Latin hands by treaty between the western emperor Frederick II and the Ayyubid sultan. Western pilgrims had, regularly made their way to the Holy Land prior to the Crusades, and the protection of Christian sites, especially the Holy Sepulchre, had long been an issue amongst Christian rulers. But the period of the Latin Kingdom of Jerusalem in the 12th century was a time of intense interaction between indigenous communities and the incoming Latins on a new scale. Now the Latins were present on a permanent basis, and in the position of power.

Models of cultural interaction between incoming Latin 'colonial' powers and the settled communities, both Christian and Muslim, need refining in the light of the special circumstances of the Latin Kingdom, especially now that the applicability of the concept of colonialism is itself a matter of debate.[1] The concept of an exclusively bipolar western and eastern 'Crusader' art has been challenged, to include a third, indigenous, component.[2] It is this more complex model of cultural interaction that will be further applied here, to discuss the interrelations between the Latin settlers and the diversity of indigenous groups.

---

[1] See the Symposium discussion 'The Crusading Kingdom of Jerusalem - The First European Colonial Society?' reported in B Z Kedar (ed.), *The Horns of Hattin: Proceedings of the Second Conference of the Society for the Study of the Crusades and the Latin East* Jerusalem and Haifa 2-6 July 1987. Jerusalem and London, 1992, 341-66.

[2] See L-A Hunt, 'Art and Colonialism: The Mosaics of the Church of the Nativity in Bethlehem (1169) and the Problem of "Crusader" Art', *Dumbarton Oaks Papers XLV*(1991), 69-85.

Orthodox and Separated:
the indigenous Christian communities in the Latin Kingdom of Jerusalem

The indigenous Christian communities should not be treated as a homogeneous mass.[3] They comprised two major groupings, who represent the pecking order as it stood before the First Crusade in 1099. The first were the Orthodox, or Melkite community, the native Chalcedonians, amongst whom the Greeks were the most influential, because of the interest and protection given them by the Byzantine emperor. (Each of the Christian groups were and are, by their own definition, 'Orthodox'. To avoid confusion, I am applying the term here to the Melkites. For the same reason, I use the term 'Syrian' in an ethnic sense.)[4] The Orthodox held primacy over the diverse Christian communities in Jerusalem because of being the only one with a patriarch - the others had bishops with their patriarchs elsewhere - with whom the authorities negotiated over shrines, and ecclesiastical matters.[5] To these can be added the Arabic and Syriac-speaking Orthodox Christians and the Georgians. These Orthodox remained the majority amongst indigenous Christians in the Latin Kingdom of Jerusalem.[6] The other major group was formed from those belonging to the separated or non-Chalcedonian churches, the 'Monophysite' Armenians and Jacobites: predominantly Syrians, with Copts and Abyssinians.[7] The Nestorian community of the Church of the East represented a much smaller group.[8]

---

[3]   On the indigenous Christian groups: B Hamilton, *The Latin Church in the Crusader States: The Secular Church*, London, 1980, esp. chaps. 7, 8, 12, 13. On their minority status see J. Prawer, 'Social Classes in the Crusader States: The 'Minorities', in N P Zacour and H W Hazard (eds.), *The Impact of the Crusades on the Near East*, K.M. Setton, gen. ed., *A History of the Crusades* V, London, 1985, 59-115; see also the older E Cerulli, *I Etiopi in Palestina* I, Rome, 1943. In a useful recent survey, H Dajani-Shakeel, 'Natives and Franks in Palestine: Perceptions and Interaction', in M Gervers and R Jibran Bikhazi (eds.), *Conversion and Continuity: Indigenous Christian Communities in Islamic Lands, Eighth to Eighteenth Centuries*, Pontifical Institute of Mediaeval Studies, Papers in Mediaeval Studies 9, Toronto, 1990, 161-184, considers Muslim-Latin and Latin-native Christian relations. R B Rose, 'The Native Christians of Jerusalem, 1187-1260', in Kedar (ed.), *The Horns of Hattin*, 239-249, concentrates on the Christian communities.

[4]   The problem arises primarily over the term 'Melkite'. Originally applied (as its linguistic origin in the Arabic *malik*, 'king', implies), to those affiliated to the imperial, Byzantine Church, in the late 17th century, it was adopted by the Uniate Church.

[5]   Rose, 'Native Christians', 239, 248 with note 29.

[6]   Hamilton, *Latin Church*, 188

[7]   For the ambiguous usage of the words 'Syrian' and 'Jacobite' see A Palmer, 'The History of the Syrian Orthodox in Jerusalem' (Part 1), *Oriens Christianus* LXXV (1991), 17-18.

[8]   See O Meinardus, 'The Nestorians in Egypt: A Note on the Nestorians in Jerusalem', *Oriens Christianus* LI (1969), 124-25.

The appearance of the Latins in the Holy Land dramatically altered this configuration. Relations between the Latins and the Orthodox, paramount at the beginning, shifted to favouring Syrian over Greek Orthodox clergy and, finally, the separated churches over the Orthodox. The crux is that relations with the Orthodox could only get worse and with the separated churches only better, with wide cultural implications.

After the Latin capture of Jerusalem, the native and Greek Christians, who had escaped being massacred like the Muslims and Jews in the city, carried on living in the patriarch's quarter, near the Holy Sepulchre (see map, fig. 1). In the early 12th century the northern, formerly Jewish, section of the city was repopulated with eastern Christians brought in from Transjordan.[9] Christians coexisted with Latins amongst a population that was a Muslim majority, with some Jews in major cities, including, eventually, Jerusalem again.[10] The indigenous Christians did not pay the poll tax, the *jizya*, as was the case with remaining native Muslims, but lost administrative control over some of their churches, especially the Holy Sepulchre and the Church of the Nativity in Bethlehem, to the Latins.[11]

Relations of the Latins with the Orthodox

The plight of the local Orthodox Christians throughout the east had been a focus of Crusading propaganda before the First Crusade in the sermons of Urban II, and further articulated in the writings of Fulcher of Chartres and William of Tyre.[12] Instigated by the reforming papacy, the Crusade was envisaged as the means of promoting unity between Rome and the Orthodox churches. The appointment to the Holy Sepulchre of the Augustinian canons in 1114 was an aspect of this.[13] Once the Latins had taken power this link also manifested itself in practical ways. In establishing itself in control over the indigenous churches the Latin church adopted existing Orthodox diocesan divisions, making changes according to political criteria and the development of particular cult centres.[14] Initially the Orthodox had expectations of their relationship with the Latins which were unrealised. Indeed, the relationship shifted over the period of Latin rule, as the Latins exercised their control. Notably, Syrians were favoured over Greeks in Orthodox episcopal appointments, altering the ethnic

[9] Dajani-Shakeel, 'Natives and Franks', 166.
[10] Dajani-Shakeel, 'Natives and Franks', 171-172.
[11] Hamilton, *Latin Church*, 169; Dajani-Shakeel, 'Natives and Franks', 171.
[12] B Hamilton, *Latin Church* 1. The Pope considered the separated churches as heretical, and, with the exception of the Armenians, had little to do with them prior to the Crusades. See also Dajani-Shakeel, 'Natives and Franks', 164, 167.
[13] Hamilton, *Latin Church*, 4, 93.
[14] Hamilton, *Latin Church*, 52, 84.

balance in the Orthodox hierarchy.[15] Cultural differences proved insurmountable, the road to unity impassable. The Orthodox felt resentment as the realisation set in that, despite the rhetoric of a single Church, in order to be taken seriously as equals they would have to be the ones expected to give ground to join the Latin church.[16] In this respect the separated churches had the edge: accepting of difference they did not share the same expectations. The Orthodox felt disillusioned. Ultimately the disenchantment of the Orthodox showed itself in their colluding in the opening of the gates of Jerusalem to the Ayyubids in 1187. They opted for liberation, just as they had wanted liberation from the Turks nearly a hundred years before, at the time of the First Crusade. Events had turned full cycle.

Relations of the Latins with the Jacobites

The attitude of western pilgrims to indigenous Christians was poor in the early days. With the exception of Saewulf (1102-03) and the Russian Abbot Daniel (1104) they in general ridiculed or despised the native Christians, an attitude which remained through to the 13th century, excepting amongst those who settled and became integrated.[17] This different attitude amongst the settled Latins, the Frankish rulers and the Latin church was largely because they saw the advantages of unity. Bernard Hamilton has contrasted the good relations between the Latins and the Jacobites as against their poor relations with the Orthodox. This positive relationship with the separated churches he attributed to the wish not to weaken the Frankish states by antagonising a large section of its existing population.[18] As a matter of policy, Church unity would have the dual advantage of strengthening both the Latin states and the Catholic church. The Frankish rulers accepted both the virtual autonomy of the separated churches and did not exercise their jurisdiction. The Latin church contented itself with the theological *status quo* as at the foundation of the Latin Kingdom, and did not muddy the waters with up-to-date controversies as they arose between Rome and Constantinople throughout the 12th century.[19] There were distinct political advantages to maintaining good relations with the indigenous churches; originally the Franks regarded the Copts, for example, as important allies against the Muslim Fatimid rulers.[20] An eye to the position of these Christians under Islamic rule no doubt remained a factor during the 12th century.

---

[15] Hamilton, *Latin Church*, 183-84.
[16] Hamilton, *Latin Church*, 186-87.
[17] Dajani-Shakeel, 'Natives and Franks', 169, 179-83.
[18] Hamilton, *Latin Church*, 210. Rose, 'Native Christians of Jerusalem', suggests, however, that relations between the Georgians and the Latins were positive throughout the 12th century, as well as beyond.
[19] Hamilton, *Latin Church*, 164-65, 189, 210. Parish organisation was left alone too: *id.*, 87.
[20] Palmer, 'Syrian Orthodox in Jerusalem' (1), 38.

Relations took place through a series of channels. These included religious and intellectual encounters effected by individuals who functioned as cultural intermediaries. Intermarriage between Latin and Armenian noble families was also a factor.[21] Morphia of Melitene, the Armenian mother of Queen Melisende, exemplifies this and probably brought up her daughters in her own (Orthodox) faith.[22] But this also had far-reaching consequences for the status of the separated churches under the rule of Queen Melisende in Jerusalem. Manuscript colophons suggest consistent positive relations between Melisende and the Jacobites between 1130 and 1148. Melisende intervened in property disputes between Jacobites and Franks. Her intervention was 'probably as important as any other single factor in removing Jacobite inhibitions about ecumenism where the Latins were concerned' according to Andrew Palmer.[23] The Church council convened in Jerusalem in 1140 may, in Hamilton's view, have been instigated by Melisende.[24] The interest and patronage of Melisende was a key issue, in which these debates would have impinged. This arguably has implications for the position of the Christian communities at the Holy Sepulchre, as will be discussed below.

The entente between the crown and the separated churches under Melisende's rule also had a political dimension. As political allies, the Jacobites and Armenians had in common with the Latins a mistrust of the Greek Orthodox.[25] This was largely due to the Orthodox association with the Byzantine state. The threat posed by Byzantium through its annexation of Cilicia under the emperor John II Comnenos in 1137-8 brought the Latin and Armenian churches together, especially as the Latin church hierarchy in Cilicia was promptly replaced with Greeks. When finally Cilicia was created into an Armenian state, the highest achievement of this entente was the crowning in 1198 of Leo II as king of Cilicia, with the kingdom established as a vassal state of the western empire.[26]

Richard Rose has shown that there was a shift in the hierarchy amongst the indigenous Christians after 1187, the year the Latin Kingdom of Jerusalem reverted to Muslim rule, when Saladin technically returned the shrines to the native Christians.[27] The Orthodox were unable to influence the reestablishment of the *status quo* as before 1099, of their primacy over the Christian communities. The Byzantine emperor was not in a position

---

[21] B Hamilton, 'The Armenian Church and the Papacy at the Time of the Crusades', *Eastern Churches Review* X (1978), rpt. in B Hamilton, *Monastic Reform, Catharism and the Crusades (900-1300)*, London, 1979, no. XII, 63 and Dajani-Shakeel, 'Natives and Franks', 172-76. Broadly on Latin-Armenian relations, see also Hamilton, *Latin Church*, 201-207.

[22] A Palmer, 'The History of the Syrian Orthodox in Jerusalem, Part Two: Queen Melisende and the Jacobite Estates', *Oriens Christianus* LXXVI (1992), 79, note 15.

[23] Palmer, 'Syrian Orthodox in Jerusalem', (II), 85.

[24] Hamilton 'Armenian Church', 65-66

[25] Palmer, 'Syrian Orthodox in Jerusalem', (II), 85.

[26] Hamilton, *Latin Church*, 86-87 argues that the union with Rome in 1198 did more harm than good in the long term, and that mutual tolerance would have been a better policy.

[27] Rose, 'Native Christians', 239-249.

to intercede effectively on their behalf, relinquishing the role of protector of the Chalcedonian community to the Georgian kingdom through its community in the Holy Land.[28] This, with the vacuum left by the departure of the Latins (excepting 1229-1244), explains the rise in influence of the 'Monophysite' communities during the period between 1187-1260. The Jacobites, Copts and Armenians succeeded in establishing their position in several of the major shrines, especially the Holy Sepulchre.[29]

The Holy Sepulchre

'The frailty of man is nowhere more apparent than here; it epitomises the human condition,' wrote Jerome Murphy-O'Connor graphically of the six communities currently represented in the Holy Sepulchre and their upholding of their rights.[30] Attitudes may not have been very different in the 12th century. The western pilgrim Theodorich, who visited the Holy Land between 1169-74, wrote: 'These are the religious sects that celebrate divine service in the church at Jerusalem: the Latins, Syrians, Armenians, Greeks, Jacobites, and Nubians. All these differ from one another both in language and in their manner of conducting divine service.'[31] He adds that 'The Jacobites use trumpets on their feast days, after the fashion of the Jews.' It is to the building and its cacophony of religious, social and political meanings for the different Christian groups, that attention may now be drawn.

The Resurrection Church functioned as a major shrine, housing Calvary and Christ's tomb, visited by pilgrims throughout the Middle Ages, as today. Indeed, given the present rather gloomy and restored condition of the building, pilgrim accounts are crucial both to a mental reconstruction of the decoration of the church as well as to an understanding of the preserved liturgical use of works of art associated with it.

A brief outline of the Holy Sepulchre's history and decoration during the 11th-12th centuries shows both how Byzantine imperial patronage consistently worked to the advantage of the Orthodox community and how the structure of the complex was altered by the Latin occupation.[32]

---

[28] Rose, 'Native Christians', 239-242, 248-49, who points to the rise in influence of the Greek Orthodox community under the Ottomans.

[29] Even though this rise in their fortunes did not survive the mid-13th century: Rose, 'Native Christians', 244-46. Rose notes (246) that the Nestorian community, isolated from both the Chalcedonian and Monophysite groupings, lost its place in the Resurrection Church in the late 13th century.

[30] J Murphy-O'Connor, *The Holy Land*, Oxford, 1986, 43

[31] *Theoderich: Guide to the Holy Land*, trans. A. Stewart, ed. R G Musto, New York, 1986, 14. By 'Syrian' he implies Orthodox and by 'Nubian' Copts.

[32] The main monographs on the structure of the Holy Sepulchre are: Ch. Coüasnon, *The Church of the Holy Sepulchre in Jerusalem* (The Schweich Lectures of the British Academy 1972), London, 1974, and V C Corbo, *Il Santo Sepolchro di Gerusalemme* (Studium Biblicum Franciscanum, Collectio Maior, Nr. 29) III vols., Jerusalem, 1981-2.

Constantine's 4th century basilica, the martyrium to the east of the rotunda, had been destroyed by the caliph al-Hakim in 1009. Between 1042-48 the Byzantine emperor Constantine IX Monomachos rebuilt the rotunda, of brick with a wooden roof and with groin-vaulted galleries (figs. 2-3). The tomb of Christ was replaced with a masonry copy of the octagonal original.[33] This galleried round church had an eastern apse (fig. 2: 71) containing the high altar. Since the Constantinian basilica was not rebuilt the main events of the Passion were celebrated in chapels in the atrium to the east of the rotunda, including the Prison of Christ (fig. 2: 318), Flagellation, Crown of Thorns and the Division of the Garments. Relics were brought from elsewhere in Jerusalem and each 'site' incorporated into the Easter liturgy.[34] These chapels were connected by a staircase down to the chapel of the Finding of the Cross (fig. 2: 309), converted from an older cistern. The chapel of Calvary (fig. 2: 200), above Golgotha where Adam was believed to have been buried, was incorporated unchanged. The centre of the world migrated from Golgotha to a new setting (fig. 2: 227) in the courtyard, just outside the main apse and marked with an aedicule, actually and symbolically equidistant between the tomb of Christ and Golgotha.[35] In addition, the rotunda itself was flanked with chapels, with that to the north (fig. 2: 126) dedicated to Mary. The row of three to the south formed part of the courtyard or parvis leading to the new main entrance to the church and were dedicated, from north to south, to St John the Evangelist (fig. 2: 501), the Holy Trinity (which incorporated the baptistery) (fig. 2: 502) and St James, the first Bishop of Jerusalem (fig. 2: 503). The patriarchal apartments on the northern side of the rotunda were extended at the gallery level.

[33] For work undertaken at the Holy Sepulchre under Constantine Monomachos: H Vincent and F-M Abel, *Jérusalem: Recherches de Topographie, d'archéologie et d'histoire II (fasc. 1-2): Jérusalem Nouvelle*, Paris, 1914, 248-59; Coüasnon, Church, 54-57, with plan, pl. IX and reconstruction, pl. XXV; T S R Boase, 'Ecclesiastical Art in the Crusader States in Palestine and Syria: A. Architecture and Sculpture', in H W Hazard (ed.), *The Art and Architecture of the Crusader States* Vol. IV of K M Setton (gen. ed.), *A History of the Crusades*, Madison and London, 1977, 75-76; Corbo, *Santo Sepolchro* II, 139-81, 229-31 with plans, II pls. 4-5; D Pringle, 'Church Building in Palestine before the Crusades', in J Folda (ed.), *Crusader Art in the Twelfth century* (British Archaeological Reports International Series 152), Oxford, 1982, 7 with fig. 1.1; R Ousterhout, 'Rebuilding the Temple: Constantine Monomachus and the Holy Sepulchre', *Journal of the Society of Architectural Historians* XLVIII (1) (March, 1989), 66-78; J Patrich, 'The Early Church of the Holy Sepulchre in the Light of Excavations and Restoration', in Y Tsafrir (ed.), *Ancient Churches Revealed*, Jerusalem, 1993, 114-16.

[34] Vincent and Abel, *Jérusalem Nouvelle*, 255-6, Ousterhout, 'Rebuilding', 71, 78.

[35] D Baldi, *Enchiridion Locorum Sanctorum*, Jerusalem, 1982, 648 no. 939 (Bernard the Monk's account of 870); Corbo, *Santo Sepolchro*, I, 159-60. Otto Meinardus pointed out to me that this positions the omphalos at the apex of an imaginery equilateral triangle, anchored by the tomb and Golgotha. Certainly contemporaries were aware of the measurements: the Russian pilgrim Abbot Daniel (1106-8) mentions that 'from the navel of the earth to the Crucifixion of the Lord and to the Place of the Skull is 12 fathoms': J Wilkinson with J Hill and W F Ryan, *Jerusalem Pilgrimage 1099-1185*, London, 1988, 128. The present marker of the omphalos is not fixed and can be moved around the west end of the choir; Glenn Bowman informs me that the favoured present-day positioning is usually right at the south side of the choir, on a line between the tomb and Golgotha.

With the work of Constantine Monomachos, the first steps were taken to incorporate the various elements associated with Christ's passion into a single whole.

This process of integration was completed by the work of the major Crusader reconstruction of the complex, consecrated on 15 July 1149, fifty years after the Latin capture of Jerusalem (figs. 4-5).[36] While the 11th-century rotunda was retained, with its flanking chapels to north and south, its eastern apse was removed, opening up the space with a large arch. Instead a new apse was built at the east end (fig. 4:529) of a new vaulted elongated choir (marked *chorus dominorum* on the plan, fig. 4). This had the effect of expanding the central space, and, for the first time, linking the rotunda with the main liturgical body of the church. The crossing of this new choir was covered with a dome, as today. In conception, as well as in the detail of its vaulting, the structure is French, poised between Romanesque and Gothic, representing a deliberate stylistic shift in the interests of the new Western rulership. At the east end of the choir the ambulatory was constructed, with radiating chapels commemorating the Prison of Christ (fig. 4: 527), the division of Christ's garments (fig. 4: 529) and the Flagellation (fig. 4: 533).[37] Conventual buildings were built to the north and south of the choir and to the east, based around the cloister of the canons. The cloister was linked to the choir through an opening (fig. 4: 528). The patriarchal apartments were enlarged. A staircase (fig. 4: 530) led down to St Helena's chapel (fig. 4: 532), built incorporating Constantinian elements, and (fig. 4: 536) up to Calvary.

Calvary itself was developed within the Crusader church. Not only was it integrated into the main structure for the first time, but it was extended, and the burial place of the Frankish kings associated with it, with their tombs (fig. 4: A, B, C) set, at the lower level, into the vestibule of the new chapel of Adam (fig. 4: 537).[38] The tombs were decorated with sculpture, as was evidenced by the tomb of Baldwin V, the seventh Latin king who

---

[36] Selectively, for the Crusader building at the Holy Sepulchre: Vincent and Abel, *Jérusalem Nouvelle*, 260-290 Coüasnon, *Church*, 57-62; Boase, 'Ecclesiastical Architecture and Sculpture', 74-84; Corbo, *Santo Sepolchro* I, 183-209. A brief but useful summary is provided by D Pringle, 'The Holy Sepulchre', in J Riley-Smith (ed.), *The Atlas of the Crusades*, London, 1990, 46-7, with reconstructed elevation reproduced here, fig. 5. The phenomenon of unifying the church struck contemporaries: William of Tyre's account is quoted by Corbo, *Santo Sepolchro*, 197.

[37] Corbo, *Santo Sepolchro*, 207-8.

[38] Five marble tombs are referred to by Theoderich: Wilkinson, *Jerusalem Pilgrimage*, 284-5; Theoderich, *Guide*, 17-18. For their former position, set in the vestibule of Adam's chapel, below Calvary: Corbo, *Santo Sepolchro* II, (*Tavole*), plate 6, marked A and B. F.

died in 1186, aged 8.[39] This practice, the burial of the Latin kings in the vicinity of the 'relic' of Golgotha, endowed Frankish rulership with sanctity. It was also in continuance, or even inheritance, of imperial practice and symbolic authority as, from the 4th century until the Comnene period, the Byzantine emperors were interred alongside relics of the apostles in the Church of the Holy Apostles in Constantinople. Also, a second access up to Calvary was built on the new south facade, to the right of the entrance, enabling the stream of pilgrims, controlled by custodians, to enter Calvary directly from the courtyard.[40] Now known as the Chapel of the Franks (fig. 4: 543), this functioned as an antechamber, and is, if anything, even more lavishly decorated than the rest of the new south facade with sculpture (fig. 7, right side). Its decoration also includes an inner tympanum, sculpted with foliage, rimmed with mosaic.[41] On the lower level, below the staircase leading up to the chapel of the Franks, was the chapel of St Mary the Egyptian (fig. 4: 543).

Constantine Monomachos had decorated the rotunda with mosaics, some of which were retained by the Latins. These included prophets in the rotunda, an Annunciation on the sanctuary arch with Christ above the altar, and the Ascension in the vault above. The Exaltation of Adam or the Anastasis, the Byzantine salvation image of Christ's Descent into Hell to redeem his ancestors, was over the altar. The 11th-century mosaic of the Anastasis in the katholicon of Constantine Monomachos' monastery at Nea Moni, Chios, (fig. 6), gives an indication of its likely appearance.[42] The chapel of Calvary was also decorated with mosaic, with the Crucifixion on the east wall and Deposition on the south, as well as mosaic in the chapel of Adam below.[43]

The Latins, whose work on the Holy Sepulchre was initiated soon after 1114, retained the 11th-century mosaic decoration, Byzantine in form for Orthodox usage. They extended it and adapted it for Latin usage by adding Latin inscriptions in places. The church's decoration was appropriate for its

---

[39] Fragments, dismembered in 1809, are reconstructed on the basis of an engraving made in the early 18th century by the Franciscan Elzear Horn. See, most recently, H Buschausen, *Die süditalienische Bauplastik im königreich Jerusalem von König Wilhelm II. bis Kaiser Friedrich II* (Österreichische Akademie der Wissenschaften: Philosophisch-Historische Klasse, Denkschrift, CVIII Bd.), Vienna, 1978, 154-77; Z Jacoby, 'The Tomb of Baldwin V, King of Jerusalem (1185-1186) and the Workshop of the Temple Area', *Gesta* XVIII/2 (1979), 3-14. See also *A Display of Crusader Sculpture at the Archaeological Museum (Rockefeller) on the Occasion of the Second Society for the Study of the Crusades and the Latin East Conference, July 2-6, 1987*, 6, 11-12.

[40] Corbo, *Sepolchro*, 194-5 with plate 40.

[41] For the sculpted tympanum: Buschhausen, 'Süditalienische Bauplastik', 147 with Abb. 947. For the mosaic: M Ayalon, 'Un mosaïque médiévale au Saint-Sépulchre', *Revue Biblique* LXXXIII/2 (1977), 237-53.

[42] For Daniel's account: Baldi, *Enchiridion*, 656; Wilkinson, *Jerusalem Pilgrimage*, 127. Figures in the base of the dome were still visible in the 17th century in the 17th century engraving of Le Bruyn: Ousterhout, 'Constantine Monomachus', 71 with fig. 70. The Anastasis at Nea Moni: D Mouriki, *The Mosaics of Nea Moni on Chios*, Athens, 1985, I, 138-9, II, pl. 128. Ousterhout, 'Constantine Monomachus', 78, comments further on the facial features of Constantine Monomachos as Solomon at Nea Moni.

[43] Daniel: Baldi, *Enchiridion*, 656; Wilkinson, *Jerusalem Pilgrimage*, 129.

context concerned with the Passion of Christ, and the salvation for mankind brought about by his death. In his account the Western pilgrim Theodoric (1169-74) adds apostles, Constantine and Helena as part of the earlier rotunda scheme.[44] Mosaics were also put in place in the apse of the Crusader choir. These comprised an Anastasis image, as there had been in the 11th-century apse. Now the scene is inscribed with Latin and described by Theoderich not just in terms of Adam but of the broader significance of the Resurrection for mankind, by reference to the other figures present.[45] Below were the Virgin, St John the Baptist and the apostles, inscribed in Latin.

Scenes which reflected preoccupations of their own, which included 'ancillary' or more historical scenes concerned with the site were also added by the Latins. These included the Finding of the True Cross, the basis of the cult of the cross in the 12th century. Another expresses the need to underline the legitimacy of the church itself, through the imagery of the replacement of the Old Dispensation with the New. This included the church replacing the synagogue decorating the choir screen. The decoration of Calvary is known from later 12th-century pilgrimage accounts to have also comprised scenes of the Passion, typological scenes and prophets, some with Latin inscriptions, either new or added to existing mosaics from the 11th-century scheme. Of this one fragment, of the Ascension of Christ, is still preserved on the chapel vault, inscribed in Latin.[46] With the inscriptions, icons and marbelling of the church, the mosaic work provided the visual imagery worshipped during the liturgical processions that took place throughout the year, with their high point at Easter. Continuity with the past in this cycle of processional worship was noted at the time.[47]

---

[44] T S R Boase, 'Ecclesiastical Art in the Crusader States in Palestine and Syria: B. Mosaic, Painting and Minor Arts', in Hazard (ed.), *Art and Architecture*, 117. In general for the decoration of the Church of the Holy Sepulchre in the 12th century see Vincent and Abel, *Jérusalem Nouvelle*, 260-90.

[45] The Latin inscription ran '*Crucifixum in carne laudate/Et sepultum propter nos glorificate/Resurgentemque a morte adorate.*' Theoderich: Baldi, *Enchiridion*, 665; Wilkinson, *Jerusalem Pilgrimage*, 281-2. Boase, 'Mosaic, Painting, and Minor Arts', 117-18, suggests, although without proof, that this was moved from the earlier high altar. For the mosaic: A. Borg, 'The Lost Apse Mosaic of the Holy Sepulchre, Jerusalem', in A Borg and A Martindale (eds.), *The Vanishing Past: Studies of Medieval Art, Liturgy and Metrology presented to Christopher Hohler* (British Archaeological Reports, International Series 111), Oxford, 1981, 7-12 does not consider the problem of the relationship with the earlier apse mosaic, but does visualize the mosaic as at the 11th century church of Hosios Lukas, as well as the seals of the patriarchs of Jerusalem and the Anastasis scene in the Melisende Psalter.

[46] '*Viri Galilaei. . .*' (Act. I, 11). The mosaic is more visible since its recent cleaning. It is attributed to the 12th century by M L Bulst-Thiele, 'Die Mosaiken der 'Auferstehungskirche' in 'Jerusalem und die Bauten der "Franken" im 12 Jahrhundert', *Frühmittelalterliche Studien* XIII (1979), 467. Boase 'Mosaic, Painting, and Minor Arts', 118, who reproduced the fragment, pl. XXX, assumed the chapel to be 12th-century work, citing parallels with Daphne and Sicily. The extent of Byzantine mosaic work as opposed to that of the 12th century at the Holy Sepulchre needs further investigation.

[47] For example, by John of Würzburg: Wilkinson, *Jerusalem Pilgrimage*, 263.

The tomb of Christ, set within an aediculed structure, was believed literally to be the place from which Christ descended into Hell 'to set man free', and where, having conquered death, his own resurrection took place. The site is thereby literally and physically holy, a factor vivid in the mind of 12th-century visitors, eager to experience this sanctity for themselves.[48] The tomb chamber itself was described by the Orthodox Russian pilgrim Abbot Daniel in 1106 as being like a small low cave, containing a shelf on which Christ's body had been laid.[49] This shelf was encased in marble, with three small windows cut in it to allow a view of the holy stone. In front of the doors to the cave was the stone on which the angel sat, and announced the Resurrection to the Holy Women. The exterior was faced in marble and surrounded by ten columns and surmounted by a silver cupola with a silver statue of Christ above, added by the Latins.[50] The main Latin adaptation of the aedicule was the conversion of the antechamber into the chapel of the angel, and altering the shape of the whole from octagonal to polygonal. The account of the Westerner, Theoderic (1169-74), takes these changes for granted, in his description of the aedicule.[51] After mentioning marble panelling, he describes the system of doors of the antechamber, by which a limited numbers of visitors are ushered in and out. Its mosaic work included the scene of the Maries at the tomb and inscriptions. Inside the tomb chamber itself the Sepulchre was decorated with marble, gold and precious stones, with the three openings for visitors to kiss the holy stone on which Christ's body lay. There was space for five kneeling worshippers in the Sepulchre itself. The exterior of the chapel was surrounded with ten columns (presumably still those referred to by Abbot Daniel), with arches between forming a cornice with a gold inscription proclaiming Christ's victory over death. At the head of the Sepulchre, to the west, was an altar encased in metal with inscriptions and painted icons and a wooden covering. The chapel as a whole was covered with gilded copper, with an aedicule surmounted with a gilt cross and dove. The work is that of the Latins, and could well have incorporated earlier elements: the ten columns referred to by Daniel and the marble-work in particular. But the Emperor Manuel Comnenos had, in 1170 contributed a gold covering to the marble

---

[48] John of Würzburg: Wilkinson, *Jerusalem Pilgrimage*, 261. See, for the early Christian period, R L Wilken, *The Land Called Holy: Palestine in Christian History and Thought*, New Haven and London, 1992, 114-17 on tactile piety.

[49] For Daniel's account: Wilkinson, *Jerusalem Pilgrimage*, 127-8; Baldi, *Enchiridion*, 784-ff; Boase, 'Ecclesiastical Architecture and Sculpture', 76; Corbo, *Sepolchro*, I, 198-9, suggests that Cosmati work is meant by Daniel's statement that the marble facing was 'like a pulpit'. He refers to the restorations of the aedicule of 1551-64 and rebuilding of 1808. Most recently on the aedicule, past and present, see M Biddle, 'The Tomb of Christ: Sources, Methods and a New Approach', in K Painter (ed.), *'Churches Built in Ancient Times' Recent Studies in Early Christian Archaeology*, Society of Antiquaries, London, Occasional Papers, 6 vol. I: Specialist Studies of the Mediterranean, London, 1994, 73-147.

[50] Sculptural fragments found in exavations are believed to be remnants of this decoration: Corbo, *Santo Sepolchro* I, pp. 198-9 and III, photos 178-88.

[51] Baldi, *Enchiridion*, 948; Wilkinson, *Jerusalem Pilgrimage*, 278-80.

tomb of Christ, reasserting the Orthodox interest in, and patronage of, the
site.[52]

The centre of the world (figs. 4-5: X) was also marked with an aedicule
decorated with mosaic work. According to Abbot Daniel, the vault of the
aedicule had a mosaic with Christ holding a scroll with an inscription
adapting Isaiah 40:12 'Behold I have measured heaven and earth with my
hand.'[53] A Western pilgrim, Saewulf (1101-3), equated Christ's measuring
with his power of salvation in his mention of 'the place called "Compas",'
where our Lord Jesus Christ with his own hand marked and measured the
centre of the world, as the Psalmist bears witness [modern Ps. 74:12]: 'But
the Lord our King has before the ages worked salvation in the centre of the
earth.'[54] By this time the centre of the earth had migrated again, so that in
the new Crusader church it was marked by concentric circles in the
pavement in the centre of the choir of the canons, with an altar above it,
within a structure lit with a hanging lamp. This is assumed to be directly
under the dome covering the crossing of the choir.[55] In his account, John
of Würzburg also associates the spot with Joseph's begging of Christ's body
from Pilate, and its anointing.[56] Here the sanctity of Christ's physical,
bodily presence and the remembering of the events of the resurrection by
pilgrims at the holy sites, close together within the church, is particularly
poignant. Pilgrims recounted events at a particular place in sequence. John
of Würzburg alluded to Christ's burial prior to the Descent into Hell, siting
the navel of the world in the centre of the choir, not far from the Place of
the Skull. The moving of the omphalos back closer to Golgotha in the 12th
century makes the events easier to visualise and stresses salvation. Placing it
under the dome of canon's choir also not only places it at the visual centre
of the church but points to its appropriation by the Latin Church.

The belief was repeated throughout the Latin occupation of the 12th
century that the centre of the world was also the site of Christ's appearance
to Mary Magdalen.[57] This scene was itself depicted, inscribed, on the right

[52] Boase, 'Ecclesiastical Architecture and Sculpture', 76.
[53] Wilkinson, *Jerusalem Pilgrimage*, 128.
[54] Wilkinson, *Jerusalem Pilgrimage*, 103; repeated by John of Würzburg, Baldi, *Enchiridion*, 665:
'. . . *operatus est salutem in medio Terrae.*'
[55] N. Kenaan-Kedar, 'Symbolic Meaning in Crusader Architecture', *Cahiers Archéologiques*,
XXXIV (1986), 110, 112, marshalls eight contemporary sources for the citing of the
omphalos in the middle of the choir.
[56] Baldi, *Enchiridion*, 665 with note 1; Wilkinson, *Jerusalem Pilgrimage*, 260.
[57] Wilkinson, *Jerusalem Pilgrimage*, 103 (Saewulf); for John of Würzburg's account, see above
note 54. This belief had apparently changed by the 14th century: Niccolò's account: N Da
Poggibonsi, *A Voyage Beyond the Seas (1346-1350)* (trans. T Bellorini and E Hoade),
Jerusalem, 1945, 17, gives the place as just outside the chapel dedicated to her at that time to
the north of the tomb of Christ.

(eastern) tympanum of the south facade portal.[58] It provides a visual cue for those entering the church, to know by which door to enter to reach the choir of the church. The representation of Christ's first appearance to a living mortal after his resurrection gives hope of salvation for all those entering the Holy Sepulchre. As Christ had redeemed Adam, so could the Christian sinner find salvation through Christ's resurrection. These beliefs surrounding the sites in the church are vital to an interpretation of the sculpted lintels of the south doorways, as will be seen.

The Latins and the indigenous communities at the Holy Sepulchre in the 12th Century

As Richard Rose has pointed out, the position of the eastern communities in the Resurrection Church was 'the final criterion of rank among Holy Land Christians.'[59] Initially the Latins planned to share the Holy Sepulchre with no-one.[60] After all this was the ecclesiastical and spiritual heart of the Latin Kingdom, and the burial place of the Latin kings. Furthermore the Latin kings and French baronage of Outremer heavily sponsored the work of rebuilding the shrines, with the Holy Sepulchre as the priority.[61] But the Latins had soon discovered the wisdom of respecting existing rituals within the church, especially that of the Holy Fire, the miraculous lighting of a lamp within the Sepulchre, the high point of the Easter ritual on Holy Saturday.[62] When the Holy Fire failed to ignite at Easter in 1101, King Baldwin I took the hint and readmitted the Orthodox.[63] Whether this was confined to the Easter ritual alone is not clear, but from 1149 the Orthodox certainly had a major altar, near the choir.[64] They also had charge of the chapel of the Holy Cross on the north side of the church

[58] Wilkinson, *Jerusalem Pilgrimage*, 261 (John of Würzburg); 287 (Theoderich). Vincent and Abel, *Jerusalem Nouvelle*, 283; Corbo, *Santo Sepolchro*, 193. Baldi, *Enchirdion*, 670, gives Theoderich's Latin text: *Ante fores ecclesiae inter duas januas Dominus Christus reverendo habitu quasi jam a morte resurgens constitit, ad cujus pedes Maria Magdalena . . . jacet Dominus Chirographum porrigit hos versus continueris: Quid, mulier, ploras. Jamjam quem quaeris, adoras. Me dignum recoli, quem jam vivum tu modo tangere noli.*

[59] Rose, 'Native Christians', 246.

[60] Hamilton, *Latin Church, 161*

[61] B Hamilton, 'Rebuilding Zion: the Holy Places of Jerusalem in the Twelfth Century', *Studies in Church History* XIV (1977), rpt. in B Hamilton, *Monastic Reform*, 114, with note 79.

[62] The ceremony is documented from the 5th century and reached its high point in the twelfth: G Bertonière, *The Historical Development of the Easter Vigil and Related Services in the Greek Church*, Rome, 1972, 29-58, 101-3. The ceremony was predominantly Orthodox although Hamilton, 'Armenian Church', 64, citing Matthew of Edessa, points to Armenian involvement in praying for the Holy Fire in 1101.

[63] A burnt column to the west of the west portal is believed by present-day pilgrims to have been the place from which the Holy Fire issued from it one Easter when the ceremony was forbidden within. I owe this observation to Glenn Bowman.

[64] According to the account of Theoderich, c. 1175: Wilkinson, *Jerusalem Pilgrimage*, 282; Hamilton, *Latin Church*, 170-71.

(shown in fig. 5), with a relic of the True Cross in a gold and silver reliquary.[65] The Holy Sepulchre soon became the predominate shrine church in the Latin Kingdom in which the liturgy was performed in both the Orthodox and Latin rites.[66]

According to Theoderich, the Armenians had control of the chapel of St Mary the Egyptian on the east side of the courtyard and the chapel of St John the Evangelist, opposite it on the west side (fig. 4: 540 and fig. 5).[67] There is debate as to whether Calvary was in Armenian or Georgian hands under Saladin, but it certainly switched between the two communities until the 15th century. Then it was turned over to the Georgians, favoured through their contacts with the Mamluk Sultans, although not without resistance from the Armenians.[68] While in Armenian hands a scriptorium functioned in the chapel of Calvary.[69] The Georgians, who had had a foothold in part of Golgotha (the chapel of Adam below Calvary) from the mid-11th century, held the key to the Holy Sepulchre between 1347-1480.[70]

The Syrian Jacobites did not possess a chapel at the Holy Sepulchre before 1168, as they were celebrating Easter at St Mary Magdalene's until that time. The Chapel of St James, the outer of the three on the east side of the courtyard, was conceded to the Syrian Jacobites, possibly in 1168 following an amicable meeting between the Latin Patriarch Amalric and Michael the Syrian Patriarch on the eve of Easter Saturday.[71] By the early 13th century the chapel of Mary Mother of God at the Holy Sepulchre was in the hands of the Copts, probably given them by Saladin after 1187.[72] By the 15th century the Jacobites apparently had two chapels within the Holy Sepulchre.[73]

To sum up: the Latins, finding that for reasons of expediency they were unable to claim exclusive usage of the Holy Sepulchre for themselves, soon

---

[65] Wilkinson, *Jerusalem Pilgrimage*, 283.

[66] Hamilton, *Latin Church*, 87

[67] Respectively: Wilkinson, *Jerusalem Pilgrimage*, 283, 287; Stewart, *Theoderich*, 15, 21. For the Armenian cathedral of St James in Jerusalem, built in the 12th century, see *History of the Hintlian, Armenians in the Holy Land*, Jerusalem, 1976, 51-56; Hamilton, *Latin Church*, 201-202 with note 1.

[68] The Georgians then retained it until the 17th century: G Peradze, 'An Account of the Georgian Monks and Monasteries in Palestine, as revealed in the writings of non-Georgian Pilgrims', *Georgica* IV/V (1937), 217-19. See also H C Luke, 'The Christian Communities in the Holy Sepulchre', in C R Ashbee (ed.), *Jerusalem, 1920-1922*, London, 1924, 49-50 and Hintlian, *History of the Armenians*, 41-42 who points out that the Armenians were compensated with the Armenian Gallery in the Rotunda, facing Calvary which they still hold today.

[69] Hintlian, *Armenians*, 42.

[70] Peradze, 'Georgian Monks', 217-18.

[71] Palmer, 'Syrian Orthodox (1)', 34.

[72] O A Meinardus, *The Copts in Jerusalem*, Cairo, 1960, 35; Palmer, 'Syrian Orthodox' (I), 35 with note 80. Palmer associates another chapel ascribed to the Jacobites in the 15th century as the chapel of Nicodemus, where the Syrian Jacobites are now to be found.

[73] Palmer, 'Syrian Orthodox' (I), 35, suggests these were the chapel of Nicodemus and a chapel of St John the Evangelist.

allowed the Orthodox back into the Holy Sepulchre, where they held chapels and worshipped in prominent positions in the church. The non-Chalcedonian 'Monophysite' Christians were, however, restricted to chapels in the courtyard until after the fall of the city to Saladin in 1187, although they enjoyed good relations with the Latins and the protection of Queen Melisende in particular. Thereafter their situation improved and they were granted their own places of worship within the church, at the expense of the Orthodox.

Artistic production

Aspects of the artistic relations between the Christian groups and their own affiliations, actual and spiritual, with the Resurrection church may be demonstrated with particular reference to the south facade of the church. A major factor was the impetus of the liturgies and processions into and within the church, especially during Palm Sunday and at Easter, with its imagery of resurrection and salvation. It is arguably a measure of the necessity for coexistence that the different artistic 'languages' of the various communities was tolerated, even acknowledged, within the decorative programme sponsored by the Latins.

The south facade of the Holy Sepulchre

The south facade of the Holy Sepulchre (fig. 7) was erected for the consecration of 1149. The formal elements - the paired arches and sculptural friezes - remain intact, as well as the portals, but for their decoration of lintels and mosaic work. The decoration reflects the political and spiritual significance of the church as a whole. The friezes are based on local Syro-Palestinian sculpture, which would have been familiar to indigenous Christian sculptors, as Nurith Kenaan-Kedar has stressed.[74] The double portal, repeated in the upper storey, adopts the regal and religious associations of triumphal entry embodied in the early medieval Golden Gate in Jerusalem.[75] Continuing Orthodox practice, Christ's entry into Jerusalem through the Golden Gate was followed by pilgrims during the Holy Week liturgy. The architectural and sculptural associations of the facade with the gate were in this typical way endowed with special symbolical significance.[76] Another local element is the bevelled voussoirs around the arches are paralleled in the Arab Bab al-Futuh in Cairo of 1087-91, as well as the Martorana in Palermo, contemporary with the Holy

[74] Boase, 'Architecture and Sculpture', 80-81; N Kenaan, 'Local Christian Art in Twelfth-Century Jerusalem', Part II *Israel Exploration Journal* XXIII (1973), 221-229.
[75] Kenaan, 'Local Christian Art', 221-22.
[76] Kenaan, 'Local Christian Art', 222.

Sepulchre facade.[77] The eastern (right) doorway has been blocked since the end of the Latin occupation, probably under Saladin's orders.[78] Thus an account of the sculpture on the facade in the 12th century must take account of the usage of both doorways, as well as the separate entry to Calvary to their right.

Now missing are the sculpted lintels over the two doorways. That formerly over the western entrance depicted Passion scenes (fig. 4: 541; fig. 9), that over the eastern (fig. 4: 542; fig. 10) a scroll inhabited with naked male figures and hybrids. The tympana of the portals, with that over the entrance to Calvary (fig. 4: 543), were decorated, with mosaics. The western tympanum depicted the Virgin and Child in mosaic, which may have resembled the Virgin and Child Enthroned in the Psalter of Queen Melisende of Jerusalem (fig. 14).[79] The eastern tympanum displayed the scene of Christ appearing to Mary Magdalene, as already observed.[80] It still shows traces of a lozenge design, perhaps the underpinning of the mosaic work. The third, Calvary, tympanum, still shows foliage decoration, with mosaic work above. Its foliage imagery has been interpreted as representing the true vine, appropriate to Calvary.[81] The strong representation of local artistic elements suggests that the Latins may have employed indigenous Christians on the south facade. Perhaps these Christians were establishing a foothold on this side of the church as early as the 1140s. It will be recalled that the 'Monophysite' Christians came to occupy chapels at this side of the church, alongside the Latin occupation of Calvary and the remaining smaller chapels.

A photograph (fig. 8) taken by the Swedish photographer Eric G Matson early this century, showing Russian pilgrims pouring out of the Holy Sepulchre on Palm Sunday, demonstrates the portals as a focal point with their lintels still *in situ*. This intersection between the sacred and the

[77] T S R Boase, 'Ecclesiastical Art in the Crusader States in Palestine and Syria: A. Architecture and Sculpture', in H W Hazard (ed.), *The Art and Architecture of the Crusader States* IV, of K M Setton (gen. ed.), *A History of the Crusades*, Madison and London, 1977, 81.

[78] Vincent and Abel, *Jérusalem nouvelle*, 283. This was observed by subsequent visitors such as Fra Niccolò da Poggibonsi in the late 1340s: see *Voyage Beyond the Seas*, 12.

[79] The mosaic is mentioned by the pilgrim Fra Nicollò of Poggibonsi in 1345: *Voyage* (trans Bellorini and Hoade), 12; it was already damaged in his day. Vincent and Abel, *Jerusalem Nouvelle*, 282; Boase, 'Architecture and Sculpture', 82, Corbo, *Santo Sepolchro*, I, 193. For the Melisende Psalter, see below, note 97.

[80] See above, note 58.

[81] Boase, 'Architecture and Sculpture', 81 with pl. 1b; L Y Rahmani, 'The Eastern Lintel of the Holy Sepulchre', *Israel Exploration Journal* XXVI (1976), 127.

profane provides as a starting point for some of the art historical issues.[82] Stephen Graham, in his account of travelling with Russian pilgrims to Jerusalem, published in 1913, vividly described this scene:

> Again next morning, Palm Sunday, the pageant at the Sepulchre was glorious, and those who penetrated to the fore of the terrible crowd of pilgrims, sight-seers, and Turkish soldiers, saw wondrous sights - many clergy in rich robes holding in their hands, some boxes of relics, others little bright-painted ikons; they saw bishops in their copes carrying Gospels, priests holding bouquets of flowers, surpliced boys with lighted candles, many with waving palms, strange, pale-faced, lank-haired monks with stove-pipe hats on their heads, and in their hands the poles of painted banners and gilt crosses. One priest held an immense olive branch, nay rather an olive tree, all hung with flowers and ornaments like a different sort of Christmas tree.[83]

The procession headed around the Sepulchre and then went down to the Golden Gate, by then already mortared up by 'suspicious Turks' fearing the fulfilment of Christ's second coming.[84]

The Matson photograph captures the time-honoured phenomenon of pilgrimage at the Resurrection church, especially at Easter, with its crush of the faithful. But it also shows the role of the south entrance portal. Here the sculpted lintels, removed in 1929, are still in place giving, a focus and direction to visitors. As now, only the left portal is open, forcing everyone in and out through the same door. But in the 12th century both doors would have been open, allowing trafficking by pilgrims and regular worshippers in and out of the building. It will be argued here that the right portal was the entry point. In addition, the third route was open to them: up the stairs to the right of the main double portal, into the 'Chapel of the Franks', leading to Calvary (fig. 7).

---

[82] I am grateful to the Christian Swedish Study Centre, and its Director, for the opportunity of attending this conference and for permission to rephotograph this plate while it was on display at the Centre. For the exhibition itself: R Hassner (ed.), *Eric G Matson and the American Colony Photographers, Jerusalem: Palestine 1898-1946*, The Swedish Institute, Stockholm, 1990. This photograph is reproduced neither here nor in *The Middle East in Pictures*, with an introduction by S Hobart, 4 Vols, New York, 1980. It is the embroidery on their collars of the pilgrims that identifies them as eastern European, of which the Russians were predominant.

[83] Stephen Graham, *With the Russian Pilgrims to Jerusalem*, London, 1913, 242.

[84] Graham, *Russian Pilgrims*, 245.

The doorways and their lintels

The lintels, removed in 1929 and now in the Rockefeller Museum, are now in a sorry state owing to the substance with which they were coated in the 1930s to prevent blistering.[85] The connexion between the two lintels, as well as their exact date in the 12th century, are issues still under discussion. Most recent commentators favour a date after the mid-century for the western lintel and its companion, suggesting a variety of Western sources and implying their insertion at some time after the consecration of 1149.[86] Studies investigating the meaning of the lintels have effectively treated them separately, by giving weight to one or the other. Viewing them together here in the context of the occupation and use of the Holy Sepulchre, including the chapels around the courtyard enables a new theory to be advanced. This views them as an intentional pair, channelling visitors in the relevant entrance, in the right portal and out of the left. Attributing aspects of the imagery to interests of the monarchy, and the popular devotion of local worshippers and pilgrims and the interests of the monarchy, as well as the Church, widens the scope of the endeavour of interpretation. The portals of the facade can then be seen as the outcome of the coordinating role of the Latins in asserting their preeminence at the Holy Sepulchre, a role reasserted in 1149. Writing of the phenomenon of stational liturgies in the early Christian period, in which movement through procession plays a fundamental part, Robert Wilken has observed that 'space is never ideologically neutral.'[87] The same is true of the 12th century, in which public liturgical processions were highly-charged political, civic events.

---

[85] Folda, 'Painting and Sculpture', 269.

[86] This contradicts Boase's acceptance of the consecration date of 1149 for the lintels: T S R Boase, 'The Arts in the Latin Kingdom of Jerusalem', *Journal of the Warburg and Courtauld Institutes* II (1938/9), 6. See A Borg, 'Observations on the Historiated Lintel of the Holy Sepulchre, Jerusalem', *Journal of the Warburg and Courtauld Institute* XXXII (1969), 40, has 1187 as the *terminus ante quem*; Rahmani, 'Eastern Lintel', 128, 1150-1180, though favours not exclude a 'somewhat earlier date'. Other views are those of H Buschhausen, 'Die Fassade der Grabeskirche zu Jerusalem', in *Crusader Art in the Twelfth Century*, ed. J Folda, BAR Int. series 152, Oxford, 1981, 84 (c. 1170); B Kühnel, 'Der Rankenfries am Portal der Grabeskirche zu Jerusalem und die romanische Skulptur in den Abruzzen', *Art Medievale* n.s. I (1987), 120-21 (third quarter of the 12th century); These views are based, however, largely on stylistic rather than historical criteria. Lindner, 'Topography and Iconography in Twelfth-Century Jerusalem,' in Kedar (ed), Horns of Hattin', 97.

[87] Wilken, *The Land Called Holy*, 114. It is also worthwhile noting that the Latin monarchs were under pressure from several interest groups amongst their own community, not just religious and ecclesiastical but also political and economic, which also manifested itself at the Holy Sepulchre. Benjamin Kedar has supported the view that an inscription in gold was put up in the rotunda in 1105, although later destroyed by King Amalric in the 1160s: B Z Kedar, 'Genoa's Golden Inscription in the Church of the Holy Sepulchre: A Case for the Defense', in G Airaldi and B Kedar (eds.), *I Comuni Italiani nel regno crociato di Gerusalemme*, Collana Storica di Fonti e Studi XLVIII, Genoa, 1986, 319-35.

The western (left) lintel

Accepting the usual identification, the scenes on the western (left) lintel (fig. 9) are, reading from left to right: 1) Raising of Lazarus 2) Mary and Martha meeting Jesus on the road to Bethany 3) Jesus sending the two disciples to fetch the ass with, below, two disciples preparing the Pascal Lamb 4) Fetching of the Ass and her Colt 5) Entry into Jerusalem 6) Last Supper.[88]

Molly Lindner has convincingly argued that the ordering of the Passion scenes on the western lintel reflected the 12th-century procession taken by pilgrims during the Palm Sunday procession. This followed Christ's own route from Bethany to Jerusalem, continuing Orthodox 11th-century practice.[89] The biblical ordering of the first two scenes is, therefore, reversed to accommodate the pilgrim's route. In the 12th-century the patriarch of Jerusalem, with the religious communities of Mount Zion, the Mount of Olives and the Valley of Josaphat, went to the tomb of Lazarus in Bethany before sunrise on Palm Sunday morning. After prayers the patriarch holding the cross led the group back to Jerusalem where they were met in the valley of Josaphat by three other Latin communities: those of the Holy Sepulchre, the Hospital of St John and Sta Maria Latina, who had previously assembled in the Templum Domini (the Dome of the Rock and site of the Presentation) for the blessing of palms. The two groups met with singing and the patriarch gave a sermon. Everyone went through the Golden Gate and processed to the courtyard of the Templum Domini.[90] Lindner points out that the Augustinians controlled all the places on the route including Bethany (Raising of Lazarus), Mt Zion (Last Supper) and the Mount of Olives (shrine of the Ascension).[91] The route went from Bethany over the Mount of Olives past the church of the Ascension into the Valley of Josaphat and through the Golden Gate. The control by the

---

[88] Alternative readings suggest reading from the centre ofthe lintel outward in both directions: see A Borg, 'Observations on the historiated lintel of the Holy Sepulchre, Jerusalem', *Journal of the Warburg and Courtauld Institutes* XXXII (1969), 36 note 29, centre outwards starting with the choice of the ass. N Kenaan-Kedar's proposal that the third and fourth scenes depicts the cleansing of temple by Christ, matched by the Latins' purging of Jerusalem of Muslim inhabitants after 1099 is also based on a reading from the centre outward: see N Kenaan-Kedar, 'The Figurative Western Lintel of the Church of the Holy Sepulchre in Jerusalem', in V P Goss and G Verzàr Bornstein (eds.), *The Meeting of Two Worlds: Cultural Exchange Between East and West During the Period of the Crusades*, Kalamazoo, 1986, 123-131. This reading is incompatable with the interaction and coexistence which is being emphasised in the present article.

[89] Lindner, 'Topography and Iconography, 81-98.

[90] Lindner, 90, citing A. Schoenfelder, 'Die Prozessionen der Lateiner in Jerusalem zur Zeit der Kreuzzüge', *Historisches Jahrbuch* 32 (1911), 584-586; H Graef, *Palmenweihe und Palmenprozession in der lateinischen Liturgie*, Steyl, 1959, 8.

[91] The Ascension itself perhaps referred to in the second scene: Lindner, 'Topography and Iconography', 95-96. Augustinian patronage, would explain, she argues, explain the presence of the last Supper, representing the Coenaculum on Mt Zion, not strictly speaking included in the itinerary.

Augustinians of the starting point at Bethany and end point at the Templum Domini, as well as the Holy Sepulchre itself, makes the association with their holdings of the Augustinians very plausible.

Accepting the first part of her argument does not necessarily, however, obligate acceptance of the exclusively Augustinian 'patronage' of the lintel. This lintel should not be viewed in isolation from the other, which opens up discussion beyond an exclusively Augustinian perspective.

The eastern (right) lintel

The eastern (right) lintel (fig. 10) is based on a design of a series of plant scrolls issuing from stylized animals' heads at their centre. The scrolls are shown in motion, turning, like wheels. Swirling around, entwined in the foliage, are naked men, with birds of prey, composite creatures with the bodies of birds and dragons' tails, with, in the centre, a centaur above a harpy.

Opinions have diverged sharply about the meaning of the right lintel. Noticing that two of the men - one in each of the outer medallions (figs. 11 a-b) - are pointing to their genitalia prompted L Y Rahmani to suggest that the lintel is rather 'a symbolic representation of sinful men, caught in the coils of hell and threatened on all sides by representations of evil.'[92] According to this interpretation, the bestiary image of the centaur is viewed as representing male lust and the harpy or siren, female seductiveness (fig. 12).[93] Positioned over the door leading to the burial place (and chapel) of Adam, it 'stands in direct contrast' with the figural lintel, with its Resurrection theme.[94]

A divergent analysis of the eastern lintel, that of Bianca Kühnel, posits its imagery as the tree of life, symbolising salvation proposed by the scenes of Passion week on the other lintel.[95] In contrast to Rahmani, she takes a positive view of the siren and centaur, based on their appearance in the *Physiologus* tradition.[96] But the situation need not be read as either black or white, especially since their appearance is not unique in Jerusalem in the 12th century. The illustrated Beatus Vir page, the opening of the 1st Psalm, in the London Psalter associated with Queen Melisende and usually dated between 1131-43, shows a centaur shooting at a siren, or harpy, across the

[92] Rahmani, 'Eastern Lintel', 120-29, esp. 127, followed by Jacoby, *Display*, 10.
[93] Rahmani, 'Eastern Lintel', 125.
[94] Rahmani, 'Eastern Lintel', 127.
[95] Kühnel, 'Rankenfries', 87-125, esp. 93-105.
[96] Kühnel, 'Rankenfries', 99. E Mâle, *Religious Art in France*, Princeton, 1978, 335, points to the frequent pairing of the centaur and the siren in 12th-century art he believes without moral meaning.

scrolls at the top of the initial, above David (fig. 3).[97] Their presence in the Psalter can be explained by the infiltration of a secular vocabulary in books for private use, in which sexual reference need not be counted out, but is not dependent on a hell-fire interpretation such as Rahmani's.[98] The overlap points to a link between sculpture and manuscripts produced at the Holy Sepulchre in the 12th century, and the impact of royal taste. Viewing the animals and men completely neutrally as redeemed through Christ as Kühnel proposes, however, is not the full story either as it does not take full account of some of the gestures and nuances of the men.

I would like to suggest that the eastern lintel complements the western one, but in a multivalent way representative of the *modus vivendi* at the Holy Sepulchre.

According to the medieval view of sexuality, unlike the modern, sex is viewed as an expendable attribute of the body in which the soul was trapped and, for this reason, usually banished to the margins of medieval art.[99] But the lintel here is not marginal but central: the focal entry point to the most holy church in Christendom. If the sculptor had intended hell-fire imagery, a Romanesque Last Judgement would have been chosen, as depicted on many portals in Europe. This is not to underplay the sexual reference, but to disassociate it from hell-fire. An alternative reading is as a allusion to mortality in the sense of the humanness, the vulnerability of those entering the church. This is as opposed to the divine nature of Christ born of Mary, reinforced with the image of the Virgin and Child above the other lintel. Here the mortal genealogy is inferred through human reproduction, with Adam the first man buried below Calvary just inside the church on this side. Sex and nakedness are a leveller, uniting all those entering the church, of whatever status, and need not imply lewdness or sinfulness.

Other men, in the upper part of the lintel (figs. 10-11a) point downward, to the liminal space of the worshipper's point of entry into the church. So entry to the church was through the right portal, and exit through the left. This is compatible with the ordering of worship within the Holy Sepulchre by custodians referred to in the pilgrims' accounts. The visitor could identify with Mary Magdalene appearing above the right portal in the *Noli me tangere* scene. She was the first mortal to see Christ after the resurrection, when he appeared to her at the site marked in the

---

[97] London, B L Egerton 1139: H Buchthal, *Miniature Painting in the Latin Kingdom of Jerusalem*, London, 1957, 12, with pl. 13; Rahmani, 'Eastern Lintel', 123, with pl. 27 (C); Wormald, 'Appendix 1' in Buchthal, *Miniature Painting*, 132-34, noted the feminine form of the prayers and argued for Melisende. The date of 1131-43 (Buchthal, *Miniature Painting*, 1) has been generally accepted, for example by J Folda, 'Painting and Sculpture in the Latin Kingdom of Jerusalem, 1099-1291', in Hazard (ed.), *Art and Architecture*, 252. Borg, 'Lost Apse Mosaic 11 offered a different view.

[98] This is even more commonly in Gothic period: see an example in M Camille, *Image on the Edge: The Margins of Medieval Art*, London, 1992, 40 with illus. 18.

[99] Camille, *Image on the Edge*, 38-9 quoting, amongst others, Michel Foucault, *The History of Sexuality I: An Introduction*, (trans. R Hurley), New York, 1978.

choir as the centre of the world, directly inside the choir from this entrance portal (figs. 4-5). She, with Martha, met Christ on the way to Bethany and was also present at the raising of her brother Lazarus at Bethany, the first two scenes represented on the left portal. The implication is that human regeneration is made possible by physical contact with the sites and relics of Christ's Passion contained within the church. The relative proximity of the left portal to the Anastasis inside the church and the right portal to Calvary, the chapel of Adam and the centre of the world is pertinent. As noted earlier, at the centre of the earth pilgrims quoted the text of Psalm 74: 12, 'But the Lord our King has before the ages worked salvation in the centre of the earth.' Identifying the dragon at the lower left of centre of the eastern lintel (fig. 10) as Leviathan in Psalm 74, within the context of the Creation, reinforces the idea of this lintel as an image of mortal salvation at the point of the creation of man, animals, earth, vegetation, and water.[100]

The correspondences between the two lintels proposes an interpretation which looks to the demands of, at different ends of the social scale, the pilgrim and the monarchy, as well as the canons and the patriarch. My contention is that the right lintel functioned as a visual sign, a point of preparation for those entering the church, to remind them of their human origins going back to Adam and their frailty, with the potential for salvation through Christ's suffering and resurrection. The exit through the left door was marked by the lintel referring to the procession from the church to join the Palm Sunday route, in a spiritual sense reenacted and replicated all year round by pilgrims. It also provided a resolution in narrative form to the issue of human origins and salvation raised in the right lintel.

The lintels' royal and spiritual association

Several factors posit a royal, as well as a popular and ecclesiastical, association with the lintels. As has been seen, the opening of the cycle of scenes on the western lintel with the Raising of Lazarus, reversing the biblical order, gives priority to the convent of Lazarus at Bethany. This convent was especially patronised by Queen Melisende whose sister Yvette

---

[100] See above, note 54. The context of Psalm 74: 12ff is of God crushing the water-monster(s) at Creation, and therefore probably at the omphalos of the earth. The monster Leviathan was in Ugaritic myth the river Litani in Lebanon, but to Psalm 74 is the river Euphrates. In Gen. 2: 10 the four rivers of the world rise in Eden and so Eden is thought of as being 'at the centre of the earth'. I owe these observations to Michael Goulder. The exact composite nature of this dragon is difficult to determine, because of the damage to the lintel. Jacoby, *Display*, 10 describes it as 'a fantastic creature with a goat's head, bird's body, hoofs and a dragon's tail'. It is worth noting that the Latins believed dragons such to be native to the east. Fulcher of Chartres described a dragon under the category of 'The different kinds of Beasts and Serpents in the land of the Saracens'. They are deadly, with venom in their tails, injuring their victims by thrashing about and by suffocation, and are crested. See F R Ryan (trans.), *Fulcher of Chartres: A History of the Expedition to Jerusalem, 1095-1127*, Knoxville, 1969, 285-86. For Kühnel's (different) comments on the dragon, see 'Rankenfries', 98.

was abbess there. William of Tyre records that she donated sacred vessels of gold decorated with gems and other objects to the convent at Bethany.[101] The Melisende Psalter's illustration of initial letters includes climbing figures, some semi-naked, with creatures of much the same type as the lintel.[102] These have been linked to the likely presence of English manuscripts at the scriptorium of the Holy Sepulchre, where the psalter was made, and recourse could have been made to these by both painter and sculptor.[103] But the link cannot be reduced to patronage and the copying of models, but may be very much closer, as a manifestation of a shared spirituality. It will be recalled that in the tympanum above the west lintel was a mosaic of the Virgin and Child, with Christ appearing to Mary Magdalene above the western lintel. Francis Wormald pointed out that both St Mary and St Mary Magdalene feature prominently in the prayers towards the end of the psalter.[104] They are both accompanied by illustrations, of the Virgin and Child as the enthroned Queen of Heaven (fig. 14) and the standing St Mary Magdalene respectively.[105] Furthermore, in the litany of saints, which precedes the prayers, the women are headed by St Mary Magdalene followed by St Martha.[106] In suggesting that the psalter was made for the private use of Queen Melisende, Wormald pointed to the devotion to St Mary Magdalene, and possibly St Martha, at the noble confraternity of the Cluniac abbey of St Mary of Josaphat, of which Melisende was probably a member and where she came to be buried.[107] What Bethany and the Holy Sepulchre have in common is being key 'stations' in the Palm Sunday processions, which passed through the Valley of Josaphat. All three share a role in the veneration to the Virgin, Mary Magdalene, and Martha. This was manifest in popular piety at one level and through the specific dedication of Melisende at another. An ally of the Church in the Latin Kingdom and a patroness of the Holy Sepulchre, she was herself crowned with her husband King Fulk at the Holy Sepulchre, in 1131.[108] This line of argument implies, that Melisende herself may have had a hand in the planning of the sculpted lintels as part of the facade and that they were indeed in position for the consecration in 1149. This was at a time when Melisende was in a position of power as

---

[101] *Guillaume de Tyre et ses Continuateurs*, 2 vols., Paris, 1879, II, Book 15, ch. XXVI, 85–86; Hintlian, *History of the Armenians*, 27-28.

[102] See Buchthal, *Miniature Painting*, pls. 14 (a-b), 15 (a-b), 16-17a.

[103] Buchthal, *Miniature Painting*, 12; Rahmai, 'Eastern Lintel', 123-24 (although he detected a 'free flow of fantasy' in the lintel); Kühnel, 'Rankenfries', 89.

[104] Wormald, 'Appendix 1' in Buchthal, *Miniature Painting*, 132-34.

[105] Buchthal, *Miniature Painting*, 9-10 with pls. 17b, 19c.

[106] Wormald, 'Appendix 1,' in Buchthal, *Miniature Painting*, 127-28.

[107] Wormald, 'Appendix 1', 127, 132. Wormald stresses the non-monastic character of the Litany, and points out that the confraternity was primarily connected to the hostel attached to the (Cluniac) abbey.

[108] For links between Melisende and the Holy Sepulchre, see R Grousset, *Histoire des Croisades et du royaume franc de Jérusalem* II, Paris, 1935, 314–316; Rahmani, 'Eastern Lintel', 128; Folda, 'Painting and Sculpture', 254.

Queen Mother (of Baldwin III).[109] The combination of eastern and western ideas in the façade is quite consistent with the work on the psalter, in which eastern Christian painters were arguably employed.[110] This is consistent with the western character of the ivory covers, with their royal emphasis, including scenes from the life of David and a Psychomachia Cycle of Virtues and Vices on the front and Deeds of Mercy on the back.[111]

A further significant royal factor is that the tombs of the Latin Kings of Jerusalem were located inside entrance to the Holy Sepulchre, just beyond the eastern entrance (fig. 4: A B C).[112] Theoderich identifies the fifth tomb, that of Baldwin II, as 'that of the father of the abbess of St Lazarus.'[113]

Again, it is important to stress the integration of the two lintels: it is not necessary to 'hive off' the western lintel to Augustinian patronage, or even privilege, and now the eastern to royal. The two were planned together to meet the needs of monarchy, clergy, the diversity of worship by the different communities, as well as the pilgrim traffic. The monarchy and the clergy were, in any case, bound by several ties. Two kings, Baldwin II and III, were canons of the Holy Sepulchre, the former especially during the time work was taking place on the church.[114] Further exemplifying the tie is the coronation ritual of the Latin kings. At his coronation the king was received by the patriarch and the clergy outside the portals of the church, and then installed assisted by barons and officials in the choir in front of the altar.[115] The ruler was thereby symbolically associated with Christ's regal triumph, both in the paired arches of the façade and the Anastasis mosaic in the apse.[116]

---

[109] H Mayer, 'Studies in the History of Queen Melisende of Jerusalem', *Dumbarton Oaks Papers* 26 (1972), rpt. in H E Mayer, *Probleme des lateinischen Königreichs Jerusalem*, London, 1983, 131, points out that 'her gifts to the Church must be viewed as an attempt to buy its political support.'

[110] For the argument that the third artist of the Psalter, who undertook the incipit pages marking the beginnings of the eight liturgical sections of the Psalter, was a Syrian, probably from Edessa see L-A Hunt, 'The Syriac Buchanan Bible in Cambridge: Book Illumination in Syria, Cilicia and Jerusalem of the Later Twelfth Century', *Orientalia Christiana Periodica* 57 (1991), 347-48. Manuscripts produced in the Holy Sepulchre scriptorium have been attributed to Armenian scribes and artists. The Paris Missal (B.N. 12056), related on palaeographical grounds to the Psalter, was written by an Armenian scribe: see Wormald, 'Appendix II' in Buchthal, *Miniature Painting*, 135. Buchthal (32) posits the work of Armenian painters in the decoration of two Gospel books (Paris. B.N. Lat. 276 and Vat. Lat. 5974) made at the scriptorium in the last quarter of the 12th century.

[111] For the covers: Boase 'Mosaic, Painting, and Minor Arts', 138-39, with note 28; J S Norman, 'The Life of King David as a Psychomachia Allegory. A Study of the Melisende Psalter Book Cover', *University of Ottowa Quarterly* L (1980), 193-201. B Kühnel, 'A Witness of Byzantine Imperial Influence in Jerusalem: The Bookcovers of Queen Melisende's Psalter', *XVIIIth International Congress of Byzantine Studies: Resumés of Communications* I, A-K (Moscow, 1991), 619-21. The front cover is reproduced in colouin Riley-Sith (ed), *Atlas*, 36.

[112] See above, notes 38-39.

[113] Wilkinson, *Jerusalem Pilgrimage*, 285; Theoderich, *Guide*, 18.

[114] Kenan-Kedar, 'Symbolic Meaning', 115.

[115] *Livre de Jean d'Ibelin VII*, in l'Academie royale des Inscriptions et Belles-Lettres, *Receuil des historiens des Croisades, Lois I, Assises de Jérusalem*, Paris, 1841, 29-31, Kenaan-Kedar, 'Symbolism', 114 with note 32.

[116] Kenaan-Kedar, 'Symbolism', 114-15.

This was cemented by the presence of the royal tombs in the Holy Sepulchre, reinforcing the special role of the church in the body politic and spiritual of the Latin Kingdom in the 12th century.

The facade of the Holy Sepulchre, then, reflects the preoccupations of the various Christian groups, including the integration of varying interests amongst the Latins themselves. It provides a public statement of this integration of the Latin Church and state, drawing on the diversity of indigenous traditions. No-one in the Middle Ages was naive about art and its visual impact, least of all in the centre of Christendom.

Orthodox artistic productivity

Finally, two icons may be selected to demonstrate the continuing presence and worship of the Orthodox within the Holy Sepulchre, and the internal shift in power on ethnic lines, from the later 12th century, from Greek to Syrian and Georgian. This shift, begun under Latin jurisdiction, continued under Muslim rule. A 13th-century icon of the Crucifixion demonstrates the continuation of the Easter celebrations at the Holy Sepulchre and their reenactment in an Orthodox monastery in Syria. The other, of the Christ of Pity (the Man of Sorrows), I will argue, was actually made for the Melkite (Greek) community at the Holy Sepulchre in the late 12th century. Its appropriation by the Georgian community is symptomatic of the shift in the hierarchy at the Holy Sepulchre from the late 12th century, alluded to earlier through the changed occupation of chapels at the church.

The Holy Fire remained an enduring symbol for the presence of the Orthodox and their spiritual authority, also attended by the separated churches. An icon, probably made in a monastery in Syria in the 13th century, and now in the monastery of the Syrians in the Wadi Natrun in Egypt (fig. 15), epitomises the reenactment of the liturgy.[117] Christ crucified is flanked by two female personifications, the left one bright red, heralding in the Holy Fire of the Resurrection of Easter. She stands with her bright flask of light combining three associations: 1) the *myrophores,* or Holy Women 2) the Church replacing the Synagogue and 3) the Wise Virgin lighting the way to paradise with a lamp. Her light gives hope to mankind, personalised as individuals climbing out of their tombs below. This is endorsed by the blood of Christ dripping down onto the skull of Adam below Calvary, baptising him, and unlocking the potential of the resurrection of man and womankind. The icon exemplifies cultural exchange and absorption through coexistence, with concepts expressed through Western imagery and style. These include the Italianate Christ and the font-shaped tombs of the rising dead to express Orthodox beliefs. It enshrines the Byzantine theological belief, popular in the Holy Land since

---

[117] L-A Hunt, 'Eternal Light and Life: A Thirteenth-Century Icon from the Monastery of the Syrians, Egypt, and the Jerusalem Pascal Liturgy', *Jahrbuch der österreichischen Byzantinistik* XLIII (1993), 349-66.

the time of Constantine Monomachos' building work in the mid-11th century, that the sins of Adam, the first man, are washed away by Christ's blood.

Preserved in the Museum of the Greek Patriarchate in Jerusalem is an icon of the Christ of Pity, set within a revetment and frame holding enamels with scenes relating to the Passion (fig. 16). The title of the icon (*O basileus tes doxes*, 'King of Glory') and the eighteen panels are inscribed in Greek. But two Georgian inscriptions, on the frame and the back of the icon, which indicate Georgian adoption of the icon. This means that the Greek enamels were incorporated into the gold embossed frame of Georgian workmanship in the 13th-14th centuries, to which a silver backing was added in the 18th. The painting of Christ was repainted or, more likely replaced, at this time. The piece, with others,was moved to the museum from the Monastery of the Holy Cross, the Georgian monastery, outside the walls of Jerusalem to the west.[118]

Paul Hetherington has shown that the central revetment, around the bust of Christ, is of a piece, including its integral late 12th-century Greek inscription, and concludes that the original icon must also have been a Christ of Pity.[119] His proposal that the enamels - reset later in their frame by the Georgians - are contemporary with those of the 12th century revetment, both technically and stylistically, can be accepted.[120] The enamels, he posits, all supplement the imagery of the Christ of Pity in elaborating the imagery of Passion around the Liturgy of Easter. He divides these into three groups, representing the events of God Friday, Easter Day and the Last Judgement respectively. To the Crucifixion imagery of Good Friday belong the central roundels of the Grieving Virgin, John, two angels, sun and moon, Longinus and the pair of standing soldiers with the group of grieving women (labelled *myrophoroi*). Others are associated with the resurrection imagery of Easter: Nicodemus and Joseph of Arimathea together with the four roundels in the bottom row depicting the tomb, the group of sleeping soldiers, the two *myrophoroi,* with the angels, one of whom is clothed in white. The third group of plaques, those at the top, are interpreted as referring to the Last Judgement. These are the two groups of standing angels wearing *loroi* and the roundel of the Etoimasia or prepared throne. They are linked by the archangels on either side of Christ's head

---

[118] One of the inscriptions is a prayer, dateable to the 13th-14th centuries when the enamels were reset. The other, on the icon's silver backing, is dated 1707. The icon is discussed by P Hetherington, 'Who is this King of Glory? The Byzantine enamels of an icon frame and revetment in Jerusalem', *Zeitschrift für Kunstgeschichte* LIII (1) (1990), 25-38. The icon is reproduced in colour in V Tzaferis, *Museum of the Greek -Orthodox Patriarchate in Jerusalem*, Jerusalem, 1985, 62. I am grateful to the authorities of the Greek patriarchate in Jerusalem for permission to view the icon and take the photograph reproduced here. For the monastery of the Holy Cross see V Tzafaris, *The Monastery of the Holy Cross in Jerusalem*, Athens, 1987; *Id.*, 'The Monastery of the Cross in Jerusalem', in Tsafrir (ed.), *Ancient Churches Revealed*, 143-46.

[119] Hetherington, 'King of Glory', especially 27-28, 30.

[120] Hetherington, 'King of Glory', 32-33. His stylistic comparison is based on the archangels on either side of Christ's halo and the angels adjacent on the frame.

and by the Psalm 23 titulus declaring the dead Christ to be the King of Glory. This text also appears in the Gospel of Nicodemus, the textual basis for the Anastasis, the Byzantine Easter image (fig. 6).[121] The image of the Crucifixion and the Anastasis are left 'to be supplied in the beholder's mind' but implicit in the image of the Christ of Pity.[122]

Hetherington puts forward an historical argument for the manufacture of such an innovative and high quality icon in Constantinople.[123] He suggests it was commissioned and sent to Jerusalem as a gift for the marriage of Theodora, a niece of Manuel Comnenos, to Baldwin III, King of Jerusalem, in 1158. As one of her personal possessions, its private use, he argues, precluded copies and explains its lack of progeny. He noted its Easter imagery and the 'genuine and, for a Byzantine artist, unique attempt to envisage the appearance of the Holy Sepulchre' in the shape of an early Christian sarcophagus, suggesting that it could have been acquired by the Georgians as early as 1163, when Theodora retired to Acre on the death of Baldwin.

Certain issues concerning the original composition and layout of panels in the original 12th-century scheme remain to be answered. But accepting Hetherington's general thesis that the enamels all belonged within the same original 12th-century context framing an icon of Christ of Pity, the argument may now be advanced that that context was a Jerusalemite one during Manuel Comnenos' direct intervention in the Holy Land, rather than a Constantinopolitan one.

The Holy Sepulchre and Jerusalem associations are more direct than Hetherington admits. The representation of the Holy Sepulchre as a sarcophagus is not the Byzantine way of depicting the tomb of Christ as he admits. It is instead the Western, or Latin.[124] A feature of the Sepulchre roundel is the three triangular gables, representing openings in the Sepulchre. Pilgrim accounts dating from the time that the panels were made, after the mid-12th century, describe the Sepulchre, as referred to above. Theoderich, during his visit between 1169-74, writes of pilgrims crawling into the mouth of the cave, which was lined with marble, gold and precious stones, to reach the Sepulchre where Christ remained for three days. There were three holes through which pilgrims could kiss the stone on which Christ lay.[125] Theoderich also noted a mosaic over the entry to the Sepulchre of the Entombment, with the Virgin and the three Maries with the angel.[126] Slightly later in his account is mention of an altar in the choir marking the spot where Joseph and Nicodemus laid out

[121] Hetherington, 'King of Glory', 31-34.

[122] Hetherington, 'King of Glory', 34.

[123] Hetherington, 'King of Glory', 35-37.

[124] N C Brooks, 'The Sepulchre of Christ in Art and Liturgy' *University of Illinois Studies in Language and Literature* VII (2), Urbana, 1921, 24-25, 62, points out that in the 11th century there was a change in the west from depicting the Sepulchre as an architectural structure to a sarcophagus, with no construction over it.

[125] Stewart, *Theodoric*, 9; Wilkinson, *Jerusalem Pilgrimage*, 279.

[126] Wilkinson, *Jerusalem Pilgrimage*, 278.

Christ's body for washing.[127] All these figures are given prominence in the panels. Furthermore, the major scenes of the Crucifixion and Anastasis are absent from the icon. While it is true that they are implicit in the Christ of Pity image, they would not be necessary if the piece were made for prayer at an Orthodox altar at the Holy Sepulchre, as these images were present in the monumental decoration, the Anastasis in the apse, and the Crucifixion in Calvary and elsewhere.[128] As mentioned above, the Emperor Manuel had had the Sepulchre encased in gold. Other metalwork is known to have been produced in, as well as made for, Jerusalem, and metalworkers are documented at the Holy Sepulchre in the 12th century.[129] I would, therefore, suggest that the Byzantine Emperor Manuel himself commissioned it at, and probably for, the church of the Holy Sepulchre.[130] The ornament on the revetment, not considered by Hetherington, support's this. The bands of repeated square pattern at the top and bottom of Christ's halo are comparable to the right side border in the Incredulity of Thomas amongst the mosaics in the Church of the Nativity at Bethlehem, completed in 1169, under the patronage of Manuel, in conjunction with Amalric, King of Jerusalem.[131] In addition, the spiky foliage of Christ's halo is comparable to the ornament below the scene of the Entry into Jerusalem at Bethlehem.[132]

The question arises as to why the Georgians in Jerusalem were resetting and reworking the group of 12th-century enamels. The scheme is consistent with the rising status of the Georgian community at the expense of the Greeks. That Georgian craftsmen were adopting, adapting and renovating Greek works of art in the 13th-14th centuries in not surprising in view of their high profile role as leaders of the Orthodox communities at the time. Probably undertaken at the Monastery of the Holy Cross, where the Georgian community was based, its imagery, incorporating the tomb of Christ in the centre bottom of the frame, may well also articulate Georgian ambitions *vis-à-vis* the Holy Sepulchre. These were eventually realized in the 15th century.

[127] Wilkinson, *Jerusalem Pilgrimage*, 282.

[128] These include Calvary (see above, note 43), the grotto chapel of the Finding of the Cross (fig. 4: 309): Corbo, *Santa Sepolchro*, I, 171-72; II, pl. 57; III, photo 113. Theoderich referred to 'a picture of the crucified one' over the door of the cloister: Wilkinson, *Jerusalem Pilgrimage*, 284. The directness of the inscription, attributing Christ's pain to the viewer, does not rule out the possibility that this was a Christ of Pity image. Stewart, *Theoderich*, 16, took it to be the Crucifixion.

[129] H Meurer, 'Kreuzreliquiare aus Jerusalem', *Jahrbuch der Staatlichen Kunstsammlungen in Baden-Württemberg* XIII (1976), 7-17. The cross reliquaries he discusses are dateable to the second quarter of the 12th century. For the four metalworkers at the Holy Sepulchre, documented in 1133 and 1160: E de Rozière, *Cartulaire de l'église du saint Sépulchre de Jérusalem*, Paris, 1849, nos. 104 and 105, cited by Meuhrer, 15 with note 47. A similar arrangement, if not imagery, of enamels around an icon frame as in the Christ of Pity is that of a portable altar formerly from the cathedral of Agrigento, attributed to Jerusalem by Meuhrer (15 with Abb. 10).

[130] For Manuel's support of the restoration of the Holy Sepulchre see Hamilton, 'Rebuilding Zion', 14.

[131] Hunt, 'Art and Colonialism', pl. 11.

[132] Entry into Jerusalem at Bethlehem: W Harvey *et. al.*, *The Church of the Nativity at Bethlehem*, London, 1910, pl. II. For the indigenous basis of the mosaics at Bethlehem see Hunt, 'Art and Colonialism', 83-85.

Conclusion

The focus, indeed and the *raison d'être* of Latin conquest of the Holy Land during the Crusades was the liberation of the sites of Christ's life, and especially his passion. Venerated by pilgrimages before the Crusades, the Holy Sepulchre occupied a prime place playing out the propaganda, spirituality and exercise of power by the Latins. But there they encountered the indigenous Christian communities who now had to adapt not only to Latin rather than Muslim rule but Latin control of the Holy sites. It is argued here than the Latins - specifically the crown and the clergy - performed a coordinating role in the administration and commissioning of art at the Holy Sepulchre, driven by the crown and acting in tandem with the church and bowing to popular and political pressure where necessary. A tactic was to play off the indigenous communities, and favour the 'Monophysite' or separated churches over the Orthodox, a situation made possible by exploiting their decline in prestige accompanying the withdrawl of involvement by the Byzantine empire by the end of the century. The art, architecture and ritual surrounding the sites of Christ's passion at the Resurrection church can be shown to express strong continuity with the Orthodox Christian past. But in other respects the Latins are innovative, developing and promoting the interests of the Latin church, through the cult of the cross and imagery of the church replacing the synagogue, as well as the legitimacy of the monarchy through the siting of the tombs of the Latin kings in the chapel of Adam. The south facade of the church, with its sculptural and mosaic programme of decoration, provides a test case of this coordinating role, with its relating of popular pilgrimage spirituality to the events inside the church, as well as the tombs of the Latin kings. The reframing in the 13th-14th centuries of the late 12th century icon of the Christ of Pity, arguably made at the Holy Sepulchre, shows appropriation by one Orthodox indigenous group, the Georgians, of another, the Orthodox Greeks, and reflects the shift in the power structure by the end of the century, once the Holy Sepulchre was back in Muslim hands after 1187.

Western Christians in the Latin Kingdom of Jerusalem soon realized that they would have to negotiate with the indigenous populations, for a range of political and social reasons. The Holy Sepulchre, like the Church of the Nativity in Bethlehem and other Holy Land sites, were sacred to each of the Christian groups, and its artistic embellishment formed an integral part of the processes of negotiation and integration which constituted coexistence. In the case of the Holy Sepulchre the ceremonies and processions of Easter, as well as the imagery of Resurrection, were stimuli to artistic production. Debates around the 'nationality' or background of particular artists may be subsumed into a wider discussion of the languages of art, in which individual groups consciously retain and develop their traditional forms of artistic production to retain their own identities.

strengths of coordinating such artistic activity in attempting to integrate the various communities. Cultural and political debate amongst the Latin and indigenous Christian groups is seen to be played out in the sphere of art with the Holy Sepulchre as the abiding focus.

fig. 1: *The Holy Sites of Jerusalem* (after T S R Boase, *Castles and Churches of the Crusading Kingdom,* London, 1967, 23).

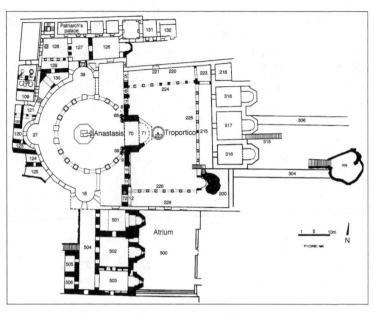

fig. 2: The Church of the Holy Sepulchre: plan of 11th-century ground-floor remains (after Corbo, *Sepolchro*, pl. 4).

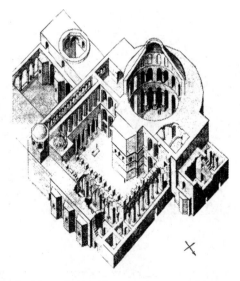

fig. 3: The Church of the Holy Sepulchre: reconstruction of the structure rebuilt in 1048 by Constantine Monomachos (after Coüasnon).

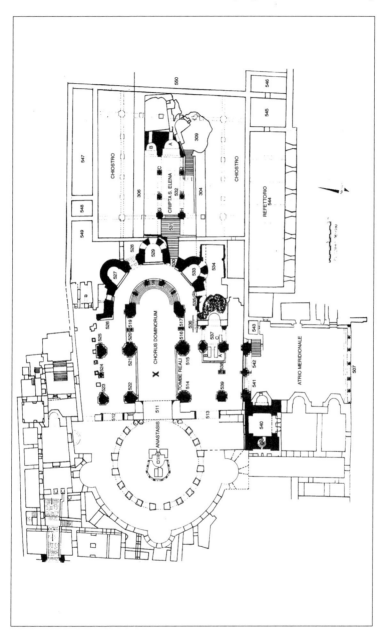

fig. 4: Ground Plan of the Holy Sepulchre at the time of the Crusaders (12th-century structures are marked in black) (after Corbo, *Sepolchro*, pl. 6).

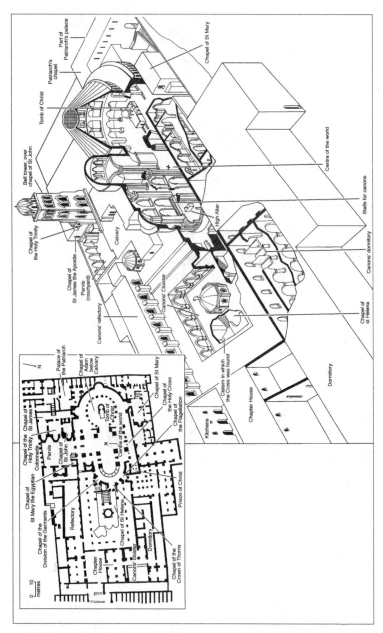

fig. 5: The Church of the Holy Sepulchre in the 12th-century (after illustration by Swanston Publishing Ltd).

fig. 6: The Anastasis, apse mosaic, Nea Moni, Chios (after Mouriki).

fig. 7: Church of the Holy Sepulchre, south facade (photo: author).

fig. 8: Palm Sunday Procession outside the Church of the Holy Sepulchre, Jerusalem, at the turn of the century. G Eric Matson Collection, Library of Congress, Washington. (Photo reproduced with permission of the Swedish Christian Study Centre, Jerusalem.)

fig. 9: Former western lintel of the South Facade, Holy Sepulchre (after C Enlart, *Les Monuments des Croisés dans le Royaume de Jérusalem Atlas II,* Paris, 1927, pl. 101, fig. 308).

fig. 10: Former Eastern Lintel of the South Facade, Holy Sepulchre (after Enlart, *Monuments des Croisés Atlas I,* Paris, 1926, pl. 100, fig. 304).

fig. 11a: Right part of former eastern lintel of the South Facade, Holy Sepulchre (after E T Richmond, 'Church of the Holy Sepulchre: Note on a recent Discovery,' *Quarterly of the Department of Antiquities in Palestine* I, 1932, fig. 1).

fig. 11b: Detail, right part of former eastern lintel of the South Facade, Holy Sepulchre.

fig. 12: Central section of eastern lintel of the South Facade, Holy Sepulchre (after Rahmani).

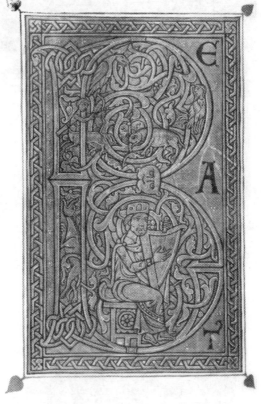

fig. 13: Initial B to Psalm 1. MS London, B.L. Egerton 1139 fol. 23v (photo: courtesy of the Trustees, British Library).

fig. 14: Enthroned Virgin and Child. MS London, Egerton 1139 fol. 202v
(photo: courtesy of the Trustees, British Library).

fig. 15: Icon, Dair al-Suryan, Wadi Natrun, Egypt (photo: author).

fig. 16: Icon, Greek Orthodox Patriarchate (photo: author, with permission of the Greek Orthodox Patriarchate, Jerusalem).

6

Tommaso Obicini (1585-1632) Custos of the Holy Land and Orientalist

Giovanni-Claudio Bottini, OFM

Among the many people who made history in the Holy Land was a remarkable Franciscan priest who was active in the Middle East during the first thirty years of the 17th century.

I do not know how many pilgrims and tourists visiting the Basilica of the Annunciation in Nazareth have noticed a tablet in memory of Fr Tommaso Obicini (1585-1632)[1] and the Amir Fakhr al-Din (1572-1635). In 1970 the Franciscans put up this memorial to acknowledge this forgotten but well-deserving Custos of the Holy Land and the amir of the Druze in Galilee on the 350th anniversary of their coming into definite possession of the Holy Place. This commemorative stone is perhaps the only marker that reminds us of this extraordinary friar and distinguished orientalist.

Through this paper I intend to offer a brief summary of his life and to outline his contribution both to oriental studies and the spread of Christianity in the East.

Tommaso Obicini was born in Nonio, a small village in northern Italy not far from Novara probably on 9 November 1585. He became a Franciscan of the Roman Province and was ordained a priest in the Basilica of St John Lateran on 20 September 1608.

---

[1] Cf. R Sbardella, *P Thomas Obicini a Novaria. De vita et operibus* (Thesis ad Lauream), Pontificium Athenaeum Antonianum, Roma, 1957; unpublished dissertation; C Balzaretti, 'Un importante ma dimenticato orientalista del sec. XVII Tommaso Obicini da Novara o.f.m.', *Novarien.* (Associazione di storia della Chiesa novarese) 19 (1989), 49-70; S De Sandoli, 'Riedizione e traduzione degli opuscoli di P. Tommaso Obicini da Novara sulle processioni nei Luoghi Santi e sull'acquisto dei santuari di Nazaret (1620) e Ain Karem (1621)', *Studia Orientalia Christiana Collectanea* 22 (1989), 175-466, a biographical profile is found in 189-200.

In the General Chapter held in Rome on 9 June 1612, Fr Obicini was named Deputy Custos of the Holy Land. He left Venice on the following 20 September and arrived in Jerusalem on 25 November. But in April 1613 he resigned as Deputy Custos to become guardian of the Franciscan friary in Aleppo, Syria.

During his seven years in Aleppo, he played a significant role in attempting to unite the Chaldeans with the Roman Church.[2] The excellent relationship Fr Tommaso established with the Chaldean Church proved to be fruitful in a variety of ways. The positive results of this relationship also lasted for many years in Jerusalem.

The Minister General of the Franciscan Order appointed Fr Tommaso Custos of the Holy Land on 14 March 1620. While travelling from Aleppo to Jerusalem, he stopped in Nazareth and expressed his deep regret to see the shrine of the Annunciation in a state of neglect. He resolved to revive the Christian faith in that city. Once in Jerusalem, he had to face a number of internal and external difficulties experienced by the Franciscan community, in addition to the problems caused by the plague that had broken out in the city the year before.

In spite of all these troubles, Fr Obicini did not lose heart. He reformed many aspects of the Franciscan life and promoted an ambitious building programme for the improvement of the shrines and friaries. He restored the Holy Sepulchre in Jerusalem and the Basilica of the Nativity in Bethlehem; he repaired the monastery in Ramleh and purchased the houses surrounding St Saviour's friary. Towards the middle of November, 1620, he paid a visit to the Amir Fakhr al-Din in Beirut and obtained the return of the shrine in Nazareth. Two weeks after that meeting, the friars were back in Nazareth! It was also due to his good offices that St John the Baptist's shrine in 'Ain Kerem was recovered by Christianity on 29 April 1621. In that same year, Fr Tommaso was confirmed in his post as Custos. On the following 6 June he went to Rome to deal with some of the problems the Custody was facing, in particular its financial difficulties and its relations with other religious and political entities. In the Eternal City, he had many fruitful meetings with the pope, the officials of the Roman curia, and the superiors of the order.

Fr Obicini thought his presence in the Holy Land was no longer necessary, so he resigned from his office in April, 1622. Soon after this, he proposed the establishment of an institute for the teaching of Arabic in

---

[2] Cf. R Sbardella, 'L'Unione della Chiesa Caldea nell'opera di P. Tommaso Obicini da Novara', *Studia Orientalia Christiana Collectanea* 5 (1960), 374-452 "published separatley as *L'opera di P. Tommaso Obicini da Novara per l'unione della Chiesa Caldea*, Cairo, 1960".

St Peter Montorio's Monastery in Rome.[3] His plan was accepted and the Congregation for the Propagation of Faith chose him to teach Arabic. Fr Tommaso spent the rest of his life in the Eternal City where he taught and acted as a consultant for the Congregation of the Propaganda. He also made his skilful contributions to the revision of the Arabic translations of the Bible.[4] His letters, however, reveal that his work was often met with misunderstanding.

Fr Obicini's love for the Holy Land was also expressed in his work as a writer. In 1623 he published five pamphlets containing the rites and texts of some pious exercises practised by the Franciscans in their sanctuaries, together with accounts of the recovery of the shrines of 'Ain Kerem and Nazareth.[5] In the same year, he wrote a booklet dedicated to the pope in which he described the deplorable state of the Christian shrines in the Holy Land.[6] He also wrote to the Medici family of Florence, soliciting their patronage for St John's in 'Ain Kerem.[7] His contacts with the East, where he was well remembered, became more intense in the years 1624-1625. From there came even appeals that he might return to the Holy Land.

Since Fr Obicini had to go back to his native region in 1626 to recover from an illness, he asked to stay in Venice to learn Persian. In this way, he could be better prepared to refute the anti-Christian book entitled 'Purifier of the Mirror', written in Persian. In November, 1629 he went back to Rome where he continued teaching at St Pietro Montorio's Institute until he died on 7 November 1632.

Fr Obicini was better known for his work on behalf of the Holy Land than as expert in Arabic and a pioneer in Oriental studies.

---

[3] Cf. A Kleinhans, *Historia studii linguae arabicae et collegii missionum Ordinis Fratrum Minorum in conventu ad S. Petrum ad Montem Aureum erecti*, Biblioteca bio-bibliografica della Terra Santa e dell'Oriente Francescano, Nuova Serie 'Documenti' 13, Quaracchi 1930, 57-72. A contemporary of his bears this witness about the excellent results this institution had over the years: 'Fr Tommaso, remaining in his Roman Province, was appointed "Lector" of Arabic in St Peter Montorio's friary where, by the grace of God, he spent most of his time teaching to many young friars belonging to different provinces of the Order. A good number of them today [1636] work in the East: administering the sacraments with admirable zeal and fervour, hearing confessions and preaching the Word of God in Arabic with great satisfaction and enjoyment of our few Catholics. Having been instructed in Christian doctrine and often nourished by the Word of God, they have again benefited from their services so lacking in the past' (G. Golubovich, *Croniche ovvero Annali di Terra Santa del P. Pietro Verniero di Montepiloso dei Frati Minori*, Biblioteca bio-bibliografica della Terra Santa e dell'Oriente Francescano, Nuova Serie 'Documenti' 10, Quaracchi 1930-1936, t. V, 1. VI, c. 206, 94).

[4] Cf. A Vaccari, 'Una Bibbia araba per il primo Gesuita venuto al Libano', *Mélanges de l'Université Saint-Joseph 10 (1925)*, 79-104; A Kleinhans, 'De collaboratoribus franciscanis in Bibliis arabicis a. 1671 editis', *Antonianum* 4 (1929), 369-386, especially 369-373.

[5] Cf. S De Sandoli, note 1.

[6] Cf. Balzaretti, 'Un importante', 62.

[7] Cf. Z Lazzeri, 'I santuari di Terra Santa e la Famiglia dei Medici', *Archivum Franciscanum Historicum* 15 (1922), 207-211.

His writings were:

(1) (in Arabic) *Isagoge Idest, breve Introductorium Arabicum, in Scientiam Logices cum versione Latina ac Theses sanctae Fidei*, Romae, 1625. The book's purpose is to introduce missionaries to the philosophical and theological concepts of the East in order to be prepared to rebut the Muslims. The first part deals with the philosophical terms of logic, the second with the tenets of the Christian faith (Arabic text with Latin translation).

(2) *Grammatica Arabica* [in Arabic], *Agrumia appellata. Cum versione latina, ac dilucida expositione*, Romae, 1631. It is a translation of the Arabic grammar by Muhammad ibn Da'ud as-Sinhaji. 'The learning of Arabic in the West has greatly improved in the last few years thanks to the translation of this grammar . . .; the latest edition by Obicini which deserves the highest degree of praise, especially for its commentary.'[8]

(3) *Thesaurus Arabico-Syro-Latinus*, Romae, 1636. A revised translation of a work by one Elia bar Shinaya, also known as Elia of Nisibis (d. 1049 or after). 'The *Thesaurus* had a considerable circulation and fortune because it was used by students of Syriac.'[9]

(4) *Scala* (= Coptic manuscripts containing grammars and vocabularies). Egyptian grammar and Egyptian-Arab-Latin dictionary. The manuscript includes an unabridged translation of the grammar by John al-Samannudi, a portion of the final part of the grammar by al-As'ad Abu 'l- Faraj ibn al-'Assal, a portion of the initial part of the grammar by John al-Wajih al-Qalyubi and a portion of the initial part of the dictionary of Abu 'l-Barakat. The translation is in Latin and Italian. There is also a Latin transcription of 17th century Coptic pronunciation in Egypt. 'The discovery of this translation singles Obicini out as one of the first to introduce the knowledge of Coptic to Europe.'[10]

---

[8] Balzaretti, 'Un importante', 66. He quotes the opinion of experts and gives a bibliographical index.

[9] Balzaretti, 'Un importante', 67. He quotes the opinion of experts and gives a bibliographical index.

[10] Balzaretti, 'Un importante', 68. Cf. also A Van Lantschoot, 'Un précurseur d'Athanase Kircher. Thomas Obicini et la Scala Vat. Copte 71. (Bibliothèque du Muséon 22), Louvain, 1948; A Kleinhans, 'Verdienste eines Franziskaners um die koptische Grammatik', *Neue Zeitschrift für Missionswissenschaft* 6 (1950), 136-138; G Giamberardini, 'Father Tommaso Obicini (†1632) O.F.M. Pioneer of the Coptic Philology', *Franciscan Studies* 25 (1965), 277-284; J Assfalg, P Küger, *Kleines Wörterbuch des christlichen Orients*, Wiesbaden 1975, 368.

Fr Tommaso is also credited with being the first scholar to have made Sinaitic inscriptions known to the Western world. We can still consult his collection of inscriptions and a report in which he recalls how the monks, on his visit to Mount Sinai, showed him an inscription attributed to the prophet Jeremiah. He made an accurate copy of it and described its symbols in a paper taken with himself to Rome. Both the inscriptions and the report are quoted by a Jesuit scholar, Athanasius Kircher, who received them from one of Fr Obicini's pupils.

Fr Tommaso left fifty-six interesting letters written between 1616 and 1631. I was most impressed by two of them. The letter of 10 January 1618, addressed to Pietro della Valle, a renowned Italian traveller, reveals his great learning and thorough knowledge of Hebrew, Syriac and Arabic.[11] His competence is also confirmed by the letter he sent to Cardinal Federico Borromeo (1564-1631) on 4 December 1623, together with a codex of the Samaritan Pentateuch, a valuable manuscript of the 10th century at earliest, which Milan's famous Biblioteca Ambrosiana still treasures.[12]

Fr Tommaso Obicini deserves a place of honour in the history of the Church both for his missionary zeal and ecumenical spirit, as it is witnessed by his attempts to unite the Chaldean Church with the Church of Rome and the return of the Basilica of Nazareth to the Christians. He is also to be remembered as one of the first generous collaborators with the Congregation of the Propagation of Faith. The Order and particularly the Custody of the Holy Land shall never forget his name and especially his exemplary and deeply-felt love for the Holy Places as well as his firm commitment to the linguistic and missionary formation of a great many Franciscans.[13] Finally, I think, he is entitled to be counted among the distinguished palestinologists and orientalists of all times.

Fr. Tommaso Obicini (1585-1632)   Amir Fakhr ad-Din (1572-1635)
on the commemorative stone at Nazareth

---

[11]   Cf. A Van Lantschoot, 'Lettre inédite de Thomas Obicini à Pietro Della Valle', *Rivista degli Studi Orientali* 28 (1953), 118-129.
[12]   Cf. R Sbardella, 'Tommaso Obicini da Novara, O.F.M. e il Cardinale Federico Borromeo', *Archivum Franciscanum Historicum* 56 (1963), 71-90.
[13]   Cf. G Graf, *Geschichte der christlichen arabischen Literatur, IV: Die Schriftsteller von der Mitte des 15. bis zum Ende des 19. Jahrhunderts. Syrer, Armenier, Kopten, Missionsliteratur, Profanliteratur,* Studi e Testi 147, Città del Vaticano 1951, 174-176; G Giamberardini, 'Il contributo dei Francescani alla cultura mediorientale', *Frate Francesco* 37 (1970), 99-111, especially 103-104; 38 (1971), 28-41.

7

Grigor the Chainbearer (1715-1749): the Rebirth of the Armenian Patriarchate

Roberta Ervine

How awesome is this place. There is none other than the house of God, and this is the gate of heaven[1]

So wrote the Armenian Bishop Hanna of Jerusalem, when in the first quarter of the 18th century he composed his history of Jerusalem. He quoted these words from the Old Testament Patriarch Jacob, in the firm conviction that Jerusalem was indeed and in truth the house of God and that it should be made to resemble the antechamber of heaven as closely as this world allows. This conviction had made it possible for Hanna, who was vicar of St James from 1717 to his death in 1733, to undertake in 1719 the massive and costly work of completely restoring the Armenian sections of the Holy Sepulchre Church a work the more remarkable for two reasons. First, because he began it upon the orders of a newly elected patriarch still in Istanbul whom he had never before seen and was not to meet in person for two more years. And secondly, because he began it at a time when the bankrupt Armenian brotherhood of St James did not have a single *qurush* in its treasury; when, in fact, most of its properties and church vessels had been seized, sold or pledged as security for the payment of its mountainous debts.

How had the rich and ancient brotherhood of St James come to be in a state of absolute poverty, and given its distressed circumstances, why would anyone order its members to begin a building project out of all proportion to its means?

To answer the first question first, it is difficult to pinpoint the exact moment in the 17th century when the decline of St James began, but it

---

[1] Hanna Erusalemac'i, *Girk' Patmut'ean Srboy ew meci k'alak'is Astucoy, Erusalemis*, Istanbul, 1807, 10.

proceeded with dreadful rapidity after the death of Patriarch Minas Amtec'i in 1704. No suitable successor to the patriarchal throne being found, the whole idea of an independent Armenian patriarchate for Jerusalem was abandoned, and the see was subsumed under the authority of the Armenian patriarch of Istanbul.[2] The patriarch of the day, Awetik' Erznkac'i, put the administration of Armenian Jerusalem into the hands of special representatives, called *nazirs*, sent to Jerusalem from the Istanbul patriarchate.[3] Although this step may have been intended to prevent financial chaos from invading the administrative void in Jerusalem, it actually caused just such chaos.

Christian Jerusalem's economic existence then as now depended upon the flow of pilgrims, whose payments and donations supported the religious institutions of the city and made it possible for them to meet the manifold exactions of the Ottoman authorities. Any interruption in the delicate cycle of income and expenditure could quickly make it impossible for a community to function. In the case of the Armenians, such an interruption was introduced as soon as the union of Jerusalem with Istanbul took place. The accommodation fees of pilgrims travelling from Istanbul to Jerusalem, usually paid upon the pilgrims' arrival in the Holy City, began to be collected instead in Istanbul itself, by representatives of the Istanbul patriarchate, before the pilgrims set sail. Each pilgrim received a certificate stating that he had paid his pilgrimage costs in full, while, the funds vital to St James' existence remained in Istanbul. There they were diverted for use in bolstering the claims of a succession of candidates to the patriarchal throne of that city.[4] The brotherhood of St James was left to provide food, housing and transportation for the arriving pilgrims as best it could.

Meanwhile, the *nazirs* sent to administer Jerusalem, as well as other relatives and friends of the various incumbent Armenian patriarchs of Istanbul arriving in the Holy City, also had their own and their families' expenses to meet. Since their tenure at St James was linked to the uncertain duration of their patron's patriarchal reign in Istanbul, it was urgent for

---

[2] Actually, the subjection of Jerusalem had begun somewhat before this point. At the instigation of Patriarch Awetik' of Istanbul, Minas was deposed in 1702 and Jerusalem was placed under Patriarch Awetik's jurisdiction. He appointed his representative or nazr to oversee the financial affairs of St James. When Awetik' fell in 1703, Minas was returned to his position, but the *nazir* of Istanbul remained in Jerusalem. An ambiguous situation was created, which Minas' death resolved.

[3] According to Tigran H T Sawalanian, *Patmut'iwn Erusalemi*, Jerusalem, 1931, I, 663, there were originally twelve lay representatives under the supervision of two clergy (Abraham Vardapet Arzuman and Step'an Vardapet Karnec'i), and an individual named Salat'iel.

[4] According to Sawalanian, patriarchal authority in Istanbul changed hands nine times between 1702 and 1714. It was held successively by Awetik' Erznkac'i, Galust Amasiac'i, Awetik' Erznkac'i for a second term, Mikayel Xarbert'c'i, Matt'eos 'Sari' Catholicos of Sis, Sahak Apuc'exc'i, Yovhannes Zmiwrnac'i, Alek'sandr Julayec'i, Sahak Apuc'exc'i for a second term, and Yovhannes Kanjakec'i, whose voluntary abdication in favour of Yovhannes Kolot ended the tragic farce. (The succession given by Patriarch Malak'ia Ormanian, *Azgapatum*, Beirut, III iii, appendix col. 51-52, differs somewhat.)

them to reap the rewards of their labours as quickly as possible. To insure that there would be sufficient funds to pay themselves, they instituted austerity measures for the monastic establishment, cutting off the brotherhood's supplies of clothing and basic necessities, and closing the refectory for months at a time. Above and beyond this, the *nazirs* also borrowed indiscriminately from various sources, using the seal of St James rather than their own signatures on the documents. No control over the amounts borrowed was possible, and no accounting of how the borrowed money had been spent was forthcoming.

By 1714, after a decade of *nazir* misrule, the monastery was at the end of its means. According to Bishop Hanna, who had been newly ordained a priest in February of that year, the *nazirs* secretly removed all of the monastery's brass vessels in a single night, and sent them into Egypt, to be melted down and sold for the value of their metal content. A similar though more gradual fate befell the monastery's gold and silver objects, many of whose workmanship was of superb quality. 'Because they did it on the sly,' wrote Hanna, 'they would sell an object worth a thousand *qurush* for barely two hundred.'[5] The monastery's holdings in real estate were also sold off under the pretence that they were being used as collateral for loans received.

Throughout the period of *nazir* control, progress reports were sent by the *nazirs* to the responsible bodies in Istanbul. Needless to say, these reports were uniformly positive; Jerusalem's house was being put in order, and all was well. As doubts about the accuracy of this rosy picture gradually began to grow in the minds of concerned businessmen and officials, events were unfolding elsewhere which would culminate in the revelation of the truth about Armenian Jerusalem's bankrupt condition and bring to the scene the man who was to send Hanna his orders to restore the Holy Sepulchre Church.

In 1704, the same year that Minas Amtec'i's death finalized the subjection of the Armenian patriarchate of Jerusalem to that of Istanbul, the famous and saintly teacher Vardan Vardapet of Bales (present day Bitlis), died in his monastery, Amrtol.[6] Shortly thereafter, seven of the Amrtol brotherhood left Bales in a group and ultimately came to settle in the monastery of St Karapet in Taron, whose brotherhood they joined, probably in 1706.[7] The monastery was in financial straits, but when one of

---

[5] Hanna, 108.

[6] Vardan died on 31 March 1704; Minas Amtec'i, on 24 November. Vardan had been appointed as Jerusalem's patriarchal legate to New Julfa by Patriarch Eliazar Ayntapc'i in 1678, and presumably his students would not have been ignorant of Jerusalem matters. Nerses Akinian, *Balesi Dproc'e*, Vienna, 1952, 254–55. The move of the seven brothers to St Karapet in Taron was a move from one monastery named for John the Baptist (the name Amrtol is a corruption of the word Amlordi, meaning 'son of the barren') to another.

[7] The seven were Bishop Grigor Sirvanc'i, his nephew Abraham Vardapet, Yovhannes Vardapet Balisec'i (Kolot), Bishop Nerses Arckec'i, Yovhannes Vardapet K'elec'i, and two priests named Gabriel and Step'annos. (G Bampuk'cian, *Yovhannes Patriark' Kolot*, Istanbul, 1984, 24.)

the new arrivals, Bishop Grigor of Sirvan, was appointed as abbot of the community, he nonetheless succeeded in renovating the churches of St Karapet and St Step'anos,[8] and in increasing the living quarters of the monastery[9]. Grigor and his associate Yovhannes Kolot, who had come with him from Bales, succeeded one another as abbot, and seconded one another's decisions.[10]

In the spring of 1710, a massive earthquake badly damaged the buildings of St Karapet, and reconstruction was required[11]. Since the work was urgent, money was borrowed to fund it. After it was completed, Abbot Grigor and the brotherhood again dispersed, this time to collect donations toward the payment of St Karapet's debts, which amounted to 13,000 *qurush*.[12] For two years, Grigor travelled through the Armenian communities of the Crimea to Adrianople, while Yovhannes organized the collection in Istanbul.

Hovhannes's arrival in the capital coincided with the time when the Armenian notables of the city had concluded that something was very much amiss in Jerusalem, despite the *nazirs'* reports to the contrary. A letter from the brotherhood of St James had been received, to the effect that the very existence of St James was in danger. Yovhannes's insight and honesty were so apparent that at the start of the year 1713, Patriarch Sahak and a group of prominent citizens,[13] called Yovhannes and commissioned him to go to the Holy City with the next pilgrimage as the new *nazir* or *vekil*, the fully empowered representative of the patriarch. He was given a modest amount of money for St James and the mission of assessing the real situation in Jerusalem. He was told to take whatever action he deemed appropriate. The entire community swore to support his decisions, to the death if necessary.[14]

When he arrived at St James in March, he found it stripped bare. The creditors, having despaired of ever recouping their losses, visited the monastery at every opportunity to seize what they could, rushing the altar during liturgy on the chance of snatching a chalice from the celebrant,

---

[8] Akinian, 327.

[9] Abp. N Bogharian, *Grand Catalogue of the Manuscripts of St James*, 1st ed., Jerusalem, 1960, V, 50. The information is from Jerusalem ms. 532, 63-69, which comprise a partial autobiography of Grigor of Sirvan, covering events from the year 1710 to the year 1717, when he was called to the patriarchal throne of Jerusalem.

[10] Karapet V Lusararian, *Gawazanagirk'* . . . *Uxtis Taronoy*, Jerusalem, 1919, 85.

[11] The date of the earthquake is given as 16 May, but the year is reported differently by different sources; Bampuk'cian gives it as 1708, following Babgen V Kiwleserian, *Kolot Yovhannes Patriark*, Vienna, 1904, 5, and Akinian, 362. Akinian, 368, in a parenthesis mentions that Kolot gives the date as 1709, referring to a colophon quoted in full in Lusararian, 127-132. Bogharian, *Vanatur*, Jerusalem, 1993, 343, gives the date as 1710, on the basis of Jerusalem ms. 532.

[12] *Catalogue*, 51.

[13] Yarut'iwn Muratean and Yarut'iwn T'evek'elean, both from the Abusheikh suburb of Istanbul; Sargis of Caesarea; the court architect Sargis Xalfaean; Israel of Istanbul; and Lut'vi, brother of the court's chief watchmaker Eusuf C'elepi. Their names are recorded in Bampuk'cian, 26, and in Hanna, 120.

[14] Hanna, 113.

bringing soldiers for nighttime raids on the monastic cells. There were no remaining church vessels.[15] In fact, there were few doors or windows left intact.[16] Moreover, a *firman* had been procured by the creditors, ordering the sale of all remaining St James properties. The *nazirs* secretly made arrangements for the sale of St Saviour's, the cemetery and monastic buildings just southwest of the Zion Gate. When the brotherhood learned of the impending sale, they were beside themselves, seeing this as the beginning of the end. They went together in tears to the creditors, begging that St Saviour's sale be postponed. As Hanna says, the hand of God touched the creditors' hearts, and they agreed, on condition that an acceptable guarantor could be found. The brothers rushed back to the monastery, to talk to Yovhannes.

Since his arrival in Jerusalem, Yovhannes had not been idle. One of his first actions had been to pay the debt for which the Armenian lamps that hung before the tomb of Christ in Holy Sepulchre Church had been seized as security. The restoration of the lamps to that most prominent of Christian places had great symbolic value; it signalled the intention of the Armenian community to resume its role as a major custodian of the holy sites. He also redeemed the garden property which divided the monastery of Holy Archangels or Dair al-Zaitun from the monastery of St James proper, thus re-uniting the main parts of the Armenian compound. The deliberation with which Yovhannes had made these redemptions left a favourable impression on the local notables. His position as the representative of Istanbul's ruling class also lent him credibility as a guarantor. Would he, the brotherhood asked, consent to bear this responsibility. Relying on the promise made him by the Istanbul community before his departure, Yovhannes agreed in the presence of the judge to personally assure repayment of eight hundred purses of money, an enormous sum. The creditors accepted his guarantee. A contract was drawn up for the beginning of payments in four years. The pasha approved, and the sultan was notified.[17]

Meanwhile Grigor was still occupied with the collection for St Karapet. Before Yovhannes left for Jerusalem, Grigor had been called to Istanbul by

---

[15] In the church of St T'oros there is preserved one of the chalices in use during this period; it is a footed tin cup, painted red on the inside and gold on the outside.

[16] Hanna, 110-111.

[17] Following the official reception, Yovhannes and the brotherhood went to Holy Sepulchre Church, to the crucifixion chapel, to begin the serious undertaking with prayer. Hanna, who was near Yovhannes as he prayed, records his words, 'Lord God of Israel, in antiquity and now, with troubled souls and heavy laden spirits we beseech your loving kindness; hear Lord the voice of our requests, and regard the sufferings of your servants. Look from your holy heaven on the misery of the church of your glory, for we know you to be a God more merciful than just, and though we have sinned before your exaltedness, yet do not remember our former sins, but speed to us your mercy, for we are reduced to great poverty. Remember the sufferings of your only begotten, holy Son, and His pure blood with which we were purchased into the adoption of you, our heavenly father. He paid the debts of our human nature with His sufferings; do you also, Lord, work this miracle in our suffering nation, and in your holy church, for you alone are our God, and beside you we know no other.' (117-118).

the patriarch to carry on the work there. He knew of his friend's mission, and when he heard that Yovhannes, in consultation with Hanna and other members of the brotherhood, had confiscated and broken the St James seal used by the *nazirs* to authenticate their borrowings, he rejoiced.

It is not clear exactly when Yovhannes returned to Istanbul, but he will not have wasted precious time, in any case. He recommended that in order to prevent Jerusalem from suffering the effects of constant changes of authority in Istanbul, it was essential to re-establish the Armenian patriarchate of Jerusalem as a separate administrative and financial entity. And it would greatly enhance the virtue of the separation, if a patriarch could be appointed for Istanbul who was a supporter of Jerusalem and for whom a long tenure in office could be guaranteed.

In the spring of 1715, while the debate over how to best carry out these recommendations was still going on, Grigor left Istanbul to return to his responsibilities as abbot of St Karapet.[18] Yovhannes stayed in the capital. Eventually, the emirs reached the logical conclusion: it was Yovhannes who was Jerusalem's guarantor. Appoint him patriarch of Istanbul, and let him choose the patriarch of independent Jerusalem. Istanbul's incumbent patriarch, Yovhannes of Ganjak, voluntarily abdicated his throne in Yovhannes's favour.[19] The manifest sense of the arrangement overrode Yovhannes's understandable objections, and he was proclaimed Patriarch of Istanbul on Friday, 12 September, 1715. By the time the liturgy was celebrated the next morning, he had already named his choice for patriarch of Jerusalem: Grigor, abbot of St Karapet.

Grigor, however, knew nothing of his appointment to the most onerous of offices. He was still en route to St Karapet when Yovhannes made the unilateral decision. Realizing that Grigor would not be easily persuaded, Yovhannes moved ahead with the process of government recognition for both his own and Grigor's appointments, as well as for the official separation of Jerusalem from Istanbul. On the other hand, he sent a special messenger to meet Grigor with a letter from the clergy and community in Istanbul: 'We have made such efforts and have done so much, and have sent after you; if you refuse to come, for whatever ill may befall the holy see hereafter, you will give account to God on the day of judgment.'[20] Also, the catholicos personally confirmed his support for Grigor's appointment, and ordered him to accept the post.[21] Grigor arrived back in Istanbul in the late summer of 1717.

Almost immediately, a general meeting of clergy and laity was convened, at which Grigor's appointment was reconfirmed. In a patriarchal

---

[18] According to *Catalogue*, 53, Grigor was already at the port awaiting departure for Pontus when Yovhannes arrived. They met there. Though no details of their meeting are given, Yovhannes will have brought Grigor up to date on the Jerusalem situation.

[19] Bp. Astuacatur Ter Yovhannesianc', *Zamanakagrakan Patmut'iwn S. Erusalemi*, Jerusalem, 1890, I, 439.

[20] *Catalogue*, 50.

[21] Catholicos Astuacatur I.

letter to Archbishop Movses, primate of New Julfa, Yovhannes Kolot described the proceedings. 'With much pleading, he desired to withdraw from this work, saying that he was insufficient for it. And when we would not allow him to turn away from responsibility for the sacred house, he stood up in the midst of the assembled people and said in the hearing of all, 'Hear me, brethren in Christ Since you will me . . . to this work, I swear to you as God and St James. are my witness, that just as we come into the world from our mother's womb naked and without possessions, and return naked thence to our original substance; so also when you release me to depart from the throne of St James, I shall return . . . whence I came naked and bearing nothing with me from that holy house And if I shall reap anything from that sacred house, for my own needs or for the needs of others, or if I shall send anything thence to St Karapet, whether it be my clothing or my food or any other necessity, or if I shall increase the belongings of my followers above what they now are, I shall answer for it to St James.'[22]

Grigor was better than his word. Already an ascetic who wore a nail studded hair shirt next to his skin, in 1718 he solemnly hung a heavy iron chain round his neck and locked it in place, vowing never to remove it until the debts of St James had been paid.[23] He was to wear it until 1726. Wearing the chain, he stood before the doors of Istanbul's churches, as if he were a penitent, humbly begging the people coming to worship not to forget Jerusalem. Aside from this, he and Yovhannes canvassed the city and its environs, preached Jerusalem at every opportunity, enlisted the help of clergy in other cities, wrote encyclicals. Grigor issued his first patriarchal order to Jerusalem, appointing Hanna as his vicar.

The public responded with generosity to Grigor's pleas for funds, but the collection met with unforeseen difficulties. In July 1718, just when a substantial sum had been gathered, a great fire swept Istanbul. Raging for thirty-four hours, it destroyed the wealthy Armenian residential district and gutted the patriarchate and cathedral. Their rebuilding took priority over everything else. All the money collected for Jerusalem was devoted to the work, which was completed in an unbelievably short seventy days.

When the work was done, the Jerusalem collection began again, from nothing. The winter of 1718 passed, and in 1719 as the deadline for the start of debt repayments approached, Grigor received word that the Greek and Latin communities in Jerusalem had been granted permission by the sultan to restore their holdings in the Holy Sepulchre Church. Fearing that the Armenians would lose their rights in the church, Grigor hastened to apply for a similar permit. It was obtained at great expense, and orders were sent to vicar Hanna to begin the restoration at once, even without funds. It

---

[22] Quoted in Bampuk'jian, 262.

[23] According to a note by Fr Mesrop Nshanian (later patriarch of Jerusalem), Grigor's shirt was still kept in the treasury of St James in the 1930s (Sawalanean, II, 692n). A chain said to be that which Grigor wore, now hangs in the St Stephen chapel of St James Cathedral. It is made of large, heavy links, with an iron cross the size of a man's chest hanging from it.

is a testimony to both men's powers of persuasion and force of will, that not only was the restoration completed by the end of 1720, but Grigor was able to meet the repayment schedule for the monastery's debts and to begin purchasing properties in Jaffa for the support of the Armenian monastery there.[24]

Once the exceptional matter of Holy Sepulchre was out of the way, Grigor's plan for the rehabilitation of Jerusalem had three priorities: to secure the pilgrim routes to Jerusalem, to make St James itself self-contained and self-supporting, and to restore the Armenian churches to the brilliance that they had had a hundred years earlier under the reign of Patriarch Grigor Paronter. So when he at last set out from Istanbul for Jerusalem in 1720, having already restored the Jerusalem properties in that city, Grigor spent time in Aleppo and in Damascus, two major stops on the overland route to Jerusalem, restoring the Armenian churches and pilgrim accommodations there and buying properties whose rents would support them. His arrangements for Jaffa, which was the first stopping place for pilgrims arriving by sea, have already been mentioned, and similar ones would later be made for Ramleh, the second station on the road from the coast to Jerusalem.

Grigor finally entered Jerusalem on 12 February, 1721. The entire population of the city turned out to greet him, even the Muslims being eager to see a man who was so well reputed. Despite the warmth of his welcome, Grigor faced great difficulties apart from the financial ones. He inherited a brotherhood divided among itself and without communal organization or spiritual discipline. The *nazir* element was still present and strongly opposed to him. By persuasion and example, he reinstituted the monastic rule and communal meals. Brothers who showed promise were encouraged, those found helpful to the work of St James were rewarded, the recalcitrant were advised and exhorted by him, but no one was punished or expelled. He made a practice of consulting with the brotherhood and involving them actively in all that went on.

Nonetheless, the discontented complained of his administration to their friends in Istanbul, and attempts were made to stir up the authorities against his building projects, and to sow discord between him and the other Christian communities. With the continual support of Yovhannes and a group of influential emirs in Istanbul, and by means of his own vigilance and his conciliatory and generous behaviour in Jerusalem, Grigor was able to maintain good relations with almost all, though his personal letters from the period show how greatly he suffered in the process.[25]

---

[24] Rooms, shops, warehouses, and a bakery are mentioned by Hanna, 129. Sawalanean, 694, specifies that Grigor's agents purchased five rooms, five shops, three warehouses, a bakery and a coffee house.

[25] A series of Grigor's letters were published in the Armenian patriarchate's journal *Sion* between 1971 and 1973.

By 1726, the original debts of the monastery had been paid in full. As they were paid, Grigor put each one's cancelled receipt in a special box, to be kept for posterity, together with his running accounts.[26] Armenian properties in Jaffa had been redeemed[27] and the monastery there completely restored and enlarged. The Holy Archangels convent had been restored, and the wooden living quarters of the nuns replaced with stone cells.

In St James itself, the changes made by Grigor transformed the monastery. The east side of the cathedral of St James backed onto a residential quarter, from which it seems to have been divided by nothing more than a courtyard. Working with Agha Melidon of Istanbul, Grigor gradually bought twelve courtyards in the residential section, with their houses. These were rebuilt in such a way that a wall was created around the whole property of St James, making it for the first time an enclosed entity. The size of the monastery doubled. With the addition of extra buildings and second storeys, St James acquired accommodations for over three hundred pilgrims.

Inside the cathedral of St James, Grigor had built a second storey chapel of the Holy Cross, restored the chapel of the Apostles and turned it into a manuscript library, enlarged the St Stephen chapel and increased the number of its altars. Iconostases for all the altars of the Armenian churches were built, including the church of St Mark, which the Armenians were keeping during the absence of the Syrian clergy from Jerusalem.

Compared to what he intended and planned, Grigor considered that had done little. But the community in Istanbul disagreed. They sent word to him that it was the will of all that he remove from his neck the chain which he had carried for eight years. His mission, while not complete, had already gone beyond his commission. In gratitude for his release, Grigor built an altar in the Ejmiacin chapel of St James, and continued his work with even more energy. He was not to rest until the day of his death in 1749, on 12 February the anniversary of his entry into Jerusalem twenty-eight years before.

He restored the monastery church in Bethlehem, and established a brotherhood established there, with a strictly ascetic rule, devoted to prayer for Jerusalem, and for the Armenian communities.[28] They were given a press, stores, kitchens and a garden. Pilgrim quarters were built on the Mt of Olives for those attending the vigil of Ascension.

St James became self-contained, with its own granary, mill, smithy, carpenters and plasterers workshops, chandlery, kitchens, gardens and winery. It had its own water supply system. Complete stores of household

---

[26] Sawalanean and Nshanian used information from Grigor's detailed accounts in preparing their history. The documents are no longer available today.

[27] According to Sawalanean, 696, eight shops had been demanded as collateral for a comparatively small loan of 11,000 *dahekan*.

[28] *Catalogue*, IV, 242, colophon to Jerusalem ms. 489.

vessels and bedding for three hundred pilgrims were maintained. All the living quarters were plastered,[29] the churches tiled. Paintings showing the life of Christ and the major events in the history of the church were made to cover the faded medieval frescoes in the cathedral. A new refectory was built, and buildings were added on the roof for the offices of the priests responsible for the pilgrims. Grigor's legates traversed the Armenian communities from the Crimea to India, and his representatives escorted pilgrim caravans from the day of their embarkation to the day of their return home. The names of the clergy, nuns and lay brothers who kept the complex St James establishment in working order were remembered by Grigor in his inscriptions. Once a year, he called them together and distributed the entirety of his own income among them.

In short the physical shape of Jerusalem's Armenian convent as it is today, with minor additions, represents Grigor's creation. The income bearing properties which he purchased for it supported its existence through the next turbulent centuries, and the refugees who flooded into it in the first decades of this century were housed in his buildings.

We owe him much. A legion of manuscript colophons attest the work of his period. You cannot walk more than a few feet in the compound without finding an inscription from his reign there are over one hundred twenty of them on stone. And you cannot attend the services for any major feast without seeing in use some of the vestments and vessels with which he filled the St James treasury. When he first arrived in Jerusalem and took an inventory of its church objects, he found three brass and four silver chalices, five lamps, one censer, twelve small crosses and one medium sized one.[30] Throughout his reign, he redeemed, commissioned and received as gifts liturgical objects of exquisite quality for the use of St James, and it is no exaggeration to say that seventy percent of what the church today possesses dates to his time. At the conclusion of this brief exposition of his works, I leave it to you, as you visit the Armenian patriarchate which he created, to judge for yourselves whether Grigor might not have said with the servant in the Gospel, 'I have done what was required of me.'

---

29 Jerusalem ms. 154 has a long colophon by Elia Vardapet, who did all the plaster and tile work for Grigor.

30 Ter Hovhanniseanc', II, 7.

8

The Copts in Jerusalem and the Question of the Holy Places

Otto Meinardus

W hoever visits Jerusalem, Bethlehem, Jericho or Nazareth in these days (1994) cannot help but notice among the clerics of the various Christian communities the Coptic desert fathers. They are easily distinguished on account of their originally Antiochene headdress. It is a tight fitting cap covering the head and neck, embroidered with thirteen yellow or white crosses representing Christ and the Apostles, the qolunsha. Around the neck and in front of the breast they wear a large black and white Coptic leather cross. They are the representatives of the Coptic Orthodox Church and His Holiness Anba Shenudah III, the 117th successor of the Evangelist St Mark. His full title is 'Pope and Patriarch of Alexandria and of all Egypt, of God's City of Jerusalem, of Nubia, the Pentapolis and all the Regions of the Preaching of St Mark'.[1]

Especially since the enthronement of Anba Abra'am I as 20th Coptic *mutran* (metropolitan) of Jerusalem and the Middle East on November 17th 1991, the Coptic presence in Israel in general and in Jerusalem in particular has acquired a new quality. In addition to some of the major restorations of old buildings, e.g., the Church of St Antony, the Church of St Helena and the passage to the large subterranean cistern, new social and educational projects, like the new College of St Antony at Bet Hanina began in August

---

[1] The inclusion of the Holy City of Jerusalem in the pontifical title dates from the Middle Ages. The Ms 253 Coptic Museum, dated 1080 AM or 1364 AD, of the Rite of Consecration of the Patriarch of Alexandria refers to the senior bishop, who places his hand upon the elected servant of God, while the archdeacon exclaims: 'The divine grace advanceth him to Archbishop of the great city of Alexandria and of all the land of Egypt and its nomes . . .' The text of the witnessing of the episcopacy is more elaborate and speaks of the 'Archbishop of the great city of Alexandria and of Babylon and of the Ethiopians and of the Five Cities in the West (Berenice, Ptolemais, Barca, Cyrene and Apollonia). Cf. Burmester, O H E, *The Rite of Consecration of the Patriarch of Alexandria*, Cairo, 1960.

1993, are tangible evidence of the Coptic renaissance which has overflowed to the Holy Land. At the same time, the age-old question pertaining to the jurisdiction of some of the holy places, namely the Dair al-Sultan on the roof of the Armenian Church of St Helena and the Chapel of the Bodiless Living Creatures and the Chapel of the Archangel Michael is presently being discussed again. In view of these recent developments some of the principal historical notes about the presence of the Copts in the Holy City should be restated.

Within the New Testament context the relationship of the Egyptians to Jerusalem can be traced to the first Pentecost when Jews 'from Egypt and the parts of Libya belonging to Cyrene were speaking in their own tongues the mighty works of God' (Acts 2: 10, 11). Upon their return from Jerusalem, these Judaeo-Christians would have formed the nucleus of the first Christian community in Egypt. With the Discovery of the Holy Cross by St Helena in May 328 AD and the subsequent construction of the Church of the Resurrection (Anastasis) over the Tomb of Jesus Christ, Jerusalem became the principal destination of Christian pilgrimages. One of the better known Egyptian woman-saints was St Mary the Egyptian, once an actress and courtesan. She had joined a group of faithful pilgrims to the Holy Land. Before entering the Church of the Resurrection she experienced a vision of the Holy Virgin who demanded from her to surrender herself completely to God and to resign from her previous ways. Realizing the incomprehensible mercy of God, she cast herself on the ground and after kissing the pavement, she went to the icon of the Holy Virgin, where falling on her knees, she begged for her intercession. Then she heard a voice saying: 'If thou goest beyond the Jordan, thou shalt find there rest and comfort.' Before crossing the Jordan, she stopped at the Monastery of St John the Baptist. Forty-seven years she spent in penance beyond the Jordan and received the Last Sacrament from St Zosimus before she died in 431.[2]

The 'Letter of Paula and Eustachium to Marcella' (386 AD) mentions among the monks of the various nations who visited Jerusalem also those coming from Egypt,[3] and the Spanish abbess, the 4th century pilgrim of Etheria, refers very clearly to the monks of Egypt or the Thebaid who used to come to the Holy City[4] The Copts are also mentioned as pilgrims to Jerusalem in the so-called 'Letter of Guarantee' attributed to the Caliph 'Umar and dated in the 15th year of the Hijra (637 AD). According to tradition, this covenant is said to have been made between the Caliph and

[2] Coptic Synaxar, *Patr. Orient.*, XVI, 286-290; Eth. Synaxar, 6 Miyazya, *Budge*, III, 784-6.
[3] Aubrey, 'Letter of Paula and Eustachium to Marcella', *Palestine Pilgrims' Texts Society*, I, 1 (*PPTS*).
[4] Bernard, 'The Pilgrimage of S. Silvia of Aquitania to the Holy Places', *PPTS*, I, 76.

the Greek Patriarch Sophronius[5] '. . . And in order that the Georgian and Abyssinians depending on the Greek Nation be well established, let all other nations that go there on pilgrimage, Latins, Copts, Syrians, Armenians, Nestorians, Jacobites, and Maronites submit to the Patriarch Sophronius of Jerusalem.'[6]

There are not many references to Coptic monks in or Coptic pilgrims to Jerusalem prior to the Crusades in the 11th century. A Christian Arabic papyrus of the 9th century refers to a Coptic lady-traveller who had returned to Egypt from Jerusalem, where presumably she had gone on a pilgrimage,[7] and John (Yuhanna) ibn Sa'id al-Qulzumi mentions that sometimes between 1047 and 1092 he went to Jerusalem and elsewhere, namely the Holy Sepulchre and Calvary.[8]

During the patriarchate of Anba Kirillus II (1078-1092) the Ghuzz or Turkomans captured Jerusalem and extended their conquests to the Egyptian frontier. The Turkoman sovereign, Sultan Galal al-Din, also known by the name King Shah, appointed a Copt, a certain Mansur al-Tilbani, to become assistant to the governor. Mansur al-Tilbani as well as his wife Mu'inah were of great help to the Christians who came to Jerusalem from Egypt and from other parts of the Middle East. At this time, the Coptic churches and monasteries in Jerusalem were confided to the Syrian Jacobites, who held the same belief as the Copts.[9] In order to avoid and misunderstanding, however, which might arise with regard to the Coptic ownership of the Church of the Jacobite Christians, Anba Kirillus II responded to the request of Mansur al-Tilbani in delegating an Egyptian bishop to consecrate the church, which was reconstructed by Mansur al-Tilbani. The consecration took place in the month of Barmahat 808 AM (1092 AD).

---

[5] The listing and the order of the Christian communities represented in Jerusalem according to this document would suggest for its composition a date during the Mamluk period. Already Augustin Scholz, writing in 1820, questioned the authenticity of the 'Umarite Covenant. Cf. Scholz, A, *Reise in die Gegend zwischen Alexandrien and Parätonium, etc.*, Leipzig, 1822, 293.

[6] Themelis, Timotheus, *Les Grecs aux Lieux Saints*, Jerusalem, 1921, 7.

[7] Anawati et Jomier, 'Un Papyrus Chrétien en Arabe', *Mélanges Islamoniques*, II, 1954, 98.

[8] The visit of John ibn Sa'id should be placed during the time of the patriarchates of Christodoulus and Cyril II. *History of the Patriarchs of the Egyptian Church* (ed. Aziz S Atiya, Yassa'Abd al-Masih, O H E Khs-Burmester), Cairo, 1959, II, iii, 358.

[9] Originally, the term 'Jacobites' from the Syrian monk Jacob Bardaeus, who died in 578 as Bishop of Edessa, was applied to the Syrian Monophysites. However, in the Middle Ages the Copts are also referred to as 'Jacobites' and the Canons of Cyril III ibn Laqlaq (1235) speak of the Coptic Jacobite Church (*Bull. de la Société d'Arch. Copte*, XIV, 141). Thietmar (1217) mentions the Jacobites who come from Egypt and who claim to be the heirs of the Pharaohs (Saint-Génois, 'Les Voyages fait en Terre Sainte par Thietmar en 1217, etc.', *Mémoires de l'Académie Royale des Sciences, Lettres et des Beaux Arts de Belgique*, XXVI, Bruxelles, 1851, 56. Jacques de Vitry (1227) and Marino Sanoto (1306) state that the Jacobites had a teacher who is said to be a certain James, a disciple of the Alexandrian patriarch. Bongars, *Gesta Dei per Francos sive Orientalium expeditionum, etc.*, Hanoviae, 1611, I, 1091-92.

From the beginning of the 12th century, the church and the monastery of St Mary Magdalene served as the spiritual centre for the Jacobites, both the Syrians and the Egyptians. The church was situated in the vicinity of the Gate of Herod, north of the Franciscan Via Dolorosa. An interesting account of the existence of the Church of St Mary Magdalene is furnished by two Syriac Codices, that of Lyons (10 February, 1138) and that of Paris (25 August, 1138). These documents refer to certain arguments between the Jacobite community in Jerusalem and a certain Frank, called Godfrey of Asha.[10] Apparently, the Jacobite community had escaped to Egypt where it had found refuge during the Latin Kingdom. After their return to the Holy City they noticed that some of their sites which they had held prior to the conquest by the Crusaders were occupied by the Franks. It was only after the intervention of Athanasius VII, patriarch of Antioch, that Baldwin I, King of Jerusalem, returned to the Jacobites their original holdings. This transfer must have occurred after 1100, the year when Athanasius VII became patriarch and before 1118, the year when Baldwin I died. It is very likely that the church and the monastery of St Mary Magdalene were temporarily in the hands of the Crusaders. In 1124, Ignatius, patriarch of Antioch, repaired the Monastery of St Mary Magdalene so that it became available again for use by the Jacobite monks. In 1137 Godfrey of Asha, after having been released by the Saracens, claimed again those sites which he had occupied. To settle the dispute, a compromise was reached and in February 1138 the Jacobites paid the sum of 300 dinars to Godfrey of Asha.[11] In 1140, an anonymous pilgrim visited Jerusalem. He had seen the Monastery of the Jacobites, wherein was the head of St James and the arm of St Stephen. He referred to the Church of St Mary Magdalene where they show some of the hair of the Patron-Saint.[12] Some of the hair of St Mary Magdalene is claimed by the Coptic monks of the Monastery of the Syrian (Dair al-Surian) in the Wadi al-Natrun.

There is good reason to assume that the Jacobite Monastery of St Mary Magdalene served both non-Chalcedonian communities, the Syrians and the Copts. An interesting colophon of the Syrian Codex 27 of the Syrian Orthodox Monastery of St Mark in Jerusalem substantiates this assumption. We are informed that the codex was completed in 1149 AD in the Monastery of St Mary Magdalene at the time of Athanasius VIII, patriarch of Antioch, and John V, patriarch of Alexandria,[13] and Ignatius III, Jacobite Bishop of Jerusalem[14] Johann of Würzburg, visiting the Holy Land in 1165,

---

[10] Martin, 'Les premiers princes croisés et les Syriens Jacobites de Jérusalem', *JA*, Nov., Dec., 1888, 471-490; Jan. 1889, 33-79. Nau, 'Le croisé lorrain Godefroy de Asha, d'après deux documents syriaques du XIIe siècle', *JA*, Nov., Dec. 1899, 421-31.

[11] Meinardus, O., 'The Syrian Jacobite in the Holy City', *Orientalia Suecana*, XII, 1963, 63, 64.

[12] 'Anonymous Pilgrims', *PPTS*, VI, 12.

[13] I.e. 1147-1166.

[14] Taylor, W R, 'A new Syriac fragment dealing with incidents in the Second Crusade', *Annual of the American Schools of Oriental Research*, XI, 1931, 120f.

refers to the Jacobite monks who possess the Church of St Mary Magdalene[15] and in the *Chronicon Ecclesiasticum* of Bar Hebraeus we read, that in 1168, Michael I, patriarch of Antioch, went for Easter celebrations to Jerusalem to celebrate the Divine Liturgy and to consecrate the Holy Chrism in the Monastery of St Mary Magdalene.[16]

Following the victory of the troops of Salah al-Din over the Crusader forces in the battle of the Horns of Hattin, 4 July 1187, the number of pilgrims from the various Christian communities of the East increased as time went on, and many of the churches felt the need to establish themselves on a permanent basis in the Holy City. In 1187, Sultan Salah al-Din granted exemption from taxes to the Greeks, Georgians, Copts and Ethiopians who came to Jerusalem on pilgrimage. By this ordinance the Sultan also confirmed the privilege of the Copts to own certain sites in the Church of the Resurrection.[17] The possibility that some Christians were evicted by the ordinances of Salah al-Din is mentioned by the 16th century Dutch traveller Ioannes Cotovicus (Iohann van Kootwyck) who visited Cyprus in 1598 and stated: There are also Maronites, Nestorians, Jacobites and Copts, fugitives from Palestine, who were driven from the realm of Saladin after the conquest of Jerusalem, and settled here, each of sect still observing its own rites.[18] At the same time it should be mentioned that the earliest reference to the presence of Copts in Cyprus occurs in an address delivered by John XIII (Yu'annis al-Misri), when he ascended the patriarchal throne on the 15th of Amshir 1199 AM (1483 AD). Among the bishops mentioned in this address there is Anba Mikhail of Cyprus (al-Kubrusi), metropolitan of Cyprus and afterwards of Rhodes.[19]

In the middle of the 13th century tensions and misunderstandings emerged between the two non-Chalcedonian communities, the Syrians and the Copts. Thus, when it was discovered that the Syrians had added some properties of the Copts to their own, and had wasted others, Anba Kirillus III (1235-1243) appointed in 1238 an Egyptian Archbishop of Jerusalem. He succeeded after much trouble in regaining the Coptic Chapel in the Church of the Resurrection and the church which was reconstructed by Mansur al-Tilbani.[20] The first Coptic Archbishop of Jerusalem was Anba Basilius I (1238-1260). The Syrian patriarch of Antioch was much distressed at this appointment and retaliated by excommunicating the newly appointed Coptic Archbishop.[21] Furthermore, the Antiochene patriarch consecrated an Ethiopian monk as

[15] Tobler, Titus, *Descriptiones Terrae Sanctae ex saeculo VIII, IX, XII et XV*, Leipzig, 1874, 132, 164.
[16] Bar Hebraeus, *op.cit.*, II, 546f.
[17] Themelis, *op. cit.*, 68.
[18] Cobham, Laude D, *Excerpta Cypria. Materials for a History of Cyprus*, Cambridge, 1908, 197.
[19] Burmester, O H E, 'The Copts in Cyprus', *Bull. de le Société d'Arch. Copte*, VII, 1941, 9.
[20] Filutaus 'Awad, *Dair al-Sultan milk al-Qibt la al-Habash*, Cairo, 1934, 17.
[21] Renaudotius, Eusebius, *Historia Patriarcharum Alexandrinarum Jacobitarum ab Marco usque ad finem saeculi XIII*, Paris, 1713, 579f.

Archbishop of Abyssinia, thus assuming a privilege which had been exclusively held by the Coptic patriarch of Alexandria.[22]

By the middle of the 13th century the Coptic Archbishopric of Jerusalem was well established. The Ethiopian *Synaxar* mentions Anba Ghobrial III (1268-1271), the 78th patriarch of Alexandria, who went to Jerusalem where he was blessed in the Holy Places. He was ordained to the priesthood in the Church of the Resurrection.[23] During the latter part of the 13th century the Copts not only had a resident Archbishop, but also monks in the Holy City. C.R. Conder states, 'that their (Coptic) bishop wore a crown like the Greek patriarchs, their monks wore white pointed cowls. They still preserved the ancient Kiss of Peace . . .'[24] Around 1280 Burchard of Mount Sion referred to the Syrians, Ethiopians and Egyptians who were among the nations residing in Jerusalem.[25] In 1287 Abu Ishaq al-Mu'taman ibn al-'Assal composed a homily addressed to the Egyptian Christians to join a pilgrimage to Jerusalem.[26]

The Western pilgrims to the Holy Land like Guilielm de Boldensele (1336), Niccolo di Poggibonsi (1346), Ludolf von Suchem (1348), the Pilgrim of Miltenberg (1350), Frescobaldi (1384), Philippe de Mézières (1384) and the Latin codices mention eight or nine Christian communities in the Church of the Resurrection, namely, the Greeks, Latins, Armenians, Jacobites, Ethiopians, Georgians, Nestorians, Maronites and the Christians of the Girdle, who are the Copts.[27] The 'Christians of the Girdle' (*Cristiani della cintura*) acquired this title already during the patriarchate of Cosmas II (851-859), when they were compelled to wear, as a mark of ignominy, girdles, while the women, to whom the girdle was a distinguishing mark of feminine modesty, were forbidden to wear them. During the reign of al-Hakim (996-1021) the Copts were forced to wear a distinctive dress consisting also of a sash around their loins. During the 13th century, the reign of Qalaun (1279-1290), the Christians were made to ride on donkeys with girdles round their wastes.[28]

There is no doubt that in the 15th and 16th centuries the Copts were established in Jerusalem and also possessed 'certain sites' in the Church of the Resurrection. The chapel 'behind the Holy Sepulchre' is repeatedly mentioned by the pilgrims as belonging to the Jacobites, e.g., Ignatios of Smolensk (1400) and the Anonymous of 1445. Generally speaking, the

[22] Kawerau, Peter, *Die Jakobitische Kirche im Zeitalter der Syrischen Renaissance*, Berlin, 1955, 67.

[23] Ethiopian Synaxar, 11 Hamlé, *Budge*, IV, 1107.

[24] Conder, C R, *The Latin Kingdom of Jerusalem 1099-1291*, London, 1897, 221.

[25] Burchard, 'Description of the Holy Land', *PPTS*, XII, 104.

[26] Abu Ishaq is the brother of al-Safi al-'Assal. Cf. Graf, Georg, 'Rede des Abu Ishaq al-Mu'taman ibn al-'Assal', *Bull. de la Société d'Arch. Copte*, VII, 1941, 51-59.

[27] Meinardus, O, *The Copts in Jerusalem*, Cairo, 1960, 19, 20.

[28] Fowler, Montague, *Christian Egypt, Past, Present and Future*, London, 1902, 70. In 1612 William Lithgow referred to the Copts 'as a sort of circumcised Christians', and still in 1666 Frantz Ferdinand of Troilo called them 'Christen della Cinte, des Gärtels wegen'. Meinardus, O, *op. cit.*, 31, 33.

Copts were still known as Jacobites, Goffites (Koster Bernd, 1463) or Egyptians (Henry the Pious, 1498).[29]

During the latter part of the 15th century the number of Copts in Jerusalem could not have been very large.[30] Francesco Suriano, writing towards the end of the 15th century, states, 'that as the Copts had left Jerusalem, when I was there, and gone to Cairo, I had no opportunity of talking to them. The Copts are least in number, and as they are few, when the sons of their priests are born, they make them deacons and subdeacons.'[31] Felix Fabri assigned to the 'Jacobite Copts' the Stone of Unction and both Peter Fassbender[32] and Arnold von Harff refer to a chapel belonging to the Jacobites which is situated behind the Holy Sepulchre.[33] At the same time there is no doubt that since the middle of the 13th century there has been regular succession of Coptic metropolitans in Jerusalem.[34]

In 1537, the Copts possessed a small chapel behind the Holy Sepulchre of Christ,[35] the altar which they still possess. It is difficult to know when they acquired this site. An interesting transaction must have taken place before the 16th century, for by that time the Franciscan friars in Egypt had the right of saying mass in the crypt of the Coptic Church of SS Sergius and Bacchus in Old Cairo. R Fedden maintains that it was a *quid pro quo* for permission granted to the Coptic Church to maintain a small room or a chapel *unita ad una parte esteriore del Ssmo Sepolcro*.[36] One of the first pilgrims to refer to the Coptic Chapel and Altar in the Church of the Resurrection was an anonymous Spanish Franciscan who visited the Holy Land in 1553.[37] By 1559 the Copts must have achieved some relative prosperity, for in that year Germanos, the Greek Orthodox patriarch, wrote to Tsar Ivan the Terrible (1553-1584). He complained of his state of poverty and mentioned that the Armenians and the Copts celebrated the Divine Liturgy in the Church of the Resurrection wearing mitres, he, the Orthodox patriarch, lacks even a mitre.[38] Leonhart Rauwolff (1573) also mentions the Copts, who have their chapel behind the Holy Sepulchre of Christ, and the

---

[29] Meinardus, O., *op. cit.*, 23, 24.

[30] Luke, H C, *The Handbook of Palestine*, London, 1922, 45.

[31] Francesco Suriano, *Treatise on the Holy Land*, Jerusalem, 1949, 92.

[32] For Fassbender (1492), Röhricht, Reinhold und H Meisner, *Deutsche Pilgerreisen nach dem Heiligen Lande*, Berlin, 1880, 258.

[33] For Von Harff (1497), Letts, Malcolm, *The Pilgrimage of Arnold von Harff Knight*, London, 1946, 203.

[34] Luke, H C, *op. cit.*, 45.

[35] As early as 1112 the Latins used to have there a parochial altar. Vincent, H and F M Abel, *Jérusalem. Recherches de Topographie d'Archéologie et d'Histoire*, Paris, 1914, II, 294.

[36] Fedden, R, 'Two Notes on Christian Cairo in the Turkish Period', *Bull. de la Soc. d'Arch. Copte*, X, 33f. The traveller Symon Semeonis (1322-24) states that the Sultan Muhammad ibn Qala'un al-Nasir (1310-41) gave the rights for the crypt of the Church of SS Sergius and Bacchus to the Friars Minor. Cf. Coquin, Charalambia, *Les Edifices Chrétien du Vieux Caire*, Cairo, 1974, I, 100.

[37] Luke, H C, *A Spanish Franciscan's Narrative of a Journey to the Holy Land*, London, 1927, 28.

[38] Callinikou, Constantine, *Ho Christianikos Naos kai ta tcloumena en auto*, Alexandria, 1922, 621.

Abyssinians, who live in the Temple of Mount Calvaria, just by the church door towards the left, and have through their lodging a peculiar way, so that, without hindrance, according to their pleasure, they may go in and out.[39] The *Codex of the Iberians* (1585-86) states clearly that the Copts, who profess the doctrine of Dioscorus, are behind the Holy Sepulchre.[40]

During the 17th century, the various Christian communities in the Church of the Resurrection suffered somewhat severely from the heavy taxes which they had to pay to their Muslim rulers. Francesco Verniore (1631) records that both the Abyssinians and the Copts have a monastery in the vicinity of the Church of the Resurrection, and that every month they had to pay some moneys to the Turks, and that every Easter, they had to apply for permission to make wine.[41] Poverty and political pressures were conducive to ecclesiastical irregularities, and a *firman*, attributed to Sultan Murad IV (1634) explicitly refers to violations of the Abyssinian properties by the Armenians.[42] In 1647 Eugène Roger observed the Coptic monks in Jerusalem and states that all monks and priests, when they perform their prayers cover their shoulders and their arms with a veil in the form of a black shawl,[43] and the Chevalier d'Arvieux (1660) saw the Copts participating in the Ceremony of the Holy Fire.[44] It is difficult to determine to what an extent the Copts participated in the Easter Celebrations of the *Hagois Phos* in the 17th century. In fact, it is questionable whether Bernard Surius (1644) was correctly informed, for according to his account 'six patriarchs participated in the Ceremony of the Holy Fire, and they were the Greek, the Coptic, the Ethiopian, the Georgian, the Nestorian and the Armenian, who locked themselves into the Chapel of the Holy Sepulchre. After the appearance of the Holy Fire, they distributed the fire to the people.[45]

The second part of the 17th century proved to be one of the most difficult periods for some of the Christian communities in Jerusalem. In 1664, the Georgians were evicted from their sites in the Church of the Resurrection, owing to being too poor to pay the necessary dues, and the

---

[39] Rauwolff, L, 'Travels in the Eastern Countries . . .' in Ray, *A Collection of Curious Travels and Voyages*, London, 1693, 352.

[40] Themelis, *op. cit.*, 46.

[41] Golubovich, G., *Biblioteca Bio-Bibliografica della Terra Santa*, N.S. I, vi, 55.

[42] Manuscript: Nolde, 'Consultation concerning the Rights of the Abyssinians', 2.

[43] Roger, Eugène, *La Terre Sainte ou Description topographique très particulière des Saints Lieux, etc.*, Paris, 1664, 417.

[44] Labat, Jean-Baptiste, *Mémoires de Chevalier d'Arvieux*, Paris, 1735, II, 13, 146.

[45] Surius, B, *Den God Turuchtigen Pilgrim*, Anversa, 1705, I, 582. Of course it is physically impossible for six hierarchs to lock themselves into the Chapel of the Holy Sepulchre. It is more likely that they participated in the distribution of the Holy Fire to their respective communities.

same fate befell the Abyssinians in 1668.[46] There is no doubt that the general penury among the Copts in Jerusalem in the 17th century was a reflection of the terrible socio-economic situation in Egypt. In 1694, the Nile did not rise and the consequent dearth found the country wholly unprepared to meet it. For some months the famine grew worse and worse, the starving mob surrounded the citadel, howling for bread, and as no notice was taken of them, they began to throw stones. Pestilence succeeded famine and the people died about the street in heaps. Though the Copts were able to maintain their holdings, Frantz Ferdinand von Troilo (1666) informs us that they were very poor.[47] In 1668, according to Michael Nau, the Copts had only one priest in the Church of the Resurrection, 'who prays alone and lights the lamps.'[48] The fact that Nau observed only one priest in the Church of the Resurrection does not necessarily mean that he was the only resident Copt in Jerusalem. He also states, that 'the nearest door of the Chapel of Calvary of the Holy Virgin leads into a church of the Copts, where they celebrate the Divine Liturgy every day.'

Two years later in 1670 Jacques Goujon confirms the impression of Nau. 'There is only one Copt, whose dwelling place is quite near the door.'[49] Yet, in spite of their poverty, the Copts retained their holy places, for Goujon speaks of the apartment of the Copts just outside the Church of the Resurrection, and O Dapper (1688) observed the Copts as being one of the nations who participated in the Ceremony of the Holy Fire,[50] and Henrich Maundrell (1697) states that only the Latins, Greeks, Armenians and Cophites keep their footing well, yet the Copts have only one monk representing their nation,[51] a fact, which is substantiated by Felix Beaugrand (1699 ?),[52] who observed the Copt holding services in the small chapel behind the Holy Sepulchre.

Throughout the 18th century the small chapel of the Copts behind the Holy Sepulchre is mentioned by the pilgrims and travellers.[53] In 1808, the Church of the Resurrection, except the eastern part, was almost entirely destroyed by fire, the dome fell in crushing the Tomb of Christ, altars and icons were consumed in the general conflagration, and the mass of ruin

---

[46] Harvey, William, *The Church of the Holy Sepulchre*, London, 1935. In 1671, the Ethiopians were forced to retreat to the roof of the Armenian Church of St Helena, where they remain to the present day. Cf. Luke, H C, 'The Christian Communities in the Holy Sepulchre', in Ashbee, C R, *Jerusalem 1920-1922*, London, 1924, 54.

[47] Troilo, Frantz Ferdinand von, *Orientalische Reisebeschreibung, etc.*, Dresden and Leipzig, 1734, 186.

[48] Nau, Michael, *Voyage nouveau de le Terre Sainte*, Paris, 1679, 145, 176.

[49] Goujon, Jacques, *Histoire et Voyage de la Terre-Sainte*, Lyons, 1672, 169, 175.

[50] Dapper, O, Asia, *oder eine genaue und gründliche Beschreibung des gantzen Syrien und Palestins*, Nürnberg, 1688, 328.

[51] Maundrell, M Henrich, *Reisebeschreibung nach dem Gelobten Lande; Darinnen die jetzige Beschaffenheit und der allerneueste Zustand des Heiligen Landes*, Hamburg, 1737, 95.

[52] Beaugrand, Felix, *Relation Nouvelle et très fidèle du Voyage de la Terre Sainte*, Paris, 1700, II, 76.

[53] Meinardus, O, *op. cit.,* 38, 39.

extended from the Chapel of St Helena to the rock-hewn tomb of Joseph of Arimathea. In the intrigues which followed at Jerusalem and Constantinople in connection with the rebuilding of the church, the Greeks secured for themselves the greater portion of the building. The Copts, however, retained their sites.

An interesting survey of the foreign constituency of Jerusalem in 1817 is provided by T R Joliffe, who speaks of 800 Latins, 2,000 Greeks, 400 Armenians and 50 Copts, who lived in the Holy City.[54] During the Easter celebrations these numbers increased, so that Augustin Scholz estimated at the time of his visit on Easter 1820, 1400 Armenians, 1200 Greeks, 30 Georgians, 300 Moscovites, 60 Copts, 15 Syrians, one Abyssinian, 20 Oriental Catholics of the Greek and Armenian rite, 4 Maronites, and 15 Franks.[55] Madden visiting Jerusalem in 1826 counted 15 Latins, 15 Greeks, 12 Armenians, 6 Copts and 4 Syrians in the Church of the Resurrection.[56] In June 1837, the cholera epidemic broke out in Jerusalem during which seven Copts died, while of the twenty-four Ethiopians only one survived.[57]

When Konstantin von Tischendorf entered the Church of the Resurrection in 1844, he remarked about 'the solitary Copts who wandered about . . . with suffering expressed in their physiognomy, as if performing an incessant act of penitence.'[58] The financial situation of the Egyptians in Jerusalem must have been rather pitiful during the middle of the 19th century, for both Francesco Cassini (1846)[59] and Karl Graul (1849)[60] speak of the poor Copts in the Church of the Resurrection. Nevertheless, Louis Enault estimated the number of Copts in Jerusalem to be about one hundred.[61] Some Copts were undoubtedly attached to the Monastery of St George in Jerusalem, which the Copts had acquired in the middle of the 18th century. We know for certain that by 1720 the Dair Mari Girgis was situated in the same locality as to-day. Moreover, the monastery seems to have possessed the following relics, which to this day attract pilgrims and visitors, namely the right arm of St George and part of the chain which was used to torture the Saint.[62]

In 1806, Ulrich Seetzen visited the Holy Land and mentioned in his description the Copts who have an unattractive and poor monastery called 'Mar Dschurdschus', and furthermore, they possess in the Dair al-Sultan a courtyard next to the Church of the Resurrection, where several married

54 Joliffe, T R, *Lettres sur la Palestine, la Syrie et l'Egypte*, Paris, 1820, 101.
55 Scholz, Augustin, *Reise in die Gegend zwischen Alexandrien und Paraetonium, the libysche Wüste
    . . . Palestine und Syrien in den Jahren 1820 und 1821*, Leipzig, 1822, 230.
56 Madden, R R, *Travels in Turkey, Egypt, Nubia and Palestine*, London, 1829, II, 131.
57 Neophytos of Cyprus, *Annals of Palestine 1821-1841*, Jerusalem, 1848, 71, 125-128.
58 Tischendorf, L F C, *Travels in the East*, London, 1847, 180.
59 Cassini, Francesco, *Le Terra Santa descritta da Francesco Cassini dell'Ordine dei Minori Riformati
    . . . dedicata a Sua Sacra Reale Maesta Ferdinando II, Re del Regno delle due Sicilie . . .*,
    Genova, 1855, II, 133.
60 Graul, Karl, *Reise nach Ostindien*, Leipzig, 1854, I, 196.
61 Enault, Louis, *La Terre Sainte: Voyage des Quarante Pèlerins de 1853*, Paris, 1854, 150-151.
62 Tobler, Titus, *Topographie von Jerusalem*, Berlin, 1853, I, 371.

priests live.[63] In a legal document of December 10th, 1820, it is stated among other things, that St George's Monastery belongs to the Copts.[64] In 1782, the Copts had already enlarged their holdings in Jerusalem by buying some houses from al-Hajj 'Abd Allah Effendi, but it was not until 1837, however, that the Copts obtained permission to build the large Coptic Khan or caravanserai in the immediate vicinity of the Monastery of St George. The site for these buildings was bought by the Copts for 8.000 piastres. The building of this Khan, which lasted for more than a year, amounted to 500,000 piastres, though most of the work was done by the Copts who gave their services free. Hanauer points out, that the Coptic Khan was built in 1838 inside the northern part of the great pool, Birkit Hammam al-Batrak (Pool of the Patriarch's Bath), traditionally known as the Pool of Hezekiah.[65]

According to A Goodrich-Freer in 1904 the Coptic archbishop in the Holy Land used to reside in Jaffa, possibly because the Copts possessed but scanty accommodations in Jerusalem.[66] The Coptic Chapel in the Church of the Resurrection, which is dedicated to the Holy Virgin, is considered by the Copts to be the holiest of all the sacred sites, for the Coptic altar is believed to be erected against the place where Christ's head rested at the time of His burial. The chapel was redecorated by Anba Timuthaus in 1901 and the icons from north to south represent the Crucifixion, Christ's Entry into Jerusalem, the Resurrection, the Mystical Supper and Christ in the Garden of Gethsemane. Above the centre icon of the Holy Virgin there is another icon of the Resurrection. Twenty-four lamps are suspended from the ceiling in the chapel. The cells of the Copts in the Church of the Resurrection are situated between columns 9, 10, and 11 of the Rotunda. The doors west of the Holy Sepulchre lead to the lodgings of the Coptic monks, occupying the first and the second floor. Generally four or five monks keep vigil in the Church of the Resurrection, though during the feasts, this number increases to ten or twelve monks.

Though the Copts do not have the right to celebrate the Divine Liturgy in the Holy Sepulchre itself (the Greeks, Latins and Armenians alone have this right), they own four sanctuary lamps which hang in the second row from the east. The other lamps in the Holy Sepulchre belong to the Greeks (13), the Latins (13) and the Armenians (13). In the Chapel of the Angel situated east of the Holy Sepulchre the Copts own one lamp, which hangs on the south side of the eastern row. Above the Stone of Unction there are eight lamps. The third lamp from the left belongs to the Copts.

The Copts process four times a year around the Holy Sepulchre. On Palm Sunday, after the celebration of the Divine Liturgy, the Copts join the Greeks, Armenians and Syrians in a procession three times around the

---

[63] Seetzen, Elrich J, *Reisen durch Syrien, Palästina, Phönizien, etc.*, Berlin, 1854, II, 20, 21.

[64] Timoteos, *Translation of Documents Bearing on the Rights over the Sultan's Monastery and other Places in Jerusalem*, Cairo, n.d., 13, 14.

[65] Hanauer, J E, *Walks in and around Jerusalem*, London, 1926, 50f.

[66] Goodrich-Freer, A, *Inner Jerusalem*, London, 1904, 123.

Holy Sepulchre. On Good Friday between 5.00pm and 7.00pm, only the Copts make a procession through the whole Church of the Resurrection, offering prayers at every altar (Greek, Latin, Armenian, Coptic and Syrian). That this is a relatively new departure is testified by Emily A Beaufort, who in 1859 saw the Good Friday Procession and mentioned that the Greek bishops and clergy were followed by a number of Copts.[67] On the Eve of Easter, about 1.30pm, the Greek Orthodox patriarch accompanied by an Armenian Archimandrite enters the Holy Sepulchre for the Ceremony of the Holy Fire. From the Chapel of the Angel the Holy Fire is passed through the southern and northern openings to the pilgrims. The Copts receive the Holy Fire through the southern opening. Then the Holy Fire is taken to the Coptic Archbishop, who during the Ceremony has remained in the Coptic Chapel of the Holy Virgin west of the Holy Sepulchre. After having received the Holy Fire, the Coptic Archbishop gives the Holy Fire to the Coptic pilgrims. Then the Greeks, Armenians, Syrians and Copts make a procession three times around the Holy Sepulchre. This procession is repeated on Easter Sunday morning when at 4 am. the Greeks, Armenians, Copts and Syrians make a procession three times around the Holy Sepulchre.[68]

Towards the north-east of the Holy Sepulchre the Copts own the Dair Mar Antunius, the Monastery of St Antony. This monastery, which in previous centuries was considered to be part of the Dair al-Sultan, was repaired in 1875 with funds provided by wealthy Copts in Egypt.[69] In 1907 the monastery was rebuilt,[70] and Baedeker (1912) states 'that the Monastery of the Copts has been fitted up as an Episcopal residence and contains cells for the accommodation of pilgrims. The church, the foundations of which are old, has been entirely restored.'[71]

The Monastery of St Antony has three churches,[72] on the ground level there is the Church of St Helena. The narthex on this church leads to the large Cistern, which is normally filled with water. The main church is dedicated to St Antony. This church has been redecorated. It was built by Anba Basilius II (1856-1899), and dedicated by Anba Timuthaus (1899-1925) in 1903. This church is adorned by numerous wall-paintings showing Biblical scenes, e.g., the Mystical Supper, the Stilling of the Storm, the Nativity, the Baptism, the Annunciation, the Ascension, Christ's Entry into Jerusalem and the Via Dolorosa, etc. The third church is dedicated to the Holy Virgin in commemoration of her apparition to the students of the Coptic College in 1954. According to the students, the Holy Virgin with the Infant Christ, St Joseph and two Angels appeared for seven consecutive Mondays at 11.30am in the study of Dr Shaker. Out of

---

[67] Beaufort, Emily, *Egyptian Sepulchres and Syrian Shrines*, London, 1862, II, 247.

[68] Meinardus, O, *op. cit.*, 72f.

[69] Wilson, R E, *Picturesque Palestine, Sinai and Egypt*, New York, 1881, I, 119.

[70] Jeffery, George, *A Brief Description of the Holy Sepulchre*, Cambridge, 1919, 58.

[71] Baedeker, Karl, *Palestine and Syria*, Leipzig, 1912, 48. The church which Baedeker mentions should be the Coptic Church of St Helena.

[72] Meinardus, O, *Monks and Monasteries of the Egyptian Deserts*, Cairo, 1961, 339.

gratitude for this event Anba Yaqubus (1946-1956), Archbishop of Jerusalem, had this room converted into a church. In commemoration of this apparition, the Coptic monks celebrate the Divine Liturgy in this church every Monday morning.

Mention has been made of the Coptic Monastery of St George on the north side of the Pool of Hezekiah in Jerusalem. The Dair Mari Girgis comprises the Church of St George and the Primary and Secondary Girls' Schools of Sitt Dimianah.

In 1994 the Coptic Orthodox school system in Jerusalem, the College of St Antony and the school of St Dimianah, included altogether about 400 students of whom 70 per cent were Muslims. These students are taught and served by 28 faculty members. The total number of Copts in Jerusalem amounts to less than 1000 persons. In Israel and in the West Bank there are no more than 2500 Copts.

Traditionally, the Metropolitan of Jerusalem and the Coptic guardians of the Holy Places used to come from the Red Sea Desert Monastery of St Antony. During the Middle Ages, from the days of Anba Basilius I (1236-1260), until the 20th century, the days of Anba Tawfilus (1935-1945), the Metropolitan of Jerusalem had jurisdiction over large sections of the Nile Delta, the provinces of Daqaliyah, Gharbiyah, Sharqiyah, Damietta, including the Dair Sitt Dimianah at Bilqas. Anba Tawfilus surrendered some of the regions which subsequently became separate dioceses, e.g., Daqaliyah, Sharqiyah and Gharbiyah. Finally, Anba Basilius IV (1959-1991) surrendered all regions west of the Suez Canal. The new jurisdictional developments as inaugurated by HH Pope Shenudah III placed the regions east of the Suez Canal, e.g., the northern Sinai, East Kantara, al-Arish and Rafah under the authority of the Metropolitan of Jerusalem.[73]

Ever since the arrival of Anba Abra'am I in Jerusalem on January 3, 1992 a new spirit of oecumenicity prevails in the Coptic archbishopric of the Holy City. Special mention should be made of the Services for Christian Unity in Jerusalem in January 1993 when clergy and laity of the various Christian communions gathered in the Church of St Antony for praise and benediction. It was also at this occasion that the Ethiopian Archbishop Anba Mattaus of Jerusalem concelebrated the Holy Eucharist with Anba Abra'am in the Church of St Antony. Indeed, the oecumenical impact of the Coptic archbishopric has made an important contribution to a more authentic and credible witness of the constantly shrinking Christian minority in the Holy Land, where nowadays no more than 2.5 per cent of the population are Christians.

---

[73] Meinardus, O, 'The Coptic Orthodox Hierarchy in 1986', *Internationale Kirchliche Zeitschrift*, 376, 1986, 4, 249-256.

In 1961 eleven Coptic monks under Anba Basilius IV (1959-1991) resided in Jerusalem.[74] In 1994 the archdiocese of Jerusalem includes all Coptic churches of the Middle East.

In Jerusalem, there are the following Coptic monks: Angelos al-Rizqati, Barnaba al-Baramusi, Makarios al-Baramusi, Bakhum al-Buli, Silvanus al-Buli, 'Abd al-Malik Anba Buli al-Qudsi, Bishoi al-Antuni al-Qudsi. The Coptic Church in Bethlehem is served by Abuna Athanasius al-Antuni, the Church of St Antony in Jericho by Abuna Nehmiya al-Antuni,[75] the traditional House of Zacchaeus on the northern banks of the Wadi Qilt, Jericho, by Abuna Sidarus al-Suriani.[76] The Coptic Church in Nazareth, where there live approximately 1000 Copts, is served by Abuna Sidraq al-Antuni. The Coptic Church in Jaffa is served by Abuna Mikhail al-Buli.

A presentation of the Copts in the Holy Land and the Question of the Holy Places would be incomplete without a reference to the thorny problem of the jurisdiction over the Dair al-Sultan, the property on the roof of the Armenian Church of St Helena and the two chapels leading to the parvis of the Church of the Resurrection. In view of the recent developments pertaining to the conflict between the Ethiopian and the Coptic Churches about the possession of the Dair al-Sultan, it might be useful to refer very briefly to some of the recent events about this ecclesiastical bone of contention in the Holy City.

The precarious ecclesiastical situation[77] pertaining to the Dair al-Sultan on the roof of the Church of the Holy Sepulchre has always reflected the delicate political climate between the Egyptians and the respective government responsible for Jerusalem. This was the case during the reigns of the various sultans and viziers of the Ottoman Empire. The discontinuance of diplomatic relations between the Arab Republic of Egypt and the Hashemite Kingdom of Jordan in 1958 led to the expulsion of the Coptic Metropolitan and eleven Coptic priests and monks from Jerusalem in the same year. After diplomatic intervention, the Coptic members of the clergy were given visitors' visas for three months with the possibility of renewal.[78] In February 1959 the tensions between the Copts and the Ethiopian residents of the site in question increased. Subsequently the Jordanian government ordered the Dair al-Sultan to be handed over to the Ethiopians.[79] 'When the Copts did not follow the dictates of the authorities, the Jordanians changed the locks and handed the new keys to the Ethiopians. But their joy over the recuperation of their ancient place of

[74] Ghobrial Anba Bishoi, Israel al-Antuni, Filutaus al-Antuni, Athanasius al-Antuni, Girgis al-Antuni al-Masri, Akladius al-Antuni, Musa al-Antuni, Butrus al-Buramusi, Bishai al-Suriani, 'Abd al-Mariam al-Suriani, Filibus al-Makari (Jericho).

[75] For the Coptic Church of St Antony at Jericho, cf. Meinardus, O, *The Copts in Jerusalem*, Cairo, 1960, 79, 80.

[76] Meinardus, O, 'The Byzantine Church of St Andrew in Jericho', *Bull. de la Société d'Arch. Copte*, XVIII, 1966, 181-195.

[77] Information received from Anba Abra'am I of Jerusalem.

[78] *Al-Ahram*, 4 January 1959.

[79] In the Treaty of Berlin (1878) the site was given to the Copts.

worship was to be shortlived only'.[80] In my study 'The Copts in Jerusalem' I have published a photo showing the Coptic deacon Riad Shehata with the key to the Church of the Four Bodiless Living Creatures.[81]

On 2 April 1961, the Dair al-Sultan was returned to the original owners, the Copts[82] and on 29 December 1962 the Copts were again the legal owners of the site in question.[83] In May 1965 constructional alterations of the Dair al-Sultan carried out by the Copts led to new deliberations between the Egyptians and the Jordanian government.[84]

During the Easter celebrations 1970 serious confrontations between the Coptic and Ethiopian monks on the roof of the Church of the Holy Sepulchre led to the forceful acquisition of the keys to the churches of the Four Bodiless Living Creatures and the Archangel St Michael by the Ethiopians. Again the seizure of the keys by the Ethiopians was possible, since Ethiopia had full diplomatic relations with Israel from 1956 to 1973 when Ethiopia followed the rest of the African nations in breaking the relations following the Yom Kippur war.

For the first time an Israeli judge entered into a conflict between two Christian communities. The Israeli High Court of Justice announced a verdict on 16 March 1971 which actually ordered the Ethiopians to hand over the keys to the Copts, unless the Israeli government would prefer to set up a commission to look into the question of ownership in this particular Holy Place. The government of Mrs Golda Meir decided to use this prerogative.[85] Coptic appeals in 1977 and 1980 have only made the Israeli High Court confirm its original decision of 1971, while an Israeli arbitration attempt led by retired High Court judge David Bacher in February 1982 produced no agreement.[86]

From 2 to 18 April 1980, the Ethiopian Patriarch-Catholicus Abuna Takla Haymanot (1976-1988), whom the Copts never recognised as head of the Ethiopian Church, visited Jerusalem where he was greeted by the Armenian patriarch. In the course of his visit he celebrated the Divine Liturgy in the Dair al-Sultan and alluded to the rights of the Ethiopians in the Church of the Holy Sepulchre. In December 1981 Pope Shenudah III reiterated his prohibition for Coptic pilgrimages to the Holy Land as long

---

[80] Stoffregen Pedersen, Kirsten (Sister Abraham), 'Deir es-Sultan: The Ethiopian Monastery in Jerusalem', *Quaderni di Studi Etiopici*, Asmara, 1987-88, 45-47.

[81] Meinardus, O, *The Copts in Jerusalem*, Cairo, 1960, 62, pl. 47.

[82] *Al-Ahram*, 3 April 1961.

[83] *Watani*, 6 January 1963.

[84] When in 1966 al-Sayyid Anwar al-Khatib, who had served the Ethiopians for 15 years as advocate, became governor of Jerusalem, he ordered that electric light and modern water supply were to be installed in the Dair al-Sultan. To this the Copts retorted not only with a request from Pope Cyril VI to King Hussain of Jordan to stop the decision of the governor, but also with a rain of stones from the roofs of the neighbouring Coptic buildings upon the Ethiopian Easter Procession in Dair al-Sultan in 1967. Cf. Stoffregen Pedersen, *loc.cit.*

[85] *Ibid.*

[86] *Ibid.*

as the Israeli government would not intervene for the rightful return of the Dair al-Sultan to the legitimate owners.[87]

On 3 April 1982 the Israeli High Court declined again to intervene on behalf of the Copts for the return of the two chapels in the Church of the Holy Sepulchre which the Ethiopians had usurped in 1970. It was argued that for such disputes and controversies the Israeli government would be the competent and responsible authority.[88] In December 1984 Anba Basilius IV, the Coptic metropolitan in Jerusalem, demanded again the restoration of the Dair al-Sultan to the legitimate owner, the Copts.[89] In February 1986 additional Coptic monks were sent from Egypt to Jerusalem for the increased responsibilities.[90]

On 14 January 1993, the Israeli government finally decided to form a ministerial commission to study again the Coptic claims of the Dair al-Sultan. The Coptic Archbishop Anba Abra'am I stated that the relationships to the Ethiopians were excellent, while his rebuke was directed against the Israeli government. Millions of Copts throughout Egypt – so the words of Anba Abra'am – awaited eagerly the very moment for the possibility to visit Jerusalem once the situation between the two communities would be solved. However, as long as the conflict remained the Coptic patriarchate in Cairo would not recommend and support pilgrimages to the Holy Land.

The Israeli commission included representatives of the Ministry of Justice, the Foreign Ministry and the Ministry of Religious Affairs. This is the second time that the Israeli government intervened in the dispute between the two non-Chalcedonian communities. Already in March 1971 under Premier Golda Meir's direction, the Israeli government designated Justice Minister Yakov S Shapiro, Foreign Minister Abba Eban, Police Minister Shlomo Hillel and Religious Affairs Minister Zerah Warhaftig to study the disputes and to make formal recommendations for a settlement. It was recommended that until a final settlement be reached, the keys to the two chapels under discussion be retained by the Ethiopians. At the same time, the members of the Coptic community should have free access to the contested sites.

From a Coptic point of view the Dair al-Sultan issue can only be solved by a transfer of the keys to the two chapels, that of the Four Bodiless Living Creatures and that of St Michael, to the Copts. The Copts possess the keys to the northern entrance to the Dair al-Sultan, moreover, Abuna 'Abd al-Malik Anba Bula resides in the cell of the abbot on the premises of the Dair al-Sultan.

[87] *Watani*, 14 December 1981.
[88] *Proche Orient Chrétien* 31, 1981, 218f.
[89] *Watani*, 2 December 1984.
[90] *Watani*, 9 February 1986.

It cannot be the purpose of this brief presentation to offer the documentary evidence or to provide a detailed description of the developments pertaining to the rights and claims of the Copts and the Ethiopians. For those interested I have described these developments from the 17th century until 1964 in my study on *The Copts in Jerusalem* and in my essays on 'The Ethiopians in Jerusalem.'[91]

[91] Meinardus, Otto F A, 'The Ethiopians in Jerusalem', *Zeitschrift für Kirchengeschichte* I/II, 1965, 112-147, 217-232.

9

The *Qeddusan:* The Ethiopian Christians in the Holy Land

Kirsten Stoffregen Pedersen

L ike most ancient national churches, also the Church of Ethiopia has been well established in Jerusalem for many centuries. Traditionally the Ethiopians living there and in the rest of the Holy Land are called *qeddusan* – the holy ones. This is not meant to describe their degree of Christian perfection, it should rather be seen as referring to the fact that they have the privilege of living in the holy places.

The oldest testimony which has hitherto reached us of the presence of Ethiopians in the Holy Land since the rise of Christianity is found in two letters from the circle of St Jerome's disciples,[1] but the Ethiopians we meet there were pilgrims, and we cannot be sure that they came from the kingdom of Aksum[2] – they might have come from other regions of East Africa, since the term 'Ethiopian' in the 4th century AD had a wider sense than it has today.

Soon, however, Ethiopian pilgrims settled near the holy places and came to form a more or less loosely organized community of ascetics. A variety of sources have preserved information about their presence here, about their situation, customs and history. We have a number of letters and book dedications from Ethiopian emperors to the Ethiopian monastery in Jerusalem; in the itineraries of European Jerusalem pilgrims we find abundant testimony, for they were always interested in meeting their African brethren in the faith and observing their liturgical customs and their way of life; the same can be said about other Christian ascetics living in Jerusalem, and among these it is particularly the Latin Franciscans, the Greeks and the Armenians who have left us interesting descriptions of the

---

[1] Ss. Paula and Eustochium to their friends nad Laeta Marcella in Rome, see J Hilberg (ed) in *CSEL*, vol. 54, Vienna 1910, esp. 46, 339-40, and esp. 107, *ibidem* vol. 55, Vienna 912, 292.

[2] The ancient capital of Ethiopia.

Ethiopians; disputes over property between the various communities and, in the 19th and 20th centuries, the building of new churches and monasteries and the acquisition of other property have furnished us with a certain number of verdicts and *firmans* from the state authorities ruling at the time; and particularly in the 19th century various Protestant missionaries have been writing about the Ethiopians in Jerusalem. Finally we have some historiographical works, both from the hands of Ethiopians living in the monasteries in the Holy Land and from foreign scholars. The manuscript collection of the Ethiopian monastery in Jerusalem holds two such works in Amharic, both of them from the late 19th or the first years of the 20th century. 57 foolscap pages, namely pages 234-290 in the ms named JE692E by professor Ephraim Isaac in 1975[3] contain a story bearing the title Tarik yä-Der Seltan and describing the history of the monastery from the days of the biblical king Solomon and until shortly before 1925. The second Amharic manuscript has no title, but instead its author has left us his name. It is Aläqa Wäldä Mädhen Arägawi who is known to have been staying in Jerusalem from 1891 till 1898 AD. This manuscript which also describes the history of the Ethiopian monastery on the roof of the Holy Sepulchre Church in Jerusalem, Dair al-Sultan, has not been taken up in Ephraim Isaac's shelf list. The reason for this is, that it was taken away to Ethiopia in the early 1960s by Ato Mäkonnen Zäwde, founder and executive secretary of the organization known as 'The Jerusalem Memorial of Ethiopian Believers'. Ato Mäkonnen used it to write pages 97-109 in his book commemorating the first ten years of his association, Yä-Iyärusalem Mätassabiya derjet yä-asser 'ammät yä-sera ermeja (Addis Abäba, 1965 EC =1973 AD). It was brought back to the manuscript library in Jerusalem only on 7th May, 1994. From an earlier listing it bears the number Qu77.[4]

Among the works of foreign scholars concerning the history of the Ethiopian Christians in Jerusalem we must first and foremost mention Enrico Cerulli's monumental book *Etiopi in Palestina*,[5] wherein the Italian scholar has described the history of the community from the earliest times till the beginning of the 20th century, quoting an impressive amount of documents. The present author has tried to follow his work up in her publication *The History of the Ethiopian Community in the Holy Land from the Time of Emperor Tewodros II till 1974.*[6]

[3]   See Ephraim Isaac, 'Shelf List of Ethiopian Manuscripts in the Monasteries of the Ethiopian Patriarchate of Jerusalem', *Rassegna di Studi Etiopici* XXX, 1984-86, 53-80.
[4]   *Qutr*, Amharic for number.
[5]   Vol. I, Rome 1943; vol. II, Rome 1947.
[6]   Jerusalem (Tantur), 1983. For a bibliography on the history of the community, see this book or two other publications by the same author, namely *Die äthiopische Kirche von Afrika bis nach Jerusalem. 2000 Jahre afrikanisches Christentum*, Trier, 1994. Kleine Schriftenreihe, Heft 21, Kulturverein Aphorism, and *The Ethiopian Church and its Community in Jerusalem*, Jerusalem 1994.

The Sitz im Leben *of the Ethiopian Church*

In order to be able to understand the development of the history of the Ethiopian Christians in Jerusalem we must first consider their place among the other ancient national Churches.

Ethiopia was christianized during the first three centuries of the Christian era. In the first quarter of the 4th century AD the royal house of Aksum embraced Christianity under the influence of a young Syrian, Frumentius,[7] and it seems to have been other Syrian theologians and ascetics, the so-called 'Nine Saints' who confirmed the Christian doctrine and faith in the East African kingdom in the 5th century AD. Frumentius became the first bishop of Aksum, but he was consecrated in Alexandria by St Athanasius, whereby the Ethiopian Church became dependent on the Egyptian Patriarchate. It has ever since its birth remained closely connected with both the Syrian and the Egyptian Church.

In that it can be compared with the much younger Church of Russia and the orthodox Churches of the Balkan, which remained quite as closely connected with Constantinople. Also in another matter its situation resembles the situation of those Byzantine Churches: quite as Constantinople fell into the hands of a Muslim nation, the Ottoman Turks, in 1453, while Russia remained a Christian state, so both Egypt and Syria were conquered by the Muslim Arabs in the 7th century AD, while Ethiopia has remained a sovereign Christian state. The Church of Russia profited from the conquest of Constantinople to declare itself autocephalous, while the Balkan Churches instead under Turkish rule became more and more dependent upon the Patriarchate of Constantinople. The Church of Greece declared itself independent in 1833, but was not recognized as such by the patriarch until 1850; the Church of Romania was organized in 1864, recognized in 1885; the Church of Bulgaria was re-established in 1871, recognized only in 1945, while the Church of Serbia was restored and recognized in 1879.

In Ethiopia the so-called Arab/Nicene canons became important for the regulation of the relationship between the Coptic (i.e. Egyptian) and the Ethiopian Church. These ecclesiastical rules are a collection of eighty canons, erroneously believed to have issued from the ecumenical Council of Nicea (325 AD). They were translated into Arabic in the 8th century AD About the hierarchy of the Ethiopian and Nubian Churches, canon 36 says:

> That the Ethiopians ought neither to create nor to elect a patriarch, because, on the contrary, their prelate should be under the authority of him who holds the see of Alexandria. There may be among them (one) in the place of the patriarch,

---

[7] See Turranii Rufini, *Historia Ecclesiastica*, Liber I, Caput IX. Migne PL vol. XXI coll., 478-80.

and he should be called Catholicos; but he has no right to create archbishops, as the patriarch has, because of the patriarch he has neither the honour nor the authority. If it happened that there be a council and that this prelate of the Ethiopians be present, let him take the seventh place, after the prelate of Seleucia [Ctesiphon, today Baghdad]. If the authority be given to him to create archbishops in his province, he will however not be permitted to appoint any of them [i.e. the Ethiopians]. Anyone who shalt not obey, the Synod excommunicates him.[8]

Needless to say, that arrangement opened the way for numerous political intrigues between Egypt and Ethiopia. Even so it stayed in force even longer than the close ties between Constantinople and the Balkan Churches. But at the beginning of the 20th century a movement of independence came up also in the Ethiopian Church, and when the last of the Coptic bishops appointed by Alexandria for Ethiopia in 1881, Abunä Mattewos, died in 1926, the Ethiopian Church leaders approached the patriarch of Alexandria with a petition that the new head of the Ethiopian Church should be authorized to consecrate bishops from among the native Ethiopian clergy. This led to lengthy negotiations between the two national Churches, but finally in 1929 a new Coptic metropolitan, Abunä Gerlos (Cyrillos) was appointed for Ethiopia, and it was agreed that he should consecrate 5 Ethiopian monks as diocesan bishops.

After the Italian occupation of Ethiopia (1936-41) the negotiations with the see of Alexandria were resumed. The Ethiopians requested full autonomy for their national Church, and again lengthy discussions followed. But in 1948 an agreement was finally reached. A decree was obtained from the Coptic Synod, that Ethiopian monks might be consecrated bishops during the lifetime of Abunä Gerlos, and that upon his death, a native Ethiopian metropolitan should be appointed.

Upon the death of Abunä Gerlos in 1951, the full autonomy of the Ethiopian Orthodox Täwahedo Church was established when Abunä Bäsilewos was chosen as metropolitan of Ethiopia by both clergy and laity, and in 1959 the autonomy was further confirmed by the elevation of the metropolitan to the rank of patriarch.

---

[8] See Giovanni Vantini, *Christianity in the Sudan*, Bologna 1981, 77 and – by the same author, *The Excavations of Faras: a contribution to the History of Christian Nubia*, Bologna, 1970, 62.

The Ethiopian community in Jerusalem during the Middle Ages

Little is known about the life of the Ethiopians in Jerusalem from the 4th till the 13th century. Cerulli is probably right when he suggests that they may have worshipped and perhaps also have been accommodated with their brethren in the faith, the Copts and the Syrians, at the St Mary Magdalene monastery near Herod's Gate in Jerusalem. Since the split in the Church caused by the ecumenical Council of Chalcedon in 451, these Churches which followed the teachings of the Alexandrian theologians insisting on the union of the divine and the human nature of Christ, were no longer in communion with the Byzantine 'dyophysitic' patriarch of Jerusalem. In the Holy Land they had their own bishop, appointed by the Jacobite[9] patriarch of Antioch, but financially they were above all supported by the see of Alexandria.

The Syrian historiographer Jacob Barhebraeus (1226-86) tells us a story which throws some light on the situation of the Ethiopians in Jerusalem in the 13th century.[10]

In 1237 a dispute broke out between the Coptic patriarch Cyril III ibn Laqlaq (1235-43) and the Syro-Jacobitic patriarch of Antioch, Ignatius, when the former, quite in contradiction to the common usage, appointed and consecrated a Coptic bishop for Jerusalem. An Ethiopian monk in the Holy City, Abba Thomas, tried to draw profit for himself from the situation by asking patriarch Ignatius to consecrate him bishop of Ethiopia. The Syrian was willing to do so, but due to resistance to the plan in various circles in Jerusalem it finally came to nothing.

Various Ethiopian emperors sent letters and gifts, among which were several books, to their compatriots in Jerusalem. The Emperor Yagbe'ä Seyon (1284-95) is known to have sent various gifts to the community in the year 1290 by way of Cairo. In 1442 the monastery in Jerusalem received from Emperor Zär'ä Ya'eqob (1434-68) a copy of the *mäshafä sinodos* with a long, dated dedication. During the reign of the same emperor the abbot of the Ethiopian monastery in Jerusalem, Abba Niqodimos, headed an Ethiopian delegation to the council of Ferrara-Firenze (1439-41), where the Roman Catholic Church tried to reach full unity with the oriental Churches.

In 1283 the Dominican friar Burcardus of Mount Sion described the Ethiopians as 'the most pious among the orientals'. The two Franciscans Fra Simon and Fra Hugo Illuminator from Ireland tell us about an Ethiopian liturgical service they attended in Jerusalem in 1323, and among the first of those who have informed us about the places where such

---

9   The name comes from the 6th century leader of the Syrian non-Chalcedonians, Bishop Jacob Baradaeus.

10   See Renaudot, *Historia Patriarcharum Alexandrinorum*, 579. J M Neal, *History of the Patriarchate of Alexandria*, London 1847, II, 31. And E Cerulli, *Etiopi in Palestina*, II, 62-76.

services took place was the Franciscan Niccolí da Poggibonsi who visited the Holy Land in 1347. According to his report, the Ethiopians at that time possessed two chapels inside the Church of the Holy Sepulchre, namely those of St Mary in Golgotha and of St Michael.

Leonardo Frescobaldi (1348) and Ogier d'Anglure (1395-96) speak of four chapels which were then in the hands of the Ethiopians. From the travel book of the German pilgrim Sebald Rieter Jr. who visited Jerusalem in 1479 we know, that the Ethiopian monks at that time possessed and inhabited a monastery situated on Mount Sion around the so-called Cave of David, where according to one tradition king David should have composed the seven penitential psalms.

The situation of the Ethiopian community in Jerusalem was thus in general quite good during the middle ages. It enjoyed the support of the Ethiopian emperors, who were then sufficiently strong to be able to protect the Christians in the Holy Land. As Sultan Barsebai in 1422 closed the Church of the Holy Sepulchre, Emperor Yeshaq (1414-29) began to persecute the Muslims in Ethiopia. And several times Ethiopian emperors reacted to persecution of Christians on the part of Muslim rulers with a menace that they would cut off the flow of the Nile so that the waters would not reach Egypt unless the persecution be stopped.

The Ethiopians in Jerusalem from 1500 till 1700

The relatively good situation of the Ethiopian community in Jerusalem was drastically changed for the worse by two events which took place at the beginning of the 16th century. In December 1516 Jerusalem was conquered by the Ottoman Turks who soon began to demand heavy taxes from their new Christian subjects. And under the influence of the success of the Turks, the Muslim emirates in East Africa began to rise against the only Christian kingdom which had remained sovereign in the region, Ethiopia. Some skirmishes over trade routes in the 1520s soon developed into a jihad, a Muslim holy war, under the leadership of a young military genius, the Somali Ahmad ibn Ibrahim al-Ghazi, whom the Ethiopians nicknamed Grañ, i.e. the left-handed. At the battle of Shembera Kure in 1529 he defeated the Ethiopian army and soon managed to invade most of the Christian kingdom, burning churches and monasteries, manuscripts and icons, and killing those who refused to embrace Islam. Had it not been for the help the Ethiopian emperor requested and immediately obtained from Portugal, it is unlikely that Ethiopia would have been able to remain a Christian country.

It is of course clear that this whole development must spell disaster for the Ethiopian community in the Holy Land. Cut off from its connection with the homeland which furthermore was no longer able to support it neither politically, nor financially, the community could not find means to

134

pay the taxes and the bribes demanded and expected by the Turkish authorities. The result was in the first place that it lost its privileges in the holy places and its monastery on Mount Sion.

Even so the 16th and 17th centuries were not an entirely negative period in the history of the Ethiopian community in Jerusalem. In 1530, hardly a year after the battle of Shembera Kure while the jihad was raging in Ethiopia,[11] the French pilgrim Maître Denis Possot found Ethiopian monks living in Dair al-Sultan. In his book *Le voyage de la Terre Sainte* he describes how he with a small group of other French pilgrims visited that place 'where Abraham fulfilled his duty of sacrificing Isaac; and the chapel is guarded by the black people called Abyssinians. And there also stands an olive tree which is still today as beautiful as it was when Abraham was about to offer up his sacrifice.'[12]

That place is also described as being in the hands of the Ethiopians in the *Itineràrio da Terra Santa* of the Portuguese Franciscan Pantaleño de Aveiro who spent a year and eight months in the Holy Land from April 1563 till November 1564.[13] Like Denis Possot, he mentions the olive tree and its connection with Abraham. Fra Pantaleño also describes the chapel called St Mary of Golgotha and situated in the forecourt of the Church of the Holy Sepulchre, on the right hand of the pilgrim as he enters, as still being in the possession of the Ethiopians. These are furthermore said to play an important part in the ceremony of the holy fire on Holy Saturday. Fra Pantaleño tells us that the Turkish soldiers admitted only two Ethiopians into the chapel of the Holy Sepulchre, and that they came out again after a good space of time with their lighted candles. From the Franciscans living in Jerusalem he had heard that previously the Greek patriarch of Jerusalem and an Armenian bishop named Andrew had been allowed inside, and that the Greeks greatly resented the change, which Fra Pantaleño found it difficult to explain.

In his *Itineràrio*[14] we also find the Ethiopians participating in the ceremonies on the Mount of Olives on the feast of the Ascension, a privilege they have since lost as well as the one of participation in the ceremony of the holy fire.

Inside the Church of the Holy Sepulchre the Ethiopians are said to occupy one chapel in the Rotunda and another which is known as the Chapel of the Mocking of Christ (chapters XXVI and XXXV).

The whole of chapter XXXII of the *Itineràrio* is an account of the Ethiopian community which the Portuguese Franciscan describes with

[11] It did not come to an end until the Ethiopian-Portuguese victory at Wäynä Däga in 1543.
[12] The book was published in Paris in 1532. 2nd edition: Paris (Leroux) 1890, 'publié et annoté par Ch. Shefer'.
[13] I owe thanks to Anthony O'Mahony for having drawn my attention to C F Beckingham's article, 'Pantaleao de Aveiro and the Ethiopian Community in Jerusalem', in *Journal of Semitic Studies*, vol. VII, 1962, 325-38. And to The Itineràrio of Fr Pantaleao de Aveiro by the same author, in Revista da Universidade de Coimbra, XXVII, 1979, 3-ll.
[14] Published in Lisbon in 1596 by Simao Lopes and reprinted in 1596, 1600, 1685, 1721 and 1732 in Lisbon, and in 1927 at Coimbra.

great sympathy, and often with admiration. In chapter XXII of his book he also speaks of an Ethiopian martyr who was burnt by the 'Moors' in the forecourt of the Church of the Holy Sepulchre, leaving a footprint in one of the stone slabs 'as though on soft wax'.

In spite of the fact that according to Fra Pantaleño the Ethiopians had thus still in the 1560s not yet lost all their privileges in the holy places, their situation was far from being good. Already at the beginning of the 16th century poverty, hunger and misery brought about that several Ethiopian monks at that time left Jerusalem and sought refuge in Europe. We find them in those days in Austria, in Florence and Rome, and even in Spain. It is probable that many of those Ethiopian manuscripts from Jerusalem which are today to be found in papal and Italian libraries reached Europe at that time with the refugees from the Holy Land.

Another, very positive result of Ethiopian monks' flight to Europe was the encounter of Ethiopian and European scholars. Two such scholars met in Rome at the end of the 15th century: The German Johann Potken, praepositus of the church of St Gregory in Cologne, and the Ethiopian monk from Jerusalem, Abba Thomas Wäldä Samuel Bähtawi (the hermit). Both of them spent several years in Rome. When Johann Potken on one occasion had attended an Ethiopian service there, his interest was aroused to such a degree that he set about to try to find an interpreter who could translate for him the Ethiopian liturgical texts from 'the Chaldean language', as he called it. In reality it was of course Ge'ez, the classical, purely Semitic language of Ethiopia.

Potken complains that even among the Jews of Rome he was unable to find an interpreter with knowledge of that language, but in the end he met Abba Thomas, and a long-lasting collaboration between the two men with prolific results took its beginning. Together they edited and published the first book ever printed in Ge'ez. It was the Psalms of David, published in Rome in 1513.

Some 30 years later another Ethiopian monk from Jerusalem arrived in Rome, Abba Petros Täsfa Seyon, who prepared for publication the four Gospels and some *anaphoras* (eucharistic texts) printed in Rome in 1548. A year later a Latin translation of the *anaphoras* became available in print.

The Italian Franciscan Francesco Verniero, who lived in the Holy Land from 1631 till 1647, again met the Ethiopian ascetics occupying Dair al-Sultan in Jerusalem.[15] He tells us that 'they own a place in front of the Shrine of the Holy Sepulchre, where there are some narrow, low and dark rooms, and there they sleep on the bare ground. They have for a church a place on calvary where they say that Abraham led his only-begotten son Isaac in order to sacrifice him. Inside the shrine of the Holy Sepulchre they have a small chapel where the soldiers divided and cast lot for the garment of Christ.' The Ethiopian participation in the ceremony of the holy fire

---

[15] See his 'Croniche ovvero Annali di Terra Santa', ed. P Gerolamo Golubovich, in *Bibliotheca Bio-bibliografica della Terra Santa*, Nuova Serie, t. VI-XX. And E Cerulli, *Etiopi in Palestina*, II, 90-91.

appears in Francesco Verniero's book in the past tense – 'These made at first, on Holy Saturday, the superstitious fire, which they call holy, through a special privilege of the Grand Turk . . .'

The Ethiopian community in Jerusalem in the 18th century

Enrico Cerulli has made it clear that a Christian Ethiopian community has been present in Jerusalem almost without interruption since the 13th century. Only for very short periods during those centuries has he been unable to find documents testifying to their presence.

One such period is the 18th century. Cerulli builds his theory of the absence of the Ethiopians in those days partly on the apparent lack of documents bearing witness to the opposite, but also on three sources which seem to show explicitly that no Ethiopian Christians were then living in Jerusalem.

The first of these sources is a report by the metropolitan of Cesarea Parthenios (later to become patriarch of Jerusalem, 1737-66), *'Istoria tees metaxy Rômaiôn te kai Armeniôn diaphoras peri tôn en Palaistinee 'agiôn topôn.*[16] The report describes the dispute and litigation between the Greek Orthodox (Rum) and the Armenians in Jerusalem concerning the right of patronage over the property of the minor non-Chalcedonian communities in the Holy City, the Copts, the Ethiopians and the Syrians. The argument of the Armenians was that those communities theologically are connected with the Armenian patriarch, while the Greeks insisted that since the Byzantine Patriarchate has from the beginning of the Christian era been paramount in the Holy Land, they – and not the Armenians were responsible for the maintenance of that property. In 1697 Sultan Mustafa II had issued a *firman* in favour of the Greeks, while Sultan Muhammad I in two documents of January and of November 1734[17] decided according to the Armenian view.

In metropolitan Parthenii report of 1734 those three communities are described as *ta dialeephthenta tria ethnee Abyssinous, Koptas kai Syrous.*[18]

Cerulli's second source is a description of the situation in the holy places drawn up in the first half of the 18th century by the guardiano of the Franciscans in the Holy Land, Padre Elzeario Horn. From this writing we can see that the Ethiopian privileges concerning the lamps in the Church of the Holy Sepulchre were preserved, but the Ethiopians themselves are related to in the past tense *fuerunt*, and it is stated that they have left *deseruerunt*.

---

[16] Published by A Papadopoulos-Kerameus in *Analekta*, vol. I, 308-86.

[17] Sha'ban 1146 and the 5th Jumada al-Akhir 1147.

[18] *Op.cit.*, I, 316. P Elzeario Horn, however, does not describe the Copts and the Syrians as being absent from Jerusalem in those days.

In a third document quoted by Cerulli, namely a report from the Custodia Terrae Sanctae of the Franciscans to the Sacra Congregatio de Propaganda Fide in 1760, it is said about the Ethiopians in Jerusalem, that they pray with the Armenians and the Copts, because they themselves have no priest.[19]

However, those lay Ethiopians who attended the Armenian and Coptic services may of course have been people living in Jerusalem quite as well as pilgrims, in which case the Ethiopian Church was in fact not absent from the Holy City in those days.

So far Cerulli. But since the 1940s when he was writing, a few additional documents have turned up, two of them in Amharic and one in Russian.

The first of the Amharic texts is the *Tarik yä-Der Seltan* of manuscript JE692E in the library of the Ethiopian orthodox archbishopric in Jerusalem. On pages 286-7 the author describes the dire economic difficulties the Ethiopian community had been suffering since the Copts in co-operation with the Greeks and Armenians during the period of Turkish rule in the country had been expelling it from its ancient possessions in the Church of the Holy Sepulchre. An Armenian archbishop Asbazazin is said to have been writing about these things in a history book he had been composing, putting a great effort into that work which took him seven years. Even chapter 35 and page 256 of his book are indicated, but hitherto it has unfortunately been impossible to identify both the author and his book.

Our Ethiopian author, however, goes on to describe the endeavours his compatriots of those days had made to improve their financial situation, while the Ethiopian government was unable to support them. They seem to have been begging fruit, wine, oil and cereals from the Christian farmers in the surrounding upland and bringing up to Jerusalem what they had gathered in that way in order to sell it there. Water they brought from as far away as 'Shiloh' (i.e. Shiloah, Silwan) and Bethany. In 1761 EC (=1769 AD) they were building monastic cells in Dair al-Sultan.

A list of names is given of those monks and nuns who 'while keeping in mind the heritage of the heavenly Jerusalem, built a house in Der Seltan in Jerusalem on earth.' It turns out that while there were five monks, there were no less than seventeen nuns at work on that project. The monks are given the usual title 'Abba' of all Ethiopian monks, lay monks as well as monastic priests, but the nuns are called by the Amharic title '*Enate*' (my mother) rather than by the more common Ge'ez '*Emmahoy*'. And these are the names: Abba Akilas, Abba Gäbrä Mikael, Abba Gäbrä Maryam, Abba Wäldä Gäbre'el, Abba 'Amdä Seyon; Enate Säbänä Dengel, Enate Sahlä Maryam, Enate Wälättä Mikael, Enate Wälättä Maryam, Enate Hirutä Sellassie, Enate Wälättä Gäbre'el, Enate 'Ammätä Seyon, Enate Essetä Maryam, Enate Wälättä Maryam, Enate Ehetä Maryam, Enate Wälättä

---

[19] Published in G Golubovich (ed.), *Biblioteca bio-bibliografica di Terra Santa*, Nuovo Serie, t.II, Quaracchi, 1922, 178.

Kidan, Enate Askalä Maryam, Enate 'Ammätä Maryam, Enate Wälättä Heywät, Enate Wälättä Täklä Haymanot, Enate Wälättä Sema'et, Enate Sälome, Enate Wälättä Dawit.

The number of the cells 'around the tomb of Christ's cross' is said to be twelve.

Our second Amharic source is the manuscript Qu77 which for so long has been missing but is now back again in the archives of the Ethiopian archbishopric in Jerusalem. The author, Aläqa Wäldä Mädhen Arägawi, tells us on pages 48-53 how an Egyptian, Abreham Juhari, in the year 1775 EC (=1783 AD)[20] was received as a guest in Dair al-Sultan by the Ethiopian monks together with his eight slaves. This gesture of hospitality towards a brother in the faith unfortunately led to several serious clashes between the Ethiopians and the Copts when the latter began to claim ownership in the monastery.

Our Russian source is the itinerary of hieromonk Meletiy from the Sarov hermitage who in 1793-94 accomplished a pilgrimage to Jerusalem. He was a well educated man with a good knowledge of both Greek and French, and after his return home he wrote a book describing his journey and the people he had met in the Holy Land. It was published in Moscow in the year 1800.

Concerning Dair al-Sultan hieromonk Meletiy writes:

> On the second day, while I was sitting at the window during a fraternal meal together with the monks[21] and looking into the courtyard of the Ethiopians, I suddenly saw the Ethiopians and the Copts engaged in a great dispute. The former expelled the latter, hitting them with sticks. The reason was that one of the Copts had been doing something inconvenient against the walls of the church.[22]

The development of the community in the 19th century

The two communities of the Copts and the Ethiopians in Jerusalem were thus on bad terms with each other already in the second half of the 18th century, and their mutual relations were not to improve during the following hundred years.

---

[20] The date is added by a later hand and it is stated that this piece of information is derived from an Egyptian document (47). The author just tells us that Abreham Juhari arrived before Emperor Tewodros (1856-68) began to rule.

[21] I.e. the Greek monks.

[22] See Catherine Pillet de Grodzinska, 'Premières notions sur l'Ethiopie parvenues en Russie de la fin du 14ème à la fin du 18ème siècle', in *Quaderni di Studi Etiopici*, vol. 6-7, Asmara 1985-86, 31-37. The author is quoting Yuriy M Kobichtchanov, 'Pin et Palmier' in Africa, in *Vstreci Tsivilizatsiy*, Moscow, Izdalstvo 'Mysl', 1970, 309.

A great wealth of documentation has been preserved from that period, and among those who have furnished us with information about the Ethiopian community is a new element in Jerusalem: Protestant missionaries. One such missionary, the Anglican William Jowett visited Dair al-Sultan on the 26-27 November 1823 and left us an interesting description of that visit. This is how he perceived the Ethiopian ascetics he met there:

> They all seemed very idle and indeed their whole object appears to be, to spend their last days in Jerusalem doing almost nothing.

The community had become so poor that it was unable to feed itself:

> At the hour we were there, about midday, we saw the poor Abyssinians receiving their daily bread. It is given them as charity by the Armenians.

And a number of the Ethiopian monks had joined or at least found lodging with other communities:

> Three or four of them have joined the Greek community; so far as I could learn this conversion had arisen from the hope of improving their condition a little, and eating more bread. They are, at present, residing at the Greek monastery of Mar Saba There are likewise two at the Armenian convent . . .[23]

In 1826 another missionary, the Swiss born Samuel Gobat, who was to become a faithful friend an protector of the Ethiopians, spent some time at Dair al-Sultan learning Amharic from the monks on his way to missionary activity in Ethiopia.

In 1838 the community suffered a devastating blow. A plague almost wiped it out, leaving only one monk and one nun alive, and when the monk left for Ethiopia in order to bring new ascetics from there to the Holy City, the Copts found a welcome occasion to lay their hands on the monastery. Another disastrous fruit of the calamity was the burning of the Ethiopian library. About that the British consul in Jerusalem, James Finn, tells the Foreign Secretary Viscount Palmerston in a letter of 30 November 1850:

> I had then a long conversation with His Lordship[24] who related to me that the Abyssinians had been formerly a flourishing body here in intercommunion with the Armenians and the Copts, having a large library and valuable documents; but that

---

[23] See E Cerulli, *Etiopi in Palestina*, II, 204-5.
[24] I.e. Bishop Samuel Gobat.

at the time of the last plague, about twelve years ago, they had all died away. The Turkish authorities, at the instigation of the Armenians, then burnt all their books and papers under the danger of infection.[25]

A quarrel between the Greeks and the Ethiopians in 1845 over a cave beneath Dair al-Sultan and a window opening on the monastery reveals an interesting little detail. The Greeks had begun to clean up the cave, using the window for that purpose, and the Ethiopians now laid claim to both. They brought the matter up in the *shari'a* court of Jerusalem but lost the case. A year later the Copts revived the dispute and tried to have the verdict of 1845 revised and changed. This made the court issue a new declaration in November 1846, in which the first verdict was upheld and the court confirmed that it had examined the documents presented by the plaintiff and found, that 'between the domain of the Copts and the cave are Dair al-Sultan and the wall of al-Dabbagha.' The *shari'a* court thus does not seem to have seen Dair al-Sultan as belonging to the domain of the Copts.[26]

When in 1846 Samuel Gobat made his official entry into Jerusalem as the second bishop of the Anglicans and Lutherans in the Holy City, the Ethiopians were there to greet him in the Amharic language they had helped him to learn 20 years earlier.

In October 1820 some necessary repair had to be carried out in Dair al-Sultan, and an Ethiopian priest living there, Abba Gäbrä Krestos, was compelled to leave. The Copts on that occasion took the keys from the cells. In 1850 the Ethiopians, who were by then more numerous, took the key of the monastery back, wherefore the Copts and the Armenians addressed the Turkish authorities with a petition that they be ordered to return the keys to the Copts. On 16 November 1850 the Jerusalem court issued a verdict in favour of the Armenians and the Copts. The same happened again in 1863, with a similar verdict being issued on 18 May 1863.

In 1852 the *de facto* rulers of Ethiopia in those days, Ras 'Ali and Dädjazmatch Wube, had addressed Queen Victoria in a letter transmitted to her by Bishop Gobat. The petition of the Ethiopian rulers was that the Queen should intervene in order to protect the Ethiopian property in Jerusalem. In fact both the Anglican-Lutheran bishop in the Holy City and the British consul, James Finn, were already trying to do so. The first of James Finn's letters to Lord Palmerston concerning the complaints of the Ethiopians is dated 30 November 1850. From that letter it becomes clear that the Copts had begun to lock the little chapel which was the only place

---

[25] Here quoted from E Cerulli, *Etiopi in Palestina*, II, 277. The correspondance of the British consulate in Jerusalem concerning the Ethiopian community in the Holy City was first published under the title *Correspondance Respecting Abyssinians at Jerusalem (1850-1867)*, presented to the House of Lords by command of Her Majesty, London 1868.

[26] See E Cerulli, *Etiopi in Palestina*, II, 211-38.

the Ethiopians had to perform their religious services in at Dair al-Sultan, and that the Ethiopians therefore had taken the keys following the advice of bishop Samuel Gobat.

Consul Finn also relates how the Ethiopians came to see him on 10 and 11 October, on which latter date he also received an Armenian delegation.

> . . . and in the afternoon a deputation of the bishops and other elders of the Armenians came to me on the same subject, declaring that the church had been well known as their property for 400 years past; that the Abyssinians are like wild beasts, going hither and thither, not fit to be trusted with property, but yet had stolen the key, and were encouraged in it by the English bishop, etc. At length I proposed, and the Armenians consented to it, that the church should be kept open to both parties till the new patriarch should arrive (and he was expected shortly), when [the matter] might be impartially examined from documents, in presence of the Bishop and myself. In a conference with His Lordship which I had after they had left me, he accused the Armenians of being cunning liars; for he knew the church and convent to have been Abyssinian properties about twelve years ago.

The keys to the upper church door remained in the hands of the Ethiopians until the arrival of the new Armenian patriarch. And the British continued to protect the Ethiopians in Jerusalem although disputes with the Turkish authorities rather ran counter to their own political interests. The correspondence continues until the summer of 1867.

In 1890 the Copts began to break down a section of the wall surrounding Dair al-Sultan, and when the Ethiopians complained to the Turkish authorities, these issued a verdict in favour of the plaintiff and ordered the Copts, to build the wall up again. The Copts who had planned to enlarge the gate of the monastery without asking the Ethiopians, were so angered by the decision of the court, that they subsequently kept the chapels of the Four Living Creatures and of St Mikael locked for the next 80 years. The Ethiopians were thus left with a very small room for the celebration of their liturgical services. Only the celebrating clergy could find place there, while the rest of the congregation had to attend the services standing outside in the courtyard in merciless sunshine, in rain or snow. This is the reason why the Turks allowed them to set up a tent chapel for the benefit of their pilgrims during Holy Week and Easter.

Beginning from the 1870s the Ethiopian community in Jerusalem was, however, also able to acquire more permanent estate. By 1860 the civil wars which had raged in their country since ever the assassination of Emperor Yoas in 1769 had finally come to an end and the central government had become sufficiently strong to allow Emperor Yohannes IV (1872-89) to extend financial and political support to the monastery in the Holy City. In November 1876 the monks acquired a property situated in the small street leading from opposite the entrance of the Greek Orthodox Xaralampos monastery in the direction of the Damascus Gate. From 1887 the house was rented out to the Latin Sisters of Charity of St Vincent of Paul, but in 1891 it became residence of the head of the Ethiopian community in Jerusalem as well as its administrative centre.

Outside the walls of the Old City of Jerusalem, towards north-west and near the new Russian cathedral of the Holy Trinity, Emperor Yohannes bought a large vineyard for the monastery. In 1884 a Ottoman *firman* was obtained, permitting the construction of a new Ethiopian church on the land. The work was begun immediately, and when Emperor Yohannes fell in the battle of Mätämma against the Sudanese Mahdists, his successor Emperor Menilek II (1889-1913) fulfilled the building. In 1893 the church was consecrated to the holy Virgin Mary under the title of Kidanä Meherät (the Covenant of Mercy). The surrounding monastery is called Däbrä Gännät (Paradise convent).

The Ethiopian Church and community in the 20th century

Both these trends, the endeavour of defending ancient rights in the Holy Places and the expansion and acquisition of new property, continued all through the following century.

The Ethiopians had attracted the attention of their new neighbours in the Old City, the Russians, who acquired land and put up their centre next to Dair al-Sultan in 1859. The Russian activity for the benefit of the Ethiopians went particularly in the direction of trying to find legal documents which could prove Ethiopian ownership in the Holy Places.

Emperor Menilek had been thinking in the same direction, and in 1905, when the relations between Ethiopia and Turkey were quite good, he sent a delegation headed by Dädjäz Mäshäshä Wärq to Jerusalem and Constantinople in order to finish the dispute over Dair al-Sultan. The work of that delegation brought forth one important fruit, namely written statements from the Greek Orthodox patriarch of Jerusalem, the Armenian patriarch, the Latin Patriarchate, the heads of the Maronite and the Syrian Jacobite Churches and of the Armenian Catholic Church as well as of the Franciscan Custos Terrae Sanctae to the effect that the disputed chapels in Dair al-Sultan were in the hands of and used by the Ethiopians until the 1890s.[27]

In 1902 another Ethiopian delegation had been sent to St Petersburg,

---

[27] These documents were published with an Amharic, English and Arabic translation by the first Ethiopian bishop in Jerusalem, Abunä Fileppos (1951-66) in his book *The Rights of the Abyssinian Church in the Holy Places*, Addis Abäba, October 1960.

143

and among its leaders was the metropolitan of the Ethiopian Church, the Copt Abunä Matthewos. On its way home that delegation had also visited Jerusalem, but the result of its work had been quite different from the one of the 1905 delegation. In the Holy City the metropolitan was reminded by his compatriots that he was a Copt and led to support their claims.

By 1914 the Russian research work at the archives in Constantinople had been so successful that the Russian government informed Addis Ababa that it would be prepared to hand the documents which had been found over to the Ethiopian government on the condition that for every twelfth holy place returned to the Ethiopians, Russia would receive two. It must be kept in mind, that since the Church of Russia was new in comparison with the ancient Middle Eastern and African Churches – it was not yet 1000 years old – it had come too late to the Holy City to be able to acquire a Holy Place of its own!

The Bolshevik revolution in Russia in 1917 of course brought all that activity to a halt. But the Russian connection even so produced one important fruit even after the revolution in the form of a report composed by a Russian expert on international law, Baron Boris Nolde. The report, *Consultation de M le Baron Boris Nolde concernant les droits de la communauté religieuse Abyssine en Palestine*, was composed at Paris in French in March 1925 and was in that same year presented to the Ethiopian government at Addis Ababa by prince Alexis Michaelovitch.

The report comprises sixteen pages and opens up with a historical consideration of the problem of ownership in Dair al-Sultan, but the main thrust of the paper is an examination of the principle of status quo in the Holy Places. The important point is to determine from which time on this principle works. Nolde points to a *firman* issued in 1250 Hijra (1834 AD) by sultan Mahmud II concerning a dispute over ownership in the Holy Places between the Greeks and the Armenians. This was the first *firman* to set up the principle of the status quo, according to which the rights should remain in the hands of those who had had them *ab antiquo,* and it should be forbidden to change them. The Ethiopians are explicitly mentioned in the *firman.*

The *firman* of Sultan 'Abd al-Majid issued on the 7th of Jumada al-Awwal 1257 Hijrah (30 June, 1841 AD) honours the same principle, and the *firmans* obtained in 1853 by the French and in 1859 by prince Menchikoff all follow the same line, as did the Berlin Treaty of 1878.

Nolde came to the conclusion that the right to Dair al-Sultan and to its chapels belongs to the Ethiopians who without any doubt were owners of the monastery and the chapels prior to 1834 and 1841.[28]

On 9 December 1917 the Turkish rule in the Holy Land came to an end through the British conquest of the country, and in 1920 the mandate for Palestine was allotted to the United Kingdom by the League of Nations.

---

[28] An English translation of Nolde's paper, with an introduction in Hebrew, was published by the Ethiopian Church in Jerusalem in September 1986 under the title *Zekuyoth ha-kenesia ha-orthodoxith ha-ethiopith ba-minzar Deir-Sultan bi-Yerushalayim.*

The text of the mandate document was approved by the League in July 1922 and came formally into effect in September 1923.

For the first time since the Crusader period the governing authority in the land was Christian. To be sure, that did not mean a return to the medieval 'Kingdom of Jerusalem'. By the beginning of the 20th century the Western world had reached a more enlightened understanding of individual rights and religious freedom than had been the case in the middle ages. But even so the Christian minority in the Holy Land could seem to be justified if it dared to nurture some hope of better and more just arrangements of its life in the Holy Places.

In 1924 such a hope dawned upon the Ethiopian community in the matter of Dair al-Sultan. In April that year the co-regent Ras Täfäri Mäkonnen (later to become Emperor Haylä Sellasie I) visited Jerusalem in person in order to try to reach a solution of the thorny problems concerning that ancient monastery. On that occasion the Greek Orthodox patriarch Damianos decided to turn over to the Ethiopians a rather large cellar (9 x 18m) situated under Dair al-Sultan, an act which would have solved the difficulties caused by the closure of the chapels perpetrated by the Copts in 1890. If the Ethiopians could have made a chapel out of that cellar, they would have had a reasonable space in which to celebrate their liturgical services, and consequently all the further unfortunate development of the dispute between the Copts and the Ethiopians over the monastery during the rest of the 20th century could have been avoided. Regrettably, the mandatory authorities saw in the planned transaction violation of the status quo in the Holy Places, and the decision of the patriarch was revoked.

At first sight it seems difficult to understand the attitude of the mandatory government in that matter. It cannot be grasped unless we consider the ill fate of the British policy in the matter of the *status quo* on a whole. There was and still is some disagreement between the various Christian communities as to what exactly the *status quo* is. During the mandatory period the rights and privileges of the Christian communities in the Holy Places were regulated in the light of the Ottoman *status quo* declarations of 1727 and 1852 as extended by later decisions issued by the secular power following the *status quo* principles.

On 21 August 1922, Lord Balfour had presented to the League of Nations a proposal for a commission to be set up concerning the Holy Places. It provided for this commission to be divided into three sub-commissions, one Jewish, one Christian and one Muslim. The Christian sub-commission should consist of a French president, three Roman Catholic representatives (Italian, Spanish and Belgian), three Orthodox representatives (one of whom should be Greek and one Russian), one Armenian and one or possibly two representatives of the Copts and the Ethiopians. The reason why they should be entrusted to the French was the fact that they ever since 1535 through their diplomatic representatives had been in the position of guarding the interests of the Catholics in the

Ottoman empire. The chairman of the whole commission (including the Jewish and Muslim sub-commissions) was to be an American Protestant.

The British proposal was discussed outside the League Council for almost five weeks. The Vatican found it outrageous on the grounds that the Christian members would be drowned in a majority of Jewish and Muslim members of the commission, and within the Christian sub-commission, the Latins would be outnumbered by other Christians not in communion with Rome. In addition to that, the American Protestant chairman would in the Vatican view have too much power.

The French then suggested the setting up of three autonomous commissions, one for each of the three religions, and a division of the Christian commission into two sub-commissions: one for the Latins and one for the Byzantine Orthodox and the Armenians. Each of these sub-commissions should comprise four members. A ninth Latin member, of French nationality, should be the president of the entire Christian commission. But to this arrangement of a French presidency the Italians objected, in view of the fact that the Latin patriarch in Jerusalem and the majority of those who took care of the Holy Places were Italians. The result of all these objection was that the mandatory authorities never managed to set up a commission concerning the Holy Places.

An important law from that period is the so-called Palestine (Holy Places) Order in Council, 1924, which laid down the following rules of conduct:

> 2. Notwithstanding anything to the contrary in the Palestine Order in Council, 1922, or in any Ordinance or law in Palestine, no cause or matter in connection with the Holy Places or religious buildings or sites in Palestine or the rights or claims relating to the different religious communities in Palestine shall be heard or determined by any Court in Palestine.

> Provided that nothing herein contained shall affect or limit the exercise by the Religious Courts of the jurisdiction conferred upon them by, or pursuant to, the said Palestine Order in Council.

> 3. If any question arises whether any cause or matter comes within the terms of the preceding Article hereof, such question shall, pending the constitution of a Commission charged with jurisdiction over the matter set out in the said Article, be referred to the High Commissioner, who shall decide the question after making due enquiry into the matter in accordance with such instructions as he may receive from one of His Majesty's Principal Secretaries of State.

The decision of the High Commissioner shall be final and binding on all parties.

In other words, the decision on ownership in the Holy Places was taken out of the hands of the courts and handed over to the government.

This became important later on in the course of the 20th century. On 22 February, 1961 the Jordanian government, which had taken over the rule of East Jerusalem after the end of the mandatory period and the Israeli-Jordanian war of 1948, decided that Dair as-Sultan with its chapels indeed did belong to the Ethiopians and ordered the Copts to give them the keys. For forty days the Ethiopians again had a church to pray in. But soon the Jordanian government under political pressure from Cairo became obliged to revise its decision. The chapels were given back to the Copts and the matter frozen.

When in February 1966 al-Sayyid Anwar al-Khatib became governor of Jerusalem he had electricity, running water and modern toilets installed at Dair al-Sultan. Because of this the Ethiopian Easter procession of 1967 was greeted by their Coptic brethren in the faith with a rain of stones. The Copts had been gathering a whole arsenal of these in the Holy Land since time immemorial appreciated weapons on their adjacent roofs. The Jordanian police had to interfere in order to restore peace, and since then the Ethiopians have every year been celebrating Easter under police protection. In the six days war of June 1967 the Israelis conquered East Jerusalem and took over the rule in the city.

During the Easter night of 1970 the Ethiopians managed to change the locks in the doors of the two locked chapels, and since that night they have thus again had a small sanctuary where they can celebrate their services. The Coptic bishop in Jerusalem, Anba Basilios, of course complained to the Israeli High Court and various international authorities, and on 16 March 1971 the Court decided that the Ethiopians should give the keys back to the Copts. But the decision comprised a condition. According to the above quoted Palestine Order in Council of 1924 the government could set up a commission with the task of examining the basic rights of possession in the monastery. And that is what the government of Golda Meir decided to do. In the meantime the chapels have remained in the hands of the Ethiopians and the passage through the sanctuary from the roof where Dair al-Sultan is situated to the parvis of the Church of the Holy Sepulchre have been kept open for everybody who might wish to use it.

The Copts have several times since 1971 been trying to bring the matter back to the court, and even the arrival of their new bishop, Anba Abraham in November 1991, which promised progress in various fields, has not brought lasting peace in the situation of Dair al-Sultan. In the summer of 1994 a new attempt was made by the Copts to obtain possession of the chapels, although they truly do not need them. Unlike the Ethiopians, they still occupy one chapel within the Church of the Holy Sepulchre, and own one church and two chapels on the roof near Dair al-Sultan.

In the field of building and expansion the 20th century has brought true progress to the Ethiopian community in the Holy Land. Emperors, empresses and nobles have continued to build new churches and monasteries in and around Jerusalem, and today the community owns no less than seven monastic settlements in addition to some twenty other properties. The monasteries are: Dair al-Sultan and the Residence of the archbishop in the Old City, Däbrä Gännät in the New City of Jerusalem, a monastery in Jericho acquired in the 1920s by a cousin of Empress Zäwditu, Lady Amarätch Wälalu who became a nun in Jerusalem; the Qeddest Sellasie (Holy Trinity) monastery at the traditional site of Christ's baptism, built by the consort of Emperor Haylä Sellassie, Queen Männän, in 1933; the Meskabä Qeddusan monastery with its cemetery, for which the land was acquired in the 1950s by Abunä Fileppos and Emperor Haylä Sellasie I, while the buildings were put up in 1974 by archbishop Matthewos, leader of the community 1972-77 and again since 1992; and finally the Däbrä Sälam monastery in Bethlehem, consecrated in February 1990 by Abunä Atenatewos, Archbishop in Jerusalem 1984-92.

The number of the Ethiopian monks and nuns living in Jerusalem has been varying from time to time. Due perhaps to the newly ended period of Italian occupation in Ethiopia there were more than 100 in the 1940s. In 1994 there are sixty and thus place for a few more.

One may hope that the more positive trend of progress which took its beginning in the 1870s, may continue and finally overcome the darker aspects of the life of the Christian communities in the Holy Land.

10
Travellers and Pilgrims in the Holy Land: the Armenian Patriarchate of Jerusalem in the 17th and 18th century

Kevork Hintlian

This paper examines two areas in the history of the Armenians in the Holy Land which have not yet been adequately researched. One is the Armenian travel literature to the Holy Land mainly between the 17th and 18th century, and the other the institution of *nuncios* or emissaries. Before embarking on these relatively virgin areas one should touch on the evolution of the Armenian Church and community in the Holy Land.

For two millennia Palestine, Asia Minor and Armenia have shared a common history as part of the Roman, Byzantine and later early Arab empires. The contacts have been political, economic and cultural. In the middle of the 1st century BC, an Armenian monarch, Tigranes, reached as far as Acre in his conquests of the region. After Armenia adopted Christianity as the state religion in 301 much national attention was focused on the Holy Land. In his letters St Jerome mentions Armenians among pilgrims from various nations visiting the Holy Land. Armenian monks were among the founders of desert monasticism in Palestine. St Euthymius, an Armenian bishop from Melitene, is considered as the organiser of Judean monasticism. According to Cyril of Scythopolis, Armenian monks prayed in their own language at Mar Saba in the 6th century. Archaeological evidence in the 19th century and as recently as 1990, indicates that around Jerusalem there were about a dozen Armenian monasteries.[1] Rich mosaic floors with Armenian inscriptions from the Byzantine period substantiate historical information that Armenian royal and princely families patronised monasteries in the Holy Land.

---

[1] During road building for route Number 1 in 1990 north of the Damascus Gate the ruins of a whole monastic complex with chapels, burial chambers and living quarters and a 6th century mosaic floor with an Armenian inscription was unearthed.

In the Crusader period, the particularly close connections of Armenian Cilicia with the Crusader kingdom saw the consolidation of the Armenian community in Jerusalem. During this period, good relations are reflected by the fact that the first three Crusader queens of Jerusalem; Arda, Morphia and Melisend were from Armenian princely families. According to Ayyubid sources, in 1187, when Saladin captured Jerusalem, there were as many as 2000 Armenian residents in Jerusalem.

According to Armenian sources the history of the establishment of the Armenian patriarchate goes as far back as Caliph 'Umar in 637. In the Byzantine and Crusader periods, Armenians were present within the Holy Places, and that centuries-old attachment and defence of the Holy Places was to shape their vocation and orientation for centuries to come. The sense of Christian responsibility for maintaining the fabric and a living liturgical presence on the Holy Sites was to become the spiritual and historic objectives for which they had to go through enormous hardships and sacrifice.

The order of St James throughout the ages has given priority to three areas: first, maintaining a presence in the Holy Land close to the sanctuaries; second, serving the Holy Places; third, hosting and accommodating the pilgrims. To fulfil these obligations entailed tremendous efforts and imposed a financial burden on the monks of St James Monastery. Encouraging pilgrimage to the Holy Land was seen as maintaining and strengthening the contacts with the Mother Church in the homeland and diaspora. Spiritually, the Holy Places were a source of inspiration for the pilgrims and pilgrimage quickly became an important source of income for the community if not the only one. Jerusalem has constantly been in the national consciousness of the Armenian people. Kings, queens, members of the royal families, clergy, merchants, peasants, people of all walks of life have visited Jerusalem and embellished its churches with their gifts. Up to the 15th century, all these voyages were undertaken by individual means. But as time went on, and Palestine became part of the Ottoman empire, organizing pilgrimages was transformed into a system on the initiative of the Armenian patriarchate of Jerusalem.

The Holy See of Jerusalem appointed a permanent representative in Constantinople, a patriarchal vicar (known as *vekil*), and he resided in special quarters known as Yerusaghematun (Jerusalem House). His tasks included maintaining contact with the Ottoman Porte authorities, staying in touch with the Armenian Patriarch and Armenian magnates in Constantinople, and overseeing the activities of the *nuncios* (emissaries), known in Armenian as *nviraks*. One of the first recorded instances of a *nvirak* is Bishop Abraham of Egypt, who went on a fundraising mission to Tabriz in 1444.[2] Given the needs and the chronic shortage of funds in Jerusalem, there should have been many preceding him. Already in the

---

[2] Aghavnouni, Bishop Mekerditch, *Miapank Yev Ayzhelouk* ('Monks and Visitors'), St James Press, Jerusalem, 1929, 3.

16th century, we find emissaries of the Holy See in far-flung places like India, Crimea, Livorno, Poland, the Balkans, Russia and most towns of Turkey. Their main duty was to organize pilgrimages, make the practical arrangements like hiring ships and sometimes accompany them to the Holy Land, then their name would change into *hraviraks* (inviter to the Holy Land). Each *nvirak*, upon appointment, was equipped with a *kontak* (encyclical), a beautifully decorated scroll, which he showed to the local ecclesiastical authorities, as his document of empowerment. He read this scroll from the altars of the churches. The *kontak* described the Holy Places, the economic plight of the patriarchate, solicited funds for the upkeep of the Holy Places, and urged every Armenian believer to perform the holy act of pilgrimage. The *nviraks* preached in every town and village, and travelled extensively in the Ottoman territory. They encouraged people to remember the Holy See of Jerusalem in their bequests. Their function included locating and collecting funds from previous bequests, and most important to collect the annual contributions intended for Jerusalem from every village and town church. There were regular contributions in the thousands of Armenian churches of the Ottoman empire plus all the local artisan guilds made their separate financial gifts. People would also contribute manuscripts in their family possession and sacred objects. Today, many objects in the Jerusalem church collection have been brought over by emissaries, including many unique artifacts from India. The church treasury includes objects from the four corners of the earth such as filigree lamps, ivory croziers from the Far East, and superb 16th-17th century embroidery from Armenian workshops of Smyrna and Constantinople, manuscripts from Isfahan, Bombay, Astrakhan, Crimea, Rumania and Poland. It is recorded in ms. colophon no. 1925, that Bishop David was sent as an emissary to Erzroum in 1627, he saved the famous Bible of Erznka, which was in the captivity of Abagha Pasha, through the help of Sirak of Van.

The *nviraks* were carefully selected, they had to be well-versed in negotiations with the civil and ecclesiastical authorities, good and convincing preachers, and competent financial organizers. Among their credentials was knowledge of several languages and usually previous overseas mission experience. although their missions were well-defined their task was not easy. They had to travel in areas where conditions of public security were not ideal such as in the hinterland of Anatolia. The Armenian population in Anatolia was under constant harassment by the local governors and subjected to exorbitant taxation. Travel was a risky undertaking, and often *nviraks* were robbed by highwaymen. This was no less true on the sea, the Mediterranean was infested with pirates even in the 18th century. We read in Aghavnouni, 'Nvirak Boghoss, in 1702, raised 200 purses of gold in Constantinople for the Holy See of Jerusalem, while he was on his way by ship to Jerusalem, in the Susam channel, pirates from a Venetian warship went overboard and robbed him and the pilgrims.'[3]

[3] *Ibid.*, 430.

The mother see of Etchmiadzin also had its needs and its *nviraks*. To be able to visit the Communities of New Julfa (Isfahan and India) both within the jurisdiction of Etchmiadzin and particularly affluent between the 17th to the 19th century, they needed the permission of the Catholicos or the local Primate in New Julfa who was the Archbishop of the Diocese of Far East.

Those emissaries who were within the confines of the Ottoman empire were for institutional and practical reasons in constant touch with the patriarchal vicar in Istanbul who facilitated this task by coordinating with the civil and ecclesiastical authorities. From time to time they reported about their progress and difficulties. In colophons of Armenian manuscripts we find interesting remarks. In one entry a *nvirak* records: 'Arrived in Babylon (Baghdad), received well by the notables. Babylon is besieged by the Persian Army.' Another emissary wrote: 'The roads are unsafe. I am at the Armenian hospice in Aleppo. The British *baleoz* [Consul], handed me over to the camel-drivers and gave me a letter of recommendation.' In another incident, an emissary describes how around the island of Cyprus their ship was attacked by pirates, resulting in the robbing of all the passengers. One of the difficulties was to find a ship ready to sail before Easter. Due to unforeseen conditions of security, sometimes no captain dared to take to the seas so Greeks, Jews and Armenians pooled their resources to hire a ship jointly. Most captains of passenger ships in the Mediterranean happened to be Greek. We learn from another entry 'Captain Dimitreus was beheaded and his goods confiscated.' Many emissaries did not make the journey back. Bishop Isahak Ter Krikorian died in Jeddah in 1847 on his way to Jerusalem from India. His remains were brought to Jerusalem in 1849. We read that a certain Fr Andreas of Zile, died upon arrival in Bombay in 1773 and was buried in the English cemetery.[4] It would be very revealing to research the lives of hundreds of Jerusalem emissaries in the last 500 years as it constitutes an important chapter in the history of the Armenian patriarchate of Jerusalem. It is to be noted that some of them rest in the Armenian cemetery of Mt Zion, with a full account of their travels, engraved on their tombstones.

Although there is ample material about travel notes of pilgrims to the Holy Land in the Mamluk and early Ottoman period yet we cannot call it travel literature in the modern sense of the word. We will consider the accounts of four travel pilgrims from the 17th and 18th century and explore the itineraries and some of their observations on the daily life of the local inhabitants. The first one is that of Simon Tpir (Deacon) of Poland. In 1614 Simon the deacon embarked on an extensive voyage to the Holy Land which included Italy, Turkey, Egypt, Syria and Palestine. He has detailed observations about the topography, culture and religion of each of these countries. His descriptions of Egypt and Turkey offer rich

---

[4] Entries from unpublished diaries from the Manuscript Library, Armenian Convent, Jerusalem.

ethnographic material for the students of the history of these land. He came to Palestine via the Sinai desert; he writes:

> There were a hundred of us, we had an escort of 80 soldiers plus many mules. We left Cairo, after 8 days of travel we reached Katia, halfway to Jerusalem. We paid *ghafar* [protection money], half a piaster for a donkey, one piaster for a horse, two piaster for a camel. Five days later we arrived to Gaza, then continued to Ramleh. The road to Jerusalem is rocky, we came to Nebi Samuel. We entered the city with hymns. I gave my horse to an old man, and myself I went on foot. The Armenian clergy received us in a big procession with joyous hymns. While the patriarch received us at the entrance of the Cathedral of St James. In the monastery, there are forty cisterns, millers, scribes, candle-makers, tailors, goldsmiths, rosary makers, wine makers. There are emissaries [*nviraks*], who are sent to foreign countries. There was a bishop called Lucas who was sent to Poland as emissary. I was asked to be a scribe, and I began writing *kontaks* to be sent with *nviraks* to all the world, and to the churches and to the wealthy. As a rule every pilgrim should be fed free for three days. The next day the patriarchate requested the authorities to open the door of the Holy Sepulchre, as it is locked and sealed and there is only a hole through which they introduce food. The patriarch asked the qadi [judge of the *shari'a* court] for the door to be opened, as the qadi had the seal and the key, he came accompanied by the *kehya* [inspector] and the *soubashi* [superintendent]. They would charge 4 golden coins, women two, and priests no charge. Franks had to pay 9 golden coins. They would not open for small groups of 5 or 6 people. Then we went to the Monastery of the Cross. We were hosted by the Georgian monks who gave us a meal. Jerusalem is very dry and rocky, but it is fertile. Full of fruit trees, the hills and the valleys are full of olive trees. There are watermelons, pomegranates, peaches, figs and honey. There is strong wine, which is so strong that you have to dilute it with water. There are very few Christians in town. There are four monasteries, Armenian, Greek, Frank and Serb. There are no lay Franks, only clergy. These monasteries pay a lot of tax. And the morning of Palm Sunday, the superior of the Franks, mounted on a donkey, preceded by monks. They come down the Mt of Olives with olive and date branches, and enter the city and pass by the Gate of St James, and the Armenians wait for the procession, and receive them with honours. During the Holy Week, the parvis of the Holy Sepulchre is like a bazaar of holy objects. On Holy Friday, the doors of Holy Sepulchre are open, each pilgrim

pays 4 golden coins, and they can stay until Saturday evening. The Ethiopians do not pay *ghafar*, because of the waters of the Nile. They lead the procession of the Holy Fire and bring out the light first, and they dance around the Tomb of Christ where they play music with cymbals and chant *Kyrie Eleison*. During the pilgrimage season, in front of St James Monastery, it is like a fair or bazaar, where you will find everything, food and clothing. On Maundy Monday, we went to Jordan accompanied by the pasha. We pay two piasters per person.[5]

Simon the Deacon stayed two years in the Holy Land and provides an excellent picture of the daily life in Palestine. Besides being close to the then Patriarch Krikor of Baronter, he was very involved in the life and work of the Monastery of St James. He admired the hermit called Abdal.

And there is a hermit called Abdal, he never uses donkey or horse and wanders everywhere on foot. He stays usually in Aleppo, he begs and asks charity for Holy Jerusalem, everybody loves and honours him. He wears a sack, he is barefooted and bareheaded, his feet and knees are hardened like a camel because he prays daily. He eats once every three days has no coat, and is like a dervish. They kiss his hand, he sends 3000-4000 piasters to Jerusalem to support Patriarch Krikor of Baronter. There are other men and women who give all their jewellery for the Love of Christ.

The next traveller to be considered is Jeremiah Keomurdjian, 1649; he writes:

On 3 August we set sail, reached Rhodes on 15 August, left on 21 August, a Frankish ship approached us and we made away quickly. Arrived in Jaffa 23 August, and celebrated the Feast of Jeremiah, arrived in the much-desired city of Jerusalem on 28 August, received by the clergy, the Armenian residents and by the pilgrims. In the morning of 29 August, we, all the pilgrims, went to Holy Sepulchre for thanksgiving and then the whole day visited the Holy Sites. And on the 16 September, went to Mar Saba, where hermits pray in caves. There we stayed overnight in the Monastery of Mar Sabas, visited his tomb, and left after 3 days. 30 March was the Palm Sunday of the Franks and the Superior of the Franks came down the Mt of Olives on a donkey, like the Lord, and all the nations of Jerusalem; Greeks, Armenians, Muslims and Jews, men an women, old

---

[5] Simon Tpir, *Oughekroutoun Simon Tpir Lehatzou* ('The Travels of Deacon Simon of Poland'), trans. by Fr Nerses Akinian, Mekhitarist Press, Vienna, 1933.

and young, sat outside the city walls to watch the procession. Then the superior of the Franks entered through the Zion Gate singing Hosanna, and passed the Gate of St James Monastery and went to the Franciscan Convent. The following year, the custom of riding on the donkey was removed by the order of the pasha. On 8 April, we went to River Jordan, and on the 9 April, we descended into the Holy Water. The Pasha of Jerusalem accompanied us with drums and trumpets, and in front of us were many armed Arabs under the command of the pasha, as a precautionary measure against the thieves. On 13 April, Saturday (Holy Fire Day), we entered the Holy Sepulchre, and each one occupied a place previously arranged for us, and all eyes were set on the life-giving Tomb of the Lord, some had tears in their eyes, some were sighing, and others were beating their breasts, and others crying for their sins and asking forgiveness for their sins. And the Greek Arabs danced around the Tomb, and carried each other on their shoulders, they sang, praised the Lord, and after the procession, the Tomb roared and the Tomb shone with light. On Monday we left for Ramleh, hired three small ships to Sidon, then at night we reached Beirut.[6]

And in the first part of 18th century, we get the first detailed guidebook of the Holy Land compiled by Hanna Vardapet, a close associate of Patriarch Gregory the Chain-Bearer. The book which is interspersed with contemporary historical information, became the standard guidebook for the Armenian pilgrims, first published in 1727, it went into four editions, the last being in 1806. The book which comprises of 353 pages, has two full pages of advice to the pilgrims before setting out. We read on page 43, 'For the love of Christ one has to go to Jerusalem and confess all your sins and sell your belongings for your travel expenses. You have to go through discomfort. By spending your money on your travel to Jerusalem you store wealth in Paradise.' He goes on: 'Confess your sins, make your testament, give up bad habits, be humble and laconic.' He describes the first night of arrival at the Hoketoun (hospice for pilgrims). 'At night, the father confessor comes, as appointed by the father superior, one confessor for men and another for women, and awakens the pilgrims, then takes them to the church of St James, and gives each two candles and the pilgrims enter the tomb chapel of St James walking on their knees, while the priests sing hymns. And the same night they are taken to the Holy Sepulchre, they kiss the divine doors and come back to St James Monastery.' We read in another place: 'The next day they visit after confessing their sins Holy Sepulchre, at night they form a procession around the tomb of Christ, and

---

6 Neshanian, Bishop Mesrop, *Orakroutioun Yeremia Chelebi Komundjiani* ('Diary of Jeremiah Keumurdjian'), St James Press, Jerusalem, 1939.

in the morning they take part in the mass. On their return to the Monastery, they are received by the patriarch who confers on them the title of *mahdess* [*hadji*], and they go to the common dining hall to lunch with the monks.' Hanna describes about 300 sites but devotes a long description to Holy Sepulchre. He adds, 'There are the tombs of the Latin Kings, one of Godfrey and the other of Baldwin. I couldn't know the names of the rest.' About St Abraham in the parvis of Holy Sepulchre, he says 'once it belonged to the Ethiopians.' Referring to the St Saviour's he writes: 'Franciscans have many rooms and gardens, they are mainly supported by Spanish kings, once it belonged to the Georgians and was called St John, Muslims call it Dair al-'Amud.' 'St Anne is in ruins it is called Salahiyya.' Then he writes about Hebron, Beit Jala, whose residents are 'Greek Arabs' and Gaza. He recommends a visit to the desert monasteries: St Jerasimos (Monastery of the Lion), St Chariton and Mar Saba with 'its 8 chapels and 2 towers of defence.'[7]

Another traveller who visited in 1721 was a clergyman from Constantinople called Zvar Jiyerji. His account is very revealing about the voyage. As his stay extended over nine months (September to May), he describes in great detail the life of the pilgrims, the local conditions, the economic life of Jerusalem and identifies some institutions in the life of the residents of the city.

> We passed by Tekirdagh, Gallipoli. On 18 September we landed at Rhodes, where we stayed for 15 days. There our papers were verified, but on the eve of our voyage, there was a sudden roaring of the sky, the sailors and the captain were not on board, we ran to the deck. Because of the storm all the ships returned to harbour. We thanked the Lord and St James, and we had to stay another 7 days. We visited the Greek metropolitan at Rhodes, who obtained an undertaking from the Greek captain of the ship that he will take us to Jaffa and nowhere else. Metropolitan Ignatius was fond of birds, he had many kinds in cages. Next day the metropolitan accompanied by the clergy and the congregation went on board, and blessed the ship. Then there were two artillery volleys, and we set out. It was 15 October, we were 17 ships destined to Jaffa. We arrived on Sunday 21 October, we kissed the thin sand. We prayed because the Lord had deemed us worthy. It had taken us 7 days from Rhodes. On Monday the Agha of Jaffa died. We wanted to go to Jerusalem, there were no camels. The fortress of Jaffa is full of cannons. At midnight, the Janissaries came with camels, we all woke up and placed our loads on the camels. Our papers were verified once more. We set out, our

---

[7] Hanna Vartapet, *Kirk Badmoutyan Srpo yev Metri Kaghakis Asdoutzo Yerusaghemis* ('History of the Holy and Great City of God, Jerusalem'), Constantinople, 1782.

group was surrounded by armed Janissaries. On arrival at Ramleh, we paid *ghafar* (pilgrim protection money). From Ramleh to Jerusalem it took six hours. On a bridge, we paid two *zolatas*. When we arrived at St Abraham's Gate (Jaffa Gate) it was dark, all the Armenian clergy were there. In the monastery an old friend, called Petros, sent me a mug of blessed wine. That evening we slept a bit, the sexton woke us up, each of us lit two candles, then we proceeded to the Holy Sepulchre, and on the way we recited prayers for our sins, we lit our candles, came back and slept.

In another context he writes: 'When we go out of the small door of the parvis of the Holy Sepulchre, to your right, there is a garden where they grow cabbages, here are the tanners [today's *dabbagha*], if you move on, there is St Stephen's Church [St Redeemer's presently], which is a prison now, all the ones who owe money are detained there, the only ones who can take them out are the creditors. Then on the street of the mosque is the Mehkame [court-house], where there is a fountain.'

As to their trip to the River Jordan:

We set out with Damascene muleteers, Jericho is a big plain, when we arrived, we had 27 *bayraks* [banners] preceding us. I saw a lot of tents, I had my own tent. Then we went to the River, with the pasha of Jerusalem. I baptized 5 people and then a priest called Gabriel, baptized me, and I filled water in the canteen. Then back to Jericho, the governor had collected 10 purses, he was afraid of the bedouins, early in the morning we began riding to Jerusalem. A few days before Palm Sunday, Arab villagers come to Jerusalem then they go on a pilgrimage to Nebi Moussa for eight days. There is a mountain near the spot of the stoning of St Stephen's, where I found 3000 women sitting to watch the ceremony.[8]

Revd Jiyerdji offers an extraordinary and uncommon description of the city of Jerusalem, which I hope to translate in a forthcoming book. An anthology of Armenian travellers to the Holy Land will shed new light on behavioural and historical patterns in 16th-18th century Palestine. The observations of Armenian travel writers (because they were Easterners) were clearly different from the observations of their European counterparts. One advantage they had was the length of their visits which would be from one to two years or more which allowed them to make more informed comments. Also they were not easily impressed with every new detail since they were themselves from the east but focused on the

---

[8] Zvar Jiyerdji Oghlu, *Oughekroutioun Zvar Jiyerdji Oghlu Kahanayi (1711-1712)*, ('Travels . . .'), Venice, 1867-69.

unique aspects of Palestinian life which they observed, whether the religious or the daily social life.

Historically the one single important source of revenue of the Armenian patriarchate was pilgrimage, which was heavily dependent on safety factors at sea and on land. In times of civil strife and epidemics, Jerusalem was deprived of its flow of pilgrims. So many times, the Armenian patriarchate would resort to national solicitation campaign, we have an early example as recorded by the contemporary chronicler Grigor Daranaghtsi 1613: 'Abbot General of the Armenian Monastery of Varak; Fr Barsegh visited Jerusalem, and witnessed with great pain the economic plight of the Holy See. Along with Bishop Martyros, he toured the regions of Van and Bitlis. A wealthy Armenian of Bitlis, called Karapet donated "seven loads of silver" then they came with a large number of wealthy Armenians to Jerusalem and repaid all the debts.'[9]

During the Ottoman domination in Palestine (1517-1917), the excessive taxes drained all the resources of the Holy See. The most dreaded tax was the annual tribute known as *muqta'a*. Once a year, the governor of Damascus (the highest Ottoman functionary of the region), would arrive with a large retinue of subordinates and troops to collect taxes. During their entire stay in Jerusalem their expenses were borne by the taxed subjects, and they would return with taxes and gifts. Sanjian writes:

> On his annual visit to Jerusalem in the spring of 1827, the governor of Damascus demanded an additional sum of 180,000 piasters from the 3 major communities for the 'needs of his army'. When the Armenians explained their total inability to pay their share, some thirty soldiers were sent to the Monastery of St James to bastinado the monks. Consequently, they were forced into paying not only this special exaction but also an additional sum of 130,000 piasters in fines.[10]

Whenever an Ottoman official was appointed to Jerusalem, they would receive from the Christian Communities what was called the *kudumiye* [arrival tax]. When a new patriarch assumed office he had to offer expensive gifts to the Ottoman functionaries. When a governor terminated his term of office, he obtained from each patriarchate the sum of 5,000 piasters for travel expenses for his new assignment.

The Porte had to approve restoration, the permit had then to be confirmed by the governor of Damascus and registered in the court of Jerusalem. To expedite matters, one had to pay bribes on all levels. More was spent for the fee for the imperial permit and gifts, rather than expenses for materials and labour. Each time a new sultan ascended the imperial

[9] Neshanian, Bishop Mesrop, *Jamanagroutioun Grigor Vardapet Kamakhetzvo* ('Chronicles of Grigor Daranaghsti'), St James Press, Jerusalem, 1915, 324–329.

[10] Sanjian, Avedis, *The Armenian Communities in Syria Under Ottoman Dominion*, Harvard University Press, Cambridge, 1965.

throne the patriarchate was compelled to have permits of construction and restoration revalidated. One of the most common means of extortion was the imposition of forced loans, with exorbitant rates of interest, and other illicit taxes (like *'ubudiya, ikramiya, sanjakiya*) not sanctioned by imperial authority. There were also self-styled tax collectors of *ghafar* (so-called protection tax for pilgrims). In such a situation neither the revenues of the patriarchate nor its expenditures could be predicted. The size and deficit in the budget depended on the fortunes of pilgrimage and the exactions of the Ottoman officials.

The 19th century was a turning point for all communities. The Armenian community grew and pilgrimage reached an annual peak of 10,000 persons. We know of 5 guidebooks published in the space of 50 years. As a result of pilgrimage the income increased, and many new institutions sprang up. In 1833, Patriarch Zakaria opened the first printing press in town. Then the Crimean War occurred. For three years not a single pilgrim came. The resources of the monastery dried up. Patriarch John took the fateful decision to base the monastery's economy on property. In the following year, when pilgrims flooded Jerusalem. With the revenue, he bought rocky land immediately outside the Jaffa Gate. In this way, he was to become the first person to think of income-bearing real estate outside the city walls. Patriarch John built the new seminary and patriarchal residence. His successor, Yessayi Garabedian, was an artist. He was to become the pioneer of local photography in Palestine in 1855. After the First World War, Armenian refugees from the genocide flooded Palestine. Their numbers reached 20,000. Today, the Armenian community of Jerusalem happens to be the oldest living Armenian community outside their homeland, and a repository of Armenian art and tradition.

11

English Protestant Pilgrims of the 19th Century

Thomas Hummel

The 19th century saw Protestant pilgrims to Jerusalem and the Holy Land taking their place, somewhat reluctantly at first, beside their Roman Catholic and Orthodox brethren. In the forefront of this phenomenon are the English Protestants who begin to frequent the area in unprecedented numbers. Also the popularity of Holy Land pilgrimages was not confined to those who actually travelled to Palestine. As can be seen by the thousands of volumes which appeared between 1815 and 1900 the Holy Land was vicariously visited by many who stayed at home. There was obviously an interest in the 'Land of Jesus' which captured the imagination of Victorian England. Why, in light of a strong Reformation tradition rejecting the efficacy and practice of pilgrimage, did these English Protestants make the journey and then in many cases decide to share their experience with the reading public? What sites did they want to visit and what spiritually did they hope to find there? Finally, what were the theological assumptions underlying and justifying their experience? These are the questions this paper seeks to elucidate.

The English travellers to the Holy Land during the 19th century came in many guises and occasionally disguised. Some were there primarily to convert the Jews to Christianity either as an act of charity or as a preparation for the return of the Messiah based upon a pre-millennialist eschatology. Another component of the English religious presence were those who sought to reach out to fellow Christians in the Eastern and Oriental (Armenian, Coptic, Syriac, Ethiopian) Churches and chose Jerusalem as the place to best engage in that ecumenical activity. There were, of course, those who also hoped that such contact with English Protestantism would lead to a purifying of these ancient Churches who were believed by some to be in the stranglehold of superstition and needing the liberating effects of exposure to the Bible freed from debilitating traditions. Others came to further British geo-political interests, especially its interest in propping up the failing Ottoman empire and countering the influence of Russia and France in the area. Ever since Napoleon's foray into the area at the beginning of the century Britain was concerned that a power vacuum caused by the collapse of Ottoman control might create opportunities for others, notably France or Russia, to move in and potentially control access to India. With the opening of the Suez Canal in 1869 this became an even more crucial policy objective of the British government. The English schools and hospitals which were the creation of the various missionary groups tended to further both the religious and the imperialistic goals and thereby combined the religious and the political. There were also English adventurers who sought out the exotic and found Palestine, with its ancient communities representing a multiplicity of religions each with their own peculiar traditions, customs and costumes, a delight to behold. The rise of science during the century brought another group of academics, explorers and military personnel who wanted to systematically study the land of the Bible. Their purposes were varied with some wanting to elucidate the biblical history with more accuracy, some wanting to prove the 'truth' of the Bible and others wanting to provide maps and other tools for possible future military uses. All of these English visitors, however, are not the concern of this paper except that the English pilgrims came from the same culture and therefore were influence by and possibly identified with the aspiration of one or more of the groups described. They all came from a Britain supremely confident in its political, cultural, economic and usually religious superiority.

The Protestant Reformation strongly condemned the whole idea of pilgrimage, linking it with the late medieval practice of indulgences and the cult of the saints. Luther, Calvin and the Anglican reformers were all adamant that one could not earn merit by performing acts of piety, including pilgrimages, and that in fact salvation was granted as a free gift from Christ and one only needed to accept it with faith and gratitude. In England this attitude was enforced by the government's abolition of the monastic guardians of the pilgrimage sites and then destruction of the local cultic monuments such as Thomas à Becket's tomb in Canterbury. Politics and theology colluded in rooting out the pilgrimage as a physical journey and it became predominately a spiritual journey, given its paradigmatic expression in Bunyan's *Pilgrim's Progress*. English Protestants, of course, still visited the old pilgrimage sites including Jerusalem but they did so as envoys, explorers or tourists.

During the 19th century, however, the English Protestants, hesitatingly at first but later more boldly and confidently, felt comfortable calling their journey to Jerusalem a pilgrimage. The shift has a number of causes from technology to theology, as we shall see, but the tension between the Reformation assertion that pilgrimages bring no merit and that God is as much in England as in Jerusalem and the spiritual enrichment gained by the travellers remained a problem for many.

One explanation for the proliferation of English pilgrims over the century was technological. The development of steamships made travel to the Eastern Mediterranean safer, quicker and cheaper. The increasing British presence in the area also made the voyage politically safer and culturally more comfortable. British interests expanded in Palestine proper with the opening up of Jerusalem to a Western political presence under the rule of the Egyptian Muhammad Ali in the 1830s which continued with the return of Ottoman rule in the 1840s. A resident British consul and a British missionary presence later supplemented by an Anglican Bishopric in Jerusalem all provided a home for English visitors to the city. The British were also becoming increasingly engaged during this time in Egypt making it a secure base from which to venture forth into surrounding territory. The opening of the Suez Canal in 1869 made Egypt even more central to British travellers as they stopped their on the way to and from India and it was easy to extend one's itinerary to include the Holy Land.

1869 was a pivotal year for English pilgrimage because it marked the first of Thomas Cook's famous tours to Egypt and the Holy Land which became such a popular way to make the journey. Cook's reputation became so great that he was asked to organize the tour for the Prince of Wales and later the German Kaiser. But his most important contribution was opening up the Holy Land to people of limited means through his proto-package tours. By 1882 Cook tours had facilitated over 5,000 visitors to come to Jerusalem. Although these numbers were small in comparison with the 10,000 or more Orthodox and Armenian pilgrims coming every year it was a great increase in the Protestant presence. The clients of Mr Cook, called 'Cookies' by the locals, were provided with their own dragoman (guide), tents to avoid staying in the primitive conditions of local monasteries or hostels, tame animals (horses or donkeys) to ride, and imported British food (including on at least one occasion beer). The attempt was to make the trip as 'civilized' as possible to cater to the sensitivities of the English middle-classes. It was also organized to meet their religious aims, so that Cook's Tours published their own guide with suitable biblical passages to illuminate the religious significance of the sites as they were being visited. [*Thomas Cook*, Brendon, p. 139]

The technological advances, imperialistic and political advancements and organizational advantages all combined to make a trip to the Holy Land cheaper, safer, quicker and more comfortable but that still does not explain why people desired to go. Part of the answer lies in the cultural institution of the 'Grand Tour'. It had long been a part of the 'education' of the upper classes to have a Grand Tour to the cultural sites of Europe and the Romantic Movement with its invocation of ancient glories and appreciation of picturesque ruins gave an added impetus to the trip. With greater accessibility in terms of comfort and cost the less well endowed, primarily the middle class, could partake in the experience as well. If communion with the ruins of Greece and Rome could bestow wondrous blessings as described by Byron *et. al.* upon those with a classical university education, how much more ennobling to the soul would be the view of the very land where God had enacted His sacred history, especially for those whose primary literary experience was the Bible. The expansion of the Grand Tour to include the Holy Land and the extension of the participants to the middle and even occasionally the working class meant that the journey could be understood in one way as a new facet of an already established educational venture.

But for an increasing number of visitors the old category of tourist was not sufficient to explain their presence. The Holy Land was not just another historical site to be compared with Rome or Athens. The Revd Cuthbertson, a Wesleyan minister, expressed this sentiment when he wrote how the classical sights are wonderful and instructive and celebrated by great works of literature but 'the imperishable interest attaching to Palestine does not rest upon such a foundation as these. It is the land chosen by God as a sanctuary.' [Cuthbertson, p. 42] Here the emphasis has shifted from one of education to one of worship, from the classroom to that of the church. These visitors, increasingly acknowledging their status as pilgrims rather than tourists, set off to see the sites where the Bible took place with the expectation that the experience would expand their understanding of scripture and deepen their faith. After all one of the primary reasons for going to church was to hear the Word of God preached and in the experience find Jesus who was then worshipped with hymns and prayers and upright lives. For those pilgrims going to the Holy Land was not a matter of earning credit with God but like going to church, a place to find Him speaking to you through His Holy Word. This than is the religious reason why most of these Protestant pilgrims bother to travel to the Holy Land – because there they expect that the Bible will be more clearly understood and more forcefully and graphically experienced. As controversy after controversy developed over the century centring on the Bible's scientific validity, historical accuracy and spiritual truthfulness the Holy Land was seen as a place where the Bible seemed to be both vivified and verified.

The itinerary of the English Protestant pilgrims was much more varied at the beginning of the century than at the end, primarily because of the development of the proto-package tour. The earlier and more adventurous visitors frequently came overland from Egypt visiting Sinai and other biblical sites on the way to Jerusalem. This was more time consuming, physically taxing and expensive so was an infrequent and, therefore, more exotic route. The normal journey involved a sea voyage to the 'port' of Jaffa where, because there was no real harbour, the passengers were loaded onto small rowboats and brought ashore. This was one of the most dangerous aspects of the trip and there are frequent accounts of people drowned as this transfer of human cargo was attempted in rough seas.

This introduction to the Holy Land seemed *apropos* to a number of authors who saw this chaotic disembarkation as a severing of one's last links to the West and its comforts. The act of being tossed into small boats commanded by strangely dressed Arabs became a real rite of passage into the exotic world of the East. Once on shore the onslaught of sellers, beggars and agents for various services from hotels to hire camels seems to have combined with the heat, smells and dust to induce a cultural vertigo. The advice was to immediately locate a trustworthy dragoman - either one provided by the tour organizer or one recommended by previous visitors. Once a dragoman was obtained it would then be his job to do all the negotiations necessary to find lodgings, hire the horses and supplies for the trek up to Jerusalem. It was a frequent complaint from travellers that dragomen would agree on a price and then once the journey began demand more to go on, leaving the client in an impossible situation. This reputed unreliability provided Thomas Cook with one of his most valuable selling points. His tours were pre-paid with meals, lodgings and guides all included and attracted all sorts and conditions from the humble shoemaker to Mark Twain and the emperor of Germany. [*Thomas Cook: 150 Years of Popular Tourism*]

As the century progressed the journey from Jaffa to Jerusalem became easier and more comfortable. Initially it would take two to three days with overnight stays in one of the convents along the way. Before 1846 this trip usually included an unscheduled stop in the village of Abu Gosh where a tariff was collected by the villagers. This involuntary baksheesh could be avoided by having Turkish soldiers as escorts. The colourful outfits of the dragomen along with the antics of the soldiers escorting the groups made for a rather fairlike atmosphere.

In the 1880s the journey from Jaffa to Jerusalem could be accomplished by carriage in 9 hours as it was by the Revd Thomas. [Thomas, p. 68] By the 1890s this same journey along the Plain of Sharon and up the hills to Jerusalem was completed in a few hours by rail. Those who travelled both ways lamented the ease of the rail journey and found the failure to first view Jerusalem shimmering in the distance only to be finally attained after an arduous series of hills and valleys, to be a spiritual loss. There was theological symbolism, they felt, in the trip because after a long ascent the view of the city of God in the distance gave hope and comfort in the hard journey remaining just as the heavenly Jerusalem comforts those who have the vision of faith for the journey of life. This connection of the pilgrim's journey of faith had, of course, a deep resonance among the English who would be familiar with Bunyan's *Pilgrim's Progress*.

The first glimpses of the object of this trip - that is Jerusalem - struck these English pilgrims in various ways. Some were overcome with the sight of the walled city with domes glowing - here they said is truly the earthly symbol of the kingdom of God. Others mocked the romantics who broke out into pious exclamations or maudlin tears and saw only a rather bedraggled small town whose power is not displayed to the eyes but hidden away only to be unlocked by those who approach it with the eyes of faith. [Tweedie, p. 10] The majority had the ambiguous reaction of seeing the city shimmering in the sun and being moved but wary of falling into an idolatrous attitude and mistaking the symbol for what it symbolizes. Especially those who had been prepared for what awaited them inside the walls were hesitant to prostrate their hearts to the town. The tension between the heavenly Jerusalem and the earthly one, which made an important theological point, was also reflected in the tension between the Jerusalem of the Romantic imagination and the reality of a small rather economically deprived town in the hinterland of the Ottoman empire.

Once inside the city those who were initially enamoured with the symbol quickly became aware of the mundane reality. Early in the century the lodgings would have been almost exclusively in the Latin, Greek or Armenian convents. The Armenian convent was almost universally viewed as the most clean, modern and therefore civilized of the lot. By late in the century hotels, hostels and other facilities became available giving a wider range of accommodation. Although until quite late the 'Cookies' lived in tents outside the walls trusting no native accommodations.

In Jerusalem the English pilgrims were, of course, interested in the whole panoply of sacred sites. The Holy Sepulchre was primary but the Temple Mount and Dome of the Rock(once they were open to non-Muslims), the Garden of Gethsemane, Mount of Olives, Church of the Ascension, the house of the Last Supper, the Tomb of the Virgin were all *de rigeur*. The Protestants travelled the Via Dolorosa but did not have the same programmed stations of the cross as the Roman Catholics. For the English Protestants the sites that moved them most were the landscape sites - the Mount of Olives and the Garden of Gethsemane - while they were more distrustful and their reactions more ambiguous towards the traditional Holy Places. Although many English visitors made an effort to be in Jerusalem for Easter it was not seen as a major bonus and for some the large numbers of other pilgrims, especially the ubiquitous Russians, made trips at other times of the year preferable.

Once they had successfully 'done' Jerusalem these peripatetic pilgrims would begin a trip to the major gospel sites, travelling to Bethlehem, Hebron, the Dead Sea (also a natural wonder), Jericho, the Jordan River, Tiberias (to the Lake of Galilee), Nazareth, and Mt Tabor. Other places of historical interest such as the desert monastery of Mar Saba, the Samaritan community or Crusader ruins might also be added in for variety. At each of these sights there were favourite locations which seemed to capture the Protestant imagination and other places which left them unmoved.

Bethlehem was an ambiguous site with many finding the Grotto of the Nativity both a likely location for the manger and the grotto itself iconographically acceptable. Others dismissed it as a fraud, finding inspiration in the nearby 'authentic' grotto of St Jerome whose presence gave sanctity to the complex. The other sites, like the Milk Grotto were rejected out of hand as tourist traps. The Shepherd's Field in the outskirts of the town, although lacking any definitive proof for its appellation, did give the Protestant imagination a vision of the landscape of the events surrounding the nativity and was, therefore, suitably appreciated.

Hebron had the grave of Sarah but what these Protestants most commented upon was the hostility and surliness of its Muslim inhabitants. If Christian Bethlehem was familiar and friendly, Islamic Hebron seemed to them foreign and sinister. The Oak of Mamre outside of town, however, again marked a dubious but evocative landscape open to imaginative reconstruction.

The Dead Sea may have been a biblical site but its inclusion on the Protestant itinerary seems to have been more a result of its strange location and properties. It was almost a requirement to test its buoyancy and healing powers as well as commenting on its lack of marine life and location as the lowest spot on earth. Not one Protestant that we read drew the connection between the fresh water of the Jordan (baptism) with the dead, salty water of the Dead Sea (death and judgement) which figures among the Russian pilgrims.

The Jordan River did, of course, elicit from the Protestants thoughts about baptism and they bathed in its waters but frequently it was to wash off the salt of the Dead Sea or to find relief from the desert heat, only rarely was it part of a ceremony of re-baptism, although Baptists were an exception. But even 'Cookies' were provided with bottles in order to capture some of the water to take back for family christenings. And there were readings of appropriate texts from the Bible at the site. In fact this was a major feature of the Protestant pilgrimages. At each of the sites mentioned in the Bible that text would be read along with suitable prayers and hymns. Often, if there was an ordained clergyman on the tour he would be asked to give a brief, sometimes not so brief, address on the importance of the events which had taken place at the spot. If there were several clergy in attendance they tended to take turns.

At Jericho, for instance, the pilgrims would read the Joshua story of the conquest of the city and listen to a commentary about the land and its being a gift to Israel and they probably also heard of how that gift had been lost through failing to recognize God's Messiah. Here the biblical history and a theological commentary upon that history joined with a contemporary judgement about the condemned status of the land about which we will have more to say later. This emphasis upon the Old Testament as well as the New Testament sites and texts was mostly a Protestant phenomenon. The Orthodox and Catholic pilgrims were attracted to Old Testament sites only when it was a part of their iconographic tradition and usually when it symbolized a Christian event or doctrine. The Protestant acquaintance with the Bible as a whole and especially with its history and geography meant they had a special interest in and affinity for those Old Testament sites where special acts of God or history had taken place. This stopping off at both New and Old Testament historical and geographical sites and reading from the Bible, however, was not of their own invention but one of the earliest forms of Holy Land pilgrimage practised by Origen and Egeria.

The Sea of Galilee was one of the Protestant's favourite spots not only because it was here that the teaching and preaching of Christ mostly took place but because the sites were the landscapes themselves and not buried inside churches and encumbered with encrusted icons and flickering, oily smelling lamps. The seashore where Jesus broke bread and ate fish with the disciples, the lake where Jesus escaped from the crowds and calmed the waves, the hillside of the beatitudes all these were there in seemingly undiluted form. There Jesus could be almost seen to inhabit the place. Once the ruins of Capernaum were discovered that also was a place beloved because it was not monumentalized and the site remained 'pure'. The ruins were seen as especially *apropos* because it was cursed and to have been destroyed was a sign of God's judgement. As Jesus said: And you Capernaum, will you be lifted up to the skies? No, you will go down to the depths. If the miracles that were performed in you had been performed in Sodom, it would have remained to this day. But I tell you that it will be more bearable for Sodom on the day of judgment than for you. [Matthew 11: 23-24] Equally the lack of a fishing industry (most travellers comment on there being only one or two boats on the whole lake) was a sign of the fall of this place from grace. It was here that seeds of God's Word were sown but hard hearts and closed minds failed to recognize it and the seeds bore no fruit. So the landscape was seen as mirroring that failure as well as witnessing to Jesus' life.

The same could not, of course, be said of Nazareth. Along with Bethlehem this was one of the centres of Christianity in Palestine. Again the manners and dress of the people made them familiar and friendly like those of Bethlehem. What attracted attention, however, were the schools and hospitals which the various Christian communities were building in competition with one other. The Protestant's especially, were active in this way and so many pilgrims saw in Nazareth a prelude to the transformation of the whole region into a modern society if only the missionaries' work could continue unabated. The traditional sites in the city, the place of the annunciation, Mary and Joseph's house, etc., were mostly rejected as apocryphal and often mocked by the Protestants. But they were enthralled by the Virgin's Fountain because here at the town's well was obviously the place to which Mary would have come to draw water and would have most likely brought the baby Jesus just as the Nazareth's mothers still brought their children. Here, they felt, was an indubitable place where the early life of Jesus was manifested and where the present residents provided an almost theatrical presentation of a beloved scene from the sacred story.

Within sight of Nazareth was Mt Tabor which some traditions identified with the mount of transfiguration, but many Protestants felt more convinced by the case for Mt Hermon further north. For those with a more extensive program Caesarea Philippi (Banas), Mt Hermon and Damascus were all part of the tour. This allowed the inclusion of a major Pauline site which might be supplemented later by visits to Corinth, Ephesus, etc. on the voyage home. The itinerary of the Cook Tours tended to be a bit more extensive including sites in Lebanon on the way to and from Damascus. Also the Cook Tour usually included a trip to the antiquities of Egypt as well. For those whose tour ended with the Galilee they would either return to Jerusalem or continue on to Beirut to begin their trip home.

The English Protestant pilgrims in addition to visiting these Holy Sites were also interested in placing what they saw around them into their own historical, social, political as well as religious paradigms. Therefore, they frequently travelled to indigenous villages and talked with those people whose language skills and inclination made them available for interrogation. Often the people they saw and the places they went were determined by where English schools were located, which meant a rather skewed sampling of opinion.

When the English Protestants set out on their journeys to the Holy Land most of them were ambivalent about what they were going to experience. On the one hand, for many this was a trip of a lifetime taking them to a faraway and exotic place. But it was even more a voyage through time, back to the biblical period where they would be able to see the scenes from the Bible, so much a part of their mental baggage, re-vivified in a new and, they hoped, transforming way. On the other hand, as Protestants they were wary of any suggestion that there was any virtue or grace inherent in the place itself. It was not the land that was holy but the holy thoughts and experiences which it could elicit if approached in the appropriate way. And the appropriate way included eliminating any superstitious or idolatrous ideas that treading on the hallowed soil of Palestine sanctified the pilgrim. This sounded dangerously like the indulgence system, in this case grace bought from God not with donations but with a costly trip. It was also felt that the magnitude of God's presence was not greater in the Holy Land than anywhere else - after all God resided in the hearts and souls of believers not in things - neither bread and wine nor rocks and soil. So the Protestant pilgrim strongly rejected any concept of Catholic sacramentality. Most came already warned that they would discover great superstition, idolatry and fraud perpetrated by dissolute monks who desecrated the Holy Sites with their fanciful rituals. Therefore, it was with an expectation of illumination of biblical truth interspersed with the false idols of human error that these pilgrims confronted the reality of Jerusalem the town and the surrounding countryside.

It is not surprising that these expectations, reinforced by the theological assumptions of their Bible centred, sacramentally suspicious Protestantism, should be largely realized by their exposure to the Holy Land itself. Most people see and interpret reality based upon their presuppositions and expectations and the English Protestant pilgrims were no exception. For these voyagers from a distant land most of the traditional Holy Sites were a great disappointment because they found that the 'language' of piety permeating these places - that is, the iconography, the rituals, the pious customs - were foreign. This feeling of being an alien in the home of the

Christian gospel was very disconcerting because it called into question the universality, adequacy and legitimacy of their own view of the Christian religion. If this strange manifestation of seeming mumbo-jumbo was really Christian then their failure to resonate with it was a judgement on their own understanding. Consequently the Protestants tended to dismiss the Orthodox, Armenian, and Latin shrines and their rites as superstitious folklore at best and a conscious fraud perpetrated by the anti-Christ at worse.

This lead the Protestants to vigorously criticize those sites dominated by this alien iconography and piety. The prime target of their outraged sensibilities was the Holy Sepulchre. Here in concentrated form were the various Eastern Orthodox, Oriental Orthodox and Roman Catholic rituals and iconography not only confronting the Protestants but contending with each other for attention and space.

The result was that the Holy Sepulchre became viewed as a modern version of the Israelite Temple of Jerusalem. And just as Herod's temple had been taken over by money changers and robbers and had promoted ritualistic sacrifice instead of moral improvement so the nurturing of these vices were what many pious Protestants perceived in the temple of Jesus resurrection. Their response was that the temple of Jesus should be cleaned out of these inappropriate elements just as Jesus had cleaned out the temple in his own day.

Of all the aspects of the Holy Sepulchre which distressed these Protestant visitors nothing could compare with the Holy Fire ceremony on the Saturday before Easter. It was both the boisterous nature and miraculous claims of the event which so upset the English. Dean Stanley called it 'probably the most offensive delusion to be found in the world.' [*Sinai and Palestine*, p. 469] C L Neil's opinion was that it was 'The greatest fraud of all time.' [*Rambles in Bible Lands*, p. 134] and Treves says of the Holy Fire: 'it is only to be equalled by those degrading religious orgies which are to be met with in the forests of savage Africa.' [p. 77] But since they had neither the influence nor the power to clean out the Holy Sepulchre these Protestant pilgrims left the Holy Sites to their 'deluded' brothers and sought out instead those places where the spirit of Jesus could still be found. This tended to be in the landscape and small villages where the biblical stories could be visualized.

Out of the city the landscape could speak with an eloquence that had been drown out and buried by centuries of misdirected devotion. Later in his book Sir Frederick Treves opines:

> It was in this plain and unassuming country that the religion of Christ was taught. It was taught in the simplest language, in words that a child could understand, and by means of illustrations drawn from the lowliest of subjects. There was in the teaching no stilted ritual, no gorgeous ceremony, no foreshadowing of the princely prelate or the chanting priest. It

was a religion associated with such sounds as the splash of a
fisherman's net in the lake, the patter of sheep, the call of the
shepherd, the tramp of the sower across the fields. [p. 87]

This was the Jesus they sought and it was on Olivet or on the shores of
the Sea of Galilee or the Garden of Gethsemane that this image could best
be evoked.

Theological foundations

The Jesus of the land rather than the sites was of the essence to these
Protestant pilgrims as their accounts and even the titles of their books
proclaimed. The 'land' seemed to serve for them two interconnected
theological functions. First of all it was in a very important and also very
Protestant way a sacrament, and secondly it was a way of responding to the
growing apprehension among the English literary classes that the Bible may
not be historically true. Let us look at each of these in turn.

The Holy Land as a sacrament is an idea mentioned by a number of
pilgrims and at first glance it seems an odd designation for these Protestants
to use. But it is quickly evident that this is a very Protestant understanding
of sacrament. John Kelman writes in his book *The Holy Land*:

> A journey through the Holy Land may reasonably be in some
> sort a sacramental event in a man's life. Spiritual things are very
> near us, and we feel that we have a heritage in them; yet they
> constantly elude us, and need help from the senses to make
> them real and commanding. Such sacramental help must surely
> be given by anything that brings vividly to our realization
> those scenes and that life in the midst of which the Word was
> made flesh. The more clearly we can gain the impression of
> places and events in Syria, the more reasonable and convincing
> will Christian faith become. [Kelman, p. 3]

Later he explicates this thought more closely:

> The sacramental quality of the Holy Land is of course felt most
> by those who seek especially for memoirs and realizations of
> Jesus Christ. Within the pale of Christianity there are several
> different ways of regarding the land as holy, and most of them
> lead to disappointment. The Greek and Roman Catholic
> churches vie with one another in their passion for sites and
> relics there, and seem to lose all sense of the distinction
> between sublime and grotesque in their eagerness for
> identifications. A Protestant counterpart to this mistaken zeal is
> that of the huntsman of the fields of prophecy . . . [those who

try and read the signs of the end times]. Apart from either of these are others less orthodox but equally superstitious who have some vague notion of occult and magic qualities which differentiate this from other regions of the world . . . It is wiser to abandon the attempt at forcing the supernatural to reveal itself, and to turn to the human side of things as the surest way of ultimately arriving at the divine. [Kelman p. 5-6]

The proper understanding of the sacrament, therefore, is to understand its power to bring the Bible and its stories and characters alive, a dramatic way of impressing them more vividly on the memory and the imagination. In this sense the Holy Land was not just illustrative but makes Jesus and the Bible real in the same way that Jesus is real in the Lord's Supper - a memory which re-presents Him to those who participate in faith. This re-presentation for most Protestant commentators on the Holy Land seems, however, to be more than just a memory (Zwingli) but a making Jesus present, albeit spiritually, once again (Calvin). In this way the relationship to the land is probably more related to the sacramental theology of Calvin than of Zwingli.

Another phrase used to express this same idea is that the Holy Land is a fifth gospel or another Bible. J M P Otts, an American but with an attitude very representative of the English Protestants, says of his book;

> . . . this is not a 'book of travels', though it never could have been written if the author had not travelled in Palestine; for it is the result of the careful reading of the Gospels in the lights and shades of the land where Jesus lived and taught. When so read it is found that the land of Jesus so harmonizes with the four written Gospels, and so unfolds and enlarges their meaning, that it forms around them a Fifth Gospel. [*The Fifth Gospel: The Land Where Jesus Lived*, p. 5]

Otts draws the term from Renan's use of it in his Life of Jesus but he gives it a very different meaning because whereas Renan saw the Bible as a human story mistakenly made divine, Otts sees the Bible as a divine story made human and therefore fundamentally sacramental.

The purpose of the Bible like the Lord's Supper is to make Jesus come alive in hearts and imaginations and this is what the Holy Land can do, he feels, to those who approach in faith. Tweedie reiterates this common Protestant theme when he comments:

> A visit to the Land of Promise, so long the land of grief and oppressions, furnishes a thousand proofs and confirmations of the Bible. It is indeed a second Bible, all responsive to the first. [Tweedie, p. 102]

To the extent that the Bible stands at the centre of the Protestant faith as the primary vehicle of God's communication to His people, then the Holy Land as a revealer of the Bible and its meaning is itself a form of revelation making it a channel of grace - a sacrament. [Whether the Bible is the archetypal sacrament or whether Jesus is, is a theological dispute we will not address and into which our authors did not delve.] Not everyone can travel to the Holy Land, of course, and it is not necessary, in fact, because those who do so can communicate and preserve their experiences (just as the original disciples did) through books about the Holy Land and, eventually, photographic essays. These allowed others to come to know the Jesus who the Holy Land proclaims but whose true domain is in the hearts of believers. This is one explanation for the plethora of Holy Land books produced in English in the 19th century.

These Holy Land books were usually attempts to capture the ability of the Land to witness to Jesus and the Bible which had so impressed and captivated the traveller. Scenery was minutely described and correlated with the appropriate biblical text which it illustrated or vivified. Initially these had a few etchings or watercolours but with the development of photography in the mid-19th century it became common to supplement the text with pictures. It was only a short time before books like Thompson's *The Land and the Book* appeared which coordinated scenes from the Holy Land and biblical text so that a person could have the edifying effects of a pilgrimage in one's own living room. As stereoscopic prints were developed (with the appropriate biblical reference conveniently printed on the card) the realism of this home tour increased. Those pilgrims who actually visited Palestine also wanted to purchase pictures as souvenirs which gave birth to a burgeoning photographic business in Jerusalem. This began with foreign visitors like Firth but eventually a native studio is created by Yessayi Garabedian at the Armenian Convent. Later his student, Kirkorian, owned his own studio and the American Colony (a religious community in Jerusalem) started taking and selling souvenir photographs, albums, stereoscopes and postcards to tourists.

At the same time that the ability of the Holy Land to vivify the Bible and make it come imaginatively alive is viewed as sacramental, it is equally important for the Protestants to reject the idea of the Land having any intrinsic merit. One example of this is the Revd James Cuthbertson who waxes poetic on the sites and their moving quality and then seems obliged to say:

> I pay little attention to what men designate the value of identical places, for the good reason that no merit or moral value can belong to the place *per se*. The stupendous facts of the Death, the Resurrection, and the Ascension of Christ being for all times and all ages, their influence can be borne in upon the soul as well in one country as another. Men are to be saved, not by pilgrimages to some distant shrine, not by any

human efforts - the living, the Divine Christ alone can save from sin and future peril. [Cuthbertson, p. 61]

Here the doctrine of salvation by grace through faith alone seems to stand in tension with the Holy Land as a sacrament. But the tension is not so much resolved as the primacy of faith and the rejection of the merits of pilgrimage are tagged onto a description of the powerful nature of the Holy Land experience. This was the common solution.

The second theological function which the Holy Land served for Protestant pilgrims was to give renewed credence to the Bible as it came under attack from the corrosive effects of historical and scientific criticism. The majority of those visiting the Holy Land as faithful pilgrims were vague about the nature of the criticism being levelled against the Bible. It was not a specific intellectual problem or set of problems that concerned them but rather an uneasiness that old assumptions no longer stood so confidently against the powers of unbelief. Living as they did in the midst of a century where the 'Bible story' was being dissected into a whole host of different and often contending sources they felt their religious foundations shake as the *Zeitgeist* or the March of Mind seemed to threaten the Bible as the Word of God. In the increasingly industrialized, secularized and scientized West the Bible seemed to be losing its credibility. It spoke of miracles, it drew upon exotic and quaint characters and customs. The Bible was becoming increasingly marginalized from real life. To these people the Holy Land seemed to provide 'evidence' of the truth of the Bible because if 'read' properly the topography, the geography and the study of the customs of the area seemed to make the Bible sensible and therefore credible once again. It was not a specific response to specific attacks but a generalized feeling that because the imagery, customs and atmosphere of the Bible meshed so thoroughly with the Holy Land itself that it gave renewed confidence to those who did not want to accept the new sanitized and demythologized Bible being created in Western universities.

This argument that the Holy Land is an 'evidence' for the truth of the Bible and therefore Christianity is well framed by Otts in his *Fifth Gospel: The Land Where Jesus Lived.*

> Thus the well-informed and observant traveller in the land of the Bible will find more to confirm its truth and unfold its meaning while journeying through the land where Jesus lived, than he could ever gather from whole acres of printed evidences of Christianity. [p. 31]

This evidence for the truth of the Bible, however, unlike the evidential theology developed by John Locke, is not based upon logical argument but upon the persuasiveness of the experience of the Holy Land in relationship to the Bible story and the resonance created by the juxtaposition of the two. In this way it is part of the shedding of the Enlightenment's search for logical evidence and a turn to the more Romantic concern with experiential persuasion.

But there were a minority of pilgrims who were aware of the intricacies surrounding the discussion on the nature of the Bible and the type of truth it meant to convey. They had read Strauss' and Renan's *Life of Jesus*, they had read or read about the ideas of biblical interpretation promulgated in *Essays and Reviews*. For these people the collapse of the Jesus Christ of tradition, the Jesus of divine power (miracles) and prerogative (judge), created by historical criticism challenged them to return to the Jesus of Galilee, the man who stood behind the myth created by nineteen hundred years of obfuscating tradition. Owen Chadwick comments of these in *The Secularization of the European Mind*:

> For some religious men of the middle nineteenth century the 'discovery' of the historical Jesus gave a marvellous fresh food for their faith. They had known, or had hardly known, a remote figure of ritual, and now perceived the humanity at last. They felt they could begin where the apostles began – come to a man because he was such a man, and then slowly find conviction that more was in him than men. [Chadwick, p. 226]

Well, what better place to begin this search for the 'historical' Jesus than in the Land of Jesus – this same sentiment we have already seen expressed by Kelman when he said: 'It is wiser to abandon the attempt at forcing the supernatural to reveal itself, and to turn to the human side of things as the surest way ultimately arriving at the divine.' [Kelman p. 3] The Holy Land was, therefore, for some not only a way to get behind the Jesus of the Church but also to get behind the Jesus of the Bible to the historical Jesus and confront him personally (as the disciples did) and out of this personal relationship rediscover the Jesus of faith.

The Orthodox accused the Protestants of wanting to worship the historical Jesus and leaving behind the divine Jesus – the Logos of God. This heresy they felt stood behind the Protestant rejection of the Orthodox iconography which encased the sacred sites. Those icons, the Orthodox felt, made clear that it was not the acts of a human Jesus which made the place special but that in those acts God was manifesting Himself in a unique way.

The English Protestants, however, were operating from another image of Jesus, one which had taken root in Anglicanism and became a major focus in 19th century theology, hymns and devotion. For these Protestants Jesus was the man who had lived on earth, experienced life as a real human being with its temptations, anxieties and fears but was and is also at one with God. This Jesus is truly human and therefore can sympathize with the human condition but he is also at one with God and serves as the Great High Priest who pleads our cause. As J B Sumner, later Archbishop of Canterbury, wrote in a sermon 'On the Person and Offices of Christ', 'He is God with power to save: He is Man, with tenderness to pity: he has loved you, as no man ever loved his nearest friend, he is with you, to strengthen your faith, he is with God, to intercede for your transgressions.' [Sumner, *Sermons on the Principal Feasts of the Christian Church*, p. 123, quoted from a yet unpublished article 'The Priestly Christ of Anglican Hymnody: A Forgotten Perspective' by Christopher Hancock]

This image of Christ as the Great High Priest taken from Hebrews explained the ability of the Protestants to focus on the historical Jesus without losing the uniqueness of his divinity which made him a saviour. It also explained the failure of those Protestants to feel any need for any other immediate or sympathetic intercessors, either saints or Mary. Jesus was the Great High Priest in heaven but he was also present in faith - transcendent but imminent. This Christology seems to stand behind the English Protestant search for the historical Jesus. (For further elaboration on the theme see Hancock's article.)

For others the significance of the Holy Land was in the ability of its geography to open up the Bible to a deeper understanding of its meaning. These pilgrims felt there was an interaction between geography and Bible which like the symbiotic relationship between history and the Bible, and science and the Bible could deepen the faith rather than destroying it. Dean Stanley, the famous biographer of Thomas Arnold, was such a personage. A leading figure of the Broad Church faction his preface to Sinai and Palestine argued that although it is easy to exaggerate the significance of the relationship of the Sacred History and the geography of the Holy Land it is, if properly used, a fruitful one. He goes on to enumerate six specific ways that the connection can be helpfully employed.

In all cultures history is influenced by geography so the geography of the Holy Land helps explain the biblical culture and therefore the Bible itself. Secondly, the geography is bound to effect the images which a culture's poets and philosophers will use, so knowing the land will be useful in elucidating their thought. One example of this is the new appreciation of such passages as 'The shadow of a great rock in a weary land' [Isaiah 22: 2] after seeking the cool shade even of a rock in the boiling heat of Palestine. [Cuthbertson, p. 129] Third, the geography can be used to explain specific actions such as why Jesus went to certain towns (the road network) or battles were conducted in certain ways (the topography of the battlefield). Fourth, the coincidence of biblical narrative and geography provides a presumption or evidence of it fundamental truthfulness.

It is impossible not to be struck by the constant agreement between recorded history and the natural geography both of the Old and New Testament. To find a marked correspondence between the scenes of the Sinaitic mountains and the events of the Israelite wanderings is not much perhaps, but it is certainly something towards a proof of the truth of the whole narrative. To meet Gospel allusions, transient but yet precise, to the localities of their early origin. Such coincidences are not usually found in fable of Easter origin. [p. xix-xx]

Fifth, beyond the real connection between the Bible and the Land rests the ability of the places, especially the landscape, to vivify the biblical story because 'the framework of life, of customs, of manners, even of dress and speech, is still substantially the same as it was ages ago.' [p. xxiv] Finally, 'the whole journey, as it is usually taken by modern travellers, presents the course of history as a living parable before us, to which no other journey or pilgrimage can present any parallel.' [p. xxvi] Here he means that a pilgrimage allows the Bible to be seen as a sacred history or drama rather than a set of proof texts. A drama or holy history where God is not the history itself but revealed through it. This would accord with the approach Thomas Arnold took to the Old Testament. For Stanley the ability of the Holy Land to re-present the Bible stories (the sacramental) and the evidential nature of the coincidence of land and text are combined with other factors to underline the value of a pilgrimage for English Protestants. So these six factors collectively give the Holy Land a special appeal and provide an argument for Christianity's truth, a position reinforced during his second visit when he accompanied the Prince of Wales to the Holy Sites.

Besides the theological significance of the Holy Land as the revealer of Jesus (sacramental) and its function as evidence of the truthfulness of the Bible it was also seen as witnessing to the superiority of Western culture and the Protestant religion. Almost all the English commentators who wrote about the Holy Land in the 19th century saw it as a land which was cursed. The physical manifestation of this curse was seen in the desolation of the land, especially in the decay of a once fertile land into scrub and desert, and in the diseased populace, suffering from not just physical disease but from economic, political and spiritual disease as well. The reason for this curse was again almost universally identified with the consequences of rejecting the overtures of God.

> The incompleteness of Syria [Holy Land] - the thing in which her life has been most lamentably unfinished - was her response to the revelation of her God. She never was at pains to understand it; she never fully opened her heart to its new progress, nor felt her high destiny as the bearer of good tidings to the world. She never seriously set herself to obey its plainest ethical demands. The wreckage is her price paid for the neglect. No man nor nation can finish any task to perfection, who has not done justice to such revelation of God as his heart and conscience have received . . . Right dealing with revelation is the secret of all efficient performance. [Kelman, p. 203]

The rejection of Jesus and God's condemnation of Israel leading to the destruction of the Temple and the exile of the Jews reinforced by the Islamic conquests and its rejection of the finality of the Gospel were all interpreted as bringing about a curse on the land and its people.

And so the 'Land of Milk and Honey' was transformed into the land of death.

> Never was symbolism more appropriate than that of the Holy Fire in the Church of the Holy Sepulchre. The very heart and soul of [the Holy Land] is a tomb - the reputed grave of Jesus Christ. To this day the chief pilgrim song repeats with exultant reiteration the words, 'This is the Tomb of Christ.' . . . It is not, however, the victory over death that impresses one as the spirit of [the Holy Land]. It is death itself, unconquered, mysterious, and dark. [Kelman, p. 228-9]

This theme of a land cursed because it has rejected God's revelation is supported by comparing the cities of Hebron and Bethlehem. The first is an Islamic town and as such despite an outward appearance of thriving fields is a place as 'stagnant as a deserted pond . . . It is moribund with a vengeance! The sullenness of people you meet on the road give a token of its spirit before you enter . . . Women draw aside their veils to curse us as we passed. Stones flung by unseen hands behind walls.' [Kelman, p. 233] Bethlehem is a different story. As Conder comments in *Tent Works*, 'Christian villages thrive and grow, while the Moslem ones fall into decay.' [p. 314] Bethlehem represent 'the contrast between Christianity and Islam, between the vitality of the religion of progress and civilization, and the hopeless stagnation of a fatalistic creed.' [p. 314] Often, as these extracts show, the characteristics that breed sloth and dishonesty are seen as being encouraged by Islam, especially the idea of fatalism.

With the theme of the 'cursed land' the theological concern with evidences for the truth of Christianity and by extension the falsity of Judaism and Islam begins to become transformed into a more overtly political concern. It is not merely that the condition of Palestine shows its denial of God but that to turn to pure Christianity, that is English Protestantism, can mean a revival of the land. The theological point transforms itself into an imperialistic one.

As the English visitor compared Palestine under the Turks with those parts of the Orient which they controlled, especially Egypt, they felt that they had sufficient evidence that British rule brought not only economic prosperity but 'freedom' to the native populations. That is freedom from the political tyranny of the Ottoman empire and its rapacious taxes, freedom from the caprice of local governor, freedom from a corrupt bureaucracy, freedom from an enslaved judiciary, and cultural freedom for the persecuted minorities, especially Jews and Christians. For many English pilgrims the foundation of their own society with its obvious political, economic and moral success and therefore the instrument for lifting the curse from Palestine was the Protestant Church. It was hoped and expected that the Protestant Church of England through its mission churches, hospitals and schools would change the face of Palestine. This would be accomplished by educating the next generation in Western (Protestant) political, social and religious values. Once they had culturally 'converted' the native population the next step would be obvious - British rule. Bishop Hannington during his visit in 1884 stopped at a Druze village with an English mission school. There he was told by the local sheikhs that 'the topic which is nearest to their hearts is English occupation' in order to drive out the Turks and bring real civilization. Kelman also saw the expansion of Western technology such as the telegraph and railroads along with the expansion of trade and tourism and the economic prosperity it brings as essential but warns that the real salvation of Palestine will reside not in technology but in faith.

> Interesting and important as all this advance of Western progress is, it is not from it that the resurrection of the Holy Land must be expected. There, as elsewhere, the chief danger of the present time is that of godless civilization, whose purely secular and materialistic prosperity may prove to be more of a curse than a blessing after all. [Kelman, p. 290]

So the real hope of Palestine lies in its religious conversion to the Protestant faith from which all sorts of material blessings as well as spiritual ones will flow. Then the landscape itself will be transformed. Where there are deserts and deserted villages trees and crops will grow again and the land like the people will be redeemed. Eustace Martin, a pilgrim who published his *Visit to the Holy Land, Syria and Constantinople* in 1883 sums up this attitude:

> The whole legislative wisdom of the British people is, I believe, in every land honoured, the activity of commerce, their respect for and support of public order, the sense of duty which is insensible to danger, their civil and religious freedom, their enterprise and industry; I believe that all those qualities and natural characteristics have sprung from and been developed by the teaching of the Bible. It is the great book of reform. [Martin, p. 104]

Reform in religion will therefore lead to reform in social, political, and economic conditions and that in turn will redeem the land.

This quasi-messianic role for Britain had a great deal to do with the willingness of Britain to exert time and energy to bring about the 'liberation' of Palestine during the First World War and its fascination with their role as occupiers. The idea that with religious and political redemption the land would return to a fruitful and forested state also helps explain the West's glorification of Israel's re-forestation and making the desert bloom projects. Here the 19th century ideal of the West redeeming the fallen Holy Land was being realized even if by the very people whose denial of Jesus was blamed for its decline into misery. But by then for many people the line between religion and culture was not very clear and as the imperialism of Christianity waned with the expansion of secularism the imperialism of Western culture continued unabated.

The interconnection of the religious and the imperialistic ideals of the 19th century Protestants was not unique of course. The Russians, during that same period, provided assistance and support to its many pilgrims with a similar combination of religion and politics. In our own time the state of Israel encourages the pilgrimage to Jerusalem of large numbers of American Jewish teenagers with an obvious political component. These real political considerations, however, should not blind us to the significant shift in Protestant attitudes towards pilgrimage to the Holy Land which takes place during the 19th century and the set of strongly Protestant theological attitudes which are used to justify the enterprise. These are: 1) the ability of the Holy Land to act as a sacrament in the sense of re-presenting the Biblical story; 2) the experiential evidencing of the truthfulness of the Bible produced by visiting the Land of the Book; 3) the quest for the human Jesus of the Bible based upon the Christology of Jesus as the Great High Priest; and 4) the illumination of the Bible which a thorough study of the geography of the Holy Land would bestow upon those who undertook the task. Behind all of these theological justifications stands the Reformation principle of *sola scriptura*. What makes the Holy Land special to the Protestants is its connection with the Bible, it is where Protestant pilgrimage begins and its end is to make that Bible come alive back in the drawing rooms of England.

Bibliography

Baggley, John. *Doors of Perception: Icons and Their Spiritual Significance*, London: 1987.

Bartlett, W H. *Walks About The City and Environs of Jerusalem*, London: 1844.

Bell, Revd Charles D. *Gleanings From a Tour in Palestine and The East*, London: 1883.

Brendon, Piers. *Thomas Cook: 150 Years of Popular Tourism*, London: 1991.

Brinton, John. *Tour in Palestine and Syria*, London: 1893.

Carradine, Revd Beverly. *A Journey to Palestine*, St Louis: 1891.

Charley, Sir Charles. *The Holy City*, London: 1902.

Clark, Francis and Harriet. *Our Journey Around The World*, Hartford: 1895.

Condor, *Tent Works*, London: 1878.

Crombie, Kelvin. *For the Love of Zion,* London: 1991.

Cunningham, James. *Pilgrims in Palestine*, Edinburgh: 1905.

Cuthbertson, James. *Sacred and Historic Lands*, London: 1855.

Davies, J G. *Pilgrimage Yesterday and Today*, London: 1988.

Durbin, John. *Observations in The East*, New York: 1845.

Gadsby, John. *My Wanderings: Being Travels in The East in 1846-47, 1850-51, 1852-53*, London: 1881.

Gray, Andrew. *A Pilgrimage to Bible Lands*, London: 1903.

Hannington, James. *The Last Journals of Bishop James Hannington*, edited by E.C. Dawson, London: 1888.

Hertslet, Reginald. *Jerusalem and the Holy Land in 1882*, London: 1883.

Hopwood, Derick. *Russian Presence in Syria and Palestine: 1843-1914*, Oxford: 1969.

Jowett, William. *Christian Researches in Syria and the Holy Land*, London: 1825.

Kabbani, Rana. *Europe's Myths of Orient*, London: 1986.

Keith, Alexander. *Evidence of The Truth of The Christian Religion, Derived From the Literal Fulfilment of Prophecy; Particularly as Illustrated By the History of the Jews, and By The Discoveries of Recent Travellers*, Edinburgh: 1832.

Kelman, John. *The Holy Land*, London: 1904.

King, Mrs. *Dr Liddon's Tour in Egypt and Palestine in 1886*, London: 1891

Kushner, David (ed.). *Palestine in the Late Ottoman Period*, Jerusalem: 1986

Leach, Charles, MP. *The Romance of the Holy Land*, London: 1911.

Leighton, William H. *A Cook's Tour to the Holy Land in 1874*, London: 1947

Lent, William. *Holy Land From Landau, Saddle and Palanquin*, New York: 1899.

Luke, Henry Charles. *Ceremonies at the Holy Places*, London: 1932.

Martin, Eustace M. *A Visit to the Holy Land, Syria and Constantinople*, London: 1883.

Meen, Joseph. *Geography of Palestine*, London: 1860.

Miller, William. *The Least of All Lands*, London: 1888.

Neil, C Lang. *Rambles in Bible Lands*, London: 1905.

Neil, Henry. *Neil's Photographs of the Holy Land*, Philadelphia: 1893.

Neil, Revd James. *Palestine Explored*, London: 1882.

Olin, Revd Stephen. *Travels in Egypt, Arabia, Petra, and the Holy Land*, New York: 1843.

Osborn, Revd Henry. *The Pilgrim in the Holy Land*, London: 1860.

Otts, J M P. *The Fifth Gospel: The Land Where Jesus Lived*, London: 1893.

Ousterhout, Robert (ed.). *The Blessings of Pilgrimage*, Urbana: 1990.

Paxton, Revd J D. *Letters from Palestine*, London: 1839.

Ridgway, Revd James. *Sketches From the East: Illustrating Church Doctrine and Practice*, Oxford: 1893.

Schaff, Philip. *Through Bible Lands*, London: 1889.

Shaffer, E S. '*Kubla Khan' and the Fall of Jerusalem: The Mythological School in Biblical Criticism and Secular Literature 1770-1880*, Cambridge: 1975.

Shepherd, Naomi. *The Zealous Intruders: The Western Rediscovery of Palestine*, London: 1987.

Stanley, A P. *Sinai and Palestine*, London: 1910.

Taylor, Bayard. *The Land of the Saracen*, New York: 1857.

Thomas, Revd Joseph. *Oxford to Palestine*, London: 1890.

Thomson, W M. *The Land and the Book*, London: 1870.

Tibawi, A L. *British Interests in Palestine: 1800-1901*, Oxford: 1961.

Treves, Sir Frederick. *The Land That is Desolate: An Account of a Tour in Palestine*, London: 1913.

Tuchman, Barbara. *Bible and Sword*, New York: 1956.

Turner, Victor and Edith. *Image and Pilgrimage in Christian Culture*, Oxford: 1978.

Tweedie, Revd W K. *Jerusalem and Its Environs*, London: 1873.

Warburton, Eliot. *The Crescent and the Cross*, London: 1845.

Warner, Charles Dudley. *In the Levant*, Boston: 1877.

Wilken, Robert L. *The Land Called Holy*, New Haven: 1992.

12
Culture and Image: Christians and the Beginnings of Local Photography in 19th Century Ottoman Palestine
Ruth Victor-Hummel

The heightened political, scientific, archaeological and religious interest in the Holy Land in the nineteenth century found an ally in the burgeoning technology of photography. The first daguerreotypes produced outside of Europe were taken in the Middle East in 1839 by Frederic Goupil-Fesquet and the painter Horace Vernet.[1] In 1849 the French Ministry of Education sent Maxime Du Camp accompanied by Gustave Flaubert to photograph sites in the Holy land and Egypt. Their efforts published in 1851 as *Egypt, Nubie, Palestine et Syrie* contained 125 photographic prints.[2] This was a milestone in the history of photography and printing for it was one of the first major publications with original photographs. The West, captive to the relentless currents of social and political dislocations flowing from the urbanization and mechanization of the Industrial Revolution, looked at the Orient and a pre-industrial Holy Land with romantic eyes.

It was the epitome of nineteenth century technology, the ever evolving photographic process, which provided the West the means to impose its images on the Middle East. The political opening of the Holy Land in 1830 under Muhammed Ali and his son, Ibrahim Pasha, and the initiating of the Tanzimat reforms in 1839 made it possible for Westerners to penetrate more easily and safely in the biblical lands; for example, the following consulates were established in Jerusalem – British (1838), Prussian (1842), French (1843), USA (1844), Austrian (1845), Russian (1858). Organizations were founded to promote scholarly interest in the Orient (Société Asiatique in 1842, Royal Asiatic Society in 1823 and the

---

[1] *Excursions Daguerriennes -vues et monuments les remarquables du globe*, Paris, Lerebours, 1842.
[2] Maxime Du Camp, *Egypte, Nubie, Palestine et Syrie*, Paris, Gide et Baudry, 1851.

American Oriental Society in 1842). And so they came – the missionaries, artists, explorers, writers, politicians and tourists, each with their own agenda.

We will discuss how the local populations of the Ottoman Empire received this new technology, why the Christians in the Empire were the first to embrace photography and then use Yessayi Garabedian, a pioneer of Jerusalem photography, as a case study to elucidate how photography was transmitted to and through the Christians in the Holy Land.

There has been much discussion about the anti-iconic attitudes of the native Muslim and Jewish population of the Ottoman Empire (see Nir, Perez, Cizgen, Gavin). Although The Quran does not explicitly prohibit the making of images but only their worship, there are some *hadiths* which condemn the creators of images to the pains of hell.[3] And, of course, representational art is not usually found within a mosque or a synagogue.

But the Ottoman sultans quickly embraced and exploited the new technology. When Sultan Abdulaziz visited Europe in 1863 he brought photographs of himself taken by the Abdullahian Frères as gifts to the monarchs of Europe. And in 1893 and 1894 Abdul Hamid presented to the Library of Congress and the British Museum fifty-one albums containing 1,819 photographs intended to convey the natural beauty, the architectural heritage and the modern innovative nature of Turkish institutions. Carney Gavin writes that these albums, 'as sent abroad must be acknowledged as the first comprehensive visual report formally dispatched by the Islamic world to humanity at large – and thereby as a uniquely significant event.'[4]

Hundreds of additional photographic albums survived the ransacking of Yildiz Palace where Adbul Hamid created a photographic studio for his personal use and enjoyment. So here are Sunni sultans being photographed for the edification of their subjects, taking photographs themselves and using photographs as imperial propaganda in the West.

So we need to continue to search for reasons why the Muslim (and the Jewish) inhabitants of the Holy Land did not embrace this new technology. An experience of mine in 1987 mirrors a story cited by Nir and suggests various motives for a 'rejection' of being photographed. In the late 1890s in Ain Balatah F M Deverell terrified a young girl carrying a baby on her back when he tried to photograph her. Deverell mused that it was concern for

---

[3] Engin Cizgen, *Photography in the Ottoman Empire, 1839-1919*, Istanbul, Haset Kitabevi AS, 1987, 15. Cizgen quotes from *Sahih -i Buhari Muhtesari, Tecrid-i Sarih*, book 6, to illustrate that The Qur'an prohibits the worship of pictures but it is the *hadiths* which condemn the creators of life-size images. 'Aisha, wife of the prophet Muhammad, speaks:
Once I bought him a pillow. It was adorned with pictures of animals. When our Prophet saw it, he stood at the door refusing to come in. That moment I felt anger on his face. I said, 'O Prophet of God, let me ask forgiveness of God and of you, but I do not know what my fault is!' Muhammed said, 'What is this pillow doing here?' When I said 'O Muhammed, I bought it for you to sit on.' Muhammed replied, 'The makers of this will surely find pain on the Day of Judgment and they will be asked to give life to animals.'

[4] Carney Gavin (ed.), *Imperial Self-Portrait: The Ottoman Empire as revealed in The Sultan Abdul-Hamid II's Photographic Albums*, Cambridge, Harvard University, 1989, 5.

the baby that caused the girl to shun his camera.[5] When my colleague, a sociologist from Baltimore, approached a young woman holding an infant in her arms outside her village in a remote corner of Baluchistan in southern Pakistan, she quickly covered herself and the child with her shawl and started to run away from him. He immediately interpreted her actions as fear of his camera which he had lifted up to indicate his desire to take her picture. But when I appeared over the horizon she stopped, smiled and uncovered the baby so I could admire his handsome features. When I tentatively pointed to my camera she laughed demurely, then signalled her acquiescence to my request (to the surprise of my companion). Perhaps Deverell and my colleague underestimated the effect of their male presence on the local standard of female modesty.

The earliest photographers assumed that any resistance of the native population to being photographed stemmed from anti-iconic restrictions or superstition (spirit or soul snatching). But tradition and local custom perhaps played an even more important role. Even though strict injunctions against image making existed in Judaism, Jews allowed themselves not only to be photographed but patronized local photographers in Jerusalem.[6] The reaction of the Muslim and Jewish population of the Holy Land to the new technology from the West most probably was driven by a complex array of local traditions and customs re-enforced by anti-iconic attitudes.

So why did the Christians of the Ottoman Empire and the Holy Land embrace photography? Three factors seem crucial: 1) Christians possessed the skills necessary for the mastery of early photography, 2) they had easy access to the essential chemical and material elements of the technology, 3) they were encouraged by their community leaders to exploit photography both for cultural and economic reasons.

The pioneers of photography in Europe were artists, painters, engravers, chemists, or scientists (or a combination of several of these metiers). This is not surprising since great technical expertise was required in order to produce a photograph or to experiment with the technology.[7] Examining one phase of the wet collodion process exemplifies the special skills required to be a successful early photographer.

In 1851 the wet collodion process produced such sharp clear negatives that it quickly superseded the calotype negative process. This new process required glass plates which needed to be coated with silver salts in a collodion solution of alcohol, ether, guncotton (cotton and the potentially explosive nitric acid). While still wet the glass negative was exposed and the latent image was immediately developed before the emulsion had time to dry. Photographers jealously guarded these collodion recipes which

---

[5] Yeshayahu Nir, *The Bible and the Image: The History of Photography in the Holy Land, 1839-1899*, Philadelphia, University of Pennsylvania Press, 1985, 177.

[6] *Ibid.*, 131.

[7] No only was expertise in the mixing of chemical compounds necessary to the first photographers but also the fine skill of an artist for the colouring and altering photographs.

required skill, portable darkrooms and impeccable timing.

The Greeks and Armenians were well-known throughout the Ottoman Empire for their skills in metallurgy, paper manufacture, dyeing and pharmacology (for example, the Dadian family who controlled the arsenals of the Ottoman sultans). These talents and skills easily transferred to photographic expertise especially when coupled with the tradition of sending Christian craftsman to Constantinople or Europe for additional training where they were exposed to the latest techniques.

Internal trade within the Ottoman Empire was regulated by the Muslim guilds but the foreign trade was primarily in the hands of European merchants. The capitulations which ceded enormous economic advantage to the Western powers enabled the European commercial and consular agents to import photographic equipment and chemical elements at very low custom duties – duties prohibitive to the Muslim population. Because of their cultivated linguistic prowess the native Christians served as the dragomen, honorary consuls or vice-consuls for the European powers. So they too could import goods at the lower custom duties.

The long tradition of pilgrimage to the Holy Land has always provided the local Christians with economic rewards. Pilgrims had always wanted *objets de piété*, religious souvenirs to verify their spiritual and physical journey to those in their city or village. Tattoos on the arm recording the year of pilgrimage above the Jerusalem cross were a permanent certification of the journey. Now photography provided new souvenirs, new witnesses to the veracity to the pilgrim's sojourn. As we shall see, the clergy understood the need of the pilgrim and the potential of the new technology.

By investigating the career of Yessayi Garabedian, Armenian patriach of Jerusalem from 1865-1885, a pioneer of local photography and the creator of the first Jerusalem photographic studio, we can chart how this new technology was introduced and flourished in the Holy Land.

Born in 1825 in Talas outside of Kayseri in central Anatolia, Garabedian soon earned the sobriquet 'Ouzounian', the tall one. Charles Dudley during a visit to the Armenian patriachate in 1875 affirms the validity of the epithet in his book *In the Levant*:

> He is probably the handsomest potentate in the world. He is tall, finely proportioned man of fifty years. He was clad in black cloak with the pointed hood of the convent which made a fine contrast to his long full beard turning white, his complexion is fair, white and red and his eyes are remarkably pleasant and benignant.[8]

In 1840 Yessayi was sent to Constantinople to study carpentry in one of the *esnafs*, Armenian craft guilds. An apprenticeship in an *esnaf* was

---

[8] Charles Dudley Warner, *In the Levant*, 5th ed., Boston, James P Osgood, 1877, 141-442.

common practice for Armenians living outside the urban centres of the Ottoman Empire. His early predilection for working with his hands would manifest itself throughout his life in his calligraphy then his passionate experimentation with galvanization and photography techniques.

When he was nineteen, Yessayi travelled to Jerusalem to begin his theological studies in Jerusalem where he was placed with David Vartabed to prepare for the priesthood there being no seminary at this time. It was not long before Yessayi's strong, perhaps stubborn, will brought him into conflict with David and provoked Patriarch Kriakos to relegate him for his disobedience to candle-making for the Holy Sepulchre. But in 1848 he was sufficiently in the good graces of the patriach that he was sent to Constantinople for six months and ordained priest on the Feast of the Holy Cross in 1851.

Soon after his ordination Yessayi wrote to the Armenian National Council in Constantinople requesting the establishment of a seminary, museum and a reform of the printing press. Unfortunately he had not informed John, the new patriach, of his letter which lead to his suspension from priestly duties for three months. But he quickly convinced the patriach of his genuine concern for the Armenian Community in Jerusalem and he was not only forgiven by him but empowered to create a seminary, museum and re-organize the printing press.[9]

The patriach's confidence unleashed Yessayi's energy and gargantuan appetite for experimentation. For the museum the young priest classified and catalogued 1,400 manuscripts clearly giving evidence of the beauty of his calligraphy and the dexterity of his hands. Inspired by the work of the Franciscans of San Saviour he experimented with galvanization processes which greatly frustrated him but the lessons learned he quickly transferred to his printing press.[10]

During this time (1855 to 1857) James Barclay, a physician and missionary from Virginia and James Graham lay secretary of the London Jews Society lived and worked in Jerusalem. Barclay assisted the Muslim architect renovating the Dome of the Rock and he himself discovered a sealed gate in the south wall of the Haram, which became known as Barclay's Arch or Gate. On his return to America he published *The City of the King* which included engravings from photographs he took in the Holy Land. James Graham, also an amateur photographer, inducted Diness, a converted Jew, into the mysteries of photography.[11] We are not certain about Yessayi's contact with either of these men but it is important to know that these resident foreign photographers were working in Jerusalem for in his autobiography he writes about his fascination in 1857 for this new *arhest*:

---

[9] Yessayi Garabedian, *Autobiography* (published in the journal *Sion*), Jerusalem, St James Press, 1938, 45.

[10] *Ibid.*

[11] Carney Gavin, *Capturing the Holy Land*, Cambridge, Harvard University Press, 1993, 18.

> He [Yessayi] wants to follow the craft [*arhest*] of photography
> with the intention to familiarize the nation [Armenians] with
> the Holy Places through photographs and, after some time to
> photograph all the antiquities and monuments of Armenia.
> This I consider a patriotic act.[12]

Yessayi referred to photography as *arhest* instead of using the Armenian word for art, *arvest*.[13] Although the two words are closely related Yessayi himself regarded photography as a demanding craft requiring extensive training and experimentation. He understood the potential power of the photograph to preserve a heritage not just to produce an *objet de piété* and had already experimented and succeeded in photographing portraits and scenes.[14] Fired with his passion to pursue the *areva-nekar*, Armenian for 'sun-picture', he beseeched Patriarch John's acquiescence to his request to study the craft of photography in Constantinople. Permission granted, he spent six months pursuing the 'craft' with urban practitioners including Vortik Aga son of the chief court carpenter and Nerse Bey Dadian of the famous Armenian family who controlled Ottoman munitions.[15] It is interesting to note that both had expertise in the manual and technical skills which necessary for photographers at the time.

Yessayi returned to Jerusalem shortly before the death of his benefactor, Patriarch John, in December 1860 after which he was promptly elected one of the members of the seven-man Holy Synod.

Three *vartabed* were candidates for patriach – Sahak, Hagop and Yessayi. After a letter arrived from Constantinople from the Armenian Council of Deputies asking him to be patriach, Yessayi not only declined the offer but removed his name from the list of candidates by using the pretext that it was necessary for him to perfect his craft of photography. In fact Hovahannes Spartalian of Smryna, who had met Yessayi on his pilgrimage to Jerusalem, offered to pay his expenses to Europe.[16]

So in April of 1863 Yessayi set out for Manchester where he studied his beloved craft with Armenian compatriots for three months before setting out for a two month stay in Paris.[17]

In the French capital he again found and learned from the local Armenian photographers what he desired to know – 'after much hard work I learned and acquired the technique of making stereoscopes.'[18] And

---

[12] Garabedian, 46.

[13] Dickinson J. Miller, 'The Craftsman's Art: Armenians and the Growth of a Photographic Tradition in the Near East, 1856-1914', MA thesis American University of Beirut, 1982, 6.

[14] Tigran Savalanian, *History of Jerusalem*, vol II, Jerusalem, St James Press, 1931, 1135.

[15] Garabedian, 46.

[16] *Ibid.*, 46.

[17] Bishop Moushegh Seropian, *The Armenian Community of Manchester*, Boston, Publishing House 'Azk', 1911, 30-31.

[18] Yessayi Garabedian, 'Photographic Manuals' (Published in *The Grand Catalogue of St James Manuscripts*, vol. VIII, Archbishop Norayr Bogharian, ed. Jerusalem, St James Press) Ms. 2773, 45.

through his sponsor Spartalian he bought all the instruments and technical equipment he needed for Jerusalem.

Albert Rhodes, American consul in Jerusalem from 1863-65, gives us an informative account of his visit with Yessayi in 1863:

> I was afterwards conducted into the library of the convent and made acquainted with the monk Isaiah [Yessayi], the librarian, who was the only inmate of the convent, who had been as far west as Paris and London. He appeared to be a good-natured unpresuming monk. He showed me some manuscript – books made in the 11th century, in which the writing, and especially the decorations around the margin, were skilfully executed. He had studied photography in London, and had a little gallery with an apparatus, on the top of the convent, where he took pictures. He appeared to be very fond of photography, and gave me a *carte-de-visite* portrait of himself.

This presentation of a photograph of himself to guests would become a familiar gesture. Rhodes continues:

> The unpretending monk Isaiah, a short time afterwards, doubtless much to his own astonishment, was elected to the patriarchate of Jerusalem by the synod in Constantinople, when he was obliged to give up his cherished photography as inconsistent with his newly-acquired dignity.[19]

In 1864 Yessayi did become patriach much against his own desires but he did not abandon his beloved 'craft'.[20] On his return from his installation in Echmiadzin he spent several months in Constantinople where he again sought out Armenian photographic expertise. Here he met the legendary Abdullahian Frères whom Sultan Abdulaziz in 1863 had proclaimed official court photographers. In 1858 the brothers (Kevork, Vichen and Hovsep) had purchased the photographic studio created by the German chemist Rabach during the Crimean War.

The brothers' backgrounds was well-suited to Rabach's studio and photography. Kevork spent six years studying art at the Mourad Raphaelian School in Venice and Vichen was renowned as an outstanding miniature artist which made his ability to retouch images a valuable asset in Rabach's studio.[21] Yessayi valued their knowledge and insights into the secrets of new technology. In his manuals of photography he recorded:

---

[19] Albert Rhodes, *Jerusalem As It Is*, London, Maxwell, 1965, 101-102.
[20] Savalanian, who did not share Yessayi's love of photography, writes that 'the patriarchal scepter was hardly capable of snatching from his hands his craft and instruments.' In Tigran Savalanian, *Biographical Memories*, Cairo, Tarpenian, 1900, 120.
[21] Miller, 14.

> In Istanbul Abdullahian taught me a method. He taught me in writing then he came to my office in Yerusaghematin [residence of the delegate of the Armenian patriach of Jerusalem][22]

The sharing of technical information involved a great sense of trust and commitment between mentor and student. In the same manual he preserves a letter sent to him in 1865 by Vichen Abdullahian:

> We are confident of your absolute secrecy [the recipe for preparing borax had just been revealed]. We hope that you will be prudent and not jeopardize our interests on any occasion.[23]

Immediately upon his return to Jerusalem as patriach, Yessayi set out to create a school of photography in the Armenian Convent of St James.[24] This was a time when photography demanded journeys on horseback and donkeys carrying all the bulky cumbersome necessaries of the portable darkroom. Patriachs could not be seen on the Mount of Olives or other public venues with their heads covered and buried under the black cloth which was an extension of the camera. So Yessayi assembled around him apprentices from the urban centres and hinterland of the Ottoman Empire. He created his photographic manuals to assure the progress of his recruits and pass on his hard-won technical expertise:

> I wrote this manuscript not as a pretence to men or as self-praise, but as an example and an encouragement for artisans and novices who after trying many times despair and give-up, so they lose the fruits of their hard work and they lose as well the future benefits. One triumphs if one perseveres with determination, this has been true for me most of the time.[25]

Yessayi's chief disciples were Deacon Garabed Krikorian and Ezekiel Vartabed Kevorkian both from Smyrna. They eventually left the ranks of the clergy to pursue their own passion for photography but not before they

---

[22] Yessayi Garabedian, *Manuals*, ms. 2775, 109.

[23] *Ibid.*, 121.

[24] Archbishop Malachia Ormanian, *Azkapatoum*, Jerusalem, St James Press, 1927, 4208:
For the purpose of the craft [photography] he stayed in Constantinople for four months afterhis consecration in Echmiadzin. When he reached Jerusalem he embarked on developing photography and on the roof of St Theodosius [St Thoros] he built an atelier for photography while in the patriarchate he had a special room for galvanization. And all his attention he turned to perfecting and being productive in these crafts.
Yessayi was also engaged in reforming and improving the seminary, printing press and museum upon his return to Jerusalem.

[25] Garabedian, *Manuals*, ms.2775, 155.

and Yessayi trained a number of Armenians from Jerusalem and others who returned to their own towns and cities to practice their newly-acquired craft.[26] Amongst the most notable were the Stepanian brothers from Talas, the Tutundjian brothers from Kharpert, the Soursourian brothers also from Khapert and Garabed Yazedjian of Jerusalem.

Krikorian, himself, is a good example of how photographic knowledge was transmitted. After leaving the deaconry in 1885 and marrying Carimeh, a Lebanese deaconess of the Lutheran Church, Garabed Krikorian set up his own photographic studio in Jerusalem. When Kaiser Wilhelm II visited the Holy City in 1898, Krikorian extensively photographed the royal entourage and began to use 'Königl. Preuss. Hof-Photograph' (the Prussian Emperor's Court Photographer) on his colophon. Following the tradition of studying abroad, one of his three sons pursued photography in Cologne. And another son, Jean, married the niece of Khalil Raad an Arab who apprenticed with Krikorian. A rift had developed between the Krikorian and Raad over the issue of whether Raad should open his own photographic atelier. The marriage in 1915 brought peace to both men and their ateliers.[27]

From 1865 to 1885 Yessayi's workshop flourished as thousands of pilgrims and locals passed through the portal of the Convent of St James in order to record their images. The pilgrims desired to capture the triumph of their journey to the Holy Land to send to relatives abroad or to carry home. Most of the surviving images are of the *carte-de-visite* (2 x 3in) or cabinet (4 x 5in) size which were so popular in Western Europe in the latter half of the 19th century. Both sizes were convenient to send to loved ones or to serve as small tokens of appreciation to a gracious host or gifts to a welcomed guest as this 1882 encounter between Henry Field and Yessayi illustrates:

> He [Yessayi] seemed to wish to keep me in memory, by requesting my photograph, which of course I blushingly declined. Dr Post [of the Syrian College in Beirut], however, appropriated it, and sent it to him; and he returned the compliment by sending me his own handsome face, with his autograph . . .[28]

But the workshop also sold panoramas, prints and stereoscopic photographs of the various Holy Sites which pilgrims purchased as

---

[26] Ormanian, 4209.

[27] I am greatly indebted to Mrs Alice Krikorian Mushabak of Jerusalem, the great-great grandaughter of Krikorian, for generously sharing the details of her family history during several interviews in 1991.
Located along the outside of the city walls just before Jaffa Gate, Krikorian's studio continued to operate until it was destroyed during the 1948 war.

[28] Henry Field, *Among the Holy Hills*, 5th ed., New York, Charles Scribner's Sons, 1890, 28-29.

mementos and souvenirs of their pilgrimage.[29] The expeditions to photograph these sites in Jerusalem, Bethlehem, Hebron and the Galilee demanded careful planning and considerable expense. When people proposed to Yessayi that he curtail the work of the seminary, printing press and especially the photographic workshop, 'he would answer,"These are the demands of the times and our nation." And he continued to add to the debt.[30]

Yessayi continued to experiment and to cultivate the foreign contacts so crucial to keep *au courant* with the latest technological advances. The following account of his relationship with a fellow photographic enthusiast illustrates his insatiable curiosity and how closely technical secrets were guarded even amongst friends:

> In 1867, the resident consul of Austria in Jerusalem, had gone for a vacation to Vienna and on his return he had brought a new device. When he came to visit me at the Convent, he took from his lap a packet of albumenized paper and said,'Watch, do you see any trace of a picture on this paper?'

As Yessayi and members of the consulate watched, the Consul placed a porous paper over the treated paper and gently wetted it with a sponge. When a picture immediately materialized:

> Mr Pascal and the rest of the entourage were all astonished. He [the Consul] gave several of these papers to me as a present.

Yessayi experimented with the papers and when he was informed that the Consul planned to return to Vienna in the near future when he completed his tour of duty in Jerusalem, he asked the Austrian to send him the formula for preparing the papers. Without a moment's hesitation, the Consul promised to send the desired information. But after some time:

> I [Yessayi] received a letter, in which he was sorry his [photography] master has reserved this secret to himself and does not wish to teach anyone, for which he asks pardon. When I got this negative answer, I was obliged for two years to try all chemicals and salts which are used in photography. I experimented, and at last . . . the secret . . . became slowly apparent.[31]

---

[29] Surprisingly few panoramas and large photographs of Holy Land scenes from the St James atelier seemed to have survived. Most of the extant material is *carte-de-visite*, cabinet, and stereographic images. In 1994 Mr Schiller of Ariel Press graciously brought to my attention an album of panoramas and vues produced by the Convent and now in a private collection.

[30] Savalanian, History p.1140.

[31] Garabedian, *Manuals*, ms. 2775, 154.

In his manual Yessayi diligently recorded secrets of the presensitized albumen paper for the edification of his students – he was always vigilant to maximize an opportunity to enhance their skills and recruit new talent to explore the latest techniques from Europe. Hagop Pascal (mentioned above) was instrumental in facilitating the acquisition of the necessary chemical and technical supplies for Yessayi's atelier.[32]

In 1869 because of his extraordinary service to Emperor Franz Josef during his visit to Jerusalem, Hagop Pascal was promoted from chancellor to vice-consul of the Austrian consulate.[33] This energetic and accomplished Armenian was a close friend to Yessayi and committed to his goal of nurturing the photographic studio. In his capacity of vice-consul Pascal was able to import from Vienna the chemicals, paper and technical equipment necessary to maintaining the Yessayi's studio. As an employee of the Austrians Pascal acquired these materials under the capitulations which granted him the status of a European living in the Ottoman Empire. This greatly reduced the duties these items required from a subject of the Ottoman Empire.

Yessayi's death in 1885 marked the end of a photographic atelier within the confines of the Convent of St James. But his passion for photography inspired a new generation of Armenian photographers who in turn would transmit their skills to other parts of the Ottoman Empire and beyond. His life and photographic career provide a potent example of why and how Christians embraced the powerful new technology from the West.

---

[32] Bishop Mekerditch Aghaunouni, *Monks and Visitors to Armenian Jerusalem*, Jerusalem, St James Press, 1929, 331-32.

[33] As dragomen or vice-consuls, Greeks and Armenians often provided the link between the foreign consulates and the local population. Hagop Pascal Muradian's linguistic skills and negotiating abilities made him a valuable asset to the Austrians. During his pilgrimage to Jerusalem Emperor Franz Josef wrote to the Empress Elisabeth that Pascal was, '. . . one of the most intelligent and inventive people I met.' In Georg Nostitz-Rieneck (ed.), *Briefe Kaiser Franz Josephs an Kaiserin Elisabeth,* Vol I, Vienna, 1966, 111.

Young Armenian pilgrim couple from the Caucasus photographed at the Armenian convent studio in 1881. Photographs were the souvenirs *par excellence* of a journey to the Holy Land.

192

Turkish officials photographed by Krikorian in front of the train which inaugurated the Jaffa to Jerusalem railroad in September, 1892.

The colonnaded basilica of the Church of the Nativity in Bethlehem is an example of the photographs of the Holy Places produced by the Armenian convent workshop (1865-85) for sale to pilgrims.

Two deacons, Krikorian (right) and Ismaelion (left) who studied under Patriarch Yessayi Garabedian in the Armenian convent studio. After leaving the diaconate Krikorian established his own photographic workshop.

A unique photograph of the Holy Selpuchre taken from the roof of the Greek Orthodox convent of St John by Yessayi Garabedian in 1861. In the foreground are the remains of the Crusader church of St Maria Latini upon which the Lutheran church of the Redeemer was built at the end of the century.

An official portrait of Patriarch Yessayi Garabedian taken by his students at the Armenian convent studio. Note the decorations received from different European monarchs.

13

Jerusalem and the Holy Places in European Diplomacy

Roger Heacock

A Brief theoretical remarks

This research is predicated on the distinction between memory and history. The former, memory, is an act of emotion and will, based on subjective identity, instant, unmediated recollection, the transmission of traditions. Its academic tools are literary criticism, oral history, ethnography. It is a totalizing process, which sometimes possesses a strong metaphysical component. The latter, history, is based on written period documents, which need, for the purpose of confirmation, to be related to one another and to the physical and cultural archeology of their production. It is a mediated and documentary exercise. In establishing this dichotomy, we are pointing to the two poles of belief and knowledge, although each pole blends with the other at their point of contact. The characteristic process of the act of memory is resurrection, the characteristic historical act is re-creation.

Each of these two phenomena have their necessary place in human individual and collective life. Problems arise when they overlap, for the combination results in the perception of reality through the promotion of myths, and the frequent fusing of this perception with policy-making. The social role of the historian is to call for the maximum delimitation of the two spheres of memory and history, in the higher interests of both and of those who produce them, that is to say human beings in general.

The question of Jerusalem and the Holy Places is only one of the areas in which the confusion between memory and history as defined above has through the ages contributed to the accumulation of contradictions within and among societies. And it is to their proper delimitation that the present paper is devoted.[1]

---

[1] Cf. Frank Alvarez-Pereyre, ed., *Milieux et memoires, Jerusalem*, 1993, 151-155 (intervention by Michel Guerin).

B Some current methodological trends

Just a few years after the collapse of the Berlin wall, one is justifiably surprised by the resurgence of pre-Cold War and even pre-World War one rhetoric in the analyses of world events by politicians, social scientists and ordinary people. Of relevance to the present study, for example, is the recent description by the Russian ambassador to Tel Aviv of 'his country's interest in Israel as deriving from historic ties such as Russian pilgrimages to the Holy Land and the Russian religious institutions . . .'[2]

Although it might seem hard to believe that a high-ranking official Russian envoy could have made such a statement, and although any particular quotation might actually have been taken out of context, this type of analysis is frequently encountered in the current generalist and specialized literature of the social sciences, and one has the feeling that seventy years of failed ideological confrontation which long nourished the thinking of politicians, academics and ordinary people gave way at least passingly to a new plunge back into the depths of time.

Historians are no exception to the rule, and chauvinistic themes are springing up once again everywhere, especially but not only where they were harshly suppressed for half a century, notably by Stalinist and neo-Stalinist regimes in Eastern Europe and elsewhere.[3] It therefore behoves the historian, whatever may be her or his particular field, to explore old and new avenues of inquiry in the quest for a balanced and convincing view of the past, and by implication the present.

C The historical evidence

I Introduction: from prehistoric through Crusader times

The site of Jerusalem and its environs has from time immemorial – from Canaanite and pre-Canaanite times – contained consecrated and important holy places. And it is due to them, and not to any intrinsic economic,

[2] Moshe Zak, 'Russian Soldiers – Here?', *Jerusalem Post*, 18 March, 1994.

[3] One clear example of this occurs in recent Balkan historiography, going back more than a decade. Consciously or unconsciously, Balkan historians, notably those from South Slav areas, were prefiguring the political confrontations which they helped to conjure up. Cf. 'Historiography of the Countries of Eastern Europe', *The American Historical Review*, 97 (4) October 1992, 1011-1117: Piotr S. Wandycz, 'Poland', Jiri Koralka, 'Czechoslovakia', Istvan Deak, 'Hungary', Keith Hitchens, 'Romania', Ivo Banac, 'Yugoslavia', Maria Todorova, 'Bulgaria'. This is not to say by any means that the phenomenon was entirely absent during the preceding period. On the contrary, Cold War rhetoric, especially on the western side (precisely because of the atmosphere of relative creative freedom which existed) could and did often go hand in hand with traditional, ethnically based values. But the strengthening of chauvinism, whether through violent aggression as in Bosnia, or through the success of right-wing extremist political parties, is clearly connected to academic *a priori* or *ex post facto* rationalizations thereof.

strategic, or political importance, that it became the subject of litigation among the great powers over the centuries and the millennia.[4]

During the period of ancient Rome, Jerusalem was a small and unimportant provincial town. It is for this reason that, because of the intensity of religious feeling centred in the area, the Romans tended to underestimate the potential for civil strife until it was too late. During the 1st century AD, and after Rome's destruction of the Temple in 70 AD, Jerusalem was converted by emperor Hadrian into a 'splendid pagan Roman colony, to be called Aelia Capitolina,' whose importance was largely symbolic.[5] In the meantime, the centre of Jewish civilization in the Roman empire had moved to Alexandria, a large and vibrant multi-ethnic city. Even though they were no longer prevented from residing in Jerusalem, they almost unanimously chose not to. And although there was still some dissidence among them, since Roman religious toleration was based on the free choice of ones deities, sacrifices being symbolically made to the Roman deities as well, a kind of recognition of the legitimacy of the Roman state and a definition of oneself as a loyal *civis*. This was unacceptable to some among the Jews, and so Jewish uprisings recurred in the Roman empire (for example in 115-116), but away from Palestine.[6] Meanwhile, with the Christianization of the empire, Jerusalem, while still acknowledged as an honoured see was, both before and after emperor Constantine's Council of Nicaea, subject to the metropolitan of Caesarea, the regional capital.[7]

During the period of Byzantine rule over Syria, Jerusalem was likewise promoted in official and unofficial mythmaking to a status totally out of proportion with its true, rather modest, standing in relation to other places. When the Persians launched their westward campaigns under emperor Khusro II (590-628), the eastern Roman empire was faced with the biggest Persian offensive ever. The Persians captured Antioch (611), Damascus and Tarsus (613), Jerusalem (614); in league with the Avars, they laid siege to Constantinople itself (617-626). Eventually, emperor Heraclius defeated Khusro on the Tigris, and the Byzantines reoccupied the territory they had lost. Of significance to the present argument is the myth which then arose, that Heraclius had fought the entire war for the purpose of recuperating the

---

[4] Maxime Rodinson, *Israel et le refus arabe – 75 ans d'histoire*, Paris, Editions du Seuil, 1968, 7. '[O]nly the imagination of starving nomads could consider Palestine as "the land where milk and honey flowed."' See also Michel Foucher, 'Israel-Palestine: quelles frontieres?', *Herodote*, 29-30, 1983, 106. In placing Jerusalem in 'neutral terrain', Foucher is talking as a geographer. But he notes the same was true at the time when the biblical David conquered it: 'the "good country" was the coastal plain,' he notes, and the Jerusalem area was 'a good country only for those who came from. . .the desert' (*loc. cit.*). And Roberta Straus Feuerlicht, *The Fate of the Jews*, New York, Times Books, 1983, 11, points out that, although 'Jerusalem was not a Jewish city,' David decided to build his capital there, because it 'lay midway between the two halves of his kingdom.'

[5] L P Wilkinson, New York, Alfred. A Knopf, 1974, 147.

[6] *Ibid.*, 140-146.

[7] A H M Jones, *The Decline of the Ancient World*, New York, Holt, Rinehart and Winston, 1966, 45.

True Cross which the Persians had stolen from Jerusalem in 614, so as to restore it to the Holy Sepulchre. In fact, it was of course a Byzantine war for survival, and it well illustrates the place of memory (in the sense defined above) in the creation of myth and the distortion of history.

The Latin kingdom of Jerusalem, founded by the crusading Franks after the city's capture in 1099 with the attendant slaughter of its population, witnessed the substitution of Orthodox by Latin ecclesiastics. Nonetheless, the majority throughout the kingdom was not Latin Christian, but was rather made up of Muslims, Jews, and Greek, Armenian, Syrian and Palestinian Christians.[8] The Roman Catholics in fact represented a dominant feudal minority. This model, once established, was repeated during different phases of the city's history, most recently in 1967. The will of the population of the Holy Land is, for reasons of state, not consulted in determining its political, civil and religious status. And as for church building, it was, 'for the most part, a symbol of dominion, in which the original local Christianity could largely be ignored, except insofar as sectaries might be occasional allies in the necessary vigilance of crusading life in Outremer (the current name for the Crusading Kingdom, or "Beyond-the-Sea"), the very name expressing the priority of the European connection.' In other words, through this precocious form of settler colonialism, the Franks were exporting not only their values, but their political priorities, which were European, and in which Jerusalem as a living city in and of itself played a secondary part.[9]

When the Third Crusade, led by Richard the Lionhearted, resulted in a compromise deal being struck with Saladin through their treaty in 1192, whereby all Christian pilgrims were guaranteed free access to the Holy Places, the Greek Orthodox were given control over the Christian churches.[10] The kingdom of Jerusalem, shorn of its former capital since 1187, was, in the eyes of the Crusaders themselves becoming more and more useful as a mere hinterland for the merchants of Venice, Genoa and Pisa.[11] Richard Coeur de Lion had no great interest in Latin control of the Holy Places. This reality became all too manifest through the notorious Fourth Crusade, in which the 'mercantile dimension of the European factor began to be central,' while 'the traditional motif of pilgrimage and holy Palestine remained to underwrite and promote it. An unholy alliance of devices and devotion came into play.'[12]

---

[8] Cf. Francois Ganshof, *The Middle Ages – A History of International Relations*, New York, Harper and Row, 1970, 93.

[9] Kenneth Cragg, *The Arab Christian – A History in the Middle East*, London, Mowbray, 1992, 102-103.

[10] Ganshof, *op. cit.*, 177.

[11] Cf. Roger Heacock, 'The Frankish Wars, Venice and the Rise of the West', in *The Frankish Wars and Their Influence on Palestine*, Birzeit, Birzeit University Press, 1994, 84-96.

[12] Cragg, *loc. cit.*

II Early modern Europe

The European powers' fascination with the Holy Places declined after their expulsion from Palestine in 1291, both because the Mamluk and Ottoman rule excluded any interference on their part for several hundred years, and because the shift in the centre of gravity from the Mediterranean to the Atlantic transferred their horizons from the southeast to the west.

The rhetoric of kings and philosophers shifted accordingly, and the promised land, by the 16th century, was conceived as American rather than Palestinian in shape (with the resulting slaughter and spoliation of indigenous Americans in preference to indigenous Muslim and Christian Arabs). And during the seventeenth and eighteenth centuries, religion as a driving force or ideological cover for the foreign and domestic policies of states declined, after the great convulsions of the Reformation and Counter Reformation had died down.[13]

Nonetheless, the powers still had residual interests in the Holy Land, and France, first among them, moved to assert them as she strengthened her ties with the Sublime Porte, under the reigns of their respective sovereigns Francis I and Suleiman the Magnificent. The rapprochement between them took shape in 1525 (in common opposition to the Habsburg empire), and what was later to be called the regime of Capitulations thus began, first and foremost in respect of French citizens and property. The Greek Orthodox church in the Holy Land, representing the largest single group of Christians, continued to insist on its privileges, seconded after 1600 by the Russian orthodox church and state. This was all the more the case when Peter the Great, representing the 'Third Rome', declared himself the legitimate successor to Greek religious sovereignty. And so a usually lethargic battle by proxy was waged on and off between the 'Latin' interests of the French state and the 'Orthodox' interests of Russia. Because of the very mode of administration of the Ottoman empire, where each religious community dealt with its own civil and religious affairs, it was inevitable, despite its privileged relationship with France and fundamental hostility towards Russia, that Orthodox interests would eventually gain the ascendancy.[14] Shortly after having granted France the Capitulations of 1740 (which were in fact a restatement of those promised in 1535, 1604 and 1673), the treaty of Kuchuk Kainadji, imposed by a victorious Russia on the Ottomans in 1774, called the French (and Latin) privileges into question. And the disorders which occurred among Orthodox subjects of the sultan in 1757 occasioned a definitive reversal in policy on the question of control over the Holy Places. A *firman* accorded the Orthodox control over and administration of the most important among them, reversing once and for all the advantages acquired by the Latins under French pressure up

---

[13] H G Koenigsberger, *Early Modern Europe, 1500-1789*, London, Longman Group, 1987, 222-223.

[14] This balancing by the Ottoman empire of internal and external considerations illustrates Charles de Gaulle's dictum that 'states have no friends, only interests.'

to 1740. The Ottoman empire, as opposed to the European powers, was of necessity sensitive to the demands of its subjects (in this instance the Orthodox), and indifferent to the quarrels, although subject to the power politics, of the Christian Holy Places.

Despite the reversal this represented for the French government, the latter did not see these developments as much of an inconvenience until around a hundred years later, when Napoleon III (a much more secular ruler than the pre-Revolutionary Bourbons) needed ideological buttresses for his activist foreign policy. For the Catholic Church and for the Latin subjects of the sultan (who were anyway a small minority) it was experienced as a great humiliation, which endured until the final collapse of the Ottoman empire itself.

III Jerusalem and the birth of the contemporary world, 1799 to 1919

Distant and non-strategic foreign ventures decrease in the calculations of states when questions of life and death to governing regimes or to the homeland itself arise.

It is thus perfectly normal that the French revolution should have turned first France, and then the other countries of Europe which were caught up in its consequences for a quarter of a century after 1789 away from the struggle for influence in the Holy Land. At the same time, the French and European ideologues of the Enlightenment and the Revolution saw in the events of 1789 the emergence of a system of ideas and a movement which should inspire the 'dormant' civilizations of the east, including those of the Ottoman empire.[15] And issues surrounding the Holy Land came back into the forefront as a result of Napoleon Bonaparte's Egyptian campaign and its Palestinian side-venture. The very motivations for the campaign (1798-1799) are linked to the theme of the present study. In addition to achieving new military glories in view of reaching the pinnacles of power in France, and to delivering a blow to his enemy Great Britain by impeding her communications with Southeast Asia, he saw himself and his expedition as bringing the glories of modern civilization back to what the French Enlightenment (in the person, for example, of Condorcet) considered to be the mother of ancient civilizations, Egypt, which had long been an integral part of the Arab world. Typically for Napoleon's expansionist wars, he wrapped his Egyptian-Palestinian campaign in the ideology of liberation, since it was intended to overthrow the obscurantist Mamluks and launch an indigenous (that is to say, an Arab) renaissance.

The unintended effect of the Napoleonic invasion was that it did in fact galvanize the Egyptians against the invader for the purpose of expelling him. At the same time, it precipitated the downfall of the Mamluks and the

---

[15] Cf. Thierry Hentsch, *L'orient imaginaire. La vision politique occidentale de l'est méditerranéen*, Paris, Editions de Minuit, 1988, 166-191.

beginnings of modernization in the Egypt and Fertile Crescent of Muhammad Ali. And it produced the first strands of polarization between Arab-Islamic and Ottoman-Islamic mobilizing themes.

Interestingly enough Bonaparte, because of his convoluted diplomacy and excessive ambitions, alienated his natural allies, the Ottomans, and France lost further ground in the Holy Land. Great Britain did not, however, fare much better, because of the resistance it encountered. Russia maintained its privileged positions, although the Sublime Porte offered no further concessions to any of the powers or their (sometimes unwitting) local religious surrogates.[16]

> Napoleon had left without ever even reaching Jerusalem, but it was really he who was responsible for introducing modernity to the town. For with his arrival in Egypt, the entire East awoke. Grandiose plans for Egypt's economic and intellectual development were drawn up. An Arabic printing press – Egypt's first, was brought into the country. A survey was made of Egypt's economic resources and another of its archeological treasures. To counter French influence in Egypt, British trading representatives in the Middle East began to build up British power along the coasts of the Persian Gulf and the Red Sea. Exactly as the crusaders had, the French and British attempted to divide up the East. Their competition was to have a profound effect on Jerusalem, for it unleashed the nationalism of Arab and of Jew.
>
> The French and British were joined by others, by Russians and Germans, who also tried to exploit the awakening nationalism of the Arabs. The Germans attempted to use the Jews too for a while. All four European powers began to play an increasing role in the history of Jerusalem, making each of their political moves under the veil of religion.[17]

During the first half of the 19th century, the coastal Palestinian towns increased in importance as the Ottoman empire was progressively absorbed into the European-dominated world economy. Akka was the Palestinian power centre, as opposed to inland towns like Jerusalem. At the same time, Palestine itself (and the *Bilad al-Sham* in general) became a source of conflict, because of their importance to Muhammad Ali in his efforts to preserve and extend his Egyptian power base. 'As long as Egypt is a part of the Ottoman empire, its autonomy can only be guaranteed against the possible reestablishment of the direct authority of the Porte through its control over the Syrian points of access to its territory.'[18]

[16] Cf. Jacques Fremeaux, *La France et l'Islam depuis 1789*, Paris, Presses Universitaires de France, 1991, 39-46.

[17] Norman Kotker, *The Earthly Jerusalem*, Mew York, Charles Scribner's Sons, 1969, 233-234.

[18] Henri Laurens, *Le royaume impossible – La France et la genèse du monde arabe*, Paris, Armand Colin, 1990, 84. The author notes that this was to be one of the motivations of British policy towards Palestine from the beginning of the 20th century to 1920.

Similar geopolitical considerations meant that France and Britain both rejected out of hand the notion of any partition of the Ottoman empire, during the first part of the 19th century. France could not tolerate an increase in Russian influence, which would have thwarted her designs as the major Mediterranean power; Britain was intent on maintaining the land routes to India. When Muhammad Ali conquered Palestine in 1831-1832, the stage was set for an intensification of great power conflict in the area, with ever-greater jockeying for position over the Holy Places. France chose Egypt's camp as a way of gaining influence in the Arab world. At the same time, she was extending her hold over Algeria, against the resistance of the Amir Abdel Qader. Together, the successes of Egypt and Algeria in the 1830s were to confirm the rise of Arabism, and the gradual transformation of the question of the Holy Places and of Palestine in general into a national one, in addition to the enduring religious one. The far more religiously tolerant regime of the Egyptians in Palestine made it possible for Christian, and notably Protestant, missionaries, to pursue their activities more freely. This is of course the time of the opening of the first European consulates in Jerusalem (Great Britain, 1838, Prussia, 1842) and of the joint Anglican-Lutheran (that is to say, British-Prussian) bishopric in the Holy City (1841). The other European powers were of course not far behind in the religious/diplomatic domain (Russian archimandrite in Jerusalem, 1844, Russian consul in Jerusalem, 1858, Latin patriarchate of Jerusalem, re-established after six centuries, 1847). The mixture of European consuls and clerics in Jerusalem in due time complemented the combination of ambassadors and bankers in Constantinople.

Britain, Austria, Prussia and Russia of course firmly opposed Muhammad Ali's rise. France was isolated and Muhammad Ali thwarted in his advance. But Britain proposed as a compromise (one that was not implemented) that in addition to being accorded hereditary rule over Egypt, he be recognized as master of the *pashalik* of Akka. This *pashalik* was defined as the southern part of Syria, bordered by a line going from Ras al-Naqoura on the Mediterranean to the northern tip of lake Tiberias, along the Jordan River and the western edge of the Dead Sea to the Red Sea at the Gulf of Aqaba and north to Suez, that is to say, something very close to mandatory Palestine.[19]

Contemporaneously with these events, Protestant millenarian thought, based on the accomplishment of biblical prophesies, was on the rise in Europe, and had been ever since the revolutionary period. Germans, Britishers, Americans, Swiss, all became involved in the movement. And their governments, for reasons of high policy, promoted this evangelical approach, which involved restoring Israel (under the protection of the Western Christian powers of course). In 1840, the British foreign secretary, Lord Palmerston, noted that 'it would be of manifest importance to the sultan to encourage the Jews to return and to settle in Palestine because the

---

[19] *Ibid.*, 102 and 196 note 54.

wealth which they would bring with them would increase the resources of the sultan's dominions; and the Jewish people, if returning under the sanction and protection and the invitation of the sultan, would be a check upon any future evil designs of Mehmet Ali or his successor.'[20] The themes of the return of the Jews, Protestant proselytizing and British (and to a lesser extent Prussian) strategic and economic aims were thus all clearly interconnected.

Meanwhile, the French worked hard, by promoting the Greek Catholic sect, to counter the influence of Russia over the Ottoman empire, which the latter promoted by demanding recognition as the official protector of Orthodox subjects. The Greek Catholics had split off in the 18th century in part to combat ethnic Greek domination over the Orthodox in Syria (which was reinforced after Greece won its independence). The sect was finally recognized officially by the Porte in 1831, something considered a great coup for French diplomacy (as was the contemporary rise of Maronite power in Lebanon). The Ottomans were caught in a difficult squeeze, since, as we have seen, they tended naturally to favour the Orthodox, but most feared the influence and designs of Russia.

The clash of the various Christian communities focussed on Jerusalem, although other areas housing Holy Places had long been integrated into the political arena, notably Bethlehem, Tiberias and its environs, and Nazareth.[21] Some chiliastic English and Scots favoured the establishment of a Judeo-Christian kingdom under British protection. French legitimist circles dreamt of restoring the Latin kingdom of Jerusalem under the legitimist pretender, the Duke of Bordeaux.[22] Meanwhile, the idea of internationalizing the Holy City (to keep it out of another European power's hands) began to be promoted by Prussia. As for the Ottoman empire, it found itself, at mid-century, navigating in ever more difficult waters, as it tried to reject encroachments (such as British claims to extend their protection over the Jews – Protestants were not very numerous – and Russian demands concerning the Orthodox), even as its grip on the affairs of Jerusalem was slipping due to the concerted pressures of powers which nonetheless insisted they were opposed to presiding over the disintegration of the Ottoman state.

IV The Crimean War

The case of the Crimean war is too well-known to go into in great detail. Out of the prolongation of the types of religious quarrels described above,

[20] Barbara W Tuchman, *Bible and Sword – England and Palestine from the Bronze Age to Balfour*, New York, Ballantine Books, 1956, 175. For the significance of the Protestant missionary movement, see J Hajjar, *L'Europe et les destinées du Proche-Orient (1215-1848)*, Paris, 1970.

[21] For a full listing of the principal Holy places which became the subject of disputes among various Christian sects, see L Thouvenel, *Nicolas Ier et Napoleon III – Les préliminaires de la guerre de Crimée*, Paris, Calmann Levy, 1891, XXIV-XXVI.

[22] Laurens, *op. cit.*, 115.

and notably that between the Latins and the Orthodox, there emerged a confrontation between Russia and France, with the Ottomans attempting to preserve the status quo.[23] Where the local parties at hand were concerned, the question of the Christian Holy Places and who was to control which ones of them was, as ever, essential. But for the European powers, other considerations of internal or foreign policy were paramount. In the words of one French source, '. . . the reasons which determined the attitude adopted by the government of the French republic seem, it must be recognized, to have been inspired by considerations of internal and parliamentary policy, rather than by a jealous concern for the maintenance of our age-old traditions in the Orient.'[24] Furthermore, '[t]he Holy Places issue was particularly useful because it tended to divide Russia from Austria, a Catholic state . . . the demarche could usefully serve to weaken the Holy Alliance, as well as affronting Russia.'[25] From the point of view of an adventurist and Bonapartist French statesman, bent on reversing the verdict of 1815, the Holy Places issue might thus result in splitting apart the imperial alliance of Hohenzollerns, Habsburgs and Romanovs which had even held up through the upheavals of 1848. Of course, Napoleon III did not want war; he even feared it, given the existing balance of forces in Europe, but he thought that by heating up the Holy Places issue, he 'was merely using diplomatic weapons to exploit the changing situation in the interest of raising French prestige.' A further complicating factor was the Austrian position, which contested France's claim to represent the Catholics in the Holy Land.[26] As for Russia under Nicholas I, it was seeking a greater say in the Ottoman empire and its influence with the Greek Orthodox patriarch in Constantinople seemed like a convenient channel for obtaining it (although technically speaking, the patriarch was superior to Church authorities in Russia itself!). When Russia demanded the right of protection over Ottoman subjects of the Orthodox community, it was in effect aiming for a partial protectorate over the empire, since those subjects numbered some twelve million.[27] It was also, and most importantly, seeking to extend its sphere of influence in the Balkans through different means, including support for independence movements.[28] Unfortunately, it seems that Nicholas' strategic goals for the Balkans were not totally clear, which contributed to the ingredients of an

[23] Cf. Paul W Schroeder, *Austria, Great Britain and the Crimean War – The Destruction of the European Concert*, Ithaca, NY, Cornell University Press, 1972, 23-31. Events got out of hand despite the fact that France was 'weary of the Holy Places issue by this time . . .' (31)

[24] Thouvenel, *op. cit.*, 3.

[25] Ann Pottinger Saab, *The Origins of the Crimean Alliance*, Charlottesville, Va., USA, University of Virginia Press, 1977, 10.

[26] Harold Temperley, *England and the Near East – The Crimea*, London, Longmans Green and Co., 1936, 286.

[27] Temperley, *op. cit.*, 320.

[28] Vicomte de Guichen, *La guerre de Crimée (1854-1856) et l'attitude des puissances européennes – Etude d'histoire diplomatique*, Paris, Editions A Pedone, 1936, 9-37. Saab, *op. cit.*, 11.

explosive mix.[29] Britain was hostile to French manipulations of the Holy Places issue, although she was intent on furthering her sway over the small Protestant community in the furtherance of its political aims.[30] But she was finally drawn into the conflict by her own ineffectual preventive diplomacy and the fear of Russian encroachments in an area which she deemed of the utmost importance in the protection of her interests, because of the Ottoman empire's strategic location on the road to India.[31] The two wisest parties were Austria and Prussia, which managed to stay out of the Crimean war, despite their own implication in the issues (religious communities and Balkans). Sardinia, on the other hand, was drawn in, because of its overriding goal of doing whatever needed to be done to achieve Italian unification under its aegis.

The value of the Crimean war for the purposes of present study lies in its demonstration of the uses made of Jerusalem, the Holy Places and indigenous Christian communities in the complex game of European and world diplomacy. In this regard, the outcome of the war is telling. In the short run, the Crimean war was fought for the unification of Italy and Germany, for the sake of the balance of power (i.e., against Russia), and for the temporary maintenance of the Ottoman empire, although in a state of weakness and dependence. It has been claimed that these outcomes preserved the peace for a further sixty years.[32] But such a claim rests on a belief in traditional principles such as the balance of power and Eurocentrism. It would seem rather, the vantage-point now afforded to the historian, that, while few changes were made in the status of the Holy Places and communities (the interests of each of the parties balanced each other out), the stage was set in the Balkans and in the Black sea for developments leading through the conference of Berlin (1878 and the Balkan wars (1912-1913) to the outbreak of the First World War (consider the centrality in the Crimean war's settlement of the questions of the Danube Principalities of Moldavia and Wallachia, Kars, the neutralization of the Black Sea).[33]

V Historical postscript: the early 20th century

At the turn of the 20th century, the future was still opaque, although it was clear that the Eastern Question (i.e., the question of when, how and in favour of whom the Ottoman empire would collapse) was soon coming to a head. One of the forces (but at that time, by no means the greatest one)

---

[29] Saab, *op. cit.*, 13.
[30] Schroeder, *op. cit.* 24
[31] Temperley, *op. cit.*, 316-321.
[32] A J P Taylor, *Europe: Grandeur and Decline*, London, Penguin Books, 1967, 67-77.
[33] Cf. Winfried Baumgart, *The Peace of Paris 1856 – Studies in War, Diplomacy and Peacemaking*, London, 1981.

contending for influence in the area, the Zionist movement, wished to establish a base in Palestine, but its founders were not during the first decades particularly attached to control over the Holy Places. Herzl accepted as a given the future extraterritoriality of the Holy Places and Jerusalem, and at one point even accepted to exclude Bethlehem and Nazareth from the Jewish state.[34]

During the First World War the great European Entente powers favoured the internationalization of Palestine, including notably Jerusalem, Bethlehem, Nazareth and all Holy Places in the region. This was foreseen in the 1916 Franco-British Sykes-Picot agreement, to which Czarist Russia acceded, followed by Italy (Saint-Jean de Maurienne agreement, 1917). This minimalist vision of the future of the Holy Land was compatible with wartime priorities, but appeared inadequate given great power interests as they emerged after the war.

From the Catholics' point of view, 'the return of Palestine to Christian hands raised great hopes. The bells of all of the churches in Rome rang out festively to salute the entrance of British troops into Jerusalem, the 9th of December, 1917, and the liberation of the city from Muslim rule.'[35]

The Italian Catholic specialist on the Holy Places, Pasquale Baldi, wrote that:

> . . . today, the unlikely has become a fact; today, due to a prodigious combination of events, that we deem to be providential, Italy, France, England, three nations which played such a part in the holy wars, hold Jerusalem under their dominion; today, therefore, the Catholics all over the world can reasonably expect that the hour of justice has finally rung; today they can finally hope that for the sanctuaries of Palestine will be renewed the splendours of the Constantinian era, the splendours of the first century of the Crusades! . . . The question of the Holy Places today assumes a brand new aspect . . . it must not be resolved by Turkey, but by the consensus of the Nations; today it is no longer a question of counting how many Greeks are in the Ottoman empire, but how many Catholics there are in the world . . . The hour of justice, the hour of reparations is therefore about to ring: the day is about to come which the Fathers of the Holy Land have been awaiting for over a century and a half, the day in which they will be restored to their possession of the usurped Sanctuaries, to the exercise of their violated rights.[36]

---

[34] Silvio Ferrari, *Vaticano e Israele – dal secondo conflitto mondiale alla guerra del golfo*, Florence, Sansoni Editors, Florence, 1991, 10

[35] Silvio Ferrari, *op. cit.*, 9.

[36] P Baldi, *La Questione dei Luoghi Santi in generale*, Torino, V Bona, 1919, 85 and 87, quoted in Silvio Ferrari, *op. cit.*, 219, note 2.

Needless to say, this euphoria was quickly shattered, as it became clear that the British mandate over Palestine was to incorporate the Balfour declaration. The Secretary of State of the Holy See, Cardinal Gasparri, delivered a note to the Council of the League of Nations strikingly similar in its arguments to those expressed during the same period by the Palestinian-Arab delegation to the British government. In particular, he noted that the proposed mandate over Palestine, by preparing for the preponderance of the Jews over the other populations of Palestine,

> not only appears seriously to endangers the rights acquired by the other nationalities but does not seem to be in conformity with article 22 of the Treaty of Versailles, which defines the nature and the scope of all of the mandates '. . . All of this would obviously stand in contrast with a mandate which would be the instrument for the subordination of the indigenous populations for the benefit of an other nationality.'[37]

Obviously, the Vatican's positions, which were momentarily in conformity with the principles of national self-determination, and therefore with those of the Arab national movement of the time, were soon to be modified as a result of the political realities, in which the great powers, for their own individual and collective reasons, were once again dealing with questions related to Palestine and the Holy Places from the point of view of overriding strategic interests, and not as a function of the strategic interests of the people of the region. Since the Vatican was in that period anything but a great power, it was both more susceptible to ideological concerns dear to it and more capable, under certain circumstances, of identifying with popular rather than state interests.[38]

Concluding remarks

Some of the lessons of history had been learned by the time of the passing of the Middle Ages. One way for a new entity to survive in the region is integration into and of existing cultural and social systems. This was indicated by the success of kings David and Solomon and of the Islamic rulers from the 7th century AD and by the relative failure of the Romans (including their Byzantine successors) and the total failure of the Frankish (Crusader) states.

---

[37] *Ibid.*, 15-16.

[38] Note also the interesting resemblance to the logic employed by the authors of the King-Crane commission report (Henry King and Charles Crane), submitted to the American delegation to the Paris peace talks in 1919, and published in 1922. This indicates that immediately after the First World War, prominent circles in the Vatican, as well as USA government advisers, were capable of reasoning and acting in favor of peoples and causes that were marginal to the great European powers of the time.

The other recipes for control over Palestine were shown to be based on the combination of military and demographic strategies, as demonstrated by the collapse of the Crusader states. One of its principal causes was the insufficiency of Frankish settlement and the ensuing long-run numerical inferiority of Crusading armies. The European states made use of their co-religionists in the Holy Land as proxies for their policies, but (with the partial exception of Russia, which had not participated in the crusades, and which had the largest Christian community on and through which to operate) they never again made a serious effort to establish permanent direct control.

Not, that is to say, until the First World War, when the possibility for military conquest by the West again loomed large. And this time, the lesson having been learned, Britain made her move with the advantages of overwhelming military force, international acquiescence, and a strong potential for settlement through the Zionist movement, which it promoted and used in the establishment and consolidation of its mandate over Palestine.

This inevitably gave rise to rejection, resistance and struggle on the part of the indigenous Palestinians, of all religious faiths. And the resistance was of needs overcome by the use of force in the first instance and dispossession and expulsion in the end, because the demographic problem continued to be intractable even after the Second World War.

In order to rationalize or veil the harsh realities of history in the Holy Land, that history has been forced into artificial compliance with myth, through the mechanism of memory, which has been marshalled to serve the policy needs of the conquering power of the day. But the combination of memory and force, even when combined with economic supremacy and outside backing, is insufficient in the long run (because power relationships are a shifting factor) to guarantee peace, stability and security for the peoples of the region. The missing element is of course integration, which requires compromise, based on the disentangling of myth and policy, thanks to the partial renunciation of the dictates of memory in favour of those of history.

14

The Greek Orthodox Patriarchate and Community of Jerusalem

Sotiris Roussos

As its title reveals, the scope of this essay is very broad. As such the essay will cover only the most recent period, that is the 19th and the 20th centuries, modern history of the Greek Orthodox patriarchate of Jerusalem and the Arab Orthodox community. However there will be a short description of the patriarchate and the community throughout the medieval and the early Ottoman period.

The Greek Orthodox patriarchate of Jerusalem had a special character different from those of the patriarchates of Constantinople, Alexandria and Antioch. The main duty undertaken by the patriarchate is the protection and preservation of the shrines in the Holy Land. Secondly that the patriarchate and its clergy are '. . . a great monastery governing and administering, under the rule of the patriarch as its superior, not only the Monastery but also the shrines and their revenues and the whole Church of Zion and the local flock therein.'[1]

One important historical aspect of the earlier periods of the Palestinian Church is its active involvement in the various doctrinal discussions and conflicts within the Christian Church but the most important development of that period was the patriarchate's encounter with Islam, its apologetic position towards the Islamic doctrines and the cultural interaction between the Palestinian Christian community and the new Islamic state and society.

The Ottoman conquest removed the ecclesiastical power of the various Orthodox centres namely, Alexandria, Antioch and Jerusalem, and concentrated it in the patriarchate of Constantinople transforming its

---

[1] A Bertram, H C Luke, *Report of the Commission appointed by the Government of Palestine . . .*, Oxford Univ. Press, London, 1921, 18, 290.

patriarch into not only the ecclesiastical but also political leader *millet bashi* of the Greek Orthodox community regardless of ethnic divisions. The residence of the patriarchs of Jerusalem was then transferred to the capital of the Ottoman empire.

The second part of this essay will cover the developments in the patriarchate from the 19th century onwards. The salient feature of these developments is the emergence of Russian ecclesiastical and political influence in the Middle East, especially in Palestine and Syria. This influence helped and sometimes gave shape to trends such as 'church-constitutionalism' and 'church-nationalism' which dominated the affairs of the patriarchate and the community throughout this period.

The third part will analyse the situation of the Greek Orthodox patriarchate and community in view of the political changes throughout the region after the Great War. The strengthening of Arab nationalism, the attitude of the British Mandate and the role of the Greek state were important factors in the history of the patriarchate in the early 20th century. The political situation after the Second World War would bring further changes to the life of the Greek Orthodox community in Palestine.

Although ancient Christianity recognised the Church of the Holy City as the 'Mother of all Churches', the Church of Jerusalem was separated from the patriarchate of Antioch and became autonomous patriarchate only in AD 451. Its first patriarch, Juvenal, took great interest in various controversies in the Christian Church convoking a local synod in order to confirm the resolutions of the 4th Ecumenical Synod.[2]

The Church of Palestine continued to be a centre of the Church's defence against Monotheletism and Monophysitism throughout the centuries. Together with the monks of the Mount Sinai the Church of Palestine became involved in much controversy in support of the Christian orthodoxy especially in the 8th and 9th century under the new political and social circumstances after the Arab conquest and the religious challenge of Islam. The examples of Anastasios of Sinai and Theodoros Abu Qurrah of St Sabas Monastery illustrated the flourishing Orthodox controversialism.

The salient feature of the early history of the patriarchate was its encounter with Islam. Although the Islamic invasion found Oriental Christians already divided into various different communities, there was only one patriarch in the Holy Land, the Greek, *O Patriarches tou Genous ton Romaion*. In 636 Patriarch Sophronios arranged the terms of the Holy City's capitulation with the Caliph 'Umar and obtained a *firman* which gave the possession and protection of the Christian Holy Places to the patriarchate.[3]

However the most lasting effect of the Orthodoxy's encounter with Islam was the creation of a new Arab Christian identity through the

[2] T Dowling, *The Orthodox Greek Patriarchate of Jerusalem*, London, 1913, 21, 118.
[3] L G A Gust, *The Status Quo in the Holy Places*, Jerusalem 1929, 5.

arabization of the ecclesiastical language and the first Arabic versions of the Gospel during the 1st 'Abbasid century. During this period Arabic became *lingua franca* in the Muslim world. The Arabization of the Islamic government during the reign of 'Abd al-Malik spread the use of the Arabic language among the Palestinian Christians who had previously adopted the Greek language as the language of Byzantine administrative and cultural life. After 750, Theodoros Abu Qurrah and other Palestinian Orthodox scholars were writing in Arabic. Although Greek remained the official language of the Orthodox Church and liturgy, the new circumstances brought the appearance of a new Arab Orthodox Christian identity and the development of Christianity in Arabic which was now the daily language of the indigenous Orthodox population.

In 1517 the Ottoman Sultan Selim I conquered Jerusalem and changed the situation in Palestine and the patriarchate of Jerusalem. The patriarchate of Constantinople re-emerged as the powerful centre of Orthodoxy. The political weakening and isolation of the Byzantine empire had deprived Constantinople from its pre-eminence and influence among the Orthodox patriarchates. The ecumenical patriarch was now not only the religious head of the Orthodoxy, due to the fact that the other patriarchs were obliged to forward all their cases to him, but he was also the political head and representative, *millet bashi*, of all the Orthodox in the Ottoman empire.[4]

This transfer of power from the various Orthodox centres of the Near East to Constantinople induced the patriarchs of Jerusalem to move their residence from the Holy City to the capital as well. After the Ottoman conquest Patriarch Germanos was the first to move to Constantinople and establish himself under the close influence of the ecumenical patriarch and the wealthy Greek who held key posts in the Ottoman administration, the *phanariotes*.[5] However the Orthodox presence in the Holy Land did not disappear. The presence of the confraternity of the Holy Sepulchre, the abbot of which was the patriarch of Jerusalem remained in the Holy City. Various sources revealed the existence of the confraternity already from the 15th century as a Christian body of monks under the patriarch of Jerusalem. Their main responsibility was the guardianship of the Holy Places. Due to the absence of the patriarch, the confraternity assumed the pastoral care of the Orthodox community in Palestine. The previous Islamic policies of the Arabs and the Mamluks were also followed by the Ottomans. Sultan Selim recognised the religious authority and guardianship of the Orthodox patriarch of Jerusalem over the Holy Places.[6]

The decline of the Ottoman Empire from the 17th century onwards allowed the increase of Western political influence and the re-emergence

[4] N J Pantazopoulos, *Church and Law in the Balkan Peninsula during the Ottoman rule*, Amsterdam, 1984, 19.
[5] D Hopwood, *The Russian presence in Syria and Palestine 1843-1914*, Oxford, 1969, 21.
[6] 'Anairesis ton kata tou Patriarcheiou Ierosolymon . . .', *Nea Sion*, vol. 32, 1937, 448.

213

of the religious interest of the Catholic and the Protestant Churches which became evident in the 18th century and came to full bloom in the 19th century. The appearance and strengthening of Catholic Church influence was mainly due to French and Austrian support and to the active alertness of Rome. In his instructions to his ambassador to the Porte, in 1728, Louis XV made clear the French aim to spread the Roman Catholic faith in the Ottoman empire.[7] The conflict between the Orthodox and the Catholic Church over the possession and guardianship of the Holy Places had already started. Catholic powers such as Venice, Genoa and France tried to secure the possession of the Holy Places for the Franciscan monks. In particular the Capitulations of 1604, 1673 and 1740 gave the Franciscans a preponderant position in the Holy Places.

However, in 1757 the Greek Orthodox Church managed to re-assume its rights over the Holy Places. It seems that despite the attempts of Catholic powers, namely, France, Venice, Austria and Naples, the Orthodox patriarchate exercised considerable influence on Ottoman bureaucracy exploiting the Ottoman suspicion of any Western intervention.[8]

We shall deal with three main developments; the re-discovery of the Holy Land by Catholics and Protestant missionaries, the emergence of Russian influence and the Arab national awakening. The gradual disintegration of the Ottoman state weakened the power of the ecumenical patriarchate over the other Orthodox patriarchates.

At the beginning of the 19th century, British interests in Palestine were better served through increasing British influence at the Porte. The combined Protestant (Prussian) and Anglican missions initially focused on the Jewish inhabitants of Palestine. The establishment of an Anglican bishopric in the Holy Land aimed at building close relation with the Orthodox patriarchate.[9]

When the Protestant mission shifted target from the Jews to members of the Arab Orthodox community the patriarchate responded with hostility.[10] The missionary work posed a threat to the Greek Orthodox patriarchate and thus led to the growth of Greek Orthodox militancy. The long amicable links between the two Churches led the heads of the Anglican Church to stop missionary work at the expense of the Orthodox Church and in 1887, an agreement was achieved between the two Churches. The patriarch of Jerusalem welcomed an Anglican bishop in the Holy City in return for a permission for a Greek bishop to reside in London.[11]

Meanwhile the Catholic Church's presence became increasingly felt through Western influence and modernisation of the Ottoman state. The Latin patriarchate was reinstated in Palestine in 1847 and Catholic activity

---

[7] A Arberry (ed), *Religion in the Middle East*, Cambridge, 1969, 315-316.

[8] W Zander, *Israel and the Holy Places of Christendom*, London, 1971, 58-61.

[9] A L Tibawi, *British Interests in Palestine 1800-1901*, Oxford, 1961, 83-84.

[10] Chr. Papadopoulos, *Istoria tes Ekklesias Ierosolymon*, Alexandria 1910, 768.

[11] A L Tibawi, *British interests . . .*, 219-220.

also included philanthropic and social projects which provided the Arab Catholics with a variety of social services. At the same time the re-organisation and strengthening of the Greek Catholic Church was considered a great danger for the Orthodox patriarchate.[12] The activities of the Catholic Church intensified the already uneasy relations between the two Churches. The Orthodox Church strongly believed that this Catholic activity would impair the dominant position of the Greek Orthodox patriarchate in the Holy Places.

The death of Patriarch Athanasios in 1844 coincided with the ascent of Russian influence on Orthodox Church in the Middle East. From 1774 when treaties between Russia and the Ottomans gave her the role of the protector of the Christians in the Ottoman empire, Russian activity in Orthodox matters were intensified. In 1847, a Russian ecclesiastical mission was established in Palestine in the context of antagonism between the Great Powers to acquire the protection of the Holy Places and the pilgrims.[13] Russian influence continued to affect the patriarchate and led to the establishment of the Imperial Orthodox Palestine Society in 1882.

The founding members of the society included Russian scholars who supported the society as a purely educational institution, others who saw it as a means to improve the life of the fellow Orthodox in the Levant, and a small group of Panslavists who saw it as an instrument of Panslavist aims in the Near East. The Greeks in both Greece and Palestine believed that Russian involvement and, in particular, the society was to do in the Levant what the Slavonic Benevolent Society had been doing in the Balkans since 1858. That is, to assist native Orthodox Christians to develop their own religious, educational, and other national institutions at the expense of the influence of the ecumenical patriarchate.[14]

In the meantime, Russia pressed upon the Ottoman authorities that the Confraternity in Jerusalem and not the ecumenical patriarchate and the *phanar* should elect the new patriarch. The Ottoman authorities agreed and eventually Cyrillos, bishop of Lydda, against the wishes of the *phanar*, was elected patriarch in 1845.[15] Cyrillos took residence in Jerusalem and his election marked the end of Jerusalem's subordination to Constantinople.[16]

In 1872, Cyrillos refused to sign the Protocol of the Orthodox Conference which declared the Bulgarian Church schismatic. The conference turned against him and called for his deposition. This was the beginning of a long controversy between on the one hand the confraternity and the ecumenical patriarchate, and, on the other, Russia and the indigenous Arab Orthodox community. However, both Russia

---

[12] A Kreutz, 'The Vatican and the Palestinians: a historical overview', *Islamochristiana*, 18, 1992, 111-112.
[13] T Stavrou, 'Russian interest in the Levant 1843-1848', *Middle East Journal (MEJ)*, vol. 17, 91-103.
[14] T Stavrou, *Russian interests in Palestine 1882-1914*, Thessaloniki, 1963, 206.
[15] Chr. Papadopoulos, *Istoria tes Ekklesias . . .* 777-778.
[16] D Hopwood, *The Russian presence . . .* 181

and the Arab Orthodox had not been able to prevent the deposition of Cyrillos by the Jerusalem synod. This deposition sparked the Arab Orthodox national consciousness. Encouraged and assisted by the Russians the Arab Orthodox advanced demands for greater participation in the affairs of the patriarchate, the hierarchy of which was traditionally Greek.

Neither Russian diplomatic pressure on the Porte, nor control of the patriarchate's income in Russia was enough to induce the Greek synod and confraternity to accept Cyrillos. The *phanariotes* in Constantinople and the confraternity in Jerusalem found in the Ottoman authorities a valuable ally. The Porte was against the spreading of Russian influence in the Middle East. Thus, the Ottomans helped the Greeks of the empire to dominate the Orthodox Church in order to thwart Russian plans. The Ottoman government recognised the deposition of Cyrillos, and the synod elected a member of the confraternity, Procopios, new patriarch, in December 1872.

Procopios' election caused new diplomatic pressure by Russia and strong Arab Orthodox opposition and an Arab Orthodox delegation went to Constantinople to present their demands. The Ottomans were not willing to accept their demands and, frustrated, they left Constantinople. They had asked for the formation of a mixed council of lay and clerical members to administer the finances of the patriarchate, lay participation in the patriarchal election, entry in the confraternity, and improvement of their education and welfare. Procopios seemed to promise various concessions except of participation in the patriarchal election. His concessions, however, were met with anger and led to further discontent among the Arab Orthodox community.

The Arab Orthodox demands revealed two general trends that existed in the life of the oriental churches throughout the 19th century. Firstly the church constitutionalism which asked for greater, indeed decisive participation of the laity in both the patriarchal election and the administration of the church property. This trend led to great changes in the ecumenical patriarchate. In 1856, a mixed national council with a lay majority was created to administer the church's finances, and, in 1862 the new regulations of patriarchal election provided for lay participation. It was the first time after the Ottoman conquest that power was transferred from the patriarch to the laity.[17] Secondly the trend of church nationalism aimed at creating autonomous national churches with indigenous hierarchies which would use the native language as the church language. The Bulgarian Church is a case in point. It was argued, however, that the monastic character of the Jerusalem patriarchate and its position regarding the Holy Places did not allow similar radical developments in the Orthodox Church of Jerusalem.

Russian control of the patriarchate's income, through control over the pilgrimage and donations, as well as Russian diplomacy and the shift in the Ottoman policy which was now not willing to back the Greek hierarchy,

---

[17] G I Papadopoulos, *Les Privilèges du Patriarcat Oecumenique*, Paris, 1924, 245, 252.

brought, in March 1875, both the deposition of Procopios and the promulgation of the new regulations of the patriarchate giving greater say to the Arab Orthodox. The Greek confraternity and synod managed, however, to elect their own favourite, Ierotheos, in the face of Russian opposition.

Ierotheos, a staunch opponent of Russian influence, died in 1882. He managed to appease the Church reinstating the old ex-Patriarch Cyrillos in the Jerusalem hierarchy. His successor was Nicodemos, superior of the Jerusalem *metochion* in Moscow. Although he was Greek by origin he co-operated with the Russians and thus gained their support. The confraternity accused him of assisting Russian influence and its vehicle in Palestine, the Imperial Orthodox Palestine Society, at the expense of the 'Greek nation'.[18] Eventually they succeeded in forcing him to abdicate in 1890.

The synod elected the Greek patriarch of Antioch, Gerasimos, new patriarch of Jerusalem. Despite his constant concern to advance the Orthodox church and education, he did not manage to bridge the gap between the Patriarchate and the Arab Orthodox. They accused the Greek hierarchy of misbehaviour towards the Arab Orthodox and considered the Greeks unfit to have exclusive control of the income and properties of the patriarchate.[19] Gerasimos died in 1897 and once more the Greek element overcame Russian intervention and elected its favourite, Damianos, the superior of the *metochion* in Taganrog, Russia, whose reign lasted until 1931.

The Ottoman constitution in 1908 stimulated a new Arab Orthodox campaign for greater participation in the patriarchate. A committee of forty members pressed upon the patriarch demands for certain church reforms including the establishment of a mixed council of lay and clerical members to administer the property of the patriarchate. In September 1908 Patriarch Damianos proposed to them the appointment by both the patriarchate and the Arab Orthodox community of a mixed committee to discuss their demands.[20] The discussions of the mixed committee did not, however, bear any fruits. The Arab Orthodox demanded the establishment of a mixed council similar to that of the ecumenical patriarchate. Damianos refused on the grounds of the monastic character of the patriarchate and, consequently, caused serious friction.

Due to the local unrest, the Porte directed an investigation into the matter. Damianos explained to them that the regulation of the ecumenical patriarchate and the provisions of the Turkish Constitution did not apply to the patriarchate of Jerusalem, due to its particular monastic character. Damianos, however, held a series of meetings with the Arab Orthodox in

---

[18] The term 'Greek nation', *to genos*, included the Greek people inside as well as outside the borders of the Greek state.
[19] D Hopwood, *The Russia presence* . . . 181-195
[20] A Bertram, H C Luke, *Report of the Commission* . . . . 251.

order to reach a compromise. Certain members accused Damianos that during these meetings, he had promised to the Arab Orthodox the control of the patriarchate.[21]

In December 1908, the majority of the holy synod led by its chief secretary, Meletios Metaxakis, future ecumenical patriarch and patriarch of Alexandria, and Chrysostomos Papadopoulos, who was to become archbishop of Athens, acted to depose Damianos. The patriarch refused to accept this deposition. The Ottoman government, however, recognised the new *locum tenens* and consequently the deposition. Damianos then appealed to the Ottoman government to send a committee to investigate the matter on the spot.

Despite the recognition of the deposition by the patriarchates of Constantinople and Alexandria as well as the Greek government, the violent reaction of the Arab Orthodox against the deposition and the reluctance of the local military forces to suppress the violence complicated the situation. The interference of both local and central Ottoman administration, backed by Russian influence induced the ecumenical patriarch to recognise Patriarch Damianos.

In February 1910, Damianos was again recognised patriarch by the holy synod of Jerusalem. The Arab Orthodox, however, were not satisfied by the resolutions of the committee set up by the Ottomans. These resolutions provided for a mixed council of six lay Arab Orthodox and six Greek clerics. It also allowed entry of the Arab Orthodox in the confraternity but it did not provide for greater Arab participation in the patriarchal election. In fact the mixed council did not function effectively and it ceased sessions in 1913.[22] The building-up of the Arab Orthodox national consciousness, the articulation of their demands, as well as Russian influence in Palestine shaped the history of the patriarchate in the 19th century and prepared the ground for the developments during the British Mandate.

During the 19th century the struggle over the physical control of the Holy Places between the Catholics and the Orthodox became fierce. The intervention of France, the protector of the Catholics and Russia, protector of the Orthodox, internationalised the conflict. In 1850, the sultan appointed a commission to decide on the conflict between the Orthodox and the Catholics over the control of certain Holy Places. In 1852, the sultan issued a *firman* confirming the status of 1757 and thus the pre-eminence of the Orthodox Church. In 1878, the Treaty of Berlin which concluded another Russo-Turkish war stated that the *status quo* in the Holy Places would not be changed.[23]

The end of the Great War in 1918 marks the beginning of the third part of this study which covers the modern history of the Greek Orthodox Church and community in the Holy Land. In the new era the Bolshevik

---

[21] *Ibid.*, 254.
[22] D Hopwood, *The Russian presence . . .* 199-200.
[23] W Zander, *Israel and the Holy Places . . .* 53-54.

Revolution eliminated Russian ecclesiastical and political influence in the Near East and the post-war treaties brought about the dismantling of the Ottoman empire. After the end of the Great War two powers, Britain and Greece, could influence the matters of the Greek Orthodox Church of Jerusalem.[24]

During the British Mandate there were three main crises in the affairs of the patriarchate. The first from 1918 to 1921 was marked by the attempt of the holy synod to revive the 1908 deposition of Patriarch Damianos. The patriarchate faced a huge debt because it had been deprived of not only the generous contributions of Russian pilgrims but also of its income from the patriarchate's vast property in Rumania and Bessarabia. The majority of the synod accused Damianos of mismanagement of the patriarchate's finances.

For the first time in the modern history of the patriarchate, the holy synod openly asked for the intervention of Greece. The Greek Liberal government of Eleutherios Venizelos took two initiatives. Damianos was considered royalist and thus an opponent of Venizelos, and the Greek consul in Jerusalem had been persuaded by the holy synod to oppose the patriarch. As such, the Greek foreign ministry supported Damianos' deposition. On the other hand the Greek government proposed a loan by the National Bank of Greece. The Arab Orthodox feared that further Greek intervention would strengthen the Greek hierarchy at the expense of their position. Consequently they put forward demands for greater Arab Orthodox control over the patriarchate.

The British intervened by appointing the Bertram-Luke Commission in 1920-1921. The commission recognised Patriarch Damianos and consolidated his position. They moreover did not accept the interference of the ecumenical patriarchate and the Church of Greece in the affairs of the patriarchate of Jerusalem. They also set a financial commission to control the finances of the patriarchate. The commission thought that a loan from a Greek bank could lead to political interference of the Greek government in the affairs of the patriarchate and as a result they did not accept this loan. The commission feared that a Greek intervention could invite similar French or Italian activities regarding the Latins.

The second crisis led, in 1925, to the appointment of the Bertram-Young Commission as a result of the Arab Orthodox struggle for greater participation and control of the patriarchate. The selling of patriarchate's land to Zionist corporations infuriated the Arab Orthodox who were now involved in the Arab national movement. Moreover in 1922 the appointment of Bishop Cleopas as metropolitan of Nazareth faced the strong reaction of part of the local Orthodox community. Cleopas allegedly supported participation in the elections for the legislative council in Palestine which were boycotted by the Arab nationalists. The same

---

[24] The account of Greek Orthodox affairs during the British Mandate is mainly based on the author's already submitted PhD thesis, 'Greece and the Arab Middle East. The Greek Orthodox communities in Egypt, Palestine and Syria 1919-1940', SOAS, London, 1994.

position was taken by Damianos.[25] In July 1923 the first Arab Orthodox congress was convened in Haifa. Its resolutions aimed at giving the patriarchate local character which virtually meant the 'arabization' of the Orthodox Church of Jerusalem.

The report of the Bertram-Young Commission proposed the participation of the Arab Orthodox in the confraternity and greater Arab Orthodox control on the finances of the patriarchate. At the same time they turned down fresh Greek proposals to solve the grave financial problems of the patriarchate through a loan by either the National Bank of Greece or a consortium of Greek banks. However, the Greek consul thought that the commission's proposals, especially the provisions for property, education and welfare, were a fair basis for negotiation. Nonetheless the Greek foreign ministry had no policy-guidelines on the matter. Exploiting the absence of policy, Patriarch Damianos dictated his uncompromising line to the Greek diplomats. Damianos was against any compromise with the Arab Orthodox especially on the matters of property and participation of the laity in the patriarchal election. The patriarch's line supported subsequently by the Greek consul and the lack of British resolve prevented the realisation of these proposals.

The death of Patriarch Damianos in 1931 signalled the beginning of the third crisis which raised both the questions of his succession and of the modification of the internal regulations of the patriarchate. The Greek government had two main aims. Firstly the election of a highly qualified patriarch who was able to support Greek interests in Palestine. The second and more immediate aim was to avoid any reform of the patriarchate's regulations before the election of the new patriarch. The Greek government believed that the British authorities in Palestine were ready to make great concessions to the Arab Orthodox in order to win their support in major political issues in Palestine.

The Arab Orthodox, on the other hand, represented by the executive committee of the second Arab Orthodox congress, asked for proportional representation and participation of the Arab Orthodox in the assembly for the election of the new patriarch. Despite laborious discussions and long controversy in the triangle Palestine-London-Athens, there was no agreement over the reforms.

On the other hand, the Greek consul in Palestine favoured the patriarch of Alexandria, Meletios Metaxakis, for the throne of Jerusalem. Instead Archbishop Timotheos a member of the confraternity was elected. Despite Arab Orthodox reaction his election was ratified by the British in 1939.

During the British Mandate there were four factors that played an important role in the affairs of the Greek Orthodox patriarchate of Jerusalem. The Greek hierarchy, the Arab Orthodox community, the British and the Greek governments. Firstly the Greek hierarchy of the patriarchate, particularly, the confraternity of the Holy Sepulchre

---

[25]   F H Kisch, *Palestine Diary*, London, 1938, 39.

continued the ancient Greek Byzantine presence in the Holy Land. The main arguments of the confraternity that supported their rights over the patriarchate was this centuries-long Greek presence. Regarding the control of the property the hierarchy maintained that most of the patriarchate's property had come from Russian and Greek benefaction and thus the Arab Orthodox could have no claim on it.

Secondly the Arab Orthodox which constituted the vast majority of the faithful in Palestine had their own deeply rooted history, which was the fruit of the encounter between Orthodoxy and Arab culture and language from the 8th century. In 1922 the Arab orthodox community numbered about 33,000, forming almost half of the entire Christian population in Palestine. In 1930s the Arab Orthodox community numbered about 40,000, constituting the largest Christian community in Palestine.

The Arab Orthodox contribution to the concept of Palestine as distinct from that of Syria was significant. Their leading paper, *Filastin*, founded by the Isa brothers in Haifa, was an advocate of the distinct geographical and political entity of Palestine since 1911. Palestine was for them the area under the authority of the Greek Orthodox patriarchate of Jerusalem.[26] But it was the anti-Zionist trend that brought Orthodox Christians and Muslims together in the creation of the Palestinian Arab national movement. The Arab Orthodox were mainly traders, craftsmen and public servants. The Jewish immigrants acquired similar educational virtues and thus posed a threat to Christian material existence.

The traditional leadership of the Arab Orthodox community preferred co-operation with the British and the patriarchate stressing the communal Orthodox identity. In contrast there was a young generation of Arab Orthodox who stressed Arab identity and supported Arab unity. This division can been seen in the Arab Orthodox demands *vis-à-vis* the patriarchate which varied from concessions in terms of education and welfare to full 'arabization' of the Church following the ill-fated example of the 'Turkish Orthodox' Church under the Kemalist regime.[27] These trends were present among the Arab Orthodox leadership in the 1930s.[28]

The British faced a dilemma. On the one hand they sought co-operation with the relatively moderate Arab Orthodox. On the other hand, bound as they were to preserve the *status quo* in the Holy Places, they avoided the fulfilment of any Arab demands which could be seen as alteration of the status quo and consequently lead to international implications in the League of Nations. They feared that the French and the Italians were ready to exploit such a situation in order to intervene in the affairs of the Holy Places. It is evident that the issue of the patriarchate was minor for the Palestinian administration. They, thus, intervened only when the

[26] Y Porath, 'The awakening of the Palestinian Arabs', in M Ma'oz (ed), *Studies on Palestine during the Ottoman period*, Jerusalem, 1975, 358-360, 380-381.

[27] Khuri S and Khuri N, *Khulasat ta'rikh kanisat Urshalim al-urthuduksiya*, Jerusalem, 1925.

[28] 17 June 1932, Greek Consul in Jerusalem D Benetatos to Second Directorate (Athens), Visit of the Arab Orthodox executive committee to High Commissioner, 7103, B/36, A.Y.E.

controversy threatened public order, exacerbating the already volatile situation in Palestine and when a foreign power, Greece in particular, interfered in the controversy.

The Greek governments gave both political and financial support to the patriarchate. The main aim of the Greek diplomats in Palestine was to preserve the Greek character of the patriarchate. Pursuing this policy the Greek governments preferred to deal exclusively with the British. They did not consider the Arab Orthodox as a potential channel of Greek influence in the Near East. Greek trade interests were negligible in the region apart from Egypt. There were three possible explanations for this attitude. Firstly, they considered the British, as opposed to the Catholic French, friendly to the Greek Orthodox Church. The close relations between the Anglican and the Orthodox Church supported this assumption. Secondly, they did not foresee any challenge of British domination in the region. Thirdly, certain high-ranking ecclesiastics who were employed as unofficial advisors of the Greek foreign ministry, advocated close ties between the Greek nation and its political centre, the Greek state and the Orthodox patriarchates.

The aftermath of the Second World War and the collapse of the British Mandate found the patriarchate in a difficult position. The internationalisation of the Holy City provided for by the UN partition resolution of 1947 was not met with enthusiasm by the patriarchate. It seems that the Greek Orthodox Church had doubts about the role of the Catholics and particularly about Catholic influence on the high commissioner.[29] The subsequent events cancelled the plans of internationalisation. The patriarchate was now under the Jordanian government but the Arab Orthodox community had been divided into two states, Jordan and Israel.

Patriarch Timotheos died in 1955 and his death signalled a renewed controversy over the position of the Arab Orthodox in the patriarchate. In a meeting of the notables of the Arab Orthodox community in 1956, the moderates dominated, again putting forward their minimal demands. They asked for an effective share in the election of the patriarch and the management of the patriarchate's property. The Jordanian government allowed the election of the patriarch under the previous regulations while it issued new set of Regulations. Patriarch Benedictos' election was ratified by the Jordanian parliament in 1958. The new regulations endeavoured to reach a compromise but it did not satisfy either of the parties. Nonetheless for the first time an Arab archbishop was elected to the confraternity under the new regulations.[30]

[29] B Papadopoulos, 'Synoptikai paratereseis epi tou nomoschediou tes diethnopoieseos tes perifereias Ierosolymon', *Nea Sion*, vol. 44, 1949, 200-202. See also A Nachmani, *Israel, Turkey and Greece . . .* London, 1987, 108-109.

[30] S Colbi, *Christianity in the Holy Land*, Tel Aviv, 1969, 148-149.

After the Second War Greece maintained its close ties with the patriarchate and continued to provide diplomatic support. In 1958-1959 the friendly relations between the Jordanian and the Greek government played an important role in the election of the new Patriarch Benedictos.[31] Moreover, in 1990 during the negotiations which led to the recognition of the State of Israel by Greece, the Greek government placed special interest on the rights of the Greek Orthodox patriarchate. The Israeli government responded with a letter assuring that it will respect the rights of the patriarchate according to the *status quo*.[32]

The change of the international and regional scene of the Middle East in 1993 and the establishment of full diplomatic relations between the Vatican and the State of Israel created fears for the rights of the Greek orthodox Church in the Holy Places. The Greek foreign minister sent a letter to his Israeli counterpart in order to express the anxiety of the Greek Orthodox Church and community regarding the negotiations between Israel and the Vatican over the Holy Places. The Greek foreign minister feared that the Greek Orthodox rights are not taking into consideration since neither the patriarchate nor the Greek government was invited to participate in the negotiations.[33] The Israeli government responded by reassuring the rights of the patriarchate 'according to the religious status quo'.[34]

The most regrettable development in the Holy Land is the rapid emigration of the Christian population from the Holy Land. From 1967 to 1991 forty percent of the present Christian population of West Bank and East Jerusalem have emigrated. The rate of Christian emigration is twice the rate for the overall Palestinian population. The Arab Christians having achieved high educational standard and a relatively high standard of living but without prospects of economic and social security, fit the model of a migrant community.[35] The situation of the Greek Orthodox community is not different from the rest of the general Christian population. There is great danger that there will be no Christians in the land of Christ.[36] In 1992 the Greek Orthodox faithful of the patriarchate of Jerusalem in Jordan, Israel and the West Bank were approximately 145,000.[37]

The patriarchate of Jerusalem had two duties a universal and a local one. It is responsible for the guardianship of the Holy Places and the preservation of the centuries-long Greek presence in the Holy Land. It is also responsible for the guidance and service of the local Arab Orthodox

[31] T Psarakes, *Anthologio tes Ierousalem*, A A Libanes Press, Athens, 1994, 41-57.
[32] Newspaper *To Vema tes Kyriakes*, 7 August 1994.
[33] *Ibid*, 7 August 1994.
[34] *Ibid*, 14 August 1994.
[35] B Sabella, 'Palestinian Christian Emigration from the Holy Land', *Proche-Orient Chrétien*, XLI, 1991, 75-76.
[36] 'Near East. Palestine', *Eastern Churches Review (ECR)*, vol. II, 1968-1969, 327.
[37] Y Courbage and P Fargues, *Chrétiens et Juifs dans l'Islam arabe et turc*, Paris, 1992, 328.

faithful. The position of the patriarchate of Jerusalem facing new challenges reminds of an analogy mentioned by Kallistos Ware – the image of a drink of water and the glass that holds it. Can you have the drink [the life-giving water of the Orthodox tradition] without the glass [a particular ethnic or cultural context]?[38]

[38] Kallistos Ware, 'Catholicity and Nationalism: A recent debate at Athens', *ECR*, vol. X, 1978, 12-13.

15

Palestinian Christians: Politics, Press and Religious Identity 1900-1948

Qustandi Shomali

The development of the Palestinian press in the Holy Land reveals the special socio-cultural position occupied by Palestinian Christians in Palestine. The chronological and quantitative dimensions of this development reflect their important contribution.[1] The presentation of an overall view of this development, will be discussed in two stages which are fairly distinct from one another: the Ottoman period (1900-1916) and the British Mandate period (1918-1948). The survey of the press during these periods will include only a summary of the main newspapers and major figures among the journalists. The omission of any name that might be familiar must not be taken as a reflection on such a writer's stature. The task of selection has been chiefly to include the names of leading journalists. In fact, selection is inevitable in any review which attempts to cover a large era in a strictly limited space. Although the survey deals only with the press, it will give a general idea of how far the cultural and political trends have been reflected in the different newspapers. However, in order to be thoroughly acquainted with the development of the press in Palestine, and the contribution of the Palestinian Christians in particular, it is essential to know the conditions which led to the modern cultural revival in Palestine, and the development of the press in particular.

At the beginning of this century, Palestine was a province of a declining Ottoman empire and suffering from poor administration. It was in a state of isolation from the intellectual and cultural movements in the Arab world and the West. The political instability, the narrowness of the system of education, the replacement of Arabic by Turkish as the official language,

---

[1] See appendix: list of periodicals published in Palestine in the Ottoman and British Mandate periods.

and the constant living in the cultural past, resulted in the degeneration of the culture of the period which remained imitative of the past. Palestine, however, witnessed a significant cultural revival after the start of the 20th century. This revival is generally known as *al-Nahdah*, meaning renaissance. The initial impulse of *al-Nahdah* was provided by the introduction of the printing press, the opening of missionary schools, the establishment of newspapers, and the growth of the nationalist movement.

Education was the initial impetus to cultural revival. Most of the work in this field was a result of private initiative: a large number of missionary and sectarian schools were founded in the second half of the 19th century as a result of the growing interest shown by several Western countries in the Holy Land (Russia, France, England and Germany). Education in these schools was in Arabic, and stressed the history of the Arabs. Until 1908 the Ottoman government had neglected educational services in Palestine. Facilities for education in villages were non-existent and very rare in towns. The first government intermediate secondary school in Jerusalem was founded in 1889.[2] However, the number of schools run by the Ottoman government was augmented after 1908.

A second aspect of the literary revival was the introduction of the printing press. The first one was brought to Jerusalem in 1846 by French missionaries, and was known as 'Matba'at al-Aba al-Fransisiyin'. It is still operating today. Another press was established three years later by the Holy Tomb Society and known as 'Matba'at al-Qabr al-Muqaddas li' l-Rum al-Urthuduks'. Other presses soon followed: 'Matba'at London' in 1848, the Armenian press in 1866, and the British Missionary Church Society press in 1879. At the turn of the 20th century, we witnessed the establishment of several private presses owned by local people. Jurji Habib Hanania established his own press in Jerusalem in 1892, Basila Jada' established 'al-Matba'a al-Wataniya' in 1908. Najib Nassar established 'Matba'at al-Karmil' in 1909 and Elias Zaka established 'Matba'at al-Nafir' in 1913. Statistics regarding 'Matba'at Jurji Habib Hanania' shows that the number of books published by this printing house between 1892 and 1909 reached 281 in different languages among which were 83 books in Arabic.[3]

A third aspect of the cultural revival was the establishment of literary clubs and societies. The earliest of these were formed with the help of missionaries like the Palestine-German Society, which published various books about Palestine and ran many schools, among which was Talitha-Kumi, founded in 1851. The Greek Orthodox Society was established in 1882 and published hundreds of books and opened 25 different schools. Other literary societies were formed by Palestinians intellectuals: 'Jami'at al-Adab al-Zahira' was founded in 1898 by Daoud Saydawi and it included a number of well known writers. 'Jami'at Ruqiy al-Adab' was established in Jaffa in 1908 and emphasized the importance of spreading education

[2] Abdul-Rahman Yaghi, *Hayat al-Adab al-Falastini al-Hadith*, Beirut, 1966, 62-77.
[3] *Ibid.*

among the youth. Translation was another element of the cultural revival. The best scientific and literary thoughts of the West were disseminated through translations, mainly from Russian, French and English. These translations made a major contribution to the adoption of Arabic for the expression of modern ideas. It could be said that translation was the most effective of all forms of cultural contact between Western and Palestinian literatures. Nearly half of the printed Arabic books between 1900 and 1950 were either translations or adaptations of works of fiction, which gave the Palestinian reader much information about intellectual life in the West.

The fourth aspect of the cultural revival was the appearance of newspapers and magazines. The Arab press in Palestine did not develop during the second half of the 19th century as it had in other Arab countries; press development was slower and came later in Palestine, although Palestinian intellectuals had contributed to the Arabic press since the last quarter of the 19th century. The Palestinian elite, until the turn of the century, depended on Arab publications which were circulated in Palestine and which reflected common Arab nationalist aspirations. In fact, the development of Arabic language newspapers in Palestine was the initial reaction to the 1908 constitution. The Palestinians took advantage of the 1908 constitution, as did other Arab nations, and established many newspapers between 1908 and 1914. Their identity began to grow strong, both in their home press and in most Arab periodicals. 19 publications appeared in that period, 12 of them in 1908, mostly in Jerusalem, Jaffa and Haifa. This emerging press became an important vehicle of cultural revival, a medium of information about the new political developments, and an organ stressing Palestinian identity. However the constitution of 1908 was suspended a year later, many newspapers in Palestine was suppressed by the Ottomans and did not resume publication until after the First World War. The press suffered during the Ottoman period from strict rules and many newspapers were closed or suspended for weeks or months for criticising the government or advocating justice and reform. The role played by the newspapers in this period should not be underestimated. They brought about a major extension of the reading public: extension which had already been promoted by the introduction of the printing press. Books could now reach many more readers than the handwritten copies of former days. Newspapers and magazines required a different Arabic, one less ornate and one that could deal with a multitude of subjects that had not or had hardly been deemed fit to be written about before.

The Ottoman period

The first press in Palestine was established by the Ottoman government. *Al-Quds al-Sharif*, the first Arabic newspaper, was published in 1870 in Jerusalem, as were other official newspapers. Arabic was not the only language used, Turkish accompanied it as the official language of the empire. However, this newspaper included only the official news of the government, new laws and regulations. The first independent newspaper did not appear until 1904, when *al-Nafir al-'Uthmani* (1904-1930) was founded in Alexandria by Ibrahim Zakka. Then it moved to Jerusalem in 1908. It was followed by some 25 periodicals and publications, none of them on a daily basis, which were active during the decade of the Turkish rule. These newspapers included *Filastin* ('Palestine') founded in Jaffa in 1911 and the Haifa-based *al-Karmil* established in 1908 and a variety of political publications, literary magazines and shortlived underground pamphlets. Since its initial days in the Ottoman period, the Arabic press has been highly politicized and of a Christian predominance. This was followed in the mid 20s in the British Mandate period by the appearance of Muslim-owned newspapers as a counterweight to the previous Christian predominance.

The early stage of the press in Palestine developed under the Ottoman rule, to express the Palestinians aspirations for full independence from foreign rule and for Arab unity. The Palestinians elite took advantage of the democratic constitution after the Young Turk's revolution in 1908 to increase the number of newspapers. After the 1908 constitution a wave of newspapers, literary magazines and underground publications began to appear. 19 publications appeared in that period, 12 of them founded in 1908 alone in Jerusalem, Jaffa and Haifa, the three major cities to host the press since then. The total number of newspaper and magazine was 25, and 19 of them were Christian-owned. These newspapers tried to familiarize their countrymen with Western civilization by producing different articles about Western culture. The authors developed also a new Arabic style suitable for the expression of Western ideas. The social themes were no less abundant than the political themes. A considerable percentage of the writings after 1908 referred directly or indirectly to the problem of social reform known as *islah*.[4] Among the most important subjects discussed on the pages of the newspapers were, the system of education and the importance of opening modern schools, the taxes imposed by the government in the villages and the importance of raising the agricultural standard and helping the farmers, news and activities of cultural and literary associations which reflected national aspirations of the Palestinians, and the visits of famous figures in Palestine. The development of the issue of the Greek Orthodox church was discussed thoroughly on the pages of the newspapers.

The most import paper of the pioneering press was *al-Karmil* founded in 1908 by Najib Nassar, it was the most important of the 1908 papers. Its founder Najib Nassar, an Orthodox Christian, is generally considered the father of nationalist journalism in Palestine. Nassar as a journalist was among the first to foresee the dangers the Zionist movement posed to Palestinians. He was diligent about revealing the aspirations and activities of

---

[4] *Filastin* newspaper 1911-1967, Jan-Dec. 1913.

Zionists through his writings. Nassar, was a man of leading public opinion rather than a business enterprise. His opposition to the Zionist movement and its activities along with his criticism of the Ottoman policy toward Jews, twice brought about suspension of his paper. *Al-Karmil* played a important role in the Arab nationalist movement until the First World War. In his prestigious newspaper, Nassar called for an Arab conference to counter the Zionist congress which was scheduled to be held in Vienna in 1913. In 1914 he urged the establishment of an Arab organization in Palestine in order to solidify Arab goals and aspirations and to raise the people's agricultural standards. The intellectuals aroused by Nassar's encouragement, established political organization in most of the major Palestinian cities, many of which had both Muslim and Christian members, as did one in Haifa called al-Muntada al-Adabi, whose stated objectives was to revive the national movement while secretly fighting Zionism.

Khalil Baydas, a writer and journalist, founded in 1908 a literary magazine called *al-Nafa'is al-'Asriya* ('Modern Treasures Magazine') in order to publish both his own short stories and translation. He introduced a rich amount of Western thought to Arabic literature and played an important role as a leader of public opinion. He translated both novels and short stories into Arabic from the world's classics, namely from Russian.[5] At the same time al-Sakakini, a Christian intellectual, founded *al-Dustur* magazine in 1910 and contributed to the revival of Arabic, developed political sentiments as a result of the nationalist movement and contributed to the awakening by his writings in education and literature.

Meanwhile other emerging papers is Palestine was *Filastin* 1911-1967 named for the country it faithfully defended throughout its publication. It was founded in Jaffa and was the longest lived newspaper, Its founders were Orthodox Christians 'Isa al-'Isa and Yusuf al-'Isa of Jaffa. provided a good example of the role of the Arab Christians in nationalism. It played a leading role, as did *al-Karmil*, in awakening the national consciousness of the masses, against Zionist activities, and the development of literary and cultural life in Palestine. *Filastin's* policy was expressed in its first editorial: it was to be an independent paper that appreciated the constitution which had resulted in the existence of the press. Its objectives were to support every development beneficial to constructive rather than destructive nation-building. However, it remained constant to nationalism while *al-Karmil* shifted it policy in 1914. In 1913 *Filastin* was serving as an organ for intellectuals to express their nationalistic views. It continued too its leading role and was harshly critic of the authorities' policy toward Zionism for the first seven months of 1914. However the nationalistic press in Palestine, including *al-Karmil* and *Filastin* was suppressed by the Ottomans during the First World War and did not resume publication until after the war.

---

[5] Kamal l-Sawafiri, *Al-Adab al-Arabi al-Mu'asir fi Filistin*, Cairo, 1979, 361.

The British Mandate period

Palestine was consigned to Britain by the League of Nations in 1920 and the Palestinians opposed this arrangement. The events of the Buraq Wall (the Wailing Wall) in 1929, the disturbances of 1933, al-Qassam's rebellion in 1935, and the revolt of 1936 marked a relation of confrontation between Palestinians and the mandate government. The intellectual leaders were the most outspoken critics of mandate authorities. They kept alive a national consciousness through the literature they wrote during this period. Many new periodicals were founded expressing the Arab's political reactions to the British Mandate this press resumed its role as an organ for expression of political nationalism. and Arab aspiration.

During this period, in the decades between the two world wars, the social and economic development of the country had a decisive role in producing the major characteristics of the press. However, the limited size of the educated sector and the average income militated against long and expansively produced publications. The newspaper column became the chief media of expression for writers. Newspapers like *Mir'at al-Sharq* (1919-1939), *Filastin* (1911-1967), *al-Sirat al-Mustaqim* (1934-1943), *al-Jami'a al-Islamiya* (1932-34), *al-Difa'* (1934-1941); and literary magazines like *al-Fajr* (1935), *al-Muntada* (1940-1946), and *al-Mustaqbal*, became the most important forums for expression. There were 60 Arabic newspapers and 22 magazines in the British Mandate period.[6]

The press returned to Palestine in 1919 after the war and set the standard for the press of the 20s as organs of political opposition. The main targets were the British Mandate and the Jewish National Home. Many politicians who were active in the literary clubs and societies became journalists and writers. Four new periodicals were born in 1919 and some of the pre-war papers came back. The newborn periodicals were: *Suriyah al-Janubiya* ('Southern Syria'), *Mir'at al-Sharq* ('The Mirror of the East'), *Bayt al-Maqdis* and *Bayt Lahm*. The first was Muslim owned and the three others were Christian owned newspapers. *Suriyah al-Janubiya* was the first paper to appear after the British occupation and the most vigorous of that year. It reflected nationalist consciousness and emphasized Palestinian aspirations for unity with Syria, 'the mother'. *Mir'at al-Sharq* was published by Bulus Shihada in Jerusalem. In its first years the weekly paper was issued in both Arabic and English, but eventually it became an Arabic periodical. Although Shihada was an active figure in the Muslim Christian Association, he was in favour of British authority. By 1924 the newspaper was committed to the defense of the Nashashibi clan which was competing with Hajj Amin Husseini's clan for leadership of the nationalist movement. *Mir'at al-Sharq* lasted until 1939. *Bayt al-Maqdis* was published in Jerusalem by Bandali Elyas Mushahwar and appeared twice a week. The paper

⁶ Yusuf Khuri, *Al-Sahafa' al-'Arabiya fi Filistin*, Beirut, 1976, 30-141.

survived until 1926, defending nationalist views in a moderate tone. It was shut down due to economic problems, as were many other papers. *Bayt Lahm* founded by Yuhnan Dakart and 'Isa Bandak as a weekly in the town of Bethlehem, and was concerned with news of Arab emigrants in Latin America, were a good number of the city's inhabitants had fled from the war. Al-Bandak founded another periodical *Sawt al-Sha'b* ('The Voice of the People') in Bethlehem in 1922 to support his role as an active figure in the political development of the nationalist movement.[7]

The first two years of the British Mandate in Palestine was a period of political unrest. The people continued to oppose the British policy and Balfour Declaration. The newspapers participated in the unrest by encouraging the masses to continue their struggles. The press in the 20s was controlled by military supervision and freedom of expression was strictly limited. This caused journalist and other public figures to suffer under the authorities oppression. The Palestinians expressed their discontent through political groups, mass demonstrations and through a growing press which played an effective role in directing the masses. Press growth developed rapidly in the 20s shaped by social changes and political and economic factors. Under the British rule, better means of transportation and modern mass communicates were introduced to Palestine, encouraging rapid change and growth in the field of journalism. Many newspapers appeared in the 20s but all lived for only a short time. Among the new periodicals two important ones were founded in Jerusalem: *al-Quds al-Sharif* was founded by Hassan Sidki al-Dajani, a Jerusalem lawyer. It was a weekly independent newspaper which reflect the nationalists' aspirations and mirrored the Palestinian of the 20s. Abdul Latif al-Husseini founded *al-Aqsa* newspaper to defend nationalist views. It was shut down in 1929 because of the economic depression which hit the country at that time. Jerusalem added *Dar al-Mu'allimin* to its list of magazines published by Abdul Hadi and Musa Niqula. The magazine survived until 1928 as a literary and educational periodical. On the other hand, this period witnessed the return of two leading newspapers in Palestine, *Filastin* and *al-Karmil*, both of which were strong nationalist organs against both the Ottoman Empire and the interests of Zionism. However, Nassar's mood had changed under the British Mandate to sympathy for British policy. *Lisan al-'Arab* ('The Arab Tongue') founded in 1921 as the first daily newspaper in Palestine by Ibrahim Salim al-Najjar, a Lebanese Christian. His newspaper served the government interests and countered the paper *al-Quds al-Sharif*. Several debates took place between the two editors. *Al-Urdun* was a weekly newspaper published in 1923 in Haifa by Basil al-Jadi and Khalil Naser and it survived in Palestine until 1927 when Naser moved it to Trans-Jordan to publish until 1929. The most influential of these periodicals is *al-Jami'a al-'Arabiya* started by Munif Husseini, cousin of the mufti.

[7]   Najar Aida Ali, *The Arabic Press and Nationalism in Palestine*, Univesity Microfilms International, Ann Arbor, 1985, 58-74.

The loyalty of the press during the first decade of the British Mandate was apparently divided by three political groups: two of the press groups separately supported rival nationalist clans: the 'Councilites', following the mufti of Jerusalem Hajj Amin Husseini and the 'Oppositionists', following Raghib al-Nashashibi. *Al-Jami'a al-'Arabiya* was the official organ of the party of Husseini group and *Filastin*, *Mir'at al-Sharq* and *al-Sirat al-Mustaqim* supported the oppositionists. A third group of the press was devoted to the government and the British policy: like *Lisan al-'Arab* and *al-Karmil*.

At the beginning of the 1930s despite the growth of national consciousness only few new periodicals were founded, The growth of the press declined because of he unfavourable economic situation and the lack of freedom of expression. *Al-Hayat* newspaper was founded in 1930 in Jerusalem by Abdel-Jabr and Khalil al-Duzdar and it was suspended in 1938. However a new newspaper joined the press *al-Jami'a al-Islamiya* ('The Islamic League'). It was founded by al-Sheik Slieman al-Taji al-Farouky who was an active figure with the opposition parties of the 1920s. The newspaper was an independent voice in defence of the Palestinian nationalist cause until 1939 when it ceased publication. It also represented the Istiqlal party. Another newspaper *al-Difa* 'was founded in 1934 which played a important role in affecting public opinion and preparing the people for the Palestinian revolution of 1936. It was founded in Jaffa by Ibrahim al-Shanti who later became chief editor of the *al-Jami'a al-Islamiya*. *Al-Difa'* was a leader in the exposure of news in this period which caused the paper suspension for many times. Dawud al-Isa was working as an editor of *al-Difa'* and he expressed his nationalistic feeling.

Emil al-Ghoury's contribution to the field of journalism was very important He founded *al-Wahda al-'Arabiya* in 1932. His participation began earlier in support in the mufti's group through the press. *Al-Shabab* ('Youth') magazine was founded by him in 1933 and in the same year he founded *al-Ittihad al-'Arabi* ('The Arab Union') written in both English and Arabic to survive for only one year before it was suspended by the authorities. In 1935 the paper was replaced by a weekly fourteen page paper *al-Awqat al-'Arabiya* ('The Arab Times'). The paper served the party for just three months before it was suspended by the authorities for its nationalist views. Al-Ghoury temporarily gave up trying to publish another newspaper. It was in 1944 that he published *al-Wahda* in Jerusalem, in an effort to revive Hajj Amin Husseini's party and build up his image in his absence. However, during this period.Falastin was the leading nationalist newspaper and one of the most prestigious daily newspapers in the country. Its circulation was estimated at 6000 in the thirties. The editor of *Filastin*, 'Isa al-'Isa, was the most outspoken critic of Greek Orthodox patriarchate and his newspaper was open to discussion over many issues related to the greek Orthodox community. A special column entitled (*Shu'un Urthuduksiya*) was open in the newspaper to all those who wanted to write about the issues of the Greek Orthodox community. A variety of literary forms and included articles, poems and short stories were published in a 'literary page' in the newspaper. It included also political tracts, news of the serious disturbances between Arabs and Jews and the confrontation with the mandate authorities. *Filastin* continued to exist in Jordan until 1967 when it disappeared.

Resisting the administration's control of the press, a delegation of six press men, representing the leading newspapers met with the High commissioner on 3 November 1933 to express their discontent and to explain the major issues discussed by the press. Among the six representative four were Christians: the editor of the *Filastin* newspaper, Dawud al-'Isa, who expressed the journalists anger, and summarized his demands as: restrict immigration, pass legislation to control the sale of land and to set up representative institutions. Isa al-Bandak representing *Sawt al-Sha'b* who repeated *Filastin's* demands and added without fear, that the situation would continue so long as the Arabs feared for their future. More interesting were the comments of Najib Nassar the editor of *al-Karmil* who found himself in a difficult position. He said that he had been accused of being pro-British and had suffered from it, both materially and morally, Nassar by the meeting has decided to convert: 'Now I am bound to criticize the British policy'. Nassar change the name of his newspaper in 1936 to *al-Karmil al-Jadid* ('New Carmel') and he started a new chapter in the nationalist movement. *Al-Karmil al-Jadid* was suspended on 16 February 1939 for its remarks on the British policy and the editor's wife Sathij Nassar was imprisoned on February 25 for her nationalist consciousness. The other two members of the delegation are Ajaj Nuwahid editor of *al-'Arab* and Munif al-Husseini representing *al-Jami'a al-'Arabiya*.[8] During the six-month strike in 1936 Arabic newspapers were suspended 34 times and officially warned 11 times, during the two months following the strike nine Arabic newspapers were banned while only one Hebrew newspaper was suspended. During the occasional suppression of all dailies, the *Palestine Official Gazette* was used as a mass medium. It published daily news of the rebels the way the British desired. *Filastin* recounting proudly on its front page the paper's share of punishment during the six month strike, on 13 October 1936 published a story entitled 'Headed the Authorities' Anger'. The count listed the eight suspension of the paper for a total of 51 days. In the second period of the Mandate, 1930 through 1939 the Palestinian press developed its influence on the masses and grew in force and became the major factor in the process of nationalism. It grew increasingly organized following the formation of political parties in the country. The revolutionary press of the thirties played multiple positive roles of educating and agitating the masses against British-Zionist imperialism.

Most of the newspapers vanished after the Second World War and the revolutionary mood had frozen. Out of the large number of emerging newspapers, only three survived and those were in bad financial condition. Those papers were: *Filastin*, *al-Difa'* and *al-Sirat al-Mustaqim* all published in

---

[8] *Ibid.*, 117.

Jaffa and representing the major political parties in the country. The press of the third period 1940-1948 became victim of the martial environment. National news was lacking which made the press less important. The three leading dailies and only surviving newspapers, *al-Difa'*, *Filastin* and *al-Sirat al-Mustaqim* fell to the government's mercy with respect to content and allocation of newsprint. The press was not committed.[9]

In tracing the development of the Arab Palestinian press we notice that it had been determined by political, social, economic and national changes. On one hand the press developed through the important contribution of the Palestinian Christians. On the other hand it was a product of the growth of the national movement and the confrontation between Palestinian, Jews and the Ottoman and Mandate authorities. It defied the hardships of geographical and cultural isolation, lack of freedom, censorship and national oppression and exceeded the best developed press in the neighbouring states despite the uncertain social, economic and political conditions. Its role went beyond all other forces to affect the masses and strive the national consciousness.

Appendix

Arabic Press in Palestine
List of Periodicals (newspapers and magazines) published in Palestine.

The Ottoman Period (1976-1916)★

★ **Bold:** important newspapers
  <u>Underlined:</u> Christian editor or publisher

year	periodical	publisher or editor
1876	*al-Quds al-Sharif*	Ali Rimawi
1907	*al-Taraqqi*	<u>Martine Alonzo</u>
1908	*al-Asma'i*	<u>Hanna Abdullah Issa</u>
	al-Quds	<u>George Hanania</u>
	al-Nafa'is	**Khalil Baidas**
	al-Insaf	<u>Bandali Elias Mushawar</u>
	Sahyun al-Jadida	<u>Yacubus Kabinkas</u>
	al-Karmil	**Najib Nassar**
	al-Nafir	<u>Elia Zaka</u>
1909	*al-Akhbar*	<u>Bandali Hanna Urabi</u>
1910	*al-Dustur*	<u>Khalil Sakakini</u>
1909	*al-Bakura al-Sahyuniya*	<u>Zion School</u>

---

[9] *Ibid.*, 186-196.

year	periodical	publisher or editor
1911	*Filastin*	**Isa al-Isa**
	al-Akhbar al-Usbu'iya	Hanna Fadoul
	al-Haymara al-Qahira	Khalil Zakout and Najib Jana
1912	*al-Munadi*	Said Jadallah
	al-'Asa Li-man 'Asa	Najib Jana
	al-Mahaba	Fadlallah Fares
	Abu-Sadouf	Wahbeh Tamari
	al-Sa'ka	Jamil Ramadan
1913	*al-Manhal*	Muhamed Musa al-Maghrabi
	al-Quds al-Sharif	Ali al-Rimawi
1914	*Sawt al-'Uthmaniya*	Shamoun Morial
	al-Itidalal-al-Yafi'	Bakri al-Samhouri
1916	*al-Sahra' al-Musawarah*	Jamal Basha

The British Mandate Period (1919-1948):

year	periodical	publisher or editor
1919	*Surya al-Janubiya*	Aref al-Aref
	Mir'at al-Sharq	**Bulus Shihadeh**
	Bayt Lahm	Hanna Dakarat
	Bayt al-Maqdis	Bandali Elias Mushawer
1920	*al-Quds al-Sharif*	Hassan Siki Djani
	Barid al-Yawm	A Sfer
	al-Aqsa	Saleh Abdelaltif Hussieni
1921	*Jaridat Hukumat Falastin*	Palestine Government
	Raqib Suhiyun	Bulus Sim'ani
	Haifa	Elia Zaka
	Zahrat al-Jamil	Jamil Buhyri
	Lisan al-Arab	**Ibrahim Slim Najar**
	al-Sabah	Kaml Budairi
	Sawt al-Sha'b	Isa Bandak
1922	*al-Zahra*	Jamil Buhyri
1923	**al-Urdun**	**Basila Jada and Khalil Nasr**
	al-Huquq	Fahmi Hussieni
1924	*al-Jazireh*	Hassan Fahmi al-Dajani
	al-Inarah	Niqual Hanna
	al-Iqdam	Salim Hilou
	al-Karmah al-Musawarah	Wasef Yusuf
	al-I'lan	Michael Salim Najar
1927	*al-Zumar*	Khalil Zaqut
	al-Zuhur	Hannah al-Buhairi and Jamil Buhairi
	al-Jami'a al-Arabiya	**Munif al-Husieni**
	al-Nakbah al-Arabiyah	Ahmad Sameh al-Khaliki
	Sawt al-Haqq	Fahmi al-Hussieni

year	periodical	publisher or editor
1930	*al-Hayat*	Adel Jaber
1932	***al-Waqa'i al-Filastiniya***	**Government of Palestine**
	al-'Arab	Ajaj Nuwehed
	Raqib Sahiyun	**Latin Patriarchate**
	al-Karmil	**Najib Nassar**
	Mir'at al-Sharq	**Bulus Shihadeh**
	al-Jami'a al-Islamiya	**Sulieman Taji al-Farouki**
	Filastin	**Isa al-Isa**
	al-Akhbar	Bandali Hanna Urabi
	al-Sirat al-Mustaqim	Aballah al-Kalkili
	al-Wahda al-Arabiya	Emile Ghouri
1934	***al-Difa'***	**Ibrahim Sahnti**
	al-Shabab	Emil Ghouri
	al-Kkarmil al-Jadid	Bulus Shehadeh
	al-Iqtisadiyat al-Arabiya	Fu'ad Saleh Saba
	al-Fajr	Alexander Halabi
1935	*al-Awqat al-Arabiya*	Ali Hussieni
	al-Jil	Ibrahim Shanti
	al-Sa'iqa	Abdelghani al-Karmi
	al-Liwa'	Emil Ghouri and Jamal Hussieni
1937	*al-Lahab*	Adib Khuri
1938	*al-Ghad*	Daoud Fisher
1940	*al-Samir*	Munir Hadad
	al-Muntada	Abderahman Bushnaq
	al-Iqdam	Tanyous Farah Nasr
	al-Harb	Yousef Francis
	Huna al-Quds	Palestine Radio
	al-Ittihad	**Emil Tuma**
	al-Rabitah	Bishop Hakim
1945	*al-Wahdah*	Ishaq Abdelsalam Hussieni
	al-Hurriya	Najib Iskandar
	al-Hadaf	Jubriel Deeb
1946	*al-Mihmaz*	Munir Hadad
	al-Nidal	Munir al-Ghuri
	al-Dhakhira	Hussien Hussien
	al-Ra'i al-'Am	Ahmad Khalil Aqad
	al-Nidal	Emil al-Ghuri

16

The Religious, Political and Social Status of the Christian Communities in Palestine c. 1800-1930

Anthony O'Mahony

Christianity in Palestine during the early Islamic period

Although characterised by plurality, the Christian Church was, in its earliest days, one undivided community. Yet well before the time of the first Muslim conquest of Palestine in 638 AD the process of fission had commenced and a number of communities had come into being.[1] There was, however, as yet only one patriarch of Jerusalem and he it was who negotiated with the Muslim conquerors on behalf of all Christians resident in the area. The Islamic conquest of the Holy Land in the 7th-century, transformed the political and religious context and the culture within which Christianity in Palestine lived and expressed itself. A determined cultural shift took place during the early Islamic period; Christians learned how to pray in the language of their conquerors, they produced devotional and theological literature and translated the Gospels into Arabic. The monks in the monasteries of Palestine began to write theology and saints' lives in the Arabic language of the Qur'an and to translate the bible, liturgical texts, hagiographies, patristic texts and other ecclesiastical works from Greek, and sometimes Syriac, into the *lingua franca* of the Islamic caliphate. The Palestinian monasteries of Mar Sabas, Mar Chariton and St Catherine at Mount Sinai, had long been known as

---

[1] P E Peters, *Jerusalem, the Holy City in the Eyes of Chroniclers, Visitors, Pilgrims and Prophets from the Days of Abraham to the Beginnings of Modern Times*, Princeton University Press, 1985; John Binns, *Ascetics and Ambassadors of Christ: the Monasteries of Palestine, 314-631*, Oxford, Clarendon Press, 1994; and Sidney H Griffith, *Arabic Christianity in the Monasteries of Ninth Century Palestine*, London, Variorum, 1992.

important centres of Christian culture in the Holy Land. In the early period after the Muslim conquest of Palestine, scholar-monks, such as Anastasuis of Sinai (d. c. 700) and John of Damascus (d. c. 750) writing in Greek the traditional ecclesiastical language of the Melkite patriarchates in the East, had undertook to confront the religious challenge of Islam. These works of religious controversy would have been taken by refugee monks to Constantinople where they would become part of the general religious literature of Byzantium on Islam. However, by the second half of the 8th-century these Melkite monastic centres in Palestine would themselves be producing the first Christian literature in Arabic. During the early 'Abbasid period many Christian communities throughout the Islamic world would give expression to the Christian faith in Arabic the new *lingua franca* of the caliphate. With their strong involvement with scholarship and being centres of learning and spirituality for the Melkite oriental patriarchates it is not surprising that the Palestinian monastic communities would be one of the first to adopt Arabic as a mode of expression in the emergence of early Arabic Christian literature within the new Islamic milieu. This early period in the development of Arabic Christian literature in Palestine dates between the three centuries from the beginning of the 'Abbasid caliphate in 750 to the eve of the crusader period in 1050. During this period, the Islamic authorities would attempt to induce the conquered peoples to become Muslims with the promise of political and social equality. As a response, the Christian communities started to produce apologetic treatises in Arabic between 750-850 by such figures as Theodore Abu Qurrah, Anthony David of Baghdad and Stephen of Ramlah.[2] These writers and the literature which they produced would set the agenda for religious dialogue between Christians and Muslims for many generations to come.

During this period until the establishment of the crusading kingdoms relations between the various Christian communities in Jerusalem seem to have been good, in spite of the growing estrangement between Rome and Constantinople. However, with the capture of Jerusalem and the setting up of the Latin Kingdoms, the cleavage between Latin and Eastern elements in the Church became more pronounced and the Latins, under their own patriarch, enjoyed paramountcy in all the Holy Places.[3] Since there was some doubt in Eastern eyes about the validity of the appointment of the Latin patriarch, the Eastern Churches also elected a patriarch, but he

[2] S H Griffith, 'The Monks of Palestine and the growth of Christian literature in Arabic', *The Muslim World* vol. 78 (1988), pp 1-28; *idem*, 'Stephen of Ramlah and the Christian Kerygma in Arabic in 9th century Palestine', *Journal of Ecclesiastical History* vol. 36 (1985), pp 23-45; and *idem*, 'Anthony David of Baghdad, scribe and monk of Mar Sabas: Arabic in the monasteries of Palestine', *Church History* vol. 58 (1989), pp 7-19; and on Christian Arabic literature, see: Samir Khalid Samir and Jorgen S Nielson (eds), *Christian Arabic Apologetics during the Abbasid Period (750-1258)*, Leiden, E J Brill, 1994.

[3] Bernard Hamilton, *The Latin Church in the Crusader States: the Secular Church*, London, Variorum, 1980); Joseph Prawer, *The Latin Kingdom of Jerusalem: European Colonialism in the Middle Ages*, London, 1972; and *idem*, 'Social Classes in the Crusader States: the "Minorities"', in *A History of the Crusades*, University of Wisconsin Press, 1985, vol 5., 59-116.

moved to Constantinople for the duration of tenure of the crusading kingdoms. From about 1250 until about 1675 the Orthodox patriarch returned to Jerusalem but then retired once more until the middle of the 19th century. After the demise of the Crusading kingdoms the Latin patriarchate was based in Rome until its revival in 1847.

From the capture of Jerusalem by Saladin until its absorption into the Ottoman empire, Jerusalem was governed by the Ayyubids and the Mamluks of Egypt. The supremacy enjoyed by the Latins was maintained for almost a century after the fall of the city, although this period also saw the fall of the Latin Church from its prominent position and the true beginning of the constant struggle between the Latin and the Orthodox Churches for supremacy, particularly in connection with the ownership of and rights over the Holy Places. The struggle was largely confined to the three main rites recognised by the authorities, namely the Armenians, the Orthodox Church and the Latins. The other rites, although represented in the Holy Places, were generally too poor to be able to take any significant part in the struggle for authority. Nevertheless in 1384 it was reported that seven different communities (Armenians, Copts, Ethiopians, Georgians, Latins, Nubians and Syrians) were represented in the Holy Places. However, throughout the Mamluk period and the subsequent Ottoman period, the history of Jerusalem is primarily a history of continual change of status, of rights of ownership and of position among the various Christian communities in the Holy Places. It should be noted that the majority of the Christian inhabitants of Jerusalem were Eastern or Oriental Christians, whatever happened in the Holy Places. The struggle for position arose not only out of the basic rivalry between the faiths, but also out of the Muslim concept of legal ownership of religious buildings and institutions.[4]

Muslim rulers held themselves to be the legal owners of all religious buildings and institutions within their dominions, no matter the faith to which they were devoted. They therefore claimed the right to allocate them, confiscate them or close them at will. Such buildings could not be repaired or rebuilt without permission, while the building of new churches was for obvious reasons forbidden. Thus Saladin closed the Church of the Holy Sepulchre when he captured Jerusalem in 1187 until he had decided under whose jurisdiction he would place it. Similarly, the Franciscans, who had become established as official representatives in Jerusalem of the Holy See with the official title of Custodian of the Holy Land, were expelled by Imperial decree from their headquarters in the Cenaculum on Mount Zion in 1552. They finally settled in the Convent of St Saviour which they

---

[4] Moshe Gil, *A History of Palestine, 643-1099*, Cambridge University Press, 1992; and 'Al-Kuds', in *Encyclopaedia of Islam* (2nd edition).

acquired from the Orthodox patriarchate, which had itself acquired the convent from the Armenians.[5]

From about beginning of the 16th century onwards the influence of the Orthodox Church was generally greater than of the Latin, despite periods of reversion. This was a logical outcome of the conquest of Constantinople by the Ottoman Turks in 1455 and their subsequent capture of Jerusalem in 1517, since the Orthodox and the Armenian Churches were the first recognised Christian *millets*, while the Latins were usually supported by foreign states with which the Ottoman authorities were at war. The Ottoman period also saw the introduction of international politics into the controversies surrounding Jerusalem and the Holy Places. Thus France claimed the right to protect not only foreigners of Latin persuasion resident in the empire, but also Ottoman subjects who were members of the Latin, Eastern or Oriental Catholic communions. The Russians claimed a similar position in respect of Ottoman subjects with Orthodox beliefs following the Treaty of Kuchuk Kainarja in 1774 as a direct result of French intrigues and opposition to Russian ambitions.[6]

The Christian communities in Ottoman Palestine

With the capture of Constantinople in 1453 Mehmed II became the overlord of a numerous group of Christians at a time when the Orthodox Church was without a leader. The sultan ordered the election of a patriarch to the vacant seat, and by assuming the functions of the defeated *basileus* he presented in person the *dekanikon*, the patriarchial crozier, to Gennadios II. This endowed the patriarch with an authority his predecessors had never enjoyed, for to the religious jurisdiction proper to his position the Ottoman authorities added now civil power over all Christians within the

---

[5] Ammon Cohen, 'The Expulsion of the Franciscans from Mount Zion, Old Documents and New Interpretations', *Turica*, vol. XVIII (1986), 147-158; for 16th century Palestine see: A Cohen, *Palestine in the 18th century: Patterns of Government and Administration*, Jerusalem, The Magnes Press, 1973; *idem, Jewish life under Islam: Jerusalem in the 16th century*, Princeton UP, 1978; *idem, Economic Life in Ottoman Jerusalem*, Cambridge UP, 1989; Amy Singer, *Palestinian Peasants and Ottoman Officials: Rural Administration around 16th Century Jerusalem*, Cambridge UP, 1994; E Toledano: 'The Sanjaq of Jerusalem in the 16th century: Aspects of topography and population', *Archivum Ottomanicum*, vol. 9, 1984, 279-319; and D S Powers, 'Revenues of Public Waqfs in 16th-century Jerusalem', *Archivum Ottomanicum*, vol. 9, 1984, 163-202.

[6] Bernard Collin, *Le problème juridique des Lieux-Saints*, Paris, 1956, 27-65; and Anton Odeh Issa, *Les minorités chrétiennes de Palestine à travers les siècles, étude historico-juridique et développement moderne international*, Jerusalem, Franciscan Printing Press, 1976.

empire, which gave him much authority and equally great responsibilities.[7] What remained after this settlement was an autonomous body under the direct rule in religious and civil affairs of an authority dependent solely on the Ottoman authorities, in effect a state within a state.[8] The generic name given to such a system was *millet*.[9] The term *millet* indicates religion, religious community, and nation. These three basic meanings of the term were used in the Ottoman empire[10] concurrently until the Tanzimat period and afterwards. However, the *millet* system, was not an institution or even group of institutions, but rather it was a set of arrangements, largely social, with considerable variation over time and space.[11]

For administrative purposes the non-Muslim subjects of the Ottoman empire were organised into autonomous religious communities known as *millet*. The heads, both central (i.e. in Istanbul) and local, of the *millets* were chosen by the *millet* but the choice was subject to the sultan's approval, communicated in the form of an imperial *berat,* which alone enabled the nominees to assume their offices and take possession of their temporalities. The heads, both local and central, of the *millets* had an important place in the official hierarchy of the state, of which they were regarded as functionaries. In the provinces they were ex officio members of the provincial administrative councils, while those in Istanbul had the right of audience with the sultan. The heads of *millets* represented their communities in their general and personal affairs *vis-à-vis* the Sublime Porte. The autonomy of the *millets* were based on custom and praxis, which was reinforced in the 19th century by specific edicts whose general spirit is incorporated in the Khatt-i Humayun. Their affairs were conducted by the head of the *millet*, generally assisted by a council

[7] Speros Vryonis, 'The History of the Greek Patriarchate of Jerusalem as reflected in Codex Patriarchicus No 428, 1517-1805', *Byzantine and Modern Greek Studies*, vol. 7 (1981), pp 29-53; Halil Inalcik, 'The Status of the Greek Orthodox Patriarch under the Ottomans', *Turica*, vols. 21-23 (1991), pp 407-437; T Halasi-Kun: 'Gennadiosí Confession of Faith', *Archivum Ottomanicum*, vol. XII (1987-1992), 5-104; and Kemal H Karpet: 'Ottoman Views and Policies towards the Orthodox Christian Church', *Greek Orthodox Theological Review*, vol. 31 (1986), 131-155.

[8] Alexis Alexandris: *The Greek Minority of Istanbul and Greek-Turkish Relations, 1918-1974*, Athens, Centre for Asia Minor Studies, 1992, 2nd edition, 21-30.

[9] F M Pareja: 'Society and Politics', in A J Arberry (ed.): *Religion in the Middle East*, Cambridge UP, 1969, vol. 2, 459-544.

[10] 'Millet', in *Encyclopedia of Islam* (2nd edition)

[11] B Braude, 'Foundation Myths of the Millet system', in B Braude and Bernard Lewis (eds), *Christians and Jews in the Ottoman Empire*, New York-London, 1982, vol. I, 69-88. See also the following works on the evolution of the status of non-Muslims within the Islamic world: Antoine Fattal, *Le statut légal des non-musulmans en pays d'Islam*, Beirut, 1958; *idem*, 'Comment les dhimmis étaient juges en terre d'Islam', *Cahiers d'Histoire Egyptienne*, vol. 3 (1951), 321-341; *idem,* 'La nature juridique du statut des dhimmis', *Annales de la Faculté de Droit*, Université de Saint-Joseph, Beirut, 1956, 139-154; A S Tritton, *The Caliphs and their non-Muslim Subjects: a critical study of the Covenant of Umar*, Oxford, 1930; N Edelby: 'L'autonomie législative des Chrétiens en terre d'Islam', *Archives d' Histoire du Droit Oriental*, vol. 5 (1950-51), 307-351; and I de las Cagigas: 'Las minorias en el Islam y el caso palestina', *Archivos del Instituto de Estudios Africanos*, vol. 3, no 8 (1949), 65-91.

composed of both lay and clerical members. The *millets* were autonomous in spiritual matters and in certain administrative and judicial matters. Their jurisdiction embraced, in the religious sphere, clerical discipline; in the administrative sphere, the control of their properties, including cemeteries, educational institutions and churches; in the judicial sphere, marriage, dowries, divorce and alimony, civil rights, and in some *millets* testamentary dispositions. Sentences pronounced by *millet* courts, if within their competence, were executed on their behalf by the state. In the case of *millets* composed of Christians whose spiritual heads resided outside the Ottoman empire, for example in Rome or Echmiadzin (the supreme head of the Armenian Church), the spiritual head recognised by the authorities had to be a Ottoman subject in possession of the imperial *berat*. For a few years following the Ottoman conquest of Constantinople, the head of the Orthodox *millet* was more than the spiritual and temporal head of the Orthodox subjects of the empire as the sultan's original *berat* gave, but the patriarch had jurisdiction over all Christians in the empire, whatever their Church or rite. Eight years later, however, the Armenian Church under an Armenian patriarch of Constantinople was recognised as a separate community, comprising not only the Armenian Christians, but also the Latins, the Eastern and Oriental Catholic communities, the Jacobites, the Nestorians and the Copts.

A number of points should be noted concerning the jurisdiction and rights of the *millets* and their members. Firstly, the *millet* organisation applied only to Ottoman subjects, and where a particular community included foreigners, these foreigners were treated under the terms of the Capitulations. which accorded a number of privileges including that of a consular jurisdiction. Again, no community was recognised as a *millet*, unless specific formal acknowledgement was given, in the shape of an Imperial decree or other statutory instrument, and the rights and privileges accorded to each *millet* were closely defined in various decrees, *firmans* (decrees or edicts issued by the Ottoman government under the sultan's cipher). Ottoman members of other religious communities were either treated in accordance with the Ottoman civil code or were regarded as coming under the jurisdiction of one of the religious *millets*. Foreign members of religious communities not recognised as *millets* were normally treated in accordance with the terms of the Capitulations. Again, the rights and jurisdiction accorded to the *millets* did not include jurisdiction in the matter of *waqf*, or religious and charitable trust endowment constituted under *shari'a* law. A *waqf* trust, no matter the religious persuasion of the person making the endowment or its purpose could only be constituted and administered through the *shari'a* Courts.

A further restriction was applied by the Ottoman laws which forbade the succession of a foreigners to the estate of an Ottoman subject or of a non-Muslim to the estate of a Muslim, and which provided for the question of succession to be deal with in the civil courts of the Ottoman empire. An Ottoman interdiction on the owning of immovable property by foreigners or foreign corporate bodies had led to a system under which such property actually owned by foreign charitable or religious organisations was registered in the name of an Ottoman subject, with separate and unofficial registers kept recording the actual state of affairs in respect of such property. It should, however, be noted that this interdiction appears to have been circumvented in some cases. Finally, certain of the religious and charitable organisations operating within the Ottoman empire had been accorded certain privileges and exemptions from various taxes and duties.

The Christian population in Ottoman Palestine

Before the Muslim conquest, the population of Palestine was overwhelmingly Christian, divided between the Greek Orthodox, who were a mainly urban community and the Syriac speaking Christians, in the rural areas. In the centuries following the conquest, the Christian population was arabized and many converted to Islam. Nonetheless, a significant minority remained Christian. During the Ottoman period, the largest Christian community was Greek-Arab Orthodox, with various pilgrim and Holy Place Christian communities of a much smaller size (such as the Ethiopians, Syrians, Copts and Armenians). Ottoman documents examined by Ammon Cohen suggest that the Christian community retreated from the rural environs towards the main urban centres between the 16th century and the early 19th century.[12] Proportionately, there were fifty percent fewer villages with a Christian rural population in the 19th century than in the 16th. This process which started in the 16th century continued throughout the following centuries; Christian peasants never returned to the villages they had evacuated; their example was rather followed by others, thus creating a historical pattern. The underlying motivation for this migration from the rural areas to larger urban concentrations with larger Christian populations must have been the concern, real or imaginary, for their own safety and perhaps for their proper communal and religious life. Many Christians attracted by the Holy Places and the security that Jerusalem offered moved there. This was a slow and gradual migration process that went on up until the 19th century and the final result of it was a small Christian presence in the rural areas throughout Palestine.[13] The declining standards of the administrative apparatus and the diminishing Ottoman military presence outside the main towns brought about increasing incursions by the Bedouin tribes on the sedentary population. The density of settlement in 19th century Palestine was far lower than that of the 16th century, the settlement frontier

---

[12] Justin McCarthy, *The Population of Palestine: Population History and statistics of the late Ottoman Period and the Mandate*, New York, 1990, 12f.

[13] Amnon Cohen, 'The Receding of the Christian Presence in the Holy Land: a 19th Century Sijill in the light of 16th Century Tahrirs', in Thomas Philipp (ed): *The Syrian Land in the 18th and 19th Century*, Stuttgart, 1992, 333-340.

retracted and an overall figure of twenty to thirty percent decrease in the density of settlement of Jerusalem.[14] The Christian *millet* or *dhimma* status as protected people was never doubted, however in daily life some Christians found it opportune to hide their identity, pass for Muslims, or gradually or move to Christian concentrations in the main towns in Palestine. In an important Ottoman document issued by the provincial governor of Damascus on 18th October 1807[15] and which has been recently studied, concerns a very sensitive matter, the question of Christians in rural Palestine trying to hide their religious identity and pass for Muslims. The local Ottoman authorities sent orders to the Christian population living in several villages within the Jerusalem district, in which they were explicitly forbidden to make any further attempts at masquerading as Muslims 'since this would not only be contrary to the conditions laid down by Shari'a law and the very substance of Islam but would also bring the proper functioning of a Muslim state into disrepute.' At this late stage of Ottoman rule in Palestine and after so many generations of life within a Muslim society, the local Christian population could be scarcely distinguished from their Muslim neighbours. An Arab Christian could be set apart by neither his speech nor his profession. The only remaining outward sign of his distinct position in an Islamic society was his clothing and head-dress. The easiest way therefore to hide one's Christian identity was to change one's clothing and dress as a Muslim. The best way to achieve this would have been to change the mandatory black headwear for a Christian into the traditional Muslim colour, white. The validity of this restriction in the early 19th century, as well as the attempts of the Christians to hide their identity, give us a glimpse into the nature of the relationship between Christians and Muslims prior to the Tanzimat reforms which would alter existing social arrangements which were dominated by Islamic practice and *shari'a* law.

The Christian communities increased at a greater rate than the Muslim community, especially in the *sanjak* of Jerusalem in the 19th century. This increase can be explained principally by the fact that the Christian community was generally more urban and less likely to reside in rural areas where mortality was high. The growth of the other Christian communities in the 19th century was primarily through conversion, more specifically conversion from the Greek Orthodox community, this was particularly true for the Greek and Latin Catholic communities. Other groups, such as the Chaldeans, Syrian Orthodox and Syrian Catholics do not appear in the population records of Jerusalem until the end of the empire.[16]

---

[14] W D Hütteroth, *Historical geography of Palestine, Transjordan and Syria in the late 16th Century*, Erlangen, 1977, 56-63; and D H Amiran: 'The Pattern of Settlement in Palestine', *Israel Exploration Journal*, vol. 3 (1953), 65-78; 192-209 and 250-260.

[15] A Cohen, 'The Receding Christian Presence in the Holy Land'.

[16] McCarthy, *op. cit.*, 13.

Ottoman Palestine in the 19th century

Throughout the Ottoman period and until the early decades of the 19th century Jerusalem was regarded as an ordinary *sanjak* without any special significance.[17] On the whole, it was part of the province of Sham (Damascus) and subject to its governor. Its jurisdiction was limited to the Judean hills. The coastal plains from Jaffa to Gaza formed administrative units of their own: the *sanjaks* of Gaza and Jaffa. Indeed, the *sanjaks* of central and southern Palestine were, until the 19th century, of marginal importance to the Ottomans. In the 18th century, due to the decline of law and order in the empire, those *sanjaks* were neglected and went through a period of substantial decline. In the 19th century, however, this situation changed radically. New challenges facing the Ottoman government during that century aroused the need for reinforcement of Ottoman rule in the area.. Consequently, the *sanjaks* of Jerusalem and Gaza acquired a renewed importance for the Ottoman authorities.[18]

The 19th century saw the revival of interest in the Holy Land throughout the Christian world, from Ethiopia to the Americas, from Russia to England, for a great variety and complexes reasons.[19] At the beginning of the century, the Franciscans were the only representatives of Latin Christianity to be found in Jerusalem. The various Eastern Churches were represented as they had been for centuries, but with the exception of the Orthodox Church and the Armenians, their following in Jerusalem was insignificant, apart from the inhabitants of the various convents and monasteries. This is, however, hardly surprising since the population of Jerusalem at the beginning of the century was estimated to be more than 12,000.[20]

During the period between the end of the Crimean War and the beginning of the First World War, there was a general extension of all religious interests. The increase of Russian influence among the Orthodox was paralleled by a steady increase of French influence among the Latins and the Eastern and Oriental Catholic communities. In this connection the establishment of consuls in Jerusalem helped considerably, the first in the

---

[17] Butrus Abu Mannah, 'The Rise of the Sanjak of Jerusalem in the late 19th century', in Gabriel Ben-Gor (ed), *The Palestinians and the Middle East*, Ramats Gan, 1978, 21-32.

[18] B Abu Mannah, 'Jerusalem in the Tanzimat period: the new Ottoman Administration and the Notables', in *Die Welt des Islams*, N.S. vol. 30 (1990), 1-44; *idem*, 'The establishing and dismantling of the Province of Syria 1865-1888', in *Problems of the modern Middle East in Historical Perspective*, (ed) JP Spagnolo, Ithaca Press, 1992, 7-26; Haim Gerber, *Ottoman Rule in Jerusalem, 1890-1914*, Berlin, 1985; *idem* 'The Ottoman Administration of the Sanjag of Jerusalem 1890-1908', *Asian and African Studies*, vol. XII (1978), 33-76; *idem,* 'A new look at the Tanzimat: the Case of the Province of Jerusalem', in *Palestine in the late Ottoman Period*, (ed) David Kushner, Leiden, 1986, 30-45.

[19] Naomi Sheppard, *The Zealous Intruders: The Western Rediscovery of Palestine*, San Francisco, Harper and Row, 1987, 11-44.

[20] McCarthy, *op. cit.*, 15-16.

field being, as already stated, the British in 1838, followed by the French, Prussian and Sardinian consuls in 1843, the Americans in 1844 and the Austrians replacing the Sardinians in 1849. The Russians, however, were constant to be represented by an agent in Jerusalem dependent on their consulate general in Beirut, which had been there since 1839, until 1858.

The Christian communities and their institutions played a very important part in the creation of modern Palestine. The importance of Jerusalem and the Holy Land in Christianity was a historical reality, however, also of importance was its institutional expression. The jurisdiction of the Greek Orthodox patriarchate of Jerusalem possibly the oldest and most important Christian institution in Palestine extended. The patriarchate had existed without a break since the Roman period, and apparently, from the very beginning, held authority over the three Roman districts of Palestine: Palestina Prima, Secunda and Tertia. The Latin patriarchate of Jerusalem, re-established in 1847, and the Anglican bishop of Jerusalem, first appointed at the end of 1841, also held authority over the whole of Palestine. It is not surprising, therefore, that among the Christian population of Palestine, the concept of Palestine was of significance.[21] The existence of the *sanjak* of Jerusalem for almost two generations as a separate entity was of a tremendous importance for the emergence of Palestine about fifty years later. It also did much to determine the character and future of Palestinian politics, and contributed to the emergence of Palestinian nationalism of which the Christian communities were to be intimately bound up with.[22]

The Christian communities and the early growth of the Arab National Movement in Palestine

One of the most important phenomena characterising the political life of Palestine from the late Ottoman Palestine and especially during the British Mandate was the formation of a joint Muslim-Christian front within the emergence of the Palestinian Arab National Movement.[23] This was something completely new and opposed to the long tradition of Christian isolation from public life. In the course of the process of reform in the Ottoman empire in the 19th century the Ottoman government had attempted to improve the status of its Christian subjects and to give them equality with the Muslims. This process had been a source of increasing bitterness to the Muslim community and created tensions between the two communities. In a period of transformation a marginal community's power

[21] Porath, *op. cit.*, 7.
[22] Muhammad Muslih, *Urban Notables, Ottomanism, Arabism and the Rise of Palestinian Nationalism, 1864-1920* (PhD Colombia University, 1986); *idem, The Origins of Palestinian Nationalism*, New York, Columbia UP, 1988.
[23] Y Porath, *The Emergence of the Palestinian-Arab National Movement, 1918-1929*, London, 1974, 293-303.

to influence and shape the dominant community is greatest when the characteristic institutions are in the process of formation, radical modification, or destruction which the marginal community is able to accelerate and focus.[24] Arab Christians actively participated in the emerging Arab national movement because they regarded it as the opportunity to break the yoke of their marginality and to create an ideology and community sufficiently broad to encompass them as full and equal participants.[25] The influence of the Palestinian Arab Christians on the national movement in its formative stage was less marked than that of the Syrian Christians because the Palestinian Arab national movement appeared later on, in 1918, when the influence of Islam on the movement was already apparent. Nevertheless, the early years of the Palestinian Arab movement were marked by the attempt to give Christians an equal position and to disregard religious affiliation. Both Muslims and Christians recognised the Islamic content of Arab history and culture. Though the majority of national leaders, on the ideological level, carefully avoided giving an explicit definition of Arab nationalism in Islamic terms.[26] One observer commenting on the political and religious dilemma of one of the Arab Christian communities in Palestine wrote:

> In order to convince themselves - if not others - that they formed part of the Arab Nation they would have to reject what had governed the social arrangements of their community for countless generations and provided a sense of identity with their fathers and fathers' fathers. In the past they had been members of a religious community, and this membership at

---

[24] Robert Haddad, *Syrian Christians in Muslim Society: An Interpretation*, Princeton University Press, 1970, 3.

[25] S G Haim, 'Islam in the Theory of Arab Nationalism', *Die Welt des Islams* N.S. vol. 4 (1955), 124-149 and *idem*, 'Islam and Arab Nationalism', in *Die Welt des Islams* N.S. vol. 3 (1954), 201-218. For the debate on the origins of Arab Nationalism, see: Mahmoud Haddad, 'The Rise of Arab Nationalism Reconsidered', *International Journal of Middle East Studies*, vol. 26 (1994), 201-222; C Earnest Dawn, *From Ottomanism to Arabism: Essays on the Origins of Arab Nationalism*, University of Illinois Press, 1973, 3-30; and Rashid Khalidi, 'Ottomanism and Arabism in Syria before 1914: a Reassessment', in Rashid Khalidi *et al.*, (eds), *The Origins of Arab Nationalism*, Columbia UP, 1991; and the older studies by C Earnest Dawn, *op. cit.*; and S G Haim, *Arab Nationalism: an Anthology*, University of California Press, 1962. For a survey of the political situation which confronted Islam, see Jacob M Landau, *The Politics of Pan-Islam: Ideology and Organization*, Oxford, 1990; and for the role of Islam in Palestinian nationalism, see N Johnson, *Islam and the Politics of Meaning in Palestinian Nationalism*, London, 1982.

[26] Daphne Tsimhoni, 'The Arab Christians and the Palestinian Arab National Movement during the formative stage', in Gabriel Ben-Gor (ed), *The Palestinians and the Middle East*, Ramat Gan, 1978, 73-98. For political Islam during the Mandate, see D R Irvine, 'Islamic Culture and Political Practice in British Mandated Palestine 1918-1948', *Review of Politics*, vol. 45 (1983), 71-93; and U M Kupferschmidt, 'Islam on the Defensive: The Supreme Muslim Council's role in Mandatory Palestine', *Asian and African Studies*, vol. 17 (1983), 175-206; and *idem*, *The Supreme Muslim Council 1921-1937: Islam under the British Mandate for Palestine* (PhD, Hebrew University, Jerusalem, 1978).

once defined their status and set the bounds of their public as of their private activity. Loyalty did not extend beyond the community, and traffic between communities was confined to an inescapable minimum of externals. But now this religion suddenly seemed a badge of servitude. Membership of the Arab nation had a price – which Muslims, being the majority and the rulers, did not have to pay. It meant the abandonment of communal organisation and the defiant assertion that religion was a private affair, that it could not be the constitutive principle of a society, that it had no political and little social significance. This radical change of view in a matter so intimate and so fundamental came abruptly, and if only because abrupt, it must also have been violent, creating a schism and discord within the community. When therefore, outside observers reported the solidarity of Christians with Muslims, were they not perhaps unwittingly echoing the claims and professions of the victorious party in a species of civil war which had raged inside the . . . Christian community.[27]

Another version of this dilemma was composed by the authors of the Commission, Bertram and Young, reporting on the controversies between the Greek Orthodox patriarchate and the Arab Orthodox community:

National consciousness is not a matter of what ought to be felt, but of what actually is felt. No amount of eloquent reasoning could persuade the inhabitants of Alsace-Lorraine that their true national consciousness is German. Similarly no amount of such reasoning would persuade the Orthodox congregation of Palestine that they are not Arabs . . . The dearest thought to every young local Orthodox Christian is that he is an Arab, and his most cherished aspirations are those of Arab nationalism, which he shares with his Moslem fellow-countrymen.[28]

Arab nationalism as an organised political movement with ideology and aims is a phenomenon of the twentieth century. Prior to the First World War it was confined to closed intellectual circles in Damascus, Beirut, Istanbul, Cairo and Paris, and was expressed through publication of

[27] E Kedourie, 'Religion and Politics: the Diaries of Khalid Sakakini', in *The Chatham Version and other Middle Eastern Studies*, Hanover, University Press of New England, 1984, 317-350, 319.

[28] A Bertram and J W A Young, *Report of the Commission Appointed by the Government of Palestine to inquire and report upon certain controversies between the Orthodox Patriarchate of Jerusalem and the Arab Orthodox Community*, Oxford, 1926, 57-8.

newspapers and pamphlets and the formation of secret societies the majority of which did not work for Arab independence and separation from the Ottoman empire before the war.[29]

One of the first political expression of discontent with Ottoman rule and a desire for an independent Arab state occurred in Najib Azuri's (Najib Azouri) book published in 1905.[30] Azouri was born (c. 1870) in the village of 'Azur in southern Lebanon. He was a Syrian Christian, a Maronite or Greek Catholic, educated in Constantinople and Paris. He was made an assistant to the Governor of Jerusalem and served as an official in the *sanjak* of Jerusalem from 1898 until 1904, when he fled to Egypt and after a while to Paris. While he himself was not from Palestine, he was well acquainted with the local Arab Christian population in Palestine.

Azouri's only preserved book was published in French under the title: *Le Réveil de la nation arabe dans l'Asie Turquie en présence des interêts et des rivalités des puissances étrangères, de la Curie Romaine et du patriarcat oecuménique. Partie asiatique de la question de l'Orient et programme de la Ligue de la Patrie Arabe.* Azouri mentions three further works he intended to compose in *Le Réveil . . .*, and although he never wrote them they are indicative of his intended programme:

1. La Patrie arabe. étude approfondie de l'état actuel et de l'avenir des pays arabes asiatiques.

2. Le Péril Juif universel. Révèlations et études politiques.

3. Les puissances étrangères et la question des sanctuaires chrétiens de Terre-Sainte. Résumé historique et exposé de la situation actuelle.

These titles clearly set out the principal points of Azouri's political thought: i) an Arab nation which has to be established in the Arab fatherland, ii) the question of the Christian Holy Places reflecting the communal division of Christian Arabs; and iii) the beginnings of Zionist immigration. For Azouri, these three questions could only be solved if and when Ottoman rule comes to an end in Palestine. In his *Le Réveil*, Azouri deals with four principal themes: an Arab nation has to be established; Ottoman rule has to come to an end; an all-Arab Catholic church must be formed, gathering all the other Christian communities within it; and the Zionist problem. With regard to the first point the termination of the Ottoman empire, this could only be achieved with the help of European powers. Azouri developed a detailed plan of action for the Christian Arab

---

[29] E Tauber, *The Emergence of the Arab Movements*, London, 1993; and *idem*, *The Arab Movements in World War I*, London, 1993.

[30] Stefan Wild, 'Negib Azoury and His Book: Le réveil de la nation arabe', in Marwan R Buheiry (ed), *Intellectual Life in the Arab East 1890-1939*, Beirut, 1981, 92-104; and Martin Kramer, 'Azoury: a Further Episode', *Middle Eastern Studies*, vol. 18 (1982), 351-58.

communities. He denounced the constant quarrels between the various Christian communities over the Holy Places in Jerusalem and their deep internal divisions and conflicts, and places the sole responsibility for this state of affairs was Ottoman rule. Azouri further proposes the creation of an national Arabic catholic church where the language of prayer and liturgy would be exclusively Arabic. Azouri proposes that such a church should have a patriarch of its own and predicts that this new rite will absorb all the others, which would include the Orthodox communities as well within a short period of time. He implores the pope to take steps in this direction. Azouri's ideas encountered opposition from other Arab Christian thinkers.[31]

The growing Jewish immigration into Palestine and in particular the purchase of land and the establishment of new colonies caused apprehension among Arab Palestinians. But, on the whole, early expressions of Arab opposition prior to 1908 were sporadic and caused by socio-economic rather than by ideological factors. The urban professional and middle classes, predominantly Christian, resented the new Jewish immigrants. It was Arab Christians who, in June 1891, organised the first Arab protest to the government against Jewish immigration,[32] which was the first political action of this nature; for in the towns Christians and Jews had, for a long time, lived in separate quarters and practised more or less the same professions and skills.

The upheavals in the Ottoman empire in 1908 ushered in the era of the Arab press in Palestine which became the standard-bearer in the struggle against Zionism. And it was only after 1908 that a consistent activity against Jewish settlement started and which was led by two influential and important Christian owned newspapers, *Filastin* by the al-'Isa brothers (Orthodox Arabs),[33] and *al-Karmil* by Najib Nasser. Nasser organised a campaign against the purchase of land by Zionists, especially in the north, and was also the first Arab to publish a book on Zionism.[34] *Al-Karmil*, tended to support the reformist and decentralist movement within the

[31] See for example, Stefan Wild, 'Ottomanism versus Arabism. The Case of Farid Kassab (1884-1970)', *Die Welt des Islams*, N.S. vol. 28 (1988), 607-627.

[32] N Mandel, *The Arabs and Zionism before World War I*, Berkeley, 1976; *idem*, 'Attempts at an Arab-Zionist Entente 1913-1914', *Middle Eastern Studies*, vol. I, no 3 (1965), 238-267; *idem*, 'Turks, Arabs and Jewish Immigration into Palestine 1882-1914', St Antony's Papers, no 17 (1965), 77-108; and Yaacou Rosi: 'The Zionist Attitudes to the Arabs, 1908-1914', *Middle Eastern Studies*, vol. 4, no 3 (1968), 198-242.

[33] Porath, *op. cit.*, 26-27; also see the important study by Qustandi Shomali, *The Arabic Press in Palestine: bibliography of literary and cultural texts: Filastin Newspaper 1911-1967*, Jerusalem: Arab Studies Society, 1990, vols. 1 and 2, and Jerusalem Research Center, 1992, vol. 3.

[34] Najib Nasser was an Arab Orthodox Christian who, it would seem, converted to Protestantism prior to the First World War but stayed in very close contact with the Orthodox community in Palestine. He published in Haifa in 1911 *Al-Sahyuniyya: Ta'rikhula, Gharaduha, Ahamiyyatuha*. For a detailed description of his activities, see Mandel, *The Arabs and Zionism before World War I*, Berkeley, 1976, 204-277; and on his book, 252-260; see also, Y Porath, 'Anti-Zionist and Anti-Jewish Ideology in the Arab Nationalist Movement in Palestine', in Shamuel Almog (ed), *Anti-Semitism through the Ages*, Oxford, 1988, 217-226.

Ottoman empire. On the other hand, *Filastin*, opposed it vehemently, and reflected Ottoman ideology, advocating the partnership of all citizens of the Ottoman empire in one united state, with full equality for members of all religions and nationalities. The fact that the newspapers, the leaders of the campaign against Zionists, were owned mostly by Christians brought Zionist circles to believe at the time that antipathy towards Jewish immigrants was mostly confined to Arab Christians. However, such feeling also prevailed among Muslim circles, but Christians, being better educated, were better equipped to express and circulate them.[35]

We also find Christian Arabs writing poetry to Palestine, which given the prevailing themes can be seen as an early sign of a growing Palestinian national feeling. Thus the poem written by the priest Elias Marmura of Nazareth, praising the beauty of his city in tender and obvious pride, is undoubtedly a Palestinian poem:[36]

> From the valley of Jesreel a city is beheld
> Gloriously competing with the clouds
> Now turning to Tabor, now to Carmel.
> Lying there, indifferent to the waves of the sea below,
> Amused she glances at white-bearded Hermon
> While Gilboa, overwhelmed, is craving for her.

If voices were raised in Palestinian political circles in protest against Zionist settlement before the First World War, these voices became even more vociferous after the capture of Jerusalem in December 1917, and after news of the Balfour Declaration had reached Palestine. During the following years the activity which had formerly been carried on by individuals was organised by establishing political national bodies and found its expression in several dimensions.[37]

---

[35] Rashid Khalid, 'Palestinian Peasant Reactions to Zionism before World War I', in Buheiry (ed), *op. cit.*, 207-233; and *idem*, 'Social Factors in the Rise for the Arab Movement in Syria', in Said Amir Argomand (ed), *From Nationalism to Revolutionary Islam*, London, 1984, 53-70.

[36] On Arab Christians and the development of Palestinian Literature during the Mandate Period, and where we find the translation of Elias Marmura, see M Peled, 'Annals of Doom: Palestinian Literature 1917-1948', *Arabica*, vol. 29, no 2 (1982), 143-183; for the use of religious symbolism in growth of nationalism, see Stefan Wild, 'Judentum, Christentum und Islam in der Palästinensischen Poesie', *Die Welt des Islams*, N.S. vols. XXIII-XXIV (1984), 259-297; and Khalid A Suliman, *Palestine and Modern Arab Poetry*, London, 1984.

[37] Porath, *op. cit.*, 31. For the early period of British administration in Palestine, see John J McTague, *The British Policy in Palestine 1917-1922*, University of America Press, 1984; and *idem*, 'The British Military Administration in Palestine, 1917-1920', *Journal of Palestine Studies*, vol. 7 (1978), 55-76; Y Porath, 'The Political Awakening of the Palestinian Arabs and their leadership towards the end of the Ottoman Period', in M Ma'oz (ed), *Studies on Palestine during the Ottoman Period*, Jerusalem, 1975, 351-383; and *idem*, 'The Social Aspects of the Emergence of the Palestinian Arab National Movement', in M Milson (ed), *Society and Political Structure in the Arab World*, New York, 1973, 93-144.

The religious and social status of the Christian communities in the 1920s and 1930s

The First World War and its immediate aftermath had disastrous consequences for the Eastern and Oriental Christian communities. Never since the capture of Constantinople (1453) and the disappearance of the Byzantine empire had Eastern Christians suffered such damage to itself and its institutions. On the surface, nothing appeared to survive of the socio-political framework which, in the two opposing Eastern empires the Russian and the Ottoman, once sustained a Christianity closely bound up with the very structures of the two States. In Russia, the violent severance of the age-old and indissoluble links between the Church and the state following the Bolshevik Revolution created a structural void to which was soon added an ideological opposition to the Church whose consequences were incalculable. In the territories of the former Ottoman empire, the Greek-Arab Orthodox community and the Oriental Christians had to submit to another form of disintegration. The various communities emerged from the war weakened by long periods of famine and by repeated massacres, in Anatolia, in Armenia and Cilicia, in northern Mesopotamia, Lebanon and in northern Syria. The dissolution of the empire which followed the armistice of Mudros (30 October 1919) and the allied occupation of Constantinople (1919-23), and after that the institution of the mandate regimes, which gave Britain and France a privileged position in the Arab provinces in the Middle East, had important consequences for the Christian communities. Instead of dealing as in the past with a single Islamic power, the post-war socio-political situation confronted the Christians with a wide variety of regimes and forms of states, which not only provided opportunities for participation in the new entities but also divided ancient communities. In addition, the Arab nationalist inspired independence movements which developed, confronted Christians whether Copt, Melkite, Assyro-Chaldean, Syriac-Jacobite or Maronites, with new religious-political choices which in many cases split their confessional and ecclesial entity asunder between competing loyalties and states.

The origins, declaration and implementation of the British Mandate for Palestine have been the subject of intense and deep scholarly research and controversy.[38] The Mandate for Palestine was to be very different from the other mandates which had been devised for other parts of the region, Iraq,

---

[38] Henry Laurens, 'Genèse de la Palestine mandataire', *Maghreb Machrek*, no 140 (1993), 3-34; Charles D Smith, *Palestine and the Arab-Israeli Conflict*, New York, St Martin's Press, 2nd edition, 1992; Michael J Cohen, *The Origins and Evolution of the Arab-Zionist Conflict*, University of California Press, 1987; Isaiah Friedman, *The Question of Palestine: British-Jewish-Arab Relations, 1914-1918*, Transaction Publishers, New Brunswick and London, 2nd expanded edition, 1992; also see Charles D Smith's important critique of Friedman: 'The Invention of a Tradition: the Question of Arab Acceptance of the Zionist Right to Palestine during World War I', *Journal of Palestine Studies*, vol. XXII, no 2, 48-61.

Syria and Lebanon. The latter were considered to be Class A Mandates, that is territories whose independence at some point in future had been provisionally recognised subject only to the administrative assistance of the mandatory. For Syria and Iraq, the mandatory power was obliged to draw up an organic law to provide for self-government and prepare the country for independence. The Mandate for Palestine was formulated with different intentions. Palestine was given the status of a Class B Mandate, and hence was not destined for independence; the idea was not even considered in the terms of the Mandate. The British Mandatory Power in Palestine was charged with promoting the political, administrative and economic conditions to ensure the establishment of a national home for the Jewish people, while protecting the civil and religious rights of the rest of the population. Considering the terms of the Mandate, it was inevitable that the British authorities found it difficult to accommodate the different aspirations of the Arab, Muslim and Christian and the Jewish communities.[39]

The Christian communities under the Mandate: the constitutional framework

In order to provide a basis for a consideration of subsequent developments, it is necessary to summarise the position of the Christian communities under the Mandate. The Mandate for Palestine was allotted by the League of Nations to the United Kingdom in 1920, the text of the Mandate document was finally approved by the League in July 1922 and it came formally into effect in September 1923, two months after the signature of the Treaty of Lausanne. This document, together with the Palestine Order in Council 1922, as subsequently amended and modified by later Orders in Council and enactments of the Government of Palestine provided the framework within which the Christian communities in Jerusalem and in Palestine as a whole functioned.

The fundamental rights of minorities were recognised by the Mandate for Palestine. Article 2 guaranteed the civil and religious rights of all inhabitants of the country, whatever their race or religion. Article 13 of the Mandate vested in the Mandatory 'all responsibility in connection with the Holy Places and religious buildings or sites in Palestine, including that of preserving existing rights and securing free access to the Holy Places,' while Article 14 provided for the appointment of a Special Commission to 'study define and determine' rights and claims in connection with the Holy Places and the different religious communities in Palestine. Article 9 charged the Mandatory with responsibility for ensuring a complete guarantee of their rights to all inhabitants of Palestine, whether nationals or foreigners, under the judicial system to be established in Palestine, it states: 'Respect for the

---

[39] Jacob Landau, 'Mandates', in *Encyclopaedia of Islam*, 2nd edition.

personal status of the various peoples and communities and for their religious interests shall be fully guaranteed. In particular, the control and administration of *waqfs* shall be exercised in accordance with religious law and the dispositions of the founders.' Articles 15 and 16 enjoined the Mandatory to ensure freedom of worship, the right of individual religious communities to maintain schools for the education of their own members and an absence of discrimination on grounds of race, religion or language, while allowing for such supervision of religious and charitable bodies of all faiths as was required for the maintenance of public order and good government. Finally, Article 8 decreed that the privileges and immunities, including the benefits of consular jurisdiction and protection, formerly enjoyed under the terms of the Capitulations would not apply in Palestine during the period of the Mandate.[40]

These general provisions were further defined and clarified in the Palestine Order in Council 1922 which was promulgated in August 1922 and designed to form a constitutional instrument establishing the framework of the administration. The preamble to the Order stated that although British Government were committed to implementing the Balfour Declaration, this was subject to the understanding that 'nothing should be done which might prejudice the civil and religious rights of existing non-Jewish communities in Palestine.' Article 46 of the Order laid down that the jurisdiction of the Civil Courts as defined in the Order should be exercised in conformity with the Ottoman Law in force in Palestine on 1 November 1914, such later Ottoman Laws as had been or might be declared in force by Public Notice, and such Orders in Council, Ordinances and Regulations as were in force when the Order took effect, or might subsequently be applied or enacted. Matters not governed by such legislation would be treated according to English Common Law. Article 51 provided that the courts of religious communities which were established and exercising jurisdiction at the date of the Order would continue to exercise jurisdiction in matters of personal status, defined as suits regarding marriage, divorce, alimony, maintenance, guardianship, legitimation and adoption of minors, inhibition from dealing with property of persons who were legally incompetent, successions, wills and legacies, and the administration of the property of absent person. Article 54 further defined the jurisdiction of the courts of the Christian communities as:

> i. Exclusive jurisdiction in matter of marriage and divorce, alimony and confirmation of wills of members of the community other than foreigners as defined in the Order.

> ii. Jurisdiction in any other matters of personal status of such persons, where all parties to the action consented to their jurisdiction.

[40] Bernard Wasserstein, *The British in Palestine: the Mandatory Government and the Arab-Jewish Conflict 1917-1929*, Blackwell, Oxford, 2nd edition, 1991.

iii. Exclusive jurisdiction over any case concerning the constitution or internal administration of a *waqf* or religious endowment constituted before a Religious Court according to the religious law of the community concerned.

The judgements of the religious courts would be executed by the civil court procedures (Article 56). It should be noted that the above provisions applied only to Palestinian members of the communities, and that jurisdiction over foreigners who might be members of a community was exercised by the civil courts, although, in matters of personal status, a foreigner could agree to such matters being tried by the religious court applicable, with the provision that in such cases the religious courts other than the Muslim religious courts could not grant divorce to foreigners. The order provided that the term foreigner would include corporations constituted under the law of a foreign state, and religious or charitable bodies or institutions wholly or mainly composed of foreigners. The order also provided that no Ordinance should be passed which restricted complete freedom of conscience, the free exercise of forms of worship, which discriminated in any way between inhabitants of Palestine on grounds of race, religion or language, and which were in any way inconsistent with the terms of the Mandate (Article 18).

Although the position of the Christian communities was fairly closely defined by the Mandate and the 1922 Order in Council, there was no legal provision for the continuation of the network of privileges and immunities which had accrued to the communities in general or to certain members of the communities in particular under Ottoman rule. Subject to the provisions of the Mandate and the Order in Council, these privileges and immunities were generally maintained by the Mandatory Administration. It was, however, found necessary from time to time to enact ordinances to validate the continued enjoyment of the privileges, to provide further definition of rights and jurisdiction and to deal with anomalies which arose. The necessity for such legislation arose because the rights, privileges and immunities enjoyed by the religious communities were of two types. The several rights and privileges in connection with the Holy Places, as defined by Ottoman statutes, had been laid down in the Status Quo of 1757, and confirmed in 1852. During the Mandate these rights and privileges were regulated by the 1757 and 1852 statutes, as extended by later decisions of the secular power based on the Status Quo principles. However, other rights, privileges and immunities enjoyed by some or all of the Christian communities and their charitable, education and medical institutions had never been satisfactorily defined or codified. To some extent they were covered by various Ottoman *firmans* and decrees, but in some cases the relevant *firmans* were contradictory, and in others an oral grant of a privilege was never confirmed in writing. The Palestine government, therefore, took the view that any community or organisation could claim the right to enjoy a particular privilege if it could prove that it had enjoyed the privilege under the Ottomans. In addition, a number of discriminatory and contradictory *firmans* were regulated by ordinance.[41]

The millet *system under the British Mandate*

The British Mandate for Palestine whilst inheriting only part of the Ottoman empire, would nonetheless inherit many Ottoman institutions and procedures, and in particular the *millet* system. The treatment of the Christians as a religious minority by the British mandate in Palestine represented the preservation and development of the Ottoman *millet* system.[42]

The unique character of the Mandate for Palestine and its guaranteeing of the rights of the Christians as a religious minority on the one hand, and the existence of the Holy Places, sacred to the three great religions, on the other, would determine the continuation of the Ottoman *millet* system under the British Mandate.

This continuation of the *millet* system in Palestine under the British Mandate placed the Muslim community upon a completely different communal and political footing than under the Ottoman administration. The status of the Muslim community in Palestine had not been considered a separate community up until 1917, but as part of the general Islamic religious and political body which ruled the Ottoman empire. Under the British Mandate, the Muslim community came to resemble that of an Ottoman *millet*, which had previously been the status and organisation of non-Muslim communities. The Muslim community in Palestine found itself severed from the Islamic environment which it had traditional given context and meaning to its religious, political and social status. Under the British Mandate the Muslim community as the majority community found itself without a communal status and institutions, and at a disadvantage *vis-à-vis* the Christian and Jewish communities.[43]

The status of the Christians communities in Palestine was determined by the unique nature and the terms of the British Mandate. The Mandate articles provided for the continuance and development of the Ottoman

---

[41] Edoardo Vitta, *The Conflict of Laws in Matters of Personal Status in Palestine*, Tel Aviv, 1947; Frederic M Goadby, *International Interreligious Private Law in Palestine*, Jerusalem, 1926; and F M Goadby, 'Religious Communities and Courts in Palestine', *Tulane Law Review*, vol. 8, no 2 (1934), 215-235.

[42] Georges Batch, *Statut Personnel: Introduction à l'étude de la Conduite juridique des Chrétiens de Palestine sous la Domination ottomane (1517-1917)*, Rome, Pontificia Universita Lateranense, 1963; Daphne Tsimboni, 'The Status of the Arab Christians under the British Mandate in Palestine', *Middle Eastern Studies*, vol. 20 no 4 (1984), 166-192.

[43] Uri M Kupferschmidt, *The Supreme Muslim Council: Islam under the British Mandate for Palestine*, Leiden, E J Brill, 1987, 1-16; Robert H Eisenman, *Islamic Law in Palestine and Israel: A History of the Survival of Tanzimat and Sheriía in the British Mandate and the Jewish State*, Leiden, E J Brill, 1978; and: Michael Dumper, *Islam and Israel: Muslim Religious Endowments and the Jewish State*, Washington: DC: Institute for Palestine Studies, 1994, 7-24.

millet system, with the innovation that no religion was to be the state religion. But whilst the Christian communities had been used to operating as a minority religious *millet* during the long centuries of Ottoman rule in Palestine, Christian communal organisations were in a very poor state and desperately needed reviving and reforming.

The basis of recognition of religious communities by the British Mandate was the continuation of autonomous rights obtained during the Ottoman period. The first list of recognised Christian communities under the British Mandate can be found as a schedule to the Succession Ordinance 1923 and including the communities which had been officially recognised by the Ottoman government: Greek Orthodox, Latin (Roman Catholic), Armenian Orthodox, Armenian Catholic, Chaldean Catholic, Syrian Catholic. To these were added the Greek Catholic community recognised in 1923[44] and the Maronite community in 1924.[45] The amended Palestine Order-in-Council 1939 added to this list the Syrian Orthodox community, and altogether nine communities were recognised throughout the mandatory period. However, the Protestant church, did not obtain the official status of a recognised community on the grounds that it had not obtained such a status during the Ottoman period.[46]

The Christian religious courts during the Mandate

An important part of the Ottoman *millet* system was the autonomy of the non-Muslim religious law courts. This autonomy was continued under the Mandate as part of a general adoption of many elements of Ottoman procedure. Article 9 of the Mandate for Palestine provided that 'respect for the personal status of the various peoples and communities and their religious interests shall be fully guaranteed.' By the Palestine Order in Council 1922, the Civil Courts were given in matters of personal status residuary jurisdiction but the religious courts, Muslim, Christian and Jewish, were confirmed in their traditional jurisdiction over members of their respective communities.

In Palestine the Christian communal religious law courts were not well developed after the long years of Islamic governance. The majority of Palestine Christians belonged to the jurisdiction of the Greek Orthodox patriarch of Jerusalem and his Synod. For many Arab Palestinian Christians the Orthodox patriarchate of Jerusalem had long ceased to fully represent their interests.[47] There was, therefore, but little incentive for Arab

---

44 *Palestine Official Gazette*, 1 September, 1923
45 *Palestine Official Gazette*, 1 September 1924
46 See the observations of the draft Constitution of Palestine by R H Drayton, a legal secretary to the Palestine Government, 6 October, 1921. Co 733-6.
47 Daphne Tsimhoni, 'The Greek Orthodox Patriarchate of Jerusalem during the formative years of the British Mandate in Palestine', *Asian and African Studies*, vol. 12 (1978), 77-122).

Christians to claim its competence as against the *shari'a* courts in any case not affecting the vital social ideas of the community. In Palestine the jurisdiction of non-Muslim courts had been reduced to a minimum. In practice all questions of successions were brought before Shari'a courts which distributed the estate in accordance with Islamic law, or, as regards *miri* Land, to which category much land in Palestine belonged, in accordance with the Ottoman *miri* law. Christians became therefore accustomed to the application of Islamic law in cases of inheritance, and the old Byzantine law which was the traditional law of the principal Palestine Christian community, that of the Orthodox Church, became obsolete.

The British conquest of Palestine found the Christian communal courts in a desperate position with less powers than the Christian religious courts in Egypt. The substitution of a British for an Ottoman authority in Palestine did affect the jurisdiction of the religious courts of personal status. This came about principally through a change in status of the *shari'a* courts, which resulted in an extension of the jurisdiction of the Christian law courts.

The authority to maintain religious law courts was granted only to the recognised communities. The unrecognised Orthodox and Catholic churches referred their cases to the courts of their recognised sister-churches, which were subject to the same ecclesiastic law. Only the local Protestants, whose church remained unrecognised throughout the period of the Mandate, lacked this possibility. They were faced with serious legal problems concerning issues of their personal status.

Over time the Christian religious law courts in Palestine adopted *shari'a* legal principles. This was due to the length of Islamic rule and the decline of a distinctive Christian legal tradition, particularly as applied by the largest Christian community and institution; the Greek Orthodox patriarchate of Jerusalem and the Arab Orthodox community.

The Orthodox Church did possess its own body of law based upon a 14th century corpus which had been taken from an earlier Byzantine model, and had been applied by the Greek Orthodox patriarchate of Alexandria in Egypt. The Jerusalem patriarchate made use of a recent legal compilation by Karavokyros in the 19th century. However, this text was only available in Greek and thus was little used by the Arabic speaking Palestinian Orthodox Christians. The creation of an Arabic Christian legal code became one of the reformist aims of the First Arab Orthodox Congress held at Haifa in 1923.[48]

The Armenian Christian community had traditionally used a 13th century code, but its application seems to have fallen into desuetude in Palestine, although some canonical principles with regard to marriage, divorce and dowry had been maintained. In other areas Islamic law was used. The Catholic communities in Palestine used a mixture of canon and

---

[48] Anton Bertram and J W A Young, *Report of the Commission Appointed by the Government of Palestine to inquire and report upon certain controversies between the Orthodox Patriarchate of Jerusalem and the Arab Orthodox Community*, Oxford University Press, 1926.

Islamic law, and in many ways were better organised than some of the Orthodox Churches and had greater access legal jurisdiction outside the confines of the Ottoman world.[49]

The Succession Ordinance of 1923, together with subsequent amendments, marked a notable advance in the settlement of the jurisdiction of the religious courts. This law provided for exclusive jurisdiction by the several religious courts in the matters of will confirmation and concurrent jurisdiction with the civil courts and in matters relating to the succession of Palestinian members of the communities. All other cases were subject to the exclusive jurisdiction of the civil courts. It adopted the Ottoman law of succession of immovable property of AH 1331 based on the Swiss Code as the Common Law of Intestate Succession, under which daughters had an equal share in inheritance (Article 19). The ordinance affirmed the restriction of the jurisdiction of the Islamic religious courts in matters of succession to Muslims only (Section 4). Matters of interstate succession of non-Muslims were placed under the jurisdiction of their respective religious courts (Section 6). Finally, the ordinance abolished both the exclusive jurisdiction, which the *shari'a* courts had until then over succession of minor heirs of all communities, as well as the Ottoman prohibition on inheritance by a non-Muslim from a Muslim (Section 22). The ordinance provided that the religious courts would apply their special law to movable property and *mulk* land (owned absolutely, equivalent to freehold), that the civil courts would apply the relevant national law in the case of movable property and *mulk* land of a foreigner and that succession to *miri* land (owned by the state, but to which right of perpetual tenure has been granted to an individual subject to certain conditions) would be in accordance with the relevant Ottoman law of succession. This ordinance also cancelled the Ottoman ban on foreigners succeeding to Ottoman subjects, and non-Muslims succeeding to Muslims.[50]

The reform of the Christian communal waqfs

Waqfs are Islamic institutions which have played an important role in the history of Middle Eastern Islamic society. The Arabic word *waqf* (plural *awqaf*) can be loosely translated as 'religious endowment'. The origins of the *waqf* institution in Muslim society has been the focus of considerable debate amongst Muslim jurists and scholars. *Awqaf* have many forms and applications, and as an Islamic institution have evolved and changed over place and time. However, certain common characteristics determine the

---

[49] Goadby, *International and Interreligious Private Law*, 134.
[50] Finally approved in February 1923. For the full text, see in Norman Bentwich, *Legislation of Palestine 1918-1925*, Alexandria, 1926, vol. I, 350-362.

nature of the *waqf* and which have been developed over time through jurisprudential disputations.[51]

What have been the general legal characteristics determining the nature of the *waqf*. The founder of the *waqf* must have full right of disposal over his property; he must therefore be in full possession of his physical health and must be of sound mind and a free man. If the endowment is made by a non-Muslim then it is only valid if it is intended for a purpose not incompatible with Islam. In theory this ruled out a Christian endowing a Church or a monastery, but over time this rule was not always honoured in Palestine. Because of the fundamentally religious character of the *waqf*, the endowment must be of a permanent nature, which is then defined in a legal document *waqfiyya* and authorised by a *shari'a* court, and as a general rule it cannot be revoked.

Waqf land and property differed from other holdings only because of its charitable purposes. The *waqf* was one of the principal institutions for the development of basic public services in the areas of religion, education, welfare and health. The *waqf* could be of two types; *khayri* (charitable or public) or *ahli/dhurri* (family-*waqf*), a form common in 19th century Palestine. The distinction between two types of endowments did not exist in the classic formulations of Islamic Law but was a response to the social and economic changes in 19th century Ottoman empire. The *khayri waqf* was important in the founding and the maintenance of mosques, madrasas, hospitals and food centres for the poor. Family *awqaf* tended to consist of property endowed to prevent the fragmentation of land holdings within large families which often happens under the law of succession under Islam.

Throughout Islamic history and especially during the late Ottoman period, *awqaf* had undergone a continuing process of dismemberment.[52] Over time, the assets which gave the *waqf* its content would deteriorate until they were alienated, which undermined the classic and stable status of the endowment, but which reflected the need for the *waqf* institution to respond to changing social and economic conditions. The dismemberment of *awqaf* and the alienation of their assets occurred in a number of ways. The *waqf* property could be leased permanently or for a period of time at a fixed or variable rent, the creation of individual rights over the *waqf* property or assets, and/or the sale of *waqf* property, all of which was against the established principles upon which the institution of *waqf* had been initially based.[53]

---

[51] W Heffening, 'Wakf', in *Encyclopaedia of Islam*, vol. IV (1932), 1096-1103; and H A R Gibb and H Bowen, *Islamic Society and the West*, vol. I, part 2, London, 1958, 165-178.

[52] Gabriel Baer, 'The dismemberment of awqaf in early 19th-century Jerusalem', in Gad Gilbar (ed), *Ottoman Palestine 1800-1914*, Leiden, E J Brill, 1990, 299-319).

[53] On the background to the *waqf* in Palestine, see Gabriel Baer, 'Jerusalem's Families of Notables and the Wakf in the Early 19th Century', in David Kushmer (ed), *Palestine in the Late Ottoman Empire*, Leiden, 1987, 109-122; Oded Peri, 'The Muslim Waqf and the collection of Jizya in late 18th-century', in Gad Gilbar (ed), *op. cit.*, 287-297; and *idem*, 'The Waqf as an Instrument to increase and consolidate political Power: The case of Khasseki Sultan Waqf in late Eighteenth-Century Ottoman Jerusalem', in G R Warburg and G Gilbar (eds), *Studies in Islamic Society*, Haifa UP, 1984, 47-62.

The *awqaf* developed into an important socio-economic and political feature of the late Ottoman period. The extensive responsibilities and holdings of the *awqaf* especially in Palestine developed into a powerful institution which controlled large areas of agricultural land and urban property. The proliferation of *awqaf* throughout the Ottoman empire created a need for increasing state control and the establishment of a ministerial department as well as codified administrative procedures.[54] The social, economic and political transformation of Palestine in the late Ottoman period and the important revival of Christian interest in the 19th century in the Holy Land, created the climate for a growth in Christian *awqaf*. The influx of contributions which accompanied this revival enabled the various churches to purchase large amounts of property, buildings and plots of land, both urban and rural, especially in the surrounding of the Holy Places; these were usually endowed as *awqaf*. It also meant that with the increasing wealth and presence of the Christian Churches and communities in Palestine many individual Christians made religious endowments.

The establishment of *awqaf* was common to members of all the main Christian churches and communities associated with the revival of interest in Palestine: Greek and Russian Orthodox, Greek Catholic, Latin Catholic, Armenian and Protestant Churches. In the predominantly Christian towns for example Bethlehem, houses, shops, market warehouses and small factories were characteristic of the property involved and in growing commercial towns like Jaffa, which had a substantial Christian population, endowments of orchards and of urban properties were common. The main recipients of the public purpose *awqaf* were the poor of the founder's community. Churches and clergy were also important beneficiaries of *khayri awqaf*, which suggests that *shari'a* legislation prohibiting the establishment of endowments for other religious purposes, which were not Islamic, were not always applied. The leadership of the religious community would administer such *awqaf*, for the maintenance and the distribution of the usufruct among the monks and the poor.[55]

The system of public or *khayri awqaf* in particular represented a solution to certain problems facing the Christian Churches in Palestine. Public organisations not recognised by Ottoman law as legal persons or as part of the *millet* system, could not register property in their names. One device used to circumvent this prohibition was the *waqf* institution. It was possible that heads of churches, especially of those lacking formal status such as the Protestant church, registered church property as *waqf* so as to ensure their ownership rights.[56]

As regards the dedication of family *awqaf* by Christians, there being no religious succession law in Christianity, Christians traditionally adopted the

[54] J B Barron, *Mohammedan Wakfs in Palestine*, Jerusalem, Greek Convent Press, 1922, 12-18.
[55] Ron Shaham, 'Christian and Jewish Waqf in Palestine during the late Ottoman Period', *The New East*, vol. 32 (1989), 46-66.
[56] F M Goadby and M J Doukhan, *The Land Law of Palestine*, Tel Aviv, 1935, 71.

civil succession law of their place of abode. In the case of Palestine, Christians, settled issues in inheritance according to *shari'a* legal principles. This law was not always in harmony with the social reality, the Muslims used the *waqf* also to enable the dedicator to place his close family members – especially his sons – as exclusive beneficiaries, thereby precluding from his estate more distant relatives otherwise entitled to a portion, such as grandfathers and uncles. Two additional advantages accorded by the *waqf* were that it enabled the dedicator to enjoy the fruits of his property during his lifetime, while preventing the property's dissipation in the aftermath of his death.[57]

The Christian communities' population of Palestine in the 1920s and 1930s

In the early period of the Mandate the Christian population in Palestine comprised 9.6 per cent of the total population. In 1931 it was reduced to 8.8 per cent, although its absolute number increased. It has been estimated that the Christian community lost 13 per cent of its overall population during the First World War mainly through migration out of Palestine and through a 4 per cent mortality rate. The reduction in the Christian proportion of the Arab Palestinian population was the outcome of their lower birth-rate and a small amount of emigration. The Arab Christian birth-rate was smaller than that of the Muslim (37.2), than that of the Muslim population (54.7) and approximated to that of the Jews (33.2) in 1922.[58]

Migration in search of economic opportunities and political-religious freedom from the Ottoman empire to the Americas in the 19th century was particularly remarkable among the Christian communities of Palestine. The first death among the emigrants to South America, recorded in the registers of the Latin Parish Priest's office in Bethlehem, however goes back to 7 September 1796. The deceased emigrant's name was Andrea Francis Hanna Dawud from the Tarajmah Quarter in Bethlehem.[59] However, the first Christian traveller from the Middle East to the Americas did not come from Palestine, but was a Chaldean priest from Mosul, Ilyas ibn Hanna, who travelled in 1668 to Italy, France and Spain and from there took ship to the American colonies.[60] He was almost certainly the first

[57] F M Goadby, *International and Interreligious Private Law*, 128-131.

[58] P*alestine: Report and General Abstracts of the Census of 1922. Taken on the 23rd of October 1922.* Compiled by J B Barron (Jerusalem, 1923). The 1922 Census was taken for the purpose of general elections, and did not include social and economic data. The 1931 Census included data on all aspects of life in Palestine. Published: *The Census of Palestine, 1931.* Compiled by E Mills (Alexandria, 1933).

[59] Mike George Salman, 'Emigration and its effect on the extinction of Bethlehem Families', *Al-Liqa'* , vol. I, Jerusalem, 1989, 55.

[60] Ilyas b. Hanna, *Le plus ancien voyage d'un Oriental en Amérique (1668-1683)*, (ed) A Rabbath, Beirut, 1906.

Middle East traveller to visit and describe the New World, where he travelled extensively in Peru, Panama and Mexico.[61] International exhibitions held in the United States played a pioneering role in attracting Palestinian Christian merchants. Many of them came to visit the Philadelphia Exhibition in 1876, the Chicago Exhibition in 1893 and the St Louis Exhibition in 1904, bringing with them Holy Land products such as mother-of-pearl, olive wood and Nabi Moses stone, to exhibit and sell to the faithful and the curious. During the first four decades of the 20th century some families began to disappear gradually from local parish registers, resulting from collective emigration of whole families. With the coming of economic and a certain degree of political stability in Palestine under the British Mandate opportunities for communal, economic and institutional growth of the Christian communities emerged. The 1931 census returns on emigration of Palestinians and pre-war residents showed 615 Christians as compared with 610 Muslims. Christian emigration into Palestine was also proportionally greater than the Muslim community, the largest sources being from Syria and Egypt.

The largest Christian centre of population in Palestine under the British Mandate was the Jerusalem district which included the towns of Jerusalem, Bethlehem and Ramallah and the villages which surrounded them. All Christian denominations were represented in this district which was principally due to the Holy Places in the two former towns. Second in size during this period was the Northern district, which included the towns of Haifa, Acre, Nazareth, Tiberias and Safad and the surrounding villages. The communities principally located in the northern district were the Greek Catholics, the Greek Orthodox and some Maronite villages along the Lebanese-Palestine border. Yet in none of the districts or subdistricts of British Mandatory Palestine did the Arab Christian community constitute a majority of the population and only in the Bethlehem subdistrict did the Christian population constitute 45 percent of the total population, according to the census of 1931. The Christians in Palestine were dispersed and formed an intricate part of Palestinian Arab society as a whole. The 1922 census showed that 30,412 or approximately 41.5 per cent of the total Christian population were concentrated in the main towns of Jerusalem, Jaffa, and Haifa. By 1931, the Christian population in these towns was 42,291 or 46.2 per cent of the total Christian population. Christians lived in villages throughout Palestine but the majority could be found in the villages surrounding Acre, Nazareth, and Ramlah. As already mentioned, the drift of the Christian population away from isolated villages from the 16th century onwards was towards the larger settlements which traditionally had a large Christian concentration. In 1922, 24 per cent or 17,981 of the Christian population lived in what the Mandate census considered to be villages. In 1931, their number was 22,148 and remained 24 per cent of the Christian population. In 1931, approximately 11,000 or

[61] B Lewis, *The Muslim Discovery of Europe*, London, 1982, 120.

12 per cent of the Arab Christian population lived in 17 Christian majority villages. By 1931, seven villages in which Christians had formed a majority in 1922 were by that time majority Muslim. In only four villages did the Christian population not decline.

According to the 1922 census, the Christian population in Palestine was predominantly urban, with 76 per cent of the community living in small or large towns. In 1922, the Christian community constituted 28.5 per cent of the total Palestinian Arab urban population (55,043) and in 1931 this was reduced to 27 per cent when the population was 69,250. In some of the major and traditional concentrations of the Christian community, the difference in population numbers between 1922 and 1931 demonstrates a change of majority status in a number of towns. For example, in Jerusalem in 1922 the Christian population constituted 60 per cent of the total; by 1931, it had dropped to less than half. In Haifa, the major urban concentration for the Christian community in the north of the country, half of the Arab Palestinian population was Christian in 1922 (8,863); in 1931, Christians only constituted a third (13,824).

Since the middle of the 19th century, the Palestinian Christian community was in a continual process of fragmentation. The majority Christian denomination, Greek-Arab Orthodox community, was decimated by the continuing political and religious conflict between the Arab Orthodox community and the ethnically Greek hierarchy. This conflict plus the important institutional and pastoral commitment offered by the various other Christian communities in Palestine attracted a great number of Arab Orthodox Christians to become Latin or Eastern Catholics and, in some areas, Protestants. The largest Christian community, according to the British Mandatory censuses, was the Greek-Arab Orthodox Church. It declined in proportion to the Christian population, from 45.7 per cent (33,369) in 1922 to 43.5 per cent (39,727) in 1931. The Latin Catholic community increased their proportion of the total Christian population of Palestine from 19.5 per cent (14,245) in 1922 to 20.7 per cent (18,895) in 1931. The Latin Catholic community was particularly strong in the central Christian belt, particularly in Jerusalem and Bethlehem, and in the coastal town of Jaffa. The proportion of the Greek Catholic community - which was predominantly found in the northern part of the country and which was historically an extension of that communities migration out from Syria since the 18th century,[62] the total Christian community fell from 15.3 per cent (11,191) in 1922 to 13,8 per cent (12,645) in 1931. The Eastern and Oriental Catholic communities, which included the Maronites, the Armenians, the Syrians and the Chaldeans constituted 19.5 per cent (14,167) in 1922 and fell to 18.2 per cent (16,683) in 1931. The proportion of the Anglican community in

---

[62] Thomas Philipp, *Syrians in Egypt, 1725-1975*, Stuttgart, 1985, and *idem*, 'The Rise and Fall of Acre: population and economy between 1700-1850', *Revue du Monde Musulman et de la Méditerranée*, vol. 55-56 (1990), 124-140.

Palestine also fell, from 6.2 per cent (4,553) in 1922 to 5.3 per cent (4,799) in 1931. The Greek Arab Orthodox community formed a majority of the Christian population in eight of the 18 subdistricts (Gaza, Bersheba, Jaffa, Ramleh, Bethlehem, Jericho, Ramlah, and Nablus). This community formed the largest Christian denomination in Palestine, though not the majority, in seven other subdistricts, including Acre, Nazareth, and Jerusalem. The Latin Catholic community was second in size to the Orthodox and was concentrated around the Holy Places in Jerusalem, Bethlehem and Nazareth. The community was highly urbanised and Latin Arab Catholics had also recently settled in important economic centres, such as Haifa, Jaffa, and Acre. The next largest Christian community was the Greek Catholics, who were principally concentrated in the north, in the subdistricts of British Mandatory Palestine, Nazareth, Acre, Haifa, and Tiberias; in the latter two they formed the largest community in Palestine. A considerable number of Greek Catholics resided in the coastal towns, and in Tiberias a large proportion lived in the rural areas of the Galilee. Of the other Eastern and Oriental Catholic communities in Palestine, it was only the Maronites who lived outside the main centres of the Holy Places. The Maronite community was an extension of that community in Lebanon which had over time seen a movement of its population southwards from its Northern mountainous areas and which now straddled the Palestine-Lebanese border. The Maronite community formed exclusively the population of the village of Bir'im, and the largest community in al-Jish. In 1922, the community numbered 2,382 and in 1931, 3,431. The small but important Arab Anglican community mainly in Jerusalem, Ramlah, Haifa and Nazareth. Of the smaller Christian communities present in Palestine, the Armenians ere concentrated in Jerusalem, Jaffa, and Haifa; the Syrian Orthodox and Catholic communities, in Jerusalem and Bethlehem; the Assyro-Chaldeans in Jerusalem and Bethlehem; the Copts in Jerusalem, Jaffa, and Nazareth; and the Ethiopians in Jerusalem and Nazareth.

Conclusion

The Christian communities of Palestine formed a distinctive part of society, and through their numbers and geographical location they were both part and apart from the Muslim community. They shared a common linguistic and material culture, but were separated by their Christian faith and community. The fortunes of the Christians of Palestine began to change with the dawn of the modern era from approximately of the middle of the 19th century until the First World War in which the whole region suffered greatly. The period between the wars was a time of communal stability and institutional growth set against the background of profound political change which would bring a period of deep change in the later part of the 1940s.

17

Church–State Relations in Jerusalem since 1948

Michael Dumper

Introduction

Attempting to study the city of Jerusalem through the discipline of
political science gives one this feeling of stepping out into the
complete unknown. It is such an utterly unique city that no existing
models or categories appear to fit. The combination of religious and
regional political factors which in themselves are difficult enough to
disentangle are made more complex by the international interest in the
city. Such interest currently stems from the central role played by Jerusalem
not only in the possibility of a lasting political peace between Palestinians
and Israelis but also in the aspirations for the city of religious communities
throughout the world, be it Muslim, Christian or Jew. In this way the
categories and methodologies proffered by those who study urban
sociology, or by those who have suggested holy city typologies that include
the study of Mecca, Lourdes or Benares, or by those who have attempted
comparative studies of the divided cities of Nicosia, Berlin or Belfast, or by
those who have suggested the use of consociational or control models to
examine deeply-divided societies, do not encompass the multi-levelled and
multi-faceted nature of the political processes of the city. How does one
study a city where the acquisition of a single property by one religious or
political community can contribute to an uprising, make international
headlines and lead to debates in the General Assembly of the United
Nations? Or where town planning decisions provoke fears of cultural
destruction that go beyond the mere redirection of traffic flows or service
provision. How does one determine which level of political activity is the
operable and decisive one - the street level, the local municipal, the
national, the regional, the international - and which ideological constructs
or symbolisms - religious, political or ethnic - have to be deciphered in
order to reveal the dynamics of political change?

This paper will not attempt to provide the model or framework for analysis which may help to answer these questions. My own thoughts on the matter are at too preliminary a stage to do justice to such an exploration. Instead it will attempt to draw out some general themes which will help to construct such a model at a later stage. The key overarching theme is the delicate balancing act the churches have to perform to maintain their position in Jerusalem. In examining church-state relations in Jerusalem since 1948 one is struck repeatedly, for example, by a three-way tension experienced by the church hierarchies - torn between being responsive to and representative of the needs of their local constituencies, being in many ways accountable and financially dependent upon their international constituency, and being obliged to accommodate the demands of the prevailing state authorities. Conversely, the study of the state during the period in question suggests that the state also experiences a three-way dynamic whereby it seeks to balance its security needs and political aspirations for the city with the need to present an acceptable face to the local Christian population to secure a minimum level of acquiescence, with the need to avoid alienating the powerful international Christian community.

It is within this maelstrom of competing interests that the churches in Jerusalem have to function on a day-to-day level. This paper will argue that the response of the church hierarchies has been indeed to carry out a delicate balancing act between, on the one hand compromising their independence, and in some cases permitting a degree of manipulation and cooptation by the state, and on the other, performing a representative and mediating role between the state and their constituency, the indigenous laity. In doing so their long-term strategy has been that of ensuring their continued existence in the city. In this sense, the Christian hierarchy can be seen as among the original *samiduun*, or 'stay-putters', a pre-Palestinian nationalist variety whose indifference or identification to the Palestinian national movement has fluctuated according to the political forces prevailing at any given time.

The paper is divided into four parts. It begins with a brief overview of the pre-1967 period during the partition of the city into an Israeli-controlled West Jerusalem and a Jordanian-controlled East Jerusalem. It was a period where the Israeli and Jordanian governments sought to consolidate their control over their respective parts of the city in the absence of international recognition of their sovereignty over those parts. The next part deals with the immediate aftermath of the 1967 War and the main legal and administrative changes which were introduced. The third section examines in more detail the relationship between specific church hierarchies and the state. The Greek Orthodox, the Armenian Orthodox and the Latin patriarchates are taken as case studies. Finally there is a look at the impact of the *intifada* on church-state relations analysing the distinct shift that has taken place as a result both of Israeli government actions and of changes within the churches themselves. The post-Oslo Accords period of late 1993 and 1994 is not discussed. The main emphasis of this paper will be the study of the church elites and hierarchies and their relations with the Jordanian and Israeli governments. Thus the term 'churches' as used in the paper should be taken to mean primarily the ecclesiastical hierarchies and does not necessarily include the local laity.

The period of partition, 1948-1967

In 1947 the General Assembly of the United Nations accepted the UN Partition Plan which divided the area of Mandatory Palestine into an Arab and Jewish state. The Plan also recommended the internationalisation of Jerusalem for at least ten years until a suitable administration could be arranged by the inhabitants. The international area covered a much wider area than the municipal borders established by the British and included Bethlehem and Beit Jala and Beit Sahour. This was partly to establish a demographic parity between the Palestinian and Jewish population and partly a recognition of the importance of the Christian Holy Places in those towns and their predominantly Christian populations. Thus for the purposes of this paper the point to note is that the internationalisation proposal as it originally stood would have the creation, an international city with increased Christian influence as a result of a large Christian local population, greater recognition of foreign ecclesiastical administration of holy sites and, finally, through international Christian interests, expressed most notably by the Vatican with its influence over the Catholic vote in the United Nations.

Despite the fact that the plan was formally accepted by the Zionist movement as the price it needed to pay for international recognition for a Jewish state, one can understand how Zionist leaders were not at all enthusiastic about its practical implementation. They much preferred a 'functional internationalisation' of the Holy Places which would be confined to the Old City. The prospect of a Christian dominated city was one to be strenuously opposed. For similar reasons, the Partition Plan and the internationalisation of Jerusalem was rejected by the Palestinians and the Arab states. Jordan remained adamant in its rejection, conscious that the legitimacy of the regime would be strengthened if it was seen in the Arab world to be the protector of the Muslim Holy Places in the city. It, too, was wary of a Christian hegemony over Jerusalem. However, during 1949, fearing wider Jordanian political ambitions in the Arab World, the League of Arab States altered its position and accepted the internationalisation of the city. By this time Jordan had consolidated its hold over the eastern parts of the city and the West Bank.

The disagreement between the regional and international parties involved over the future of Jerusalem led to serious fighting in and around the city. Although the population of the city had already been divided to a large extent in the Mandate period by the development of ethnically segregated neighbourhoods and by political tensions, the Armistice Lines drawn up by the Jordanian and Israeli governments did not correspond to areas of predominantly Palestinian or predominantly Jewish areas of residence but cut right through the city separating the 'New City' and its western suburbs from the Old City and its eastern suburbs. In this way while many of the major holy sites of Christianity, such as the Church of the Holy Sepulchre, the Garden of Gethsemane, the Church of Ascension, were located in the Jordanian sector, the churches owned many newly-built and valuable properties in the Israeli sector. These included the Pontifical Biblical Institute, the Ratisbon and the Terra Sancta College, as well as much older properties such as the Monastery of the Cross, the Russian Compound and various sites at 'Ayn Karim. Sami Hadawi has estimated that approximately 13.40 per cent of the land of the New City, nearly all of which was to be located in Israeli-controlled West Jerusalem after the Armistice Agreements, was owned by the Christian churches.[1] During the period of partition, the churches suffered in logistical terms from the division of their administrative units between two hostile regimes. However, since both Israel and Jordan were anxious to avoid antagonising prospective Western support, it soon became possible for the clergy of the larger denominations to obtain special passes for crossing the Armistice Line.

During the partition period the Jordanian government was in a vulnerable position with regard to the Christian community in Jerusalem. The main Christian areas of settlement during the Mandate period had been in the Israeli-controlled West Jerusalem. The hostilities and partition of Jerusalem resulted in the loss of their extensive properties in the western part of the city. Some Christian families were forced to become refugee squatters in the Old City, others settled in Sheikh Jarrah, American Colony or further afield in Ramallah, Beit Hanina, Beit Jallah and Bethlehem. Still others made their way to Jordan, Lebanon and the West. A Jordanian census in 1961 reveals that their numbers (including non-Arabs) in East Jerusalem had fallen to 11,000, a dramatic drop of 62 per cent.[2] In the same year there were only 1,400 Christians in Israeli Jerusalem, probably mostly foreign nationals and non-Arabs. One writer has estimated that between 1948 and 1967 the Christian population of East Jerusalem dropped from 38 per cent of the total population to just 15 per cent.[3] Many of those left were living in reduced circumstances and unable to leave the city. An Israeli census in 1967 in East Jerusalem showed that while 15.6 per cent of the Muslim population of Jerusalem were refugees, as many as 37 per cent

---

[1] 'Jerusalem', Map compiled by Hadawi, S,(The Palestine Arab Refugee Office, New York, n.d.). A former official in the Palestine government, Hadawi based this map upon Palestine survey maps and taxation records.

[2] Schmelz, U O, *Modern Jerusalem's Demographic Evolution*, Jerusalem Institute for Israel Studies, Jerusalem, 1987, 63, Table 16.

[3] Prittie, T, *Whose Jerusalem*, London, Frederick Muller Ltd, 1981, (hereinafter referred to as *Whose Jerusalem*), 71. Prittie, T, *Whose Jerusalem*, London, Frederick Muller Ltd, 1981.

of Christians in the city were refugees.[4] Such dislocation led to pressures being placed upon the Jordanian government to confront the Israelis over the return of property in West Jerusalem.

In addition, the Jordanian government was also acutely conscious that due to its own impoverished condition it was itself unable to develop the city to provide sufficient services and employment for the inhabitants. During the Mandate period, the Christian communities had been provided with ample funds from abroad for the construction of schools, churches, hostels and residences and it was unlikely that the state could compete with such investment. In addition, the Jordanian government was at pains to establish its Muslim credentials as guardians of the third holy site of Islam and in this way sought to check the momentum of Christian development that had been gathering force during the Mandate period.[5] In concrete terms, these concerns were addressed by the placing of strict limitations upon the opportunities for the churches to purchase land and develop property.[6] In 1953 the Jordanian government passed a law restricting the purchase of property 'by religious and charitable organisations, which constitute branches of a foreign religious body'.[7] Similarly, since Christian run schools were more affluent, better equipped and staffed, and attracted large numbers of Muslim students, greater supervision and some restrictions were introduced. A ceiling for the number of students was set and amendments made to the curricula which included the teaching of the Qur'an.[8]

In West Jerusalem, Israeli statistics for this period reveal a dramatic change in the demographic profile of the New City. 99 per cent of the population was Jewish with only 1,500 foreign Christians remaining.[9] This is in stark contrast to other Israeli towns such as Haifa, Lydda and Tel Aviv-Jaffa where there were significant numbers of Palestinian Arab Christians

---

[4] Benvenisti, M, *Jerusalem: The Torn City*, Minneapolis, Israeltypset and the University of Minneapolis, 1976, 53.

[5] Furthermore, Jerusalem was seen as the main base for Palestinians opposed to the Hashemite regime and the government was anxious to prevent Jerusalem developing as a major urban centre in competition to its capital in Amman.

[6] Interview with Naomi Teasdale, advisor to the mayor on Christian affairs, 30.3.1993. See also Shepherd, N, *The Mayor and the Citadel: Teddy Kollek and Jerusalem*, London, Weidenfeld and Nicholson, 1987, 70.

[7] Talhami, G, 'Between Development and Preservation: Jerusalem under Three Regimes', *American-Arab Affairs*, Spring, 1986, 103.

[8] Colbi, 'Christian Establishment', 174. Interview with Naomi Teasdale, 30.3.93. The Jordanian government was also alarmed by allegations that some Christian churches had sold parcels of land and property to the Jewish National Fund during the Mandate period and it therefore sought to put in place a body of law which would prevent such activities reoccurring. In 1965, the purchase of land by churches was completely forbidden. Without presenting her sources Talhami argues that acquisitions by the churches continued surreptitiously, since in 1949 it was estimated that 91 plots of commercial land belonged to the Christian churches but by 1969 they owned 392 plots.

[9] *Ibid.*, 48.

residing.[10] A Christian Division was established in the Israeli Ministry of Religious Affairs and Christian property which had been acquired by the Custodian of Absentee Property immediately following the hostilities in 1948 was gradually released to the churches.[11] Denominations such as the Arab Evangelical Episcopal Church (Anglican) who had not been formally registered during the Mandate period had more difficulty in obtaining the release of their properties.[12] The main change brought about by the Israeli government was in the area of missionary activity. A law banning overt proselytisation was designed to protect new immigrant Jews from Protestant evangelicals.

Nevertheless, Israel was, on the whole, extremely anxious to promote good relations with the Western powers. In the absence of a strong local community whose demands would need to be accommodated, the government was given much greater latitude in cultivating Christian leaders and pursuing international recognition of its sovereignty over West Jerusalem. In addition, the encouragement and protection of Christian pilgrims was essential if tourism was to be made part of the struggling West Jerusalem economy. It is important to note, however, that the visit of Pope Paul VI in 1964 which was heralded as a new era in Vatican-Israel relations which did not lead to an exchange of diplomatic relations between the two states. The expectation by the international community that Jerusalem should be internationalised continued to hamper church relations with Israel during this period.

The immediate aftermath of the 1967 War

As is well known, the 1967 War led to the Israeli occupation of former Jordanian East Jerusalem and the extension of the Israeli municipal borders to include not only East Jerusalem but also adjacent parts of the West Bank. It is important to recall that the Israeli government did not regard its occupation of East Jerusalem and these adjacent parts of the West Bank in the same way as it is held by the international community. It was not, in the Israeli government's view, 'the belligerent occupier of enemy

---

[10] The main reason for the uniqueness of Jerusalem in this context is that all the Palestinian Arab population had fled out of Israeli-controlled territory and was not permitted to return. By the time the limited repatriation and family reunion schemes were in operation, Palestinian Arab property had been expropriated and passed onto the Jewish National Fund and government agencies concerned exclusively with the absorption of new Jewish immigrants. There was little opportunity for Palestinian Arabs with Israeli citizenship to live in the city.

[11] See Dumper, M, *Islam and Israel: Muslim Religious Endowments and the Jewish State*, Washington DC, Institute for Palestine Studies, 1994, 40 for further details.

[12] See *ibid.*, 40, note 67.

territory'.[13] To them, it was a legitimate extension of Israeli civil law over territory brought under its control as laid down by the Law and Administration Ordnance announced by the Israel Provisional Government in 1948.[14] There could be no belligerent occupation or annexation of a *terra nullus*, that is, of territory without a sovereign controlling body. Jordan's annexation of East Jerusalem had not been accepted by the international community.

The Israeli government contested the view that it was obliged to respect international legal agreements enshrined in the Hague and Geneva Conventions since in their eyes they could not apply to Jerusalem.[15] While not recognising the applicability of the conventions to Jerusalem, the Israeli government did to some extent try to work within its ambit. On 27 June, 1967, in accordance with Article 27 of the Geneva Convention, the Israeli Knesset passed the Protection of Holy Places Law, which stated:

1) The Holy Places shall be protected from desecration and any other violation and from anything likely to violate the freedom of access of the members of the different religions to the places sacred to them or their feelings with regard to those places.

2) a) Whosoever desecrates or otherwise violates a Holy Place shall be liable to imprisonment for a term of seven years.

b) Any person who does anything likely to impair freedom of access to a Holy Place or to hurt the feelings of anyone to whom a place is sacred, shall be liable to imprisonment for a term of five years.

3) This law shall add to and derogate from any other law.

4) The Ministry of Religious Affairs is charged with the implementation of the Law, and he may, after consultation with, or upon the proposal of, representatives of the religions

---

[13] For a fuller discussion on this issue, see Gershon, A, *Israel, the West Bank and International Law*, London, Frank Cass, 1978, 78-82 and Cohen, E R, *Human Rights in the Israeli-occupied Territories*, Manchester, Manchester University Press, 1985, 37-56; and Shehadi, R, *The West Bank and the Rule of Law*, New York, International Jurists and Law in the Service of Man, 1980, (hereinafter referred to as *Rule of Law*), 10ff.

[14] Law and Administration Ordinance (Amendment No 11) Law, 5727-1967, Laws of the State of Israel, Vol 21 (1966/67), 75.

[15] Article 56 of the 'Protection of Cultural Property in Time of War or Military Occupation' annexed to both the 1899 Hague Convention II and 1907 Hague Convention IV as Regulations, treat all religious and charitable institutions as private property. Destruction and wilful damage to such property is therfore, forbidden. In addition, Jordan and Israel had signed and ratified the 1954 Hague Convention for the 'Protection of Cultural Property in the Event of Armed Conflict'. This convention covers both religious buildings and *waqf* land and property on the West Bank. Similarly, Article 53 of the 1977 Geneva Protocol I (Protection of Cultural Objects and Places of Worship) and Article 16 of 1977 Geneva Protocol II (which has the same title) prohibits any act of hostility against cultural property or their use in any military effort or as an object of reprisal. This has been signed by Jordan but not by Israel.

concerned and with the consent of the Minister of Justice, make regulations as to any matter relating to such implementation.

The Protection of Holy Places Law contains one very significant omission: it did not contain any explicit reference to the maintenance of the Status Quo arrangements established during the Ottoman period and preserved by the British and Jordanians. These were arrangements primarily concerned with issues of status and precedence between the different Christian denominations but also related to the ownership of and access to Holy Places in the Holy Land. As Benvenisti points out, this was no accident, since to have done so would have placed the same irksome restrictions upon Jewish access to the Jewish Holy Places in East Jerusalem that had been in existence during the Ottoman and Mandate periods and which had led to the Wailing Wall Incident.[16]

It should be noted that between 1948 and 1967, Israel had officially recognised over twelve different Christian denominations inside Israel itself. These communities were given freedom to appoint their own clergy, to retain their independent administration over church property (save for a number of long-running disputes) and freedom to run their own schools and their own religious courts. Separated by the Armistice Lines, ecclesiastical superiors based in Jerusalem had been able to coordinate activities with their co-religionists in Israel by frequent visits across the Line. In 1967, the removal of the frontier made their life much easier.

However, they were unable to secure an unequivocal commitment from the Israeli government to maintain the Status Quo arrangements and not to intervene either in favour of one or another of the Christian communities or in communal internal affairs. This meant that their relations with the Israeli state was continually subject to pressures and piecemeal agreements. Government pronouncements on religious matters were therefore, closely scrutinized for clues of any impending changes. Even before the end of the 1967 War, the Israeli government was aware of the need to assuage Christian anxieties on this issue. On 7 June, 1967, the Israeli Prime Minister, Levi Eshkol, announced that the Ministry of Religious Affairs had instructions to establish a 'council of religious clergymen' to make 'arrangements' in the Holy Places.[17] The next day the Minister of Religious Affairs, Dr Zerah Wahrhaftig, informed the different religious communities that regulations concerning the Holy Places would be drawn up.[18] It was never made clear who would establish the council and what its composition would be. In fact it was never set up, echoing the difficulties the British Mandate authorities had experienced, nor were the regulations

---

[16] Benvenisti, *Torn City*, 263.
[17] Benvenisti, *Torn City*, 267.
[18] *Ibid.*, 101.

ever published.[19] Instead the Israeli Knesset passed the Protection of the Holy Places Law, mentioned above, and from that church leaders could see that no drastic action was to be taken over altering the Status Quo arrangements.

However, there was no question of the issue remaining dormant. The desire of the Israeli government to promote the interests of its own religious community, to acquire land for its settlement programme and to contain opposition to its occupation of East Jerusalem meant that government intervention in the churches' affairs, however discreet, was inevitable. On-going disputes between the Christian denominations intensified the anxiety that the Israeli government would side with one denomination or the other. The perceived presence, for example, of a pro-Catholic 'faction' within the various Israeli state ministries dealing with Christian affairs in the city made the situation unstable.[20] Greek and Armenian Orthodox clergy were concerned that this faction would promote Catholic claims to alterations in the Status Quo in exchange for Vatican recognition of the state of Israel and Israeli sovereignty over the city. The gradually waning support of the Vatican for the internationalisation of Jerusalem, much opposed by Israel, could be seen in this light.[21]

1967-1987

The Israeli census of 1967 estimated that there were 10,970 Christians in the new extended municipality borders of Jerusalem, amounting to 17 per cent of the Palestinian Arab population and 4.4 per cent of the total population.[22] Emigration continued to be a feature of the post-1967 period but a steady natural increase meant that the total amount of Christians, as opposed to its proportion of population, did not decrease significantly. A survey conducted by the Palestinian sociologist, Dr Bernard Sabella of Bethlehem University, in 1992 suggests that the Christian population has decreased to 2,620 families or approximately 10,000 people.[23] These figures exclude clergy, students and foreign Christians. However, the proportion of Christians in the total population of the municipality area has

---

[19] These regulations should not be confused with the 'code of behaviour' regulations one often sees at Holy Places issued by the Ministry of Religious Affairs. See *ibid.*, 104.

[20] Very crudely, the Department of External Christian Relations in the Ministry of Foreign Affairs is felt to be more concerned to reach an accommodation with the Vatican than other Israeli bodies due to the Vatican's influence in the Third World, Latin America, Central America and in the UN.

[21] Patient Israeli diplomacy has succeeded in diluting this position to a call for 'international guarantees' for the Holy Places. Benvenisti, *Torn City,* 266-270.

[22] See *Census of Population and Housing 1967,* Jerusalem, Central Bureau of Statistics, 1968, table 4, 10.

[23] Sabella, B, 'Christian emigration: A Comparison of the Jerusalem, Ramallah and Bethlehem areas.' Unpublished survey for the al-Liqa Institute, Jerusalem, 1992, 3.

decreased. In 1983 it was 3.2 per cent and in 1992 it was in the region of 2 per cent.[24] They indicate one very important point: although the Christian Holy Places continue to exercise the interest and concern of church hierarchies from all over the world, the actual numbers of indigenous Christians in Jerusalem is very low.[25]

As a result one can understand how Israeli policies towards the Christian community differed from that towards the Muslim community. Not only were the smaller numbers less challenging to Israeli sovereignty over the annexed areas, by necessity the policy is directed as much towards the international Christian community as it is towards the indigenous congregations.[26] As Mayor Kollek's political biographer writes:

> The Israeli authorities all want to make it clear to the outside world not only that Israel maintains freedom of worship and is scrupulous in its protection of the Christian Holy Places, but that the situation of the Christian community under Israel is demonstrably better than it was during King Hussein's regime.[27]

At the same time, however, while the Israeli government sought to establish harmonious relations with the different Christian communities, it was aware of the possibilities of the church hierarchies being a vehicle for opposition, both locally and internationally, to its sovereignty over the whole city. It was, therefore, not in the Israeli government's interest to antagonize the churches for three reasons. First, it did not wish to encourage a united Christian front against it. One could argue that the maintenance of divisions between the different hierarchies was part and parcel of this approach. One denomination could be played off against the other to the Israeli government's advantage.[28] Secondly, it was of paramount importance that a Christian-Muslim coalition against Israeli sovereignty should not be formed. The Palestinian nationalist sentiments of many of the indigenous Christians were countered by the Israeli government by courting senior foreign clergy. And finally, but not of least

---

[24] 1983 figures are taken from Hyman, B, Kimhi, I, and Savitzky, J, *Jerusalem in Transition: Urban Growth and change, 1970s-1980s*, Jerusalem, Jerusalem Institute for Israel Studies, 1985, 10; 1992 figures are based upon Sabella's estimates.

[25] The decline in numbers of Christians in Jerusalem is the subject of many Middle East Council of Churches discussions and international Christian conferences. See for example the declaration of the Cumberland Lodge Conference, 'Christians in the Holy Land', 28-30 May, 1993.; published in 1995 in M Prior and W Taylor (eds.), *Christians in the Holy Land*, London, 1994; cited in *Middle East International*, no. 452, 11.6.93.

[26] See Dumper, *Islam and Israel*, 101-104 for further details of this point.

[27] Shepherd, *The Mayor*, 69-70.

[28] It should be borne in mind that in this the government was in turn greatly assisted by the continuation of age-old disputes over precedence, custodianship and access. Interview, Daniel Rossing, former Director of the Christian Division of the Ministry of Religious Affairs, 14.1.93.

importance, the Israeli government was anxious to acquire or lease church-owned property in East and West Jerusalem. For this it needed not only good relations but a degree of leverage over the senior clergy. Thus the issuing of visas, discretion over the imposition of taxation and the granting of planning permission for new religious buildings were made contingent upon the churches' cooperation in selling property to the Israeli government.

It is possible to examine the unfolding relationship between the Christian churches and the Israeli government with examples of cooperation and conflict from each of the three main denominations: the Greek Orthodox patriarchate, the Armenian Orthodox patriarchate and the Latin patriarchate. From the very early days of the occupation, the Greek Orthodox patriarch sought to pre-empt any possible changes in the Status Quo which would be harmful to its hitherto pre-eminent position. It proposed that it and the Israeli government sign an official memorandum that dealt with its relations with the Israeli state. Preferring to keep its own options open, the Israeli government declined, but was able to address a number of grievances concerning the granting of visas to foreign clergy and monks, and other property and tax matters.[29] It is generally understood that until the mid-eighties relations between the Greek Orthodox patriarchate and the Israeli government and municipality were cordial and cooperative. Indeed, the patriarchate often consulted with Israeli officials whenever other Christian sects began to organise a coordinated protest against Israeli policy.[30] One reason for such cordiality was that the patriarch was also anxious to stave off Jordanian pressure to reform its appointment and accounting procedures. By cultivating Israeli support for the existing system it could counterbalance these Jordanian pressures.[31] Such cordiality also led to a close involvement in the patriarchate's affairs. There is evidence to suggest, for example, that the municipality attempted to intervene in the appointment of the new patriarch in 1983.[32]

The most controversial element in this harmonious relationship was the question of the land sales and leases by the patriarchate to the Israeli government. When discussing land sales by the Christian churches of Jerusalem to the Israeli government, two points have to been borne in mind. First, there has been a long tradition of such sales to Jewish institutions dating back to the late Ottoman period. These have been carried out by a wide-range of foreign and indigenous Palestinian bodies and individuals. The sale of land by churches is neither unique nor so much more than other landowners in the Holy Land. The fact that Israel is deemed to have the support of the Christian West places these sales in a conspiratorial context and gives them a high political profile. Second, not all lands sales should be viewed in a sinister light. Some were astute business

[29] Benvenisti, *Torn City*, 271.
[30] Shepherd, *The Mayor*, 77.
[31] Interview with Naomi Teasdale, 30.3.93.
[32] *Ibid.*, 75.

transactions designed to augment the assets of a given church and not necessarily designed to disadvantage the Palestinian community. Greater sensitivity to, consultation with and accountability to the views of the lay community may have allayed many suspicions. Nevertheless, the issue continues to be highly contentious and great care must be taken in documenting allegations. This paper offers no additional evidence to that which has been published already.

Land sales by the Greek Orthodox patriarchate to the Jewish National Fund during the partition period of the city is said to have continued after 1967. According to one source, in 1977, the patriarchate received $5 million for approximately 60 *dunams* of land in the area leading down from Jaffa Gate to the Cinemathéque on the road south to Bethlehem.[33] The land was leased for 140 years and the patriarchate was allowed to build a luxury apartment on it. Other large tracts of undeveloped real estate in West Jerusalem and smaller amounts in East Jerusalem were also said to have been sold to the Israel-Lands Administration during the 1970s.[34] To a large extent the actual sales matter less than the perception by Palestinians in Jerusalem that they took place. In the light of the concerted attempts by Israel to secure its territorial base in Jerusalem and encourage new Israeli in-migration, such transactions took on a political colouring which highly embarrassed the Palestinian Greek Orthodox congregations living in the midst of Palestinian Muslims.

Differences between the Palestinian Greek Orthodox laity and the Greek or Cypriot-born clergy of the Greek Orthodox church have long been contentious and disputatious. The issue is too complex to discuss here in any detail but a number of points should be borne in mind. Despite reforms in other parts of the world, the Greek Orthodox patriarchate of Jerusalem, who is the legal owner of all religious property and land in Jerusalem has not had, until recently, any representation of the local population among the senior clergy.[35] Over the years this has led to increasingly strident calls by the local congregation for a reform of the appointment process and for greater accountability of the financial dealings of the patriarchate. In the political climate of the Israeli occupation of East Jerusalem the perception that land sales were taking place raised the political temperature considerably.

Since the *intifada*, these calls for a greater transparency in the financial affairs of the patriarchate mounted. These culminated in the establishment of an 'Arab' Orthodox Initiative Committee who regard the patriarchate as

---

[33] Shepherd, *The Mayor*, 72.

[34] Benevenisti, *Torn City*, 260.

[35] During the Mandate period this point caused a number serious disputes which led the Mandate authorities to make a special study of the situation. See Bertram, A, and Luke, H C, *Report of the Commission. . . to inquire into the affairs of the Orthodox patriarchate of Jerusalem*, London, 1921, and Bertram, A, and Young, I W A, *The Orthodox patriarchate of Jerusalem: Report of the Commission*, London, 1926. Both reports are cited in O'Mahony, A, 'The Orthodox Christian Arab community during the British Mandate in Palestine during the 1920s and 1930s', unpublished manuscript, 1987.

having usurped the rights of the Palestinian Orthodox congregations. A conference convened in October 1992 in Jerusalem passed the following resolution:

> The Executive Committee [of the Arab Orthodox Initiative Committee] will work to amend the Laws and Regulations which define the relationship between the patriarchate and the Arab Orthodox sect, in order to redress the grievances and the injustices suffered by the members of the Arab Orthodox sect and to comply with the new developments at large. In this regard the Conference approves the amendments forwarded by the Arab Orthodox Initiative Committee, to the Laws of the Orthodox patriarchate (No 27 of 1958) that would secure the rights and the participation of the Arab Orthodox community in handling the affairs of the patriarchate and its supervision over the endowments, budgets and buildings of schools.[36]

Of particular relevance are the resolutions concerning the administration of the property of the patriarchate. This issue goes to the heart of the current dispute between the patriarchate and the Palestinian Orthodox congregation. In the context of the dwindling Palestinian grip over the eastern parts of Jerusalem as a result of the settlement policies of the Israeli government, the alleged sales of land by the patriarchate to the Israeli government is acutely embarrassing and alienates the Greek Orthodox laity from the Palestinian mainstream. In the heightened political circumstances prevailing, church lands are no longer seen by the laity as the exclusive province of the church, certainly not a Greek and Greek-Cypriot dominated church, but part of the Palestinian Arab patrimony. Resolution No 16 of the Conference states that (emphasis added):

> The conference will make sure to oversee and protect all church properties in order to curb any attempts at selling religious and physical endowments. Efforts will be made in taking inventories of the properties to be invested for the benefit of the community, for *they are considered to be an integral part of the Palestinian land*, the tampering of which is considered to be national treason.[37]

A follow-up conference held in Amman received the support and recognition of both the Jordanian government and the Palestine Liberation Organisation. For its part the patriarchate insists that land sales have been properly accounted for and are for the benefit of the Greek Orthodox community. It argues that the patriarchate must take a long-term view of

---

[36] Recommendations and Resolutions of the Arab Orthodox conference held in Jerusalem in 23 October, 1992.
[37] *Ibid.*

its presence in the Holy Land and to hand over control of its assets to the Palestinian laity would make the land and property of the church vulnerable to state pressure, whether it be Jordanian, Israeli or Palestinian. The significance of these and other developments on Israel-patriarch-Palestinian laity relations will be discussed in the next section. The point to be emphasised at this stage is that the balancing act that the patriarchate has tried to perform became increasingly unstable. Its relative autonomy of action with regard to its local constituency, the Palestinian laity, has been threatened by a perceived cooption by the Israeli state, a state whose settlement policies in Jerusalem threaten the very future of that constituency in Jerusalem. The laity was no longer prepared to accept a leadership which appeared to be working against its long-term interests.

The second case study in this paper, that of the Armenian Orthodox patriarchate, has experienced similar conflict over the issue of land sales. In the early seventies the alleged willingness of the patriarchate to sell land and property to the Israel-Lands Administration prompted the same disquiet within this community as with the Greek Orthodox.[38] In this case, the patriarchate did not lose its close connections with the Armenian laity but it led to a public rupture between the patriarchate and the Israeli government. The Armenian community is a close-knit community based almost entirely inside the Monastery of St James or in the immediate vicinity of the Armenian quarter.[39] Despite the fact that the Jerusalem patriarchate has been exempted from the democratising reforms enacted in other parts of the Armenian Orthodox church, the close living conditions of the community have meant that lay influence in the affairs of the patriarchate is strong. Since the Armenian community is reputed to be the largest landowner in the Old City and one of the largest in Jerusalem, government interest, be it Jordanian or Israeli, in the community's affairs is also strong. An example of this occurred during the Jordanian period when the intervention of the Jordanian government ensured the appointment of Patriarch Derderian.[40]

A similar event took place in the mid-eighties over the replacement of the pro-Israeli Sacristan, Archbishop Shahe Ajamian. The sacristan is responsible for the financial affairs of the community and Ajamian had been responsible for land sales to the Israeli government including land along the western slopes of the city walls from Jaffa Gate to the Dormition Abbey.[41] He maintained extremely good relations with Mayor Kollek and

---

[38] *Ibid.*, 260.
[39] See Azarya, V, *The Armenian Quarter of Jerusalem*, London, University of California Press, 1984. See chapters four and five. See also Hintlian, K, *History of theArmenians in the Holy Land*, Jerusalem, Armenian Patriarchate Printing Press, 1989, second edition, 46-50.
[40] Azarya, *Armenian Quarter*, 114-117.
[41] Shepherd, *The Mayor*, 75.

was a frequent host to the mayor's foreign guests.[42] In 1981, the Armenian patriarch attempted to replace Ajamian with an Australian citizen, Kareki Kazanjian, but found that the municipality and the Minister of the Interior were opposed to this move. Kazanjian visitor's visa was not renewed, tax exemptions for the patriarchate were withheld and repair projects not permitted. Mayor Kollek himself attempted to get Kazanjian deported.[43] Finally, the public furore over the government's intervention in the internal affairs of a church obliged the government to desist from deporting Kazanjian but he remained in Jerusalem without a residency permit. One result of this tenuous residency status is to lay him open to further government and municipality pressures.[44] Subsequent developments revealed that Ajamian and Raphael Levy, the Israeli District Governor of Jerusalem, were involved in bribe-taking, smuggling and currency offences.[45] These events provoked a great deal of tension between the patriarchate and the Israeli government and municipality, and within the Armenian community of Jerusalem itself.[46] Again, similar to developments in the relationship between the Greek Orthodox patriarchate and the Israeli state, we can see how also in the case of the Armenian Orthodox patriarchate, too close an involvement by the state disturbed the delicate balancing act that the patriarchate had been try to perform. But in this case the refusal by the local Armenian community to accept the cooption of its clergy and the close identification of the clergy with the community led to the collapse of the balancing act.

The final example to be examined is the Latin patriarchate. It is faintly ironic that, despite Israel's attempts to court Western Christendom, the most Western of the three main churches in Jerusalem, the Latin patriarchate, is the one with the most problematic relationship with Israel. The reasons for this lies both in the international plane and in local Israel-Palestinian politics.[47] The Latins, as the Roman Catholic church is called in Jerusalem, acquired much of their property and influence during their dominant position in the Crusader period. They have never completely accepted the restoration of Greek Orthodox precedence during the Ottoman period. The current importance of the Vatican's role in Jerusalem

[42] One can imagine how useful it was to have a senior dignitary from one of the Eastern Orthodox churches extolling the virtues of an Israeli administration over a unified city. Ajamian also voted against World Council of Churches conference resolutions that were critical of Israel and was hailed by Israelis as a good friend of Israel.

[43] *Ibid.*, 76.

[44] Despite being deposed Ajamian continued to appear at Israeli receptions and was granted passage to Jordan without customs checks.

[45] Shepherd, *The Mayor*, 160-2.

[46] See Azarya, *Armenian Quarter*, 218, n. 18. See also Shepherd, *The Mayor*, 76.

[47] For further detail of Vatican-Israeli relations see Khoury, F J, 'The Jerusalem Question and the Vatican', in Ellis, H F (ed), *The Vatican, Islam and the Middle East*, New York, Syracuse University Press, 1987, 143-162; Irani, G E, *Papacy and the Middle East: The role of the Papacy in the Arab-Israeli conflict, 1962-1984*, Notre Dame, University of Notre Dame, 1986, and Rokach, L, *The Catholic Church and the Question of Palestine*, London, al-Saqi, 1987.

has been its traditional support for the 'internationalisation' of Jerusalem under UN auspices. The Vatican has particular influence in these discussions since its views carry a great deal of weight with a number of Roman Catholic member states, such as Italy, the Philippines, those of South and Central America. In addition, the influence of the Roman Catholic church goes beyond that of their own community. The Pontifical Mission for Palestine is one of the largest non-governmental organisation funders in the occupied Palestinian territories and many of its projects are devoted to strengthening the Palestinian community on a non-sectarian basis.

Since 1967, there has been a gradual waning of the Vatican's support for the notion of a 'territorial internationalisation', yet it continues to insist on some form of international administration of the Holy Places. On this account it has refused to recognise the state of Israel or Israeli sovereignty either in West or East Jerusalem.[48] This firm line was subjected to great strain as German and US Catholic bishops, whose provinces are the main funders of the contemporary Catholic church, pressurized the Vatican to establish diplomatic relations with Israel. Furthermore, the Vatican is well aware how it has been completely marginalised in the current Arab-Israeli peace negotiations due to its position of non-recognition. It was not even invited to the opening session of the talks in Madrid. It was anxious, therefore, to recover what it saw as lost diplomatic ground. A further irony in Israel-Vatican relations is that it was not the pressure of the pro-Israeli groups within the Roman Catholic church which led to a rapprochement with Israel, but the Declaration of Principles signed between the Israeli government and the PLO in Oslo 1993 which prompted diplomatic recognition between the Vatican and Israel. The Declaration of Principles further marginalised the Vatican which was left isolated and to appear more pro-Palestinian than the PLO. A protocol was quickly signed in January 1994 but with the result that whatever little leverage the Vatican had over Israel in terms of diplomatic recognition was completely lost. These international developments and internal tensions had an impact upon the three-way relations between the Israeli state and senior Roman Catholic clergy and the Palestinian Catholic congregation in Jerusalem.

In contrast to the Greek Orthodox church, clergy-laity relations in the Roman Catholic church are close and Palestinians can rise up the ranks to become senior clergy. In the late eighties, for example, a Palestinian, Michel Sabbah, became the Latin patriarch for Jerusalem.[49] In addition,

---

48 See discussion of this theme in Khouri, F, 'The Jerusalem Question and the Vatican', in Ellis, K, *The Vatican, Islam and the Middle East*, New York, Syracuse University Press, 1987; Irani, G, *The Papacy and the Middle East: The Role of the Holy See in the Arab-Israeli, 1962-1984*, Notre Dame, University of Notre Dame Press, 1986, chapter two.

49 A short profile on Sabah can be found in Tsimhoni, D, 'The Latin patriarchate of Jerusalem from the First Half of the 19th Century to Present Times: Institutional and Social Aspects,' in Layish, A (ed.), *The Arabs in Jerusalem: From the Late Ottoman Period to the Beginning of the 1990s - Religious, Social and Cultural Distinctiveness, Hamizrah Hehadash*, Vol. XXXIV, 1992, Jerusalem, 1992, 127. For his role in the *intifada*, see 133ff.

there have not been the same clergy-laity tensions over, for example, land sales to the Israeli government. The Latin patriarchate and the Catholic Franciscan Order do own large tracts of land in Jerusalem but they have been very reluctant to sell to the Israeli government. It took many years before the patriarchate agreed to lease the land between the New Gate and the Damascus Gate for a park and only agreed to sell a small tract of land on French Hill in the north of the city when planning permission was repeatedly refused.[50] An indication of the strength of the Vatican's position can be partly guaged by the dispute over the ownership of the Notre Dame Hostel. Immediately after the 1967 War, the Notre Dame Hostel which had remained empty while standing on the Armistice Lines for nineteen years, was sold by a Catholic ecclesiastical order to the Hebrew University without the Vatican's knowledge. On hearing the news the Vatican put great pressure on the government and managed to have the sale revoked despite strong opposition from the university and the municipality.[51] The Hostel is now one of the largest and most prestigious hotels in East Jerusalem and the flagship of the Christian Palestinian economy in Jerusalem.

The main on-going dispute between the Roman Catholic church and the Israeli municipality is over the question of tax-exemptions for its property. This the Latins have in common with other churches and the problem stems from the Mandate period where exemptions were granted to churches for their religious property. The Jordanian government agreed to continue this practice, but after 1967 the Israeli government argued that the definition of religious property was too wide and should not include profit-making buildings. The Latin patriarchate in particular refuses to pay tax on such property on two accounts: first the UN Partition Plan accepted by Israel in 1947 included an obligation to continue such exemptions, and secondly, payment would imply recognition of Israel as the sovereign state in Jerusalem. As Naomi Shepherd argues, in itself this issue is not so important but:

> . . . it relates to the all-important question of the overall status of the churches in Jerusalem and in all the Holy Land, which is still undefined, unsatisfactory and a potential cause of conflict between the churches themselves, and between the churches and Israel. All the churches want some kind of recognised, independent status, not just a promise of free access to the Holy Places.

She goes on to argue that:

> . . . Instead of enjoying a blanket exemption from customs duties, for example, the duties are charged, the churches apply

---

[50] Shepherd, *The Mayor*, 73.
[51] Benvenisti, *Torn City*, 260; see also Shepherd, *The Mayor*, 73.

to the Ministry [of Religious Affairs], and the Ministry (if it agrees) pays the duty on the churches behalf. So exemption depends on ministerial approval and the state of the Ministry's budget.[52]

In this way the Latin patriarchate and the other churches are open to pressures over a wide range of issues from exemptions, to planning permission, to visas for new appointments. The scope for government and Municipality intervention is clear. However, the main point to be made here, is that the close coordination between the Latin patriarchate and its local constituency has prevented the patriarchate from having too close a relationship with the Israeli state.

The impact of the intifada

During the eighties, a marked change can be noted in church-state relations in Jerusalem. Some of the factors in that change can be traced to the period before the Palestinian *intifada* began in 1987 and were unrelated to this dramatic event. Nevertheless, manifesting themselves more fully during the *intifada* itself, the result was to give these changes a keener political edge. The two key factors in this change are, first, the growing demands by the Palestinian laity for the 'Palestinianization' or 'Arabization' of the clergy, and second, the shift in the locus of state authority from Israeli bodies familiar with dealing with the churches to institutions and official bodies with a more hawkish and Israeli chauvinistic agenda.

As the Palestinian laity became better educated and more cosmopolitan than their clergy during the post-1967 period, the demand for both greater involvement in the running of their respective churches increased. Similarly the growing sense of a Palestinian identity replacing the previous more sectarian, denominational one, led to a further scrutiny of the clergy's stance on the social and political issues of the day. As we indicated in the Greek Orthodox patriarchate example above, the land, the property and the administrative structures of the churches are increasingly seen by the politically active members of the laity as belonging to the Palestinian people as an embryonic nation. The appointments of Palestinians as bishops, such as Lutfi Laham for the Greek Catholics, Samir Kafity for the Arab Episcopalians (Anglicans) and Michel Sabbah for the Roman Catholics, projected politically aware, articulate and internationally well-connected individuals to the head of these churches.[53] In addition, these men were the leaders of churches who, in the main, had close contact with and were respected by their congregations and shared its political aspirations.

---

[52] Shepherd, *The Mayor*, 71.
[53] See Tsimhoni, 'The Latin Patriarchate', 126ff.

It is highly significant that after decades of uncoordinated bilateral relations with the Israeli government, these men were able to draw together all the leaders of the churches in Jerusalem to issue a series of statements highly critical of the Israeli government and its policies during the *intifada*. For example, on 27 April 1987 a strongly-worded statement was issued by the 'Heads of the Christian Communities in Jerusalem', part of which declared:

> It is our Christian conviction that as spiritual leaders we have an urgent duty to follow up the developments in this situation and to make known to the world the conditions of life of our people here in the Holy Land. In Jerusalem, on the West Bank and in Gaza our people experience in their daily lives constant deprivation of their fundamental rights because of arbitrary actions deliberately taken by the authorities. Our people are often subjected to unprovoked harassment and hardship . . . We protest against the frequent shooting incidents in the vicinity of the Holy Places . . . We demand that the authorities respect the right of believers to enjoy free access to all places of worship on the Holy Days of all religions . . . we request the international community and the UN to give urgent attention to the plight of the Palestinian people, and to work for a speedy and just resolution of the Palestinian problem.[54]

These statements can be interpreted in a number of ways. They were a reflection of a shift in the internal politics of the Jerusalem churches, where the more politically involved clergy and laity took the lead. Ritually, traditional leadership remained with the Greek Orthodox patriarchate, but politically this position was being challenged by the smaller denominations. At the same time the statements were an astute defensive move by the church leaders to guard their flanks against the criticisms of radical Palestinian nationalists and militant Muslim fundamentalists during this tense period. By publicly aligning themselves with the *intifada*, church leaders were positioning themselves alongside the Palestinian national movement to protect their congregations and their property. Finally, these statements also sent a clear signal to the Israeli government that the Christian community in Jerusalem could no longer be detached from the main body of Palestinian opinion. The signature of the Greek Orthodox

---

[54] See Documentation Section, *MECC Perspectives*, no. 8. July 1990, 75-76. The statement was signed by: His Beatitude (HB) Diadorus, Greek Orthodox patriarch of Jerusalem, HB Michel Sabbah, Latin patriarch of Jerusalem, Bishop Samir Kafity, President Bishop, Episcopal Church in Jerusalem and the Middle East, Archbishop Lutfi Laham, patriarchal Vicar, Greek Catholic patriarchate of Jerusalem, HB Yeghishe Derderian, Armenian Orthodox patriarch of Jerusalem, Bishop Naim Nassar, Evangelical Lutheran Church in Jordan, HB Basilios, Coptic Orthodox patriarch of Jerusalem, Archbishop Dionysios Behnam Jijjawi, Syrian Orthodox patriarchal Vicar of Jerusalem, Most Reverend Father Cechitelli (Order of the Franciscan Monks), Custos of the Holy Land.

patriarch, the most political conservative and pro-Israeli of the heads of Christian communities, to these statements was highly significant. It marked, at least temporarily, the failure of the Israeli government to co-opt the church hierarchies and was a blow to their land acquisition policies.

The second key factor in the changes in church-state relations has been the shift in the locus of real influence amongst the various Israeli officials and institutions dealing with the Christian community. This shift was all the more decisive since its ramifications coincided with the outbreak of the Palestinian *intifada* against Israeli rule in the occupied Palestinian territories including East Jerusalem. In the past, the main responsible bodies dealing with the Christian leaders and communities have been: the mayor's office at the Jerusalem municipality, the Christian Division of the Ministry of Religious Affairs, the Department of External Christian Relations in the Ministry of Foreign Affairs and the District Commissioner of Jerusalem. Representatives of these bodies would meet regularly to coordinate approaches to the churches.[55] All these bodies have broadly been content not to antagonise or provoke the Christian community while at the same time extracting piecemeal advantage for the Israeli government wherever possible.

After the election of the Likud coalition in 1977, hawkish and religious nationalists were appointed to key positions in the Israel-Lands Administration, the Ministry of Justice, the Ministry of Religious Affairs and the Ministry of Housing. These were the most important ministries and departments in the Likud government's strategic programme of ensuring an irrevocable Israeli Jewish dominance over the city by acquiring land and property and settling new Jewish immigrants. However, they showed less sensitivity to the churches concerns and gradually began to override the more cooperative and consultative relationship previously established.[56] For example, in 1979 and 1980 a series of arson attacks and vandalism against church property by Israeli Jewish extremists took place. The Dormition Abbey on Mount Zion, the Christian Information Centre near Jaffa Gate, the Protestant Bible Bookshop were all damaged and a Baptist church in West Jerusalem burned down.[57] While the police investigated and some people were charged the response of the Israeli government was lukewarm and uninterested.

Official encouragement of groups such as the International Christian Embassy in Jerusalem and other fundamentalist supporters of Israel was also extremely disturbing for the established Christian communities and their clergy. It should be recalled that it was in the early 1980s that Israeli settler

---

[55] Interview with Naomi Teasdale, 30.3.93.
[56] Initially the good rapport between Mayor Kollek and the then Foreign Minister, Moshe Dayan, meant that the Municipality and the District Governor, Raphael Levy, were given a free rein in their dealings with the churches; see Shepherd, *The Mayor*, 74.
[57] Shepherd, *The Mayor*, 70.

groups first started to make their presence felt in the Old City.[58] Primarily directed at sites of Jewish association in the Old City, particularly in the Muslim quarters, the churches noticed that some of the settler groups received support from organisations such as the Temple Mount Foundation which had Christian support.[59]

As the settler groups became increasingly emboldened by covert and overt government funding, their attention turned to potential sites in the Christian quarters. The revelations of official government support from the Ministries of Justice, Housing and Religious Affairs undermined the complex weave of *ad hoc* understandings and personal guarantees that constituted the structure of relationships between the churches and the government and municipality. This shift in the locus of state power came to a head when, in April 1990, the Ateret Cohanim settler group broke into St John's Hospice, hitherto owned by the Greek Orthodox patriarchate, and set up a *yeshiva* and residence for its members.[60] The attempt by the Patriarch Diodorus to enter and restore Greek Orthodox control over the building led to a physical confrontation with the result that the patriarch himself was pushed violently to the floor.

The public humiliation of the patriarch in this way symbolised the political changes taking place in church state-relations in Jerusalem. From the point of view of the Greek Orthodox clergy here was the leader of the most ancient Christian community in Jerusalem, who had cooperated with the Israeli government and Israeli officials at some risk to himself, who had acceded in the sale and leasing of precious land in Jerusalem, who had for many years successfully obstructed any concerted Christian opposition to Israeli sovereignty, who had allowed himself to be paraded in front of foreign dignitaries by municipal officials as the authentic Christian response to Israeli rule, here he was treated by some North American roughnecks as if he was of no consequence whatsoever, without the government even attempting to restore his dignity and status or make redress. What was the purpose of all this accommodation to the Israeli state if the end result was dispossession and humiliation.

The St John's Hospice incident highlighted the declining influence of those Israeli officials in the government and the Municipality who have sought to maintain the Status Quo arrangements and it marked the corresponding rise of those committed to a chauvinistic Israeli Jewish agenda for Jerusalem. It also prompted a realignment of the Greek Orthodox community behind the more nationalist church leaders in the Roman Catholic, Greek Catholic and Anglican churches. As a result of the

[58]   See Dumper, M, 'IsraeliSettlement in the Old City of Jerusalem', *Journal of Palestine Studies*, vol. XXI, no.4 (summer 1992), 32-53.

[59]   See Halsell, G, *Prophecy and Politics: Militant Evangelists on the Road to Nuclear War*, Westport, Lawrence Hill, 1986, 96ff.

[60]   They claimed that the property had been sold to them by an Armenian tenant via a Panamanian company. See *Jerusalem Post*, 'Casualties reported over Old City settlement', 17.4.1990.

St John's incident and the near-breakdown in official relations, as evidenced by a bitter public exchange between the patriarch and the president of Israel, Chaim Herzog, the Greek Orthodox patriarchate reassessed its cooperative relations with the Israeli government.[61] From the patriarch's point-of-view, there must seem little incentive to maintain good cooperative relationship with the Israeli government against the wishes of the lay Palestinian community, if those relations do not serve to preserve the property of the church and its influence in government and municipal policy. No doubt there has been a lessening of tension between the Israeli government and the Greek Orthodox patriarchate since the change of government in 1992. Nevertheless, the shift in the locus of power has continued and the election of a hawkish mayor of Jerusalem, may have exacerbated this development.

Conclusion

It is perhaps stating the obvious to say that no less since 1948 than over the past centuries the over-riding concern of the churches in Jerusalem has been to ensure their continued presence in the city. This paper has argued that this has only been achieved in the contemporary period through a balancing act of being responsive to both the state and the local community. Such an act has carried with it inherent dangers of co-option and manipulation by the state authorities. The paper has illustrated how too close a cooperation between the church hierarchies and the state destabilised that balancing act and led to its breakdown. The radicalisation of the clergy, the Palestinian *intifada* and the intervention of more chauvinistic state officials have all contributed to a new dynamic whose features are not completely revealed. In sum, the balancing acts are over until the new political configurations are established. If it becomes clear that the Israeli state authorities will remain sovereign over both sides of Jerusalem, one can anticipate a resurrection of the balancing act as the churches seek to protect their positions and assets. Conversely, while there is a possibility, however distant, that a Palestinian governing authority may exert some administrative or political influence in the city, one can anticipate the churches continuing to be more responsive to the interests of their local constituencies in order to position themselves better following any transfer of power.

---

[61] An open letter from the president to the patriarch was published in the *Jerusalem Post*, 18.5.1990. The patriarch's reply was issued in a press release 28 May, 1990, but not published. The dispute also spilled over into the diplomatic domain when the patriarch called on the Greek government to suspend attempts to improve Greek-Israeli relations. See *Jerusalem Post*, 16.5.1990.

18

Contemporary Christian
Pilgrimage to the Holy Land[1]

Glenn Bowman

Introduction: interpreting pilgrimage

It is easier to talk about pilgrimages than it is to define what we are speaking about; one knows what the speaker means when he or she refers to an activity as a pilgrimage despite the fact the activity referred to may be a visit to a small local shrine on the outskirts of the village in which one lives or a journey of several years and several thousand miles from which one might never return.[2] Is it appropriate to claim that such widely divergent practices are manifestations of the same thing? I would like, in opening this paper, to consider the category under which we group what we recognise as pilgrimages, not because of pedantry but because globalizing the term in the way we tend to forces us to focus on certain elements which seem to be common to all pilgrimages. By doing so we lose sight of anomalous features of certain types of pilgrimage such as Christian pilgrimage to the Holy Land - which, when attended to, prove to be of much greater significance than more universal features. My investigation of the category of pilgrimage then opens onto an examination of differences in perceptions of and practices relating to the Holy Land

[1] Research in the Isreali-Occupied Territories (1983-1985, 1987, 1989, 1990, 1993 and 1994) was funded by grants from the Palestine Exploration Fund, the Lady Davis Foundation, the Deya Mediterranean Area Research Centre, and the Wenner Gren Foundation for Anthropological Research.

[2] I would chose as illustration of this divergence two discriptions of pilgrimage which have been seminal to my work: Robert Hertz's description of the pilgrimage of local villagers to the Alpine shrine St Besse (Hertz, 1913), trans. (Hertz, 1983) and the narrative of the voyage of Egeria, a fourth century Christian nun from Gaul, to Palestine and then onwards (beyond the limits of the fragments of the text which remain) to Southern India to the sites commemorating St Thomas's mission to the East (Wilkinson, 1971). Further literature, reflecting the range of pilgrimage phenomena within and beyond Christian traditions, is extensive and only partially cited in the bibliography of Morinis's *Sacred Journeys: the Anthropology of Pilgrimage* (Morinis, 1992: 279-307).

between two dominant tendencies within Christianity (Orthodox and Latin). I here stress the way groups which revere the holy places and are resident outside the contested territory I will refer to as Israel/Palestine tend to reconstitute the place in accordance with their respective - and different - images of it. In closing I will demonstrate the dangers implicit in such approaches by contrasting these with the relations to the holy sites of communities (in particular Christian and Muslim Palestinians) who reside in the land and who tend to share the sites despite their variant interpretations of the significance of those places. I will close with a call to understand the sacrality of holy sites not in metaphysical and hence totalizing terms but as something profoundly of this world and therefore of vital significance to the future of inter-communal relations in the Holy Land.

The *Oxford English Dictionary* defines pilgrimage as a journey (usually of considerable duration) to some sacred place as an act of religious devotion (*OED,* 1971: 2174). In this definition - as in all other citations I came across in scanning lexicons and academic studies of the topic - the salient elements of the contemporary concept are contact with the sacred and displacement. Etymologically, however, it is displacement which gave rise to the term. Skeat traces the modern English word pilgrimage back to the Latin term *peregrinus* which signified foreigner or stranger, and points out that this noun itself devolved from the adverb *peregrine* which meant simply away from home (Skeat, 1927: 391). We cannot, of course, argue that a term's earliest form carries an essential meaning within it; Nietzsche - despite his own tendency to cite etymologies in order to undermine contemporary significations - argued that

> the cause of the origin of a thing and its eventual utility, its actual employment and place in a system of purposes, lie worlds apart; whatever exists, having somehow come into being, is again and again reinterpreted to new ends, taken over, transformed, and redirected by some power superior to it (Nietzsche, 1969: 77).

This process of appropriation is central to an understanding of Christian pilgrimage to the Holy Land. The concept of pilgrimage has a history of transformation in the course of which other concepts - such as that of seeking a source of sacred power - have been calqued onto the ordinary sense of being displaced from home. Such accretions have translated the concept of pilgrimage into something which carries implications different from those of its ordinary sense.

What I wish to show, with particular reference to contemporary pilgrimage practices in Israel/Palestine, is that this history of deletion, accretion and supplementation has given rise to a number of quite distinct forms of pilgrimage. These, despite normally being grouped in both popular and academic discourses within the rubric of Christian pilgrimage to the Holy Land, promote in their practitioners very different sets of expectations and practices. Those manifestations of sacrality sought by pilgrims from Latin traditions (Catholic and Protestant) will differ, both in appearance and significance, from those sought by pilgrims coming from places in which Orthodox or non-Chalcedonian traditions are prevalent. Pilgrims pursuits of different manifestations of the sacred have given rise to and been fostered by different sets of institutions on the ground in both the Holy Land and in the societies from whence the pilgrims come. These institutions serve, through their arrangement and elaboration of the sites and through the dissemination of materials constructing these in the imagination of pilgrims and visitors (promotional materials, guide books, descriptions of pilgrimage and the like), to create the place travellers encounter, and this place will not be the same as that encountered by visitors coming from other traditions (see Casey 1993: 3-39 on the distinction between abstract space and phenomenlogical place). There is thus not one paradigmatic Christian pilgrimage to the Holy Land pursued by several hundred thousands of Christians per annum[3] but a number of distinct models of deportment and anticipation in which pilgrims will variously engage because of the way they have learned to think of Holy Land pilgrimage and the holy places in their home environments (Bowman, 1991). The consequence of these various discursive constructions of the goal of Christian Holy Land pilgrimage is that the sacrality pursued by the various Christian pilgrims is quite diverse in so far as it is variously given form through the ways in which it is spoken, perceived and pursued. Because each community of Christians conceives of the goal of its pilgrimages according to its customs, there is in effect no single Jerusalem and enveloping Holy Land; there are as many different Holy Lands as there are cultures revering that simultaneously mythical and real place.

The implication of the compounding of the terms mythical and real in describing the Holy Lands revered by Christians (not to mention Jews, Muslims, and other significant religious communities) is that the real place is encountered through texts which imbue it with sacrality and call upon it to substantiate their claims to authority. This is not to deny that there is a materiality to the places deemed holy; people come to lay eyes and hands upon the sites their traditions have celebrated, and many of them take pieces of the places (relics, souvenirs, photographs) back to fix the stories which circulate around the names of the places with tokens of the reality of

---

[3] In 1984 a total of 1,259,000 visitors to 'Isreal' were recorded. Extrapolating from figures established by Ray Baron and Haya Fisher over an eight year (1974-1982) survey of visitor's intentions, I conclude that of these 749,000 were at least nominally Christian among which 160,000 were persons who strictly defined themselves as Christian 'pilgrims' and 220,000 came on 'Holy Land Tours' focused on the visiting of Christian sites. The remaining 170,000 came for the primary purposes of studying, working, attending conferences, recreation, or visiting friends and family (Isreal, Ministry of Tourism, 1986 and Baron & Fisher, 1983). I cite these figures rather than more up to date ones because the disruption to pilgrimage/tourism trade effected by the *intifada* and its repression made the accurate collection of later figures problematic.

the sites. Such objects - real or representations such as photographs - are, however, meaningless without the stories and traditions which set them in interpretative frameworks. Mark Twain's wonderfully incisive *The Innocents Abroad* illustrates the dialectic through which objects come firstly to be given meaning through association with a sanctified narrative and then serve to give credence to the story itself. He describes, for instance, an encounter between the pilgrim group he accompanied and the village of Madaba:

> We came to a bramble-infested inclosure and a Roman looking ruin which had been the veritable dwelling of St Mary Magdalene, the friend and follower of Jesus. The guide believed it, and so did I. I could not well do otherwise, with the house right there before my eyes as plain as day. The pilgrims took down portions of the front wall for specimens, as is their honored custom, and then we departed (Twain, 1905: II 262).

He furthermore elucidates the way in which the discourses of the pilgrims constitute the significances of the places they encounter:

> Many who have visited this land in years gone by, were Presbyterians, and came seeking evidences in support of their particular creed; they found a Presbyterian Palestine, and they had already made up their minds to find no other, though possibly they did not know it, being blinded by their zeal. Others were Baptists, seeking Baptist evidences and a Baptist Palestine. Others were Catholics, Methodists, Episcopalians, seeking evidences indorsing their several creeds, and a Catholic, a Methodist, an Episcopalian Palestine. Honest as these men's intentions may have been, they were full of partialities and prejudices, they entered the country with their verdicts already prepared, and they could no more write dispassionately and impartially about it than they could about their own wives and children (Twain, 1905: II 270-271).

Twain's tales are imbued with a corrosive humour which - perhaps - renders them dubious witnesses to the nature of something as serious as pilgrimage. A more sanctified source for examples of the way stones are in effect transfigured by expectation - or the textual imagination would be St Jerome who tells of the

> pilgrimage of an acolyte, Paula, through the holy places, [who] 'declared in my hearing that by the eyes of faith she could see [in Bethlehem's Grotto of the Saviour] the Infant Lord, wrapped in swaddling-clothes, wailing in the Manger, the Magi

adoring, the star shining above, the Virgin mother, the careful
nursing, the shepherds coming by night that they might see the
Word which had been made, and might even then declare the
beginning of the Evangelist John, In the beginning was the
Word, and the Word was made flesh' (St Jerome, 1896: 7).

Lest we are led to suspect that the esteemed Church Father is here
describing the illusions of an hysterical religiosa we must refer to another of
his letters in which he describes a similar hallucination of his own: as often
as we enter (the Lord's Sepulchre) we see the Saviour in His grave clothes
and if we linger we see again the angel sitting at His feet and the napkin
folded at His head (St Jerome, 1893: 62). I myself have listened to an
American Evangelical with whom I had visited the alleged sepulchre of
Christ in the Protestant Garden Tomb tell me that while she stood within
the tomb with me next to her she saw Christ's winding cloth folded on the
stone and an angel standing guard in the doorway (fieldnotes: May 1984).

The point of these illustrations is that we must modify our definition of
pilgrimage in a manner which may seem nominal but is in fact quite
substantial. I propose that the previously cited *OED* definition of
pilgrimage as a journey (usually of considerable duration) to some sacred
place as an act of religious devotion should instead read a journey (usually
of considerable duration) to some place rendered sacred by the religious
devotion of the pilgrim. This redefinition retains the activity of
displacement but shifts the locus of sacrality from the site to the apparatuses
of interpretation the pilgrim carries with him or her self. The site is a place
and sacrality is written over that place by the faith of the pilgrim. This faith
is socially constituted; a community, through history, articulates and
elaborates its conceptions of its relationships with divinity and then gives
expression to these relationships in the form of *sacra* or sacred things. Emile
Durkheim, building on the research done by William Robertson Smith on
the genesis of holy places in Ancient Israelite religion (Smith, 1907),
contended that collective sentiments can become conscious of themselves
only by fixing themselves upon external objects (Durkheim, 1915: 466).
Durkheim's essentially atheistic study of the *soi disant* elementary forms of
the religious life argued that individuals, imbued with a collective sense of
dependency and awe by their unarticulated relationships with the society
which both maintains them and - through language and tradition - renders
their existences meaningful, effectively displace the social power to which
they feel subordinated onto an extra-social domain and monumentalize
that power by seeing it as incarnated in certain objects or sites. The power
they recognise in those objectifications is not recognised as a manifestation
of their own communality but as something that their community, like
themselves, must reverence. The atheistic project informing Durkheim's
conceptualization of the genesis of *sacra* is not, however, essential to an
understanding of how objectifications derive their sacrality from society
while being misrecognised as things sacred in themselves by those who

make them sacred. Whether or not divinity exists in itself, it is how persons – and communities – conceive of the relations they can establish with what they perceive as divine which creates both the character of those things memorialised as sacred and the deportment with which persons approach them:

> the idea of holiness . . . is not so much a thing that characterises the gods and divine things in themselves, as the most general notion that governs their relations with humanity; and, as these relations are concentrated at particular points of the earth's surface, it is at these points that we must expect to find the clearest indications of what holiness means (Smith, 1907: 142).

The sacrality of sites is, in other words, a projection onto objects in this world of a social imagining of how humans and divinity can interrelate. The pilgrim, then, is a person who travels beyond domains marked out by largely secular concerns to a place he or she believes he or she can encounter in as pure a form as is available a model of the relationship possible between the human and the divine.

Text and context

The significance of this insight for the study of Holy Land pilgrimage devolves from the fact that the holy places body forth this socially constituted imagining for a number of distinct communities which have, in a number of disparate ways, constituted very different concepts of the relationship of divinity to humanity. In so far as this paper approaches only Christian pilgrimage to the Holy Land I am spared the task of attempting to map the various holy lands constituted amongst the plethora of distinct religious communities which revere a land central to three of the chief monotheistic religions of the world and to all of their varied offshoots. I furthermore will avoid examining specifically national variants of Holy Land imaginings among the various Christian nations which have manifested spiritual involvement with the holy places[4] since I can claim, for

---

[4] I would nonetheless here draw attention to the 19th century proliferation of nationally defined religious institutions in Jerusalem and the Holy Land (see, for a good introduction, Ben-Arieh, 1984: 184-264). Jeff Halper, in an unpublished manuscript entitled *The Other Jerusalem: The Reemergence of the Holy City (1800-1917)*, points out that as a result of the European ecclesiastical building craze which followed the Ctimean War, Austrian, French, Russian and Italian pilgrims could stay in the holy land and visit all of the revered sites without ever having to stay in a building alien to the styles of their own countries r having to hear a word spoken in any other language other than their own. If one's perception of sacrality – kenned in one's originary culture through hearing or reading stories from the *Bible* (most likely in one's natal language), joining neighbours in religious ceremonies, and the like – is to be amplified in the holy places, then the last thing one would desire is to perceive the holy *desiderata* in a context marred by voices speaking in foreign languages, people dressing and deporting themselves in

methodological reasons, that national and religious sensibilities are distinguishable things.[5] Even, however, leaving out of consideration the wide field of non-Chalcedonian communities (Ethiopian, Armenian, Syrian and Coptic Orthodox) and dedicating myself to considering solely what differences lie in the approaches to the holy places of one Orthodox tradition (Greek Orthodoxy rather than Serbian, Russian, Roumanian or others) and the linked traditions of Roman Catholicism and the various Protestantisms is to embark upon a massive endeavour. I have tried to map out these differences in some detail in another paper (Bowman, 1991) but will here point to the way the sacred character of the holy places in the eyes of pilgrims from Greek Orthodox, Catholic and Protestant traditions can be transformed radically by what might, in a short-sighted view, seem a mere slip of the pen. Between 382 and 384 St Jerome, at the bequest of Pope Damasus, translated the New Testament from Greek into Latin. In his translation of Paul's Letters to the Romans, which includes seminal passages on the consequences of Adam's disobedience, St Jerome introduced a reading of original sin which varied substantially from that expressed in the original Greek. This reading was subsequently taken up by St Augustine in his disputes with the Pelagians (see Frend, 1984: 673-683 on the Pelagian controversy) in a manner which, I will argue, produced very different conceptions of human relations to divinity in the Orthodox and Latin churches. These divergences have given rise to different conceptions of how humans approach the *sacra* and these continue to this day to influence the variant manners by which Latin and Orthodox Christians envisage the holy places. Different formulations of the approach persons are able to make to divinity lead to very different modes of practice in the holy places as well as to very different formulations of what sorts of sites and objects make visible the sacred. Different definitions of sacrality lead, in effect, to the constitution of different Holy Lands.

While Orthodoxy accepts the same biblical account of Adam's disobedience as does Latin Christianity, it interprets the consequences of that disobedience - recounted in Romans 5: 12 differently. St Jerome's

---

'foreign' ways, *etcetera*. As soon as national sensibilities were distinguishable pilgrims sought to visit the Holy Land in the company of co-nationals and to avoid, as much as possible, sites and situations penetrated by national alterity. Thus, in the late fifteenth century, the author of *Fratris Felices Fabri Evagatorium in Terrae Sanctae* (The Wanderings of Felix Fabri) - a German Dominican friar who travelled to the Holy Land twice (in 1480 and again in 1483) - comments with pleasure on the pilgrims' hospice in which he stayed in Venice on the eve of his departure for Palestine that "the entire household . . . and all the man-servants and maid-servants were of the German nation and speech, and no word of Italian was to be heard in the house". Even the host's dog was an "implacable foe of the Italians . . . German men can never agree with Italians nor Italians with us, because each nation has hatred of the other rooted in its very nature" (Fabri, 1892-1897: VII 79-81).

[5] A claim whose validity is seriously undermined by the intensity of nationalist fervour which has marked the relations of the Greek Orthodox community to the Holy Land since the early sixteenth century when Patriarch Germanos transformed the Orthodox Patriarchate in Jerusalem in to Greek enclave (see Bertram and Young, 1926: 34-78, Bowman, 1993: 436 and 443, O'Mahony 1987 and Runciman, 1970: 14f).

Latin rendition derived from the Greek Gospels reads (in the English of the Revised Standard Edition) As sin came into the world through one man, and through sin, death, so death spread to all men because all men have sinned. Orthodox interpretation of the Greek text hinges, on the other hand, on reading 'because' (*eph ho*) not - as Jerome did - as a neuter pronoun but as a masculine pronoun referring to the immediately preceding substantive, death (*thanatos*). The Orthodox passage would thus translate as: As sin came into the world through one man and death through sin, so death spread to all men; and because of death, all men have sinned (see Meyendorff, 1974: 144 for this analysis). In the Orthodox reading Adam and Eve's sin resulted in their losing their immortality, and subsequently mortality (but not mortal sin) was inherited by their descendants. Mortality causes the individual to sin because it commits him or her to the struggle for food, drink, sex and other worldly things not needed by immortal beings. The need for these sensible objects in a world of limited resources generates anger, envy, hatred and lust, and all of these - tempered by the perpetual fear of death - bind the individual to the world and prevent him or her from seeing through it to that which gives it meaning. Orthodox salvation - the bringing of the individual back into its original relationship with its divine creator - is thus achievable through the individual's detachment from worldly passions and his or her embrace of those holy things which make the immortal world visible in this vale of mortality. The Latin reading, on the other hand, contends that human mortality is consequent on humankind's inheritance of original sin. Christ's incarnation made salvation possible, but, as a result of the Latin church's adoption of St Augustine's authoritarian approach to heresy (an adoption prompted by the collapse of the Western Roman Empire and the consequent necessity of the church taking responsibility for civic order in the wake of that fall), that salvation was figured as available only to the very small number of humans who escaped the consequences of original sin through absolute and unremitting obedience to God's will in this world (see Dumont, 1982 for an elaboration of the in-worldly ethics of Latin Christianity as opposed to the transcendent ethics of Orthodox Christianity). The implications of this mistranslation were monumental and, as Robertson Smith suggested in the passage quoted above, are eminently visible at particular points of the earth's surface where relations between deity and humanity are believed to have been concentrated.

The analysis of different models of pilgrimage which follows is in part extrapolated from fieldwork I carried out in the early-eighties with pilgrim groups from a number of the twenty seven churches which regularly promote pilgrimages to the Holy Land. Although I travelled with pilgrims from a number of other religious communities (Ethiopian Orthodox, Syrian Orthodox, Coptic, Armenian Orthodox, French Catholic, and Lutheran Protestant), I have chosen to focus my analysis on Greek Orthodox, European Catholic and European and North American Protestant pilgrimages both because I carried out intensive fieldwork focused on these groups and because the responses of members of these groups to the holy places highlights tendencies I believe are symptomatic of more general proclivities I have discerned within Orthodox and Latin forms of pilgrimage. In my analyses of Greek Orthodox and Catholic pilgrimages I draw heavily on two particular groups with which I travelled. The first group was made up of forty eight Greek Orthodox Cypriots brought together from a wide area of villages and towns by a pilgrimage organiser with ties to the Jerusalem Brotherhood of the Holy Sepulchre. One group of nine men and women within the larger group came from a single village and was accompanied by its parish priest, but the guide for the group as a whole was an archimandrite (superior of a monastery), normally resident in Gaza, who came up to Jerusalem to assist with pilgrim groups during the period leading up to and including Holy Week. The second group was made up of fifteen English and Irish Catholics who were members of a lay organisation called the 'Little Way', dedicated to the performance of acts of charity and devotion in accordance with the model set by the life of St Theresa. They had been brought together through an advertisement in the organisation's journal and were being guided by a Franciscan priest, Father Raphael. My insights into Protestant pilgrimages come from a broad range of pilgrim groups and pilgrim activities at Protestant sites but I emphasize, to some degree, the activities of largely Protestant Christian Zionists who I spent considerable time with during the 1984 Feast of Tabernacles (organized by the self-styled International Christian Embassy) and those of a group of Lutherans, from the United States and Canada, who visited the holy places in 1985 in the course of an inspirational tour of charity organisations aiding Palestinians which were funded by the Lutheran church. While keeping in mind the reservations expressed by James Clifford (1988) about the possibility of extrapolating general ethnological statements from encounters with particular individuals and small groups, I will nonetheless try to indicate the ways the particular pilgrimage practices of these groups coincided with general tendencies within Orthodox, Catholic and Protestant pilgrimages. I must, however, assert that each group was distinctive in terms of its constituency, its background and the particularities of its experiences and that, therefore, the particular groups to which I refer cannot simply be presented as 'typical' representatives of the wider religious entities.

Greek Orthodox pilgrimage

Greek Orthodox Christians see life as divided into two stages. The first is a period stretching from childhood until the moment one's children are married off during which the establishment, raising and supporting of a family deeply involves one in the social world. During the latter, subsequent phase one sheds social and familial responsibilities and, in preparation for ascension after death into Paradise, turns attention to sacred things (Hirschon, 1989: 225-232 and Hart, 1992: 130ff). One's behaviour during the earlier, material, phase of life does not, except when one breaks communion with God, determine whether or not one will, after death, ascend to Paradise; lay Greek Orthodox theology assumes that the sins of the world are the results of living in a fallen world and that sinners will be punished in that world rather than in an afterlife (Campbell, 1964: 323-326). The separation of the fallen and the redeemed worlds, which is a consequence of Adam and Eve's sin of devotion to the world rather than to its creator, is in large part complete, with only the bridges of the *sacra* - those things, like icons or liturgies, which coexist in both worlds - to bring them into contact. Within Orthodoxy the divine liturgy as well as other vehicles of the sacred like icons or holy relics serve as means of allowing people to step out of illusion and see creation, as a whole, in relation to its creator: the icon's first and foremost liturgical function is making contact between the worshipper and the world of grace . . . the icon is an indispensable part of the liturgy which in its turn functions as an icon revealing the divine presence to the faithful and uniting the celestial and terrestrial church (Galavaris, 1981: 5). Greek Orthodox believers, in Greece as well as in the Holy Land, have several times told me that, when they stand within an Orthodox church - its walls and iconostasis dense with icons and its ceilings painted with stars and pictures of the Pantocrator - they stand in Paradise in the presence of God, the Virgin Mary and all the saints. Their entry into holy space serves, in effect, to presage their entry, at death, into eternity.

What is important in Greek Orthodox theology is that the Christian, as he or she approaches the moment when death will provide escape from this world, establishes full communion with God and throws off involvement with the illusion of a world that seems to exist apart from its creator. As John Campbell was told by the Sarakatsanos villagers with whom he worked in the north of Greece, humans are, because of their enmeshment in a mortal world, subject to envy and sensuality - conditions which imply an attachment to material things which leads man away from God (Campbell, 1964: 326). The extirpation of these ancestral sins through devotion to those things - holy persons, icons, and liturgies - through which God reveals that he, and he alone, creates and gives meaning to existence, enables the Greek Orthodox to enter into the Paradise which God has opened to all those who recognize its existence (this, in so far as it is available to all those who are able to cast off the bonds of mortality, is a universal redemption). Greek Orthodox pilgrims envision their pilgrimage to the holy places as a shucking off of impurities consequent on the Fall in preparation for death and resurrection. They step out of a world in which they have been deeply involved in the sins consequent on mortality and into a world which has, with Christ's life and death, partaken in the process of turning mortal into immortal flesh. Traditionally, Greek and Cypriot pilgrims come to the Holy Land in old age to prepare themselves for a good death and for their subsequent assumption into the redeemed world promised by Jesus.

Greek Orthodox pilgrimage is made up of two types of activity, although these are not necessarily arranged sequentially. The first involves the transformation of the fallen to the redeemed, while the second celebrates their consequent participation in Paradise itself. Within the first is enacted the process of the individual's own transfiguration, and pilgrims, before going on pilgrimage, prepare for this by confessing their sins. On entering the Holy Land they will, so as to mark the boundary between a world in which they have dedicated themselves to worldly concerns and one in which they will devote themselves to the eternal, have their feet washed by monks of the Brotherhood of the Holy Sepulchre who meet them at the sea or air ports. At some point during their pilgrimage they will be baptised in the Jordan River[6] in order, like Christ himself, to have the Holy Spirit descend upon them. In baptism

> the Holy Spirit purifies and recreates the nature of the child, uniting it to the body of Christ and bestowing Spirit upon it. The rite of Baptism marks the acceptance of a soul into the Church, it makes possible the remission of future sins and it releases the individual from the weight of original sin (Campbell, 1964: 219, see also Meyendorff, 1974: 193-195).

The baptism at the Jordan is, for the pilgrims, a cathartic reunification with the divine image within them which has, through the years, been tarnished and covered over by the corruption consequent on their mortality.

The second aspect of Greek Orthodox pilgrimage is collective participation in the eternity imaged in the places where Christ had worked his redemptive mission. The Holy Land, for Orthodox pilgrims, is a place that images forth the places they commemorate in their churches and icons at home. Each place has, in history, played a particular part in manifesting the divine promise of deification to the world, and so too each place - as a bridge to the eternal - has a particular significance. However, particular sites, like particular icons, provide entry into the entirety of the redeemed world and, once that entry has been effected, there is no reason to consider any moment of eternity as different from any other. The particularity of holy places visited by Greek Orthodox pilgrims is discarded as soon as it has served to bring pilgrims out of the fallen world and into communion with the saints in risen world manifest within the icon-dense churches built over

---

[6] The traditional site of the baptism, for Orthodox as well as Latin pilgrims, is located near Jericho, but this site has - since the 1967 war - been within a closed military zone. As a result, pilgrimages have shifted north to *kibbutz* which owns the area around the egress of the Jordan River from the Sea of Galilee. This site is profitably run by the *kibbutz* as an interdominational pilgrimage site where pilgrims are not only able to bathe in the river but also to buy 'relics' packed and marketed by the *kibbutzim*. There have been recent moves towards reopening the old site, but the Galilee site has in large part come to stand in for the traditional site.

or next to the memorialized sites. An historical moment is only distinct from others in the light of temporality - in eternity all moments are the same.

I was bemused, while travelling with Orthodox pilgrims, to see that the guides always presented biblical and historical information about holy places before entering onto the property of those places, and that the pilgrims were so uninterested in those details that, as the pilgrimages proceeded, the guides took to keeping the pilgrims confined to the busses until they had finished their historico-biblical sketches. Once released the pilgrims would rush impatiently into the churches and proceed around the interiors kissing all the icons without granting any - except perhaps those of Jesus and the Virgin Mary - any particular attention. For the pilgrims the interiors of churches prefigured Paradise, and, since all the saints in Paradise were present through their icons within the churches, there was no reason why a pilgrim should grant any of them, except perhaps the Lord and his mother who had effected their *metastoicheiosis*, or trans-elementation, any more attention than any other. Icons which figured forth the incidents which were supposed to have occurred on the site, and the actual remains of those places, received no more reverence than did the other icons, although some pilgrims would pay particular attention to the icons of the saints of their name days.

The one thing that, perhaps, makes the Holy Land more sacred than the other *sacra* experienced in the life of a Greek Orthodox person is that it is the most realistic icon, or representation, of the spiritual truths expressed in all Orthodox religious forms. Yet the fact that the places themselves are supposed to be the same places through which Christ walked and around which he did his work does not appear to be universally appreciated; on the same pilgrimage one can see people who kiss every available rock and drink from every body of water and others who only show enthusiasm when they are inside churches revering and commenting on icons identical to those in their home churches. Travels around the holy places are, for the Greek Orthodox, a desirable but unnecessary supplement to their pilgrimage; what the pilgrimage to the Holy Land is about, at heart, is being present in Jerusalem during the holy feasts. It is during these festivals that the significant realism of the holy places comes into play when Greek Orthodox pilgrims, in the company of thousands of other Orthodox persons from throughout the Mediterranean basin and beyond, witness, for perhaps the only time in their lives, an image of the community of mankind united in Christ.

Campbell and Hirschon, in their examinations of religion in Greek community life, have both emphasized the fact that that life is torn by a deeply felt contradiction whereby people recognize that they are one in Christ but at the same time live in a world where, because of the curse of mortality, others are for the most part perceived as ruthless competitors for scarce resources. Campbell points out that it is only during Holy Week that the Sarakatsani transcend that isolation and see themselves, at least hypothetically, as part of the community to which Christ has granted them access:

> The idea of Christ's brotherhood implies, at least, the brotherhood of the Sarakatsani of Zagori, and, by extension (although less certainly), the brotherhood of Orthodox Greeks. Christ sacrificed Himself not for one but for all. Not the least miracle of Easter is the measure of social goodwill. There is an easy warmth of greeting and attitude between unrelated men which is entirely foreign to the tense aggressiveness that is the formal idiom of social life at other times . . . The union of men in Christ is reflected at the level of social relations in an expression of ideal solidarity which for a moment breaks down the barriers which isolate family from family and community from community (Campbell, 1964: 350, see too Hirschon, 1989: 198-201).

During Holy Week in Jerusalem, and to a lesser extent during the two other feasts for which Orthodox pilgrims come to the Holy City (the Feast of the Assumption of the Virgin, and that of the Exaltation of the Cross), Greek Orthodox pilgrims are able to transcend that contradiction and see that ideal community bodied forth, as it were, in the flesh. For days the streets and churches are filled with elderly Greek and Cypriot pilgrims who are not, in any significant way, in competition with others and who, for perhaps the first time in their lives, are not in places scarred by memories of conflicts in which they have been involved. During the ceremonies that bring both the Lenten fast and the Holy Land pilgrimages to their fulfilment, all the pilgrims commemorate collectively the process of redemption they have mirrored individually or in smaller groups throughout their lives and their pilgrimage. They then engage together in the fruit of those processes. With Christ's resurrection the universal transformation of the fallen world is effected, and as that anastasis is celebrated in the Holy Sepulchre an image of mankind, united not in temporality but in eternity, is figured forth.

Latin pilgrimages

Whereas the *sacra* in Orthodoxy serves, in effect, to disengage believers from the false values of a fallen world in preparation for their admission into the redeemed world, holiness in Latin theology serves instead to impose a particular ethics on activity in that fallen world itself. In the Latin Churches knowledge of the sacred is always mobilized back towards activity in the world. The liturgy makes clear to believers the debt owed to their God who took human form and, in that form, was humiliated and judicially murdered so as to grant humankind the possibility of salvation.

The structure of sermons and devotions is designed to inspire worshippers with faith in the power of God and with models for behaving in the world in accordance with that power. Each week, and for the particularly devout each day, is dedicated to a particular saint or holy incident which provides a particular lesson on how to live one's life. Religious art, instead of - like the icon - providing a patch of clear visibility (Brown and MacCormack, 1982: 212) through which the devotee can see into Paradise, is pedagogic: it provides models for meditation which, rather than offering the meditator momentary access into the redeemed world, teaches him or her the sorts of activities that God rewards. The lessons are inspirational and meant to provoke the devotee into action in the world. Unlike in Greek Orthodoxy where one engages the sacred precisely to the degree that one's social position disengages one from the secular domain - Hirschon points out that it is women and the old who, in Greek society, are expected to be religious (Hirschon, 1989: 219-231) - in the Latin Churches people are expected, throughout the whole of their lives, to model their behaviour according to the lessons of the Church.

The great heterodoxy of Latin Christianity, spanning as it does numerous manifestations of Catholicism as well as a bewildering diversity of Protestant sects, might lead the reader to doubt whether one can talk of a Latin ontology.[7] It is, however, precisely the in-worldliness of the Latin perspective which unites most if not all of those churches, and a consequence of that inworldliness that gives them their apparent diversity. The correlate of the Church's sanctification of the world as a domain of religious action is a secularisation of the Church as a worldly institution. Walter Ullman, in pointing out that the history of Western theology after the fall of Rome made the Church the sole legislator of the secular world, also demonstrates the sources of an elitism which alienated the greater part of its members from the benefits it promised: the priests alone are functionally qualified to govern the community of Christians in the world (Ullman, 1970: 291, see also Kantorowicz, 1957). This political elitism combined with the spiritual elitism implicit in the Augustinian concept of the *massa peccati* (sinful mass) to provoke a *de facto* refusal by the Church to include its lay members in the liturgical practices meant to offer them the chance of salvation; after the fifth century the unconsecrated were in large part excluded from both the offertory and communion (Dix, 1945: 598). Thus, in effect, the lay population was subordinated to the secular rule of the Church without access to the spiritual grace which the Church claimed legitimated that rule. This exclusion was to lead, throughout the Middle

---

[7] This query is particularly pertinent when one examines the 'Eastern-rite Catholic churches' (formerly known as 'Uniates'). Eastern-rite Catholics accepted the authority of the Vatican when, during a long period of Catholic expansion into domains in which Orthodox (both Chalcedonian and non-Chalcedonian) churches had been dominant, they were offered sustenance and support from the Catholic Church in exchange for allegiance. These Christians kept their traditional liturgies, but accepted the dominion of Rome. It is difficult to say whether, with this shift in affiliation, there was as well a shift in ontology, but this vast and stimulating subject is outside the purview of this paper.

Ages, to several suppressed popular heretical movements which were, in effect, social revolutions against the hegemony of the Church. Subsequently, however, the more general spread of literacy and lay power in the late medieval period initiated a theological assault on the legitimacy of the Church. Wycliffe, Huss, and subsequent fundamentalists argued that the Bible was the sole criterion of doctrine and that it provided no sanction for the immense and corrupt power of Latin Church. In effect, the mediation of the Church as the sole vehicle of salvation existing between God and mankind was thrown into question and, while liberalisation within the Catholic Church itself promoted a greater franchisement of the people, among groups that broke away from Vatican rule the Bible was given priority as the Word of God present in the world.

The Protestant revolt initiated several new discourses on God, humankind, and moral activity. By throwing aside the authority of the Roman Church the Protestant reformers once again released the biblical text from the constraints of tradition so that it could speak new words to new contexts. The various answers which would be thrown up by the multiple Protestant sects over the next five hundred years to questions of who is worthy of redemption, what is the relationship of the sect to the world, and how is God to continue to make his will manifest in the world, are too diverse to examine here. It is, however, worth stressing the ontological continuity which survives Protestantism's rupturing of Catholic hegemony. Protestantism, like Catholicism, presents a discourse on transforming the world in accordance with a transcendental will. It retains the idea of an elect which works that will and of others, outside grace, who neither assist God nor will benefit from redemption. Divine will is still seen to be channelled through a community, more or less institutionalised in the world, which serves to interpret and articulate it and, in some cases, to impose it by force on those who do not submit to it willingly. The individual still gains, or loses, salvation in relation to how he or she accords his or her life in the world to models ordained as God-given. The chief difference is that the Protestant sects claim to draw more directly on biblical texts than on the authority of an interpretative institution for their models of behaviour and of devotion.

Catholic pilgrimage, unlike that of the Greek Orthodox, is not strictly regulated by a liturgical calendar. Catholic groups come to the Holy Land throughout the year, and while many come as individuals or in families the larger proportion come in groups active as organisations in the world outside. In large part Catholic pilgrimage is inspirational; although plenary indulgences are still given, priests and pilgrims alike spoke of them to me as atavisms. People come to the Holy Land to be renewed in their faith so that they can subsequently reengage their ordinary lives with renewed energy and a renewed sense of purpose. The idea that pilgrimage serves as a revitalization of spiritual energies drained by involvement in the labours of the secular world makes Catholic pilgrimage much more individuated than that of the Orthodox; instead of a cosmological celebration of the community of mankind in Christ Catholics engage, as individuals or in groups bound by a shared purpose, in a process of being repossessed by the power that gives meaning to their personal lives and labours. This individuation releases Catholic pilgrimage from the timetable of communal feasts. Whereas in Orthodoxy the holy places and the holy dates in the church calendar are moments at which the temporal participates in the eternal, in Catholicism the sites and the days are sources of inspiration which do not reach beyond the world but point to the appropriateness of certain activities and attitudes in the world; their significance can be meditated upon at any time and, in some sense, in any place.

Like priests guiding Greek Orthodox pilgrims, the priests taking Catholic groups around the holy sites present secular and historical information about places outside the chapels built to commemorate them (but not, as with the Orthodox guides, off the property of the holy places). However, when inside, Catholic guides continue to instruct pilgrims and talk not of the site itself but of the significance of what was alleged to have occurred there. The Catholic group with which I travelled in 1985 was taken by its Franciscan leader to the mosque enclosing the traditional site of Christ's ascension. There the priest read two biblical passages pertaining to the ascension (Matthew 28: 16 and Luke 24: 50) before telling the people that what is important is not the literal place but the actual fact of the ascension (field notes, February 1985). The pilgrims then engaged the priest in a discussion of the significance of the ascension during which one woman said that the footprint of Jesus, enshrined within the mosque, is not relevant, it is only there to assist us in the interiorization of the significance. The group then recited the Lord's Prayer and a series of ten decades (Hail Marys) after which their leader read the *virs* Galilee passage (Acts 1:11) from the Gospels and added we should stop staring at the sky and get on with the missionary call of Christ.

This pattern of drawing spiritual inspiration from a site and directing its significance back into activity in the world is typical of Catholic approaches to the holy places the community reveres. Each place has a particular significance, not only linked to what was alleged to have happened at that site but also to the way that event provides inspiration and a model for devout activity in the pilgrims lives. When available, as they usually are in Latin holy places, realist wall paintings of the events which the places commemorate are pedagogically mobilized; details of the representations are pointed out and expanded upon so that the pilgrims can interiorize events usually, although not always, drawn from the Gospels.[8] Whereas the

---

[8] In some senses, however, there is little distinction between God's work and the work done by the institution, and the individuals, God had directly inspired. Thus at St Saviour's monastery, the headquarters of the Fransiscan Order in the Holy Land, the lives of St Fancis and his followers are set up as models of inspiration in the same manner as are, elsewhere, episodes from the life of Christ and the disciples.

Greek Orthodox approach to the holy places diminishes the specificity of the places by grouping them as manifestations of Paradise, the Catholics diminish the specificity of the sites by distinguishing between the significance of the biblical events said to have happened at the sites and the places themselves. It is from the significance, not the places, that one draws inspiration, and the places serve primarily as loci where pilgrims are better able to evoke the subjects of their meditations in their imaginations. In the Chapel of the Flagellation, on the Via Dolorosa, life size paintings of Christ's judicial humiliation are designed, with the help of painted plaster extensions, to appear to project out of the walls and into the space of the chapel itself. Pilgrims can, in effect, be in the presence of these events while in the chapel and can thus be particularly moved by their experience. Furthermore, the experience of interiorization can take place away from the sites; it is the image, not the place, which is important. I noticed, on the many occasions I accompanied Catholic pilgrims on Friday processions along the Via Dolorosa, that they often kept their eyes closed in prayer as the monks who led the processions read out the appropriate Gospel passages; several pilgrims told me that they did not want images of the literal place to get in the way of the images of Christ's procession that they normally meditated on when they performed the Stations of the Cross in their home churches.

It is finally, however, communion - in which officiants sanctified by God through the agency of the Church pass on to celebrants the redemptive power of the blood and flesh of Christ which provides fulfilment to the fervour inspired in the pilgrims by meditation on sacred sites. Meditations and devotions serve to make clear to them the debt owed Christ and the consequent necessity of orientating their thoughts and actions towards his will, but it is only through liturgical channels that that spiritual orientation can be translated into a real and redemptive contact with God. It is in these liturgical celebrations, which can occur more than once a day but which in effect duplicate those in which pilgrims participate in their home communities, that the ideal relation of the individual to the divine can be bodied forth. The pilgrims, inspired and cleansed by images of the divine word made flesh in the places where that word engendered the ecclesiastical machinery of salvation, here take from the hands of that spiritual elite to which God bequeathed the keys of heaven and hell the saving flesh and blood of divinity. In my fieldtrips with Catholic groups I have seen communion given in a multitude of different sites, many of which did not concur with holy sites, and have always - at those times - witnessed the pilgrims most impassioned expressions of spiritual exaltation.

An unplanned alteration in the Little Way's itinerary revealed the primary role of the Church, through its officiants and its rituals, in mediating between God and its members. We were supposed to have a communion mass at the Franciscan chapel of Dominus Flevit (which commemorates the site at which Christ wept for the imminent destruction of Jerusalem) but arrived at the chapel an hour before the time at which we had been scheduled. Father Raphael managed, after considerable effort, to get permission for us to have mass instead in a small chapel, redolent with the fumes of cabbage being cooked for the monks' lunch, attached to a nearby building in which the attendant monks lived. I had, up to this time, noted that the pilgrims had showed curiosity at the sites we had visited but not, surprisingly, displays of strong emotion, even at places commemorating events quite signal in the career of Christ. However, during mass this coolness dissolved, and the pilgrims spent the half hour on their knees with three of the women crying throughout and several of the others breaking into tears during communion. It was there, in a chapel with only an incidental connection to the holy places and during a mass identical to those they engaged in at home, that the pilgrims seemed most to feel the presence of Christ.

Protestant pilgrimages - if one dare generalise about practices which range from Christian Zionist celebrations of the establishment of Jewish settlements on Palestinian lands in Gaza and on the West Bank to Lutheran visits to hospitals and hospices serving Palestinians established with funds drawn from congregationists - have, despite their apparent disparity, several features in common. Protestant devotions in the Holy Land, for reasons both historical and ontological, tend to be disengaged from the traditional holy sites revered by the Orthodox and the Catholics. Protestants came late to the Holy Land, and the claims of the more well-established churches to significant places, made official by the Ottoman *firman,* or edict, of 1852, were established and concretized in the shrines they maintained at the traditional holy sites. Furthermore, the Protestant desire to have an unmediated relation to the Bible means that a holy place covered over with Orthodox or Catholic churches is, in effect, a site which commemorates institutional domination rather than the truth that institution is seen to have usurped and distorted. Protestants, in general, approach the Holy Land for the same inspirational reasons as Catholics, but for them that inspiration devolves from what is interpreted as an unimpeded relationship between the individual and Christ and not, as with Catholicism, from the sense of being part of a long history during which the will of Jesus has been enacted in the world through the agency of the Church. Consequently, Protestants tend to want to witness Christ and not his putative agents and frequent places, like the area around the Sea of Galilee or the Garden Tomb in Jerusalem, where they can imagine Christ in situ rather than displaced by monuments thrown up by two thousand years of devotion to his memory.[9]

[9] W M Thomson, the Presbyterian author of *The Land and the Book* (1876), immediately follows a condemnation of 'the buffoonery and the profane orgies performed by the Greeks around the tomb on the day of the Holy Fire' with a meditation on site and sacrality: "I am devoutly thankful that no amount of learning or research can establish the remotest connection between any act of our Saviour and any one of these so-called holy places . . . since God has concealed the *realities,* we have no need of these fictitious sites to confirm our faith. We are surrounded by witnesses, and these mountains, and valleys, and ruins, that cannot be effaced or corrupted. They are now spread out before our eyes . . . This is all I care for, all that mere topography can offer. If sure, to the fraction of a foot, in regard to the sepulchre, I could no more worship in it

The Garden Tomb saliently displays the characteristic setting of Protestant Holy Land devotion. The site, which many Protestants consider the actual place of Christ's burial, is a small enclosed property outside the walls of the Old City within which is a careful reconstruction of a rich man's first century garden. Louring over this quiet orchard of olive and carob trees is a rock face which is given the appearance of a skull by the open sockets of two eroded medieval cisterns. The Garden Tomb guides, trained volunteers who are the only persons allowed to guide people while they are within the garden's confines, instruct visitors in seeing that the site before them is identical to that described in the biblical texts relating Christ's crucifixion and entombment: it is correctly located outside the walls (even though – as they do not say – the contemporary walls of the Old City, built in 1542 by Suleiman the Magnificent, are very differently placed from those of the city within which Jesus was condemned and outside which crucified); the skull-like hill above it is obviously Golgotha, the place of the skull; and the garden itself appears, even to the empty burial cave with a channel for its rolling rock door at its western end, to be the garden of the wealthy land-holder, Joseph of Arimathea (see Bowman, 1992 on the dialectical relation between pilgrim expectations and tour guide constructions of a site). Pilgrims, whether or not they are convinced that the Garden Tomb is the literal site (and there is occasional dissension on this issue), assert that it is easier to imagine Jesus here than inside that dark pile of stones they call the Holy Sepulchre (fieldnotes November 1983).

As with other Latin pilgrimages, the various Protestant pilgrimage are in large part inspirational although, as with Catholic pilgrimages, the ultimate goal of the journey is celebration of subordination of the individual will to that of divinity. Within Protestantism the concept of living according to the biblical word has a wide range of reference, calling upon some sects to separate themselves as far as possible from the secular world so as to organize personal and communal lives around biblical precepts and demanding of others that their members labour in the fields of political activism to impose their readings of biblical morals on the whole of the world around them. There is no room here to discuss this plethora of forms, but what they appear to share is the function of enabling pilgrims to feel they are integrally, and to a degree exceptionally, involved in the divine redemptive project. Protestant pilgrimage inspires pilgrims by placing them in settings where they can imagine Jesus's presence (a region like the Galilee is popular in so far as it – in some areas – can be imagined as having hardly changed since biblical times) and can thus locate themselves

---

that I could worship the boat in which he sailed over Gennesaret, or the ass upon which he rode into Jerusalem, and hence I have no need of any of these 'inventions;' and since they are perverted to an idolatry worse than the burning of incense to the brazen serpent, I would have them all removed out of my sight, that He who is a spirit may be worshipped, even at Jerusalem, in spirit and in truth" (Thomson, 1876: 679).

in unmediated - albeit visionary - contact with divinity.[10] Nonetheless, the Protestant model shares with the Catholic the concept of a divine will operating in the world with which the worshipper must align himself or herself. Protestant projects vary widely. The Christian Zionist pilgrimage examined in my Christian ideology and the image of a holy land (Bowman 1991: 116-120) linked the efforts (and the funds) of pilgrims in with what they saw as the divinely ordained project of re-establishing the Kingdom of Israel and rebuilding the Third Temple. Other church-organised Protestant pilgrimages[11] calque religious enthusiasm onto projects in which the communities are involved, whether these be humanist projects such as the building of hospitals or the support of indigenous Christian communities or more teleological projects such as mobilisation of commitment for missionary spreading of the Word of God. In all of these instances, however, contact with the sacred directs pilgrims back into the world where they are enjoined to join with an organised community which knows, and carries out, the divine will.

Conclusion: the politics of interpretation

As John Wilken has shown in a recent study (Wilken, 1992), the Holy Land has, since the time of the Babylonian exile, stood as an emblem of redemption in Judaic and Christian thought. Although one cannot assume some sort of essential continuity of significance through the entirety of that two thousand five hundred year history, there has been a thematic continuity in so far as the holy land has stood throughout and in various forms as a figure of redemption. Its holiness in the sense cited by Robinson Smith - has always implied some form of return of persons, exiled in the vale of tears of the secular world, to communion with the divine fountainhead of their being.

Implicit in this image of return is, however, a politics with a substantial impact. If images of the Holy Land are constructed in the home locales of all of the religious communities which esteem its sacrality, then what their pilgrims respectively seek out when they go pilgrimages to experience that sacrality is a more perfect version of the holiness they encounter in its degraded form in their everyday exilic lives. In so far, however, as the

[10] Interestingly, the Protestant mosel of an immediate relationship with Jesus is analogous to that related by St Jerome in the letters cited above. This is, perhaps, because the anti-institutionalism of the Protestant paradigm is most closely paralleled by the relatively pre-institutional conception of the holy evoked by St Jerome in a period preceeding both icon theology and the establishment of a worldly church.

[11] I have, in this paper, not addressed the subject of 'Chritian tourists' who travel to the Holy Land alone or in small groups. I would, were there more time, argue however that these pilgrims gain inspiration from their contacts with sites redolent with sacrality but, in the absence of the sort of programme in which an organised group might call upon them to invest their enthusiasm, 'save it up' as a means of subsequently re-enthusing the religious projects they engage in their home settings.

images of sacrality they desire to encounter are purified versions of the sacrality made evident in their home communities, they want, in the Holy Land, to encounter a cleansed rendition of their own cultural models rather than the radical cultural heterodoxy (collocated out of Jews, Muslims, atheists, tourists and a plethora of heretical so-called Christians) they are bound to come across in Israel/Palestine. A return from exile to a land in which one feels lost is not the desideratum, and the result of such a threatened loss of the Promised Land is - when political situations allow for it open warfare between the returnees and whomever else might occupy their land. One need not here limit discussion to the dislocations and destructions brought about in the 20th century by the Zionist project of returning the scattered Jewish people from their ancient exile. From the time when the Babylonian exiles returned to Israel to wage war on the non-Jewish Jews (Samaritans) who had stayed behind and created a land which did not live up to that constructed in the imaginations of the exiles, through the Crusades (when the Christian liberators of the Holy Land indiscriminately slaughtered Muslim, Jew and Eastern Christian alike in the Old City), to the present day when - as in the Christmas-time cleaning of the Church of the Nativity - the slightest deviation from the temporal-spatial boundary drawing of the *firman* of the *status quo* can lead to murderous bloodshed between the various sects guardians of the holy places, the colonising imaginations of returning exiles have given rise to violence and bloodshed. The religious imagination is, in so far as it deals with ultimate questions of ontology, necessarily totalizing, and when that imagination is able to function in a place unrestrained by secular considerations it calls up imagery of an apocalyptic sacred cleansing.

I have, over the past few years, been involved in an extended study of shared Muslim-Christian shrines in the Bethlehem region (see Bowman, 1993: esp. 433-439 on Mar Elyas). At such shrines Muslim and Christian Palestinians meet to revere holy persons and sacred objects each group variously interprets as providing access to divinity. When one questions the people who participate in these festivals one discovers a wonderful diversity of interpretations; Christians of different denominations offer different narratives of the source and the efficacy of the holy sites and Muslims, similarly, tell different tales of why they attend the festivities. Nonetheless, not only do the various interpretative communities share the sites and the times of the devotions but they also, in so coinciding, celebrate another form of community which both encompasses and transcends religious rationales for attending. In coming together to eat, dance, worship and talk at shrines such as Mar Elyas and El Khadr Palestinians of the region shadow forth, on holy ground, an image of the wider collectivity in which they all participate as residents of the catchment areas of the shrines. In such contexts religious difference retains its saliency - none of these people would deny, or surrender, their sectarian affiliations - yet it does not mark out borders traversable only by antagonism and warfare. Just as, in daily life, religious concerns are woven into the fabric of secular pursuits so, at sites and times dedicated to the pursuit of the sacred, secular co-existence provides a framework within which religion - in all its heterodoxy - can be celebrated.

It seems evident that the sharing of holy sites by persons of different religious convictions who nonetheless live together in their quotidian existences is radically dissimilar to the kind of coexistence that might be entertained by persons of similarly diverse religious affiliations who live nations, and often even continents, apart. However, in the contemporary situation, the disparity is not so obvious. In many ways the utopian fantasy of a global village has foundations in the real; not only are disparate national communities more and more bound together by economic and political cooperation but the worldwide proliferation of communications networks translates such abstract allegiances into repertoires of mutually comprehensible images. We have, for perhaps the first time in history, the ability to understand the communality which underlies our differences. If persons from the world-wide catchment area from whence Holy Land pilgrims are drawn were better to understand that those others who share the sites with them bring holiness to the places rather than steal it away they might not only recognise that the power of the place is not diminished by its dissemination among scores of sects and a handful of world religions but as well come to see the miraculousness of a land which enriches people's lives by mirroring back to them as a gift what they unknowingly bring to it.

Bibliography

Bar-on, R, and Fisher, H (1983). Pilgrimage Promotion 1983 No. Israel Ministry of Tourism.

Ben-Arieh, Y (1984). *Jerusalem in the Nineteenth Century: the Old City*. New York: St Martin's Press.

Bertram, S A, and Young, J W A (1926). *The Orthodox Patriarchate of Jerusalem: Report of the Commission Appointed by the Government of Palestine to Inquire and Report Upon Certain Controversies Between the Orthodox Patriarchate of Jerusalem and the Arab Orthodox Community*. London: Humphrey Milford.

Bowman, G (1991). 'Christian ideology and the image of a holy land: the place of Jerusalem pilgrimage in the various Christianities'. In J Eade and M Sallnow (eds.), *Contesting the Sacred: the Anthropology of Christian Pilgrimage*. London: Routledge; 98-121.

Bowman, G (1992). 'The politics of tour guiding: Israeli and Palestinian guides in Israel and the Occupied Territories'. In D Harrison (ed.), *Tourism and the Less Developed Countries*. London: Belhaven Press; 121-134.

Bowman, G (1993). 'Nationalizing the sacred: shrines and shifting identities in the Israeli-occupied territories'. *Man: The Journal of the Royal Anthropological Institute*, XXVIII (3); 431-460.

Brown, P, and MacCormack, S (1982). 'Artifices of eternity'. In P Brown (ed.), *Society and the Holy in Late Antiquity*. London: Faber and Faber; 207-221.

Campbell, J (1964). *Honour, Family and Patronage: A Study of Institutions and Moral Values in a Greek Mountain Village*. Oxford: Clarendon Press.

Casey, E (1993). *Getting Back into Place: Toward a Renewed Understanding of the Place-World*. Bloomington: Indiana University Press.

Clifford, J (1988). *The Predicament of Culture: Twentieth Century Ethnography, Literature, and Art*. Cambridge: Harvard.

Dix, G (1945). *The Shape of the Liturgy*. Westminster: Dacre Press.

Dumont, L (1982). 'A modified view of our origins: the Christian beginnings of modern individualism'. *Religion*, XII (1); 1-27.

Durkheim, E (1915). *The Elementary Forms of Religious Life* (Joseph Ward Swain, trans.). London: George Allen and Unwin.

Fabri, F (1892-1897). *The Wanderings of Felix Fabri* (Aubrey Stewart, trans.). London:

Frend, W H C (1984). *The Rise of Christianity*. London: Darton, Longman and Todd.

Galavaris, G (1981). 'The icon in the life of the church'. *Iconography of Religions*, XXIV (8); 1-21.

Hart, L K (1992). *Time, Religion and Social Experience in Rural Greece*. Lanham, Maryland: Rowman and Littlefield.

Hertz, R (1913). 'Saint Besse: étude d' un cult alpestre'. *Revue de l'Histoire des Religions* 67; 115-180.

Hertz, R (1983). 'Saint Besse: a study of an Alpine cult'. In S Wilson (ed.), *Saints and Their Cults: Studies in Religious Sociology, Folklore and History*. Cambridge: Cambridge University Press; 55-100.

Hirschon, R (1989). *Heirs of the Greek Catastrophe: The Social Life of Asia Minor Refugees in Piraeus*. Oxford: Clarendon Press.

Israel, Ministry of Tourism (1986). *Tourism 1983/1984*. Jerusalem: Central Bureau of Statistics.

Kantorowicz, E H (1957). *The King's Two Bodies: A Study in Medieval Political Theology*. Princeton: Princeton University Press.

Meyendorff, J (1974). *Byzantine Theology: Historical Trends and Doctrinal Themes*. London: A. R. Mowbray and Co.

Morinis, E. A. (ed.). (1992). *Sacred Journeys: The Anthropology of Pilgrimage*. Westport, Connecticut: Greenwood Press.

Nietzsche, F (1969). 'On the Genealogy of Morals'. In W Kaufman (ed.), *On the Genealogy of Morals and Ecce Homo*. New York: Vintage Books; 13-163.

O'Mahony, A (1987). 'The Orthodox Christian Arab community during the British Mandate in Palestine during the 1920s and 1930s'. Manuscript.

Runciman, S (1970). *The Historic Role of the Christian Arabs of Palestine*. London: Longman Group.

St Jerome (1893). 'Letter XLVI (Paula and Eustochium to Marcella)'. In W H Fremantle (ed.), *The Principle Works of St Jerome*. Oxford.

St Jerome (1896). *The Pilgrimage of the Holy Paula* (Stewart, Aubrey, trans.). London: Palestine Pilgrim Text Society.

Skeat, W (1927). *A Concise Etymological Dictionary of the English Language* (new and corrected impression ed.). Oxford: Clarendon Press.

Smith, W R (1907). *Lectures on the Religion of the Semites*. London: Charles Black.

Thomson, W M (1876). *The Land and the Book; or, Biblical Illustrations Drawn from the Manners and Customs, the Scenes and Scenery of the Holy Land*. London: T Nelson and Sons.

Twain, M (1905). *The Innocents Abroad or the New Pilgrim's Progress: Being Some Account of the Steamship Quaker City's Pleasure Excursion to Europe and the Holy Land*. New York: Harper and Brothers.

Ullman, W (1970). *The Growth of Papal Government in the Middle Ages*. London: Methuen and Co.

Wilken, R L (1992). *The Land Called Holy: Palestine in Christian History and Thought*. New Haven: Yale University Press.

Wilkinson, J (1971). *Egeria's Travels*. London: SPCK.

19

Who is the Church? A Christian Theology for the Holy Land

Naim Ateek

Introduction

I have been entrusted with the awesome task of suggesting a Christian theology for the Holy Land. My presentation will be simply an introduction to a practical theology for the Holy Land. In this paper, I will emphasize the most salient themes and agenda of this theology and point to its basic theological thrust.

Who is the Church?

On the first day of Pentecost when the Church came into being by the power of the Holy Spirit in Jerusalem, the composition of the church was defined. This same encompassing definition still applies to the church in Jerusalem and the Holy Land today. Let me explain.

It is important to note the text in Acts 2: 5 (RSV), 'Now there were dwelling in Jerusalem Jews, devout men (and women) from every nation under heaven.' The word 'Jews' is omitted by *Codex Sinaiticus*. (This is one of the oldest manuscripts of the Bible that comes to us from the 4th century.) The text therefore, reads, 'Now there were dwelling in Jerusalem devout men (and women) from every nation under heaven.' It is possible to say then, that the first believers on whom the Holy Spirit descended were Jews who were scattered in different parts of the world but who were living in Jerusalem at the time of the feast of Shavuot. Or it could be read with a broader theological implication, as *Codex Sinaiticus* suggests, that the people who were dwelling in Jerusalem at the time of the coming of the Holy Spirit represented the whole world, Jews and Gentiles alike. Acts mentions them as, 'Parthians, Medes, Elamites, and residents of Mesopotamia, Judea and Cappadocia, Pontus and Asia, Phrygia and

Pamphylia, Egypt and the parts of Libya belonging to Cyrene, and visitors from Rome, both Jews and proselytes, Cretans and Arabs . . .' (2: 9-11). For Luke, the writer of Acts, this was a significant theological statement expressing the world-wide mission of the church and stemming from Christ's commission to his disciples, 'Go to all the world . . .' For Palestinian Christians today, the second rendering of the text is preferred because it is a more inclusive definition of the church in Jerusalem. In other words, from its inception, the Church in Jerusalem reflected the universal dimension of the Gospel of Christ.

Unfortunately, denominational divisions began to appear due to theological as well as political and ethnic reasons. By the end of the 4th and 5th century, most of the Christians of the East were divided. This represented the first great rift within Christendom. By the 11th century the schism between Orthodoxy and Catholicism was in effect. Approximately five hundred years later, major divisions split the Catholic Church of the West leading to the emergence of the Anglican, Reformed, and subsequently to many evangelical traditions of Protestantism.

It took almost nineteen hundred years to complete the presence of these Christian denominations in the Holy Land. This legacy today is both a positive as well as a negative one. It reflects the richness of the Christian Church as well as its fragmentation and brokenness; its strength as well as its weakness. Positively speaking, it reflects the greatness of the Gospel in its ability to incarnate itself in the racial and ethnic molds of many languages and cultures. Indeed, it is a wonderful testimony for the Gospel that was expressed in so many exquisite liturgies of the Church. At the same time, the initial emergence and later presence in the Holy Land of many of these churches was due, to a large part, by what is assessed today as negative political or religious legacies; whether we are considering the Crusades and the establishment of the Roman Catholic Church and gradually the Eastern Catholics (Uniates) or the founding of the Anglican and Protestant churches, which was undoubtedly enhanced by the rise of Western European powers and colonialism.

Without entering a debate on whether one wants or can attribute such a phenomena to providence, it is possible to surmise that the church in the Holy Land today is composed of representatives of all the major branches of the Church in the world. It began with the indigenous Byzantine Orthodox Church, represented largely today by Palestinian Arab and Greek Orthodox Christians. Soon after, the Oriental Orthodox churches of the Armenians, Syrians, Copts, and Ethiopians emerged, followed by the various branches of Catholicism, present in the Roman and Eastern Catholic (Uniates) churches. The Anglican, Protestant, and evangelical churches represent the final stage of this development. We must also include a small number of Messianic Jews who are believers in Jesus and are trying to live their faith under very difficult circumstances.

In other words, today in Jerusalem, whether it suits our own denominational taste or not, and to the chagrin of some of our church hierarchy and people, the church in the Holy Land has come to be that body of Christians some of whom, like the parable of the labourers in the vineyard, have been in the vineyard from the beginning of the day while others are latecomers. All of them, however, are contributing to the work of the Kingdom of God.

These Christian churches, in spite of their differing origins, have all felt connected with Jerusalem and the Holy Land. They have come to feel, faithfully and intensely, that Jerusalem belongs to them or that they belong to Jerusalem. The universal dimension of the church is realized again in Jerusalem as on the day of Pentecost, with one major difference, however: fragmented by doctrinal and ecclesiastical differences, the Church's witness is weakened and the picture it reflects is that of disunity and brokenness.

The Church of the Holy Land today is therefore a rich mosaic of clergy and people; men and women, Eastern and Western, Orthodox, Catholic and Protestant, indigenous and expatriate, Palestinian and Israeli, liberal theologically and conservative, liturgical and free, traditional as well as non-conformist and modern. This fact seems axiomatic to many of us. It is, however, still resisted by some clerics and lay.

Be that as it may, I would like to emphasize that at least from my own perspective of faith, it is not the innate holiness of the city of Jerusalem that has brought all these churches here, but the holiness of our Lord Jesus Christ and what He has done in this city, through His crucifixion, death, and resurrection. For us Christians, this land is not holy because it is the promised land as Jews believe, nor is it holy because of a miraculous nocturnal journey of Muhammad as Muslims believe. It is holy because it has been sanctified by the incarnation of the Holy One. We are reminded of His presence everywhere we go. He was born in Bethlehem, was brought up in Nazareth, was baptized in the River Jordan, lived around the Sea of Galilee, died and was resurrected here in Jerusalem.

It was therefore inevitable for the events of the last two thousand years to develop in the way they did. It was theologically sound for the early New Testament church to disregard the significance of the holiness of Jerusalem because it was superseded by the significance and holiness of Christ. Indeed, the holiness of the person of Christ replaced the holiness of the place. It was equally important to de-zionize the tradition from the very beginning, as the New Testament certainly does. It was right to de-territorialize the Christian faith and emphasize its universal character. 'For God so loved the world' (John 3: 16). Yet after the 4th century, it was also natural for humans who seem to need holy places and cannot live without them, to want to sacralize space. This was certainly accomplished in this land where the drama of salvation was enacted. Any theology for the Holy Land must out of necessity take seriously this comprehensive definition and theological understanding of the Church in the Holy Land today.

Theological priorities for Christians in the Holy Land

A Developing a theology for Palestinian Christians

1 A theology of Christian unity

This comprehensive understanding of the Church is still perceived by some clerics as scandalous without any willingness to accept its positive dimensions and its unique potential. Many fierce internecine squabbles have been fought among the churches with adamant rejection of the presence of the other. Therefore, the tragedy today as one studies the Christian heritage of the Christian church in the Holy Land, is that the Church has not risen to its full stature, responsibility, and potential due largely to this perception that the heritage is scandalous rather than potentially potent. A Christian theology for the Holy Land must out of necessity take the issue of the unity/disunity of the church very seriously. The rich heritage is today marred by the lack of a unified vision for the future of the Christian faith in the land of the incarnation. We are approaching shortly the 2000 years' anniversary of the birth of Christ, yet many of us still sustain a 5th century theological mentality while we wrestle with 20th century political reality. This is part of the serious dilemma we are facing. Therefore, without any shadow of doubt, a Christian theology of the Holy Land must take seriously these considerations. I will try to outline briefly some practical theological implications of such considerations.

a The ministry of all the people of God

Statistically, the Christian community in the Holy Land today numbers less than 2 per cent of the population. We are slowly dying numerically and our divisions add to our ineffectiveness and fragility. Christian unity is both a theological and spiritual necessity as well as a strategic one. I have noticed, for example, that relatively speaking very few indigenous Christian Palestinians attend the Week of Prayer for Christian Unity. Most of them are convinced that it is not God who is blocking the road to unity but the hierarchy of our churches. Unity is willed by God but not by humans.

We have noticed in the last few years that some lay people have taken matters into their own hands. A number of our Christian communities in Israel, Palestine, and Jordan have agreed on the community level to celebrate Easter and Christmas together at the same time, with or without the blessing of their bishops. It matters to people more and more that they unify these celebrations. As we look to the future, it may be that our hope for initiative and change will have to come from the grassroots of the Christian community.

Moreover, the theology that is needed must take seriously the important ministry of the laity, both men and women. The relative ineffectiveness of the Church today is largely due to the marginalization of the laity. It has become imbedded in people's psyche in the East that the Church is really an elite group of ordained clergy that controls and runs it. The Church is composed of all the people of God. The New Testament model of ministry is closer to a horizontal rather than a hierarchical form. The members of the one body serve according to their gifts, talents, and abilities, each having an important function in the life of the body. This is not a new theology but the first theology of the Church, which is 2000 years old.

b   A living Christian witness

To talk about the unity of the Church does not mean in any way the melting of all denominations into one. On the contrary, it should mean the preservation of the rich diversity while drawing closer to each other in genuine love, coordination, and cooperation. Unity must issue in strategic planning for the ministry of the Church in the Holy Land. The importance, for example, of upgrading all church institutions to achieve a higher standard of service is an essential component of an effective church's witness. Our church institutions are our windows on society. Without improving the quality of their work, the Church's witness will be crippled. Indeed, the institutions might survive physically, but they will be unable to impact society and nation.

This leads me to address the whole issue of the witness of the Church today. The Church must define anew what it means by Christian witness in a non-Christian context, and what it means by witness in a multi-religious context. Here again our theology must be clear. Many of our institutions have simply deteriorated under Israeli military occupation. Some have lost their distinctive Christian character. Mission and evangelism are words that have negative connotations in the Middle East today. A better word for us is witness, but we must define its meaning and fill it with content. Without a viable witness the Church will only be a social institution void of any spiritual substance.

Another dimension of witness for which we must articulate a theology is that of pilgrimage. God has placed the Church here with this specific ministry to Christians and non-Christians who come from abroad. What is our theology of pilgrimage? How can we best speak to our brothers and sisters who visit us and ensure that the witness of the Holy places is communicated? Are we satisfied with the way guides are communicating the message of these places to tourists and pilgrims? If not, what can we do about it? How can we coordinate this ministry together? The Holy Land is our window on the whole world. We must discover and articulate the implications of such a theology for people here.

2 *A prophetic theology for the Church*

Witness in society must also encompass the Church's involvement in issues of justice and peace. We must have a vision for a just future. Ideally, the Church must be the conscience of the state. Thank God, that during the *intifada*, many Christians, clergy and lay, were active advocates for justice. But the church can do much more when the hierarchy is willing to work together with its laity. Some of us have been calling for an ecumenical monitoring committee to be set up by the churches so that it can monitor political events, strategize, and advise the hierarchy for possible action. In the past, the Church's action has been mostly a reaction rather than a proaction. In spite of the numerical size of the Church, it can have an important impact because of its international dimension.

To become involved in issues of justice and peace is a costly business. The Church in the Holy Land lives in a pre-Constantinian context. It needs to regain the meaning of suffering for Christ. The cross, for many of us, is attractive because it is a beautiful ornament that glitters and shines from our necks and chests but it is often rejected as a way of life. An important part of the Church's witness is to champion the cause of the poor and stand on the side of the oppressed. The Church of the Holy Land can unitedly dare to speak truth to power and if need be, suffer for it. A theology of the Christian community of the Holy Land must include a theology of suffering and the cross. It is a theology that aims to draw the churches closer together and rises to the demands of the hour.

B Developing a Christian theology of Islam

The Church of the Holy Land does not live in a religious vacuum today. The same land is holy to three religions. The Church lives in the midst of Islam and Judaism. It's place, historically and chronologically, is in the middle. The Church came from the milieu of 1st century Judaism and accepted the Jewish sacred writings as sacred Scriptures. It saw in these scriptures, a prelude to the coming of Christ and the New Testament interpreted the Old Testament from the perspective of its fulfilment in Christ. That is why there is a very conscious attempt in the New Testament to de-zionize the Jewish tradition. What is our theology of Judaism? Some of our historical churches in the Middle East refuse on theological grounds to deal with Judaism as a religion. They believe that theologically, Judaism as a religion has ceased to exist and is therefore passé, whereas in the West, since the Second World War there has been a renewed interest in Jews and Judaism. The time has to come when we should address this issue. A more urgent assignment for us is not the issue of Judaism *per se*, but Jews, Zionism, and Israel. I believe that the Church must articulate a theology of Israel.

A greater priority for us is the Church's theology of Islam. It is true that one can be enlightened by the Christian medieval writings of the past, but it is mandatory to articulate a theology of the church *vis-à-vis* Islam, today. Indeed, there is so much ignorance on both sides. With the slogans of the extreme fundamentalists, many Christians have been frightened by the prospects of modern-day Islam. Some people try to minimize the dangers and threats of the extremists. Our understanding of Islam must not be based on a reaction against the extremists. It must express a sound theology stemming from the perspective of our Christian faith and articulating our understanding of Islam today.

With due respect to a number of excellent Western Christian scholars of Islam, I would say that such a theology must be done by Palestinian Christian scholars. Our understanding of Islam is different. Our life with Muslims does not stem from academic exchange, but from real, every day life. Indeed, we can greatly benefit by the writings of Western Christian scholars, but it is not enough for us. We must discover our own points of contact with Muslims. We can, therefore, discover on the religious, theological as well as the more practical level many points that can be the basis of understanding, mutual respect and cooperation. We need a theology that would ultimately express itself in real life situations rather than formal dialogue: a theology that can begin with practical issues and yet move to the more religious and theological: a theology that has practical implications as, for example, cooperating in the realm of human rights, and move on to share our understanding of the sovereignty of God: a theology that moves beyond co-existence and solidifies the relationship between us as equal citizens of the same land and people: a theology that helps us emphasize our common Palestinian heritage and our common nationality: a theology that capitalizes on our common struggle for political freedom and independence and the unique contribution which each of us has given towards the achievement of this common objective.

This theology, however, must be faithful to what we believe as Christians. We should not be ashamed of our faith. Without degrading the faith of others, we must be true to who we are. Admittedly, we still live in the clichés of the past and in the stereotyping of one another. Much of the respect that we express to each other is superficial and lip service. This must change. Without abdicating our own deep sense of our Christian faith, we must oppose the denigration of the other religion. One way to implement this new approach must be through our Christian educational institutions. Although most of the student body in most of our Christian schools is Muslim, they leave the schools with hardly any knowledge of the Christian faith. I am not talking about evangelizing the Muslims. I am talking about a new religious curriculum that simply and clearly exposes Christians and Muslims to the basic tenets of each other's beliefs in order to dispel myths and build greater respect and understanding.

This is a very delicate task, but I believe it can and should be done. Specially trained teachers can accomplish this task with a good measure of objectivity and dignity. Tolerance should be built on knowledge rather than on ignorance. We must help our students to mature in the understanding of their Christian faith, as well as understand and respect Islam. We must help our Christian young people to shed any inferiority complex that they might have. We must insist, for example, that our understanding of God as triune is not a clever Christian philosophical way which the early church concocted in order to cover up or explain away a dilemma of the relationship between Christ and God. We believe in One God, but this One God is triune in his essence and being. This is the living faith experience of our forefathers and foremothers. It is the heart of our understanding of God in and through Christ. We say this clearly and unashamedly.

We have been living with Islam for the last fourteen hundred years. Some of us have been Arab and Christian long before they were Arab and Muslim. Living with Muslims, we have become to a small or large extent culturally Muslim. Many of us admit this but at the same time, this does not mean at all that we have ceased to be deeply committed to our Christian faith. Many Palestinian Muslims have been at one time, Christian. After the Crusades, for example, whole Christian villages switched religion *en masse* and became Muslim, in order to escape the cruelty of non-Arab Islamic regimes. We need to dispel myths of each other. We need to study history more critically and learn from the past. At the same time, we need to discover the good in each other. We have to discover and emphasize the good in Islam rather than see only its faults and discrepancies. We need to undo the residual harm which some 19th century missionary methods adopted against Islam.

At the same time, we need to challenge some modern Islamic movements in their attack on Christianity which most often is based on ignorance and prejudice. We need to insist that Muslims take the time to understand the Christian faith as Eastern Christians understand it, rather than the way they think Christians believe. We need to work with the more open minded among them. Together as Christians and Muslims in a Palestinian state, we must move towards a constitutional, democratic form of government. This may still be difficult in most of the Arab, Islamic countries, but I believe it may be easier to achieve in Palestine. Without democracy, our life with Islam could be difficult. A Palestinian Christian theology of Islam is crucial, and it must be articulated along the lines that I have outlined above.

C Developing a theology of relation with the states of Israel and Palestine

The third area for theological articulation has to do with the political sphere. Palestinian Christians must articulate a theology of relationship with the state. The Church has a long history here in the Middle East. Its relationship with power has passed through many stages. At times it has been oppressed by the state, at other times it has enjoyed special status and privilege. At still other times it has been merely tolerated. Under Israeli rule, the Church was generally treated as an integral part of the Palestinian people. Except for some expatriate Christians who at times enjoyed certain protection and some privileges, most of our people suffered as Palestinians with the rest of the community. We did not escape the confiscation of our land or deportation, incarceration, or at times the desecration of our Holy Places, etc. For Palestinian Christians, the state of Israel has been the occupier of their land, usurper of their human and political rights, oppressor and dehumanizer. With the state of Israel, we must articulate a theology that addresses an agenda of justice and human rights. For Palestinian Arabs in Israel, we must address the issue of equal democracy. A theology is needed that challenges the history of Zionism and calls for a rewriting of the history of the state so that it can comply with truth. It has to be a theology that insists on the right of Palestinians to repatriation or compensation. It has to challenge the unjust laws that have been enacted by the state in order to control and subject the Palestinians. It must be a theology that exposes the arrogance and built-in discrimination of the state. At the same time, such a theology of Israel must of necessity move forward to address issues of peace and reconciliation. It has to push for renewal and forgiveness. We are living in new, exciting times.

A theology of the state of Israel must include a section on the use of the Bible as a servant of oppression. Many Christian fundamentalists and religious Jews have used and still use certain sections of the Bible to legitimate occupation and oppression. This Palestinian articulation of theology must contribute to a more inclusive understanding of God and a deeper understanding of the Bible by emphasizing more responsible criteria, especially for the interpretation of the Old Testament.

The Church in Palestine has had a unique experience with Jews. In the West, Jews have been the victims of Western anti-semitism and discrimination. In Palestine, the Palestinians have been the victims of oppressive anti-Palestinianism, at the hands of Zionist Jews. For the first time in almost nineteen hundred years, Jews have been able to muster a formidable military force that was capable, on the ashes of the Palestinians, to establish a respectable political state for their people. Once justice is done in the establishment of a Palestinian state, the Church should be a vanguard in expressing a vision of peace and becoming an agent of reconciliation between Palestinians and Israelis.

Likewise, we have a theological responsibility for the state of Palestine. At this point, it is a message of comfort and hope to our people: a message of binding and healing: a message of support and encouragement. We have a responsibility for the making of peace and the enhancement of reconciliation.

We need to point to our painful experiences with Israel and yet work so that the same injustices will not be committed by Palestinians. We will need to lift the banner of democracy, human rights, and freedom. Ultimately, whether it be Israel, Palestine, or any other state, we must insist that our first allegiance is to the God of love who loves all people equally and who has called us to be instruments of justice, righteousness, peace, reconciliation, and love. To that end, the Church should recognize its servant role, following the example of its Lord, who came not to be served, but to spend His life in humble and loving service to others.

Conclusion

This is practical theology. It is a theology that analyzes the life of the Christian Church in the Holy Land and tries to respond realistically to its needs and concerns. It is a theology that takes seriously the predicament of the Church, both internally and externally, and yet looks outward to being light and salt in its own land. It is a theology that must come to terms with the inter-religious realities of life in the Holy Land, as it relates to Judaism and especially Islam. Finally, it is a theology that deals with the emerging new political reality of the state of Israel and the state of Palestine. The Church must be both involved and committed to the ministry and service of all people, while maintaining a prophetic role and a relationship of constant dialogue with the state. At all cost, the Church must retain its independent voice and continue to champion the cause of the poor and oppressed. In this way, it maintains its servant role in society, and follows in the footsteps of its Lord Jesus Christ.